MUCH
DEPENDS ON
DINNER

MUCH DEPENDS ON DINNER

THE EXTRAORDINARY HISTORY AND
MYTHOLOGY, ALLURE AND OBSESSIONS,
PERILS AND TABOOS, OF AN
ORDINARY MEAL

Margaret Visser

GROVE PRESS
New York

First published by McClelland and Stewart Limited, Canada

Printed in the United States of America

Library of Congress Cataloging-in-Publication Data

Visser, Margaret.
    Much depends on dinner.

    Bibliography: p.
    Includes index.
    1. Food habits.   2. Dinners and dining.   3. Food
habits—England.   4. Dinners and dinging—England.
5. Food—History.   6. England—Social life and customs.
I. Title.
GT2860.V57   1987   394.1'2   87-257
ISBN-10: 0-8021-3651-6
ISBN-13: 978-0-8021-3651-0

Illustrations by Mary Firth

Grove Press
an imprint of Grove/Atlantic, Inc.
841 Broadway
New York, NY 10003

06 07 08 09 10   10 9 8 7 6 5 4 3

Contents

*S*PECIAL THANKS are for Colin, Emily, and Joan, and for Pat Kennedy, Emmet Robbins, Nada Conić, Norma Rowen, and Alan Koval. Pierre Berton encouraged me to write this book when I had just begun work on it, and so did all the staff of CBC Radio's *Morningside*, especially Don Harron, Richard Handler, and Peter Gzowski. Vesna Vukov kindly undertook to check the chemistry sections. I would also like to thank my editors, Ramsay Derry and Sarah Reid, and Jan Walter at McClelland and Stewart.

Since Eve ate apples, much depends on dinner.

BYRON, *Don Juan*

What Shall We Have for Dinner?

*T*HE EXTENT TO WHICH we take everyday objects for granted is the precise extent to which they govern and inform our lives. The knee-high chair, the four-pronged fork, the corridor or hallway which enables us to walk into a room without having to pass through another room to do so: these determine (among other things) how and where we sit down, the manner in which we approach our food, and the thoroughness with which we live separately from others and respect the privacy and autonomy of their lives. None of these objects is necessary; many cultures eschew them altogether, and there was a time when our own ancestors lived very happily without them. We invented them, however, to fill needs: chairs, forks, and hallways were required by the sort of people we have become; having them now prevents us from being different.

The shape of chairs has kept changing over the centuries, and so have the number of prongs in and the general shape of forks, as well as the width, length, and decoration of corridors. These "accidents" or forms of things are a kind of language, speaking the *logos* of our culture, and they are a record of its life history. One of the great eye-openers of the twentieth century (like every discovery it springs from our need) is the realization that the use of humble everyday objects is not only habitual – which is to say that we cannot do without them – but that these things are "ordinary" in the earliest and fullest sense of the word also: they embody our mostly unspoken assumptions, and they both order our culture and determine its direction.

Food is "everyday" – it has to be, or we would not survive for long. But food is never just something to eat. It is something to find or hunt or cultivate first of all; for most of human history we have spent a much longer portion of our lives worrying about food, and plotting, working, and fighting to obtain it, than we have in any other pursuit. As soon as we can count on a food supply (and so take food for granted), and not a moment sooner, we start to civilize ourselves. Civilization entails shaping, regulating, constraining, and dramatizing ourselves; we echo the preferences and the principles of our culture in the way we treat our food. An elaborate frozen dessert moulded into the shape of a ruined classical temple can be read as one vivid expression of a society's view of itself and its ideals; so can a round ground hamburger patty between two circular buns. Food – what is chosen from the possibilities available, how it is presented, how it is eaten, with whom and when, and how much time is allotted to cooking and eating it – is one of the means by which a society creates itself and acts out its aims and fantasies. Changing (or unchanging) food choices and presentations are part of every society's tradition and character. Food shapes us and expresses us even more definitively than our furniture or houses or utensils do.

I think this realization first dawned on me (it is a common discovery in our day) while I was chopping onions for *sauce soubise*, a recipe which my husband and I were carefully following from Elizabeth David's *French Country Cooking*, one day about fifteen years ago. Chopping onions is not an occupation which favours dreaming. Perhaps it was boredom or annoyance or simply that when you chop onions you had better keep your mind alert, and my concentration spilled over, but I started wondering about onions. Every time anything savoury was "*cuisiné*" it seemed to require onions. They smelled strongly and stung my eyes (Why?), some were quite hard to peel and others easy (Why?), others again were red (What made them so? Where did they come from?). I had a dim memory that someone had said (Who?) that onions were the chief sustenance of the people who built the Pyramids (Was it true? Were they the same onions?). I knew that onions were used in various ways in folk medicine (What ways, and were they efficacious?).

The next day I was at the library, supposed, I remember, to be doing research for an essay on the causes and results of the Battle of Arginousai, as background to the *Frogs* of Aristophanes. Stuck for inspiration, and abstractedly flipping through the catalogue of what happens to be the largest library in Canada, I looked under the subject-heading, "Onions." There were three books listed on onions: T. Greiner, *The New Onion Culture* (1911); H. H. Laughlin, *Duration of the Several Mitotic Stages in the Dividing Root-Tip Cells of the Common Onion* (1919); and H. A. Jones and L. K. Mann, *Onions and Their Allies* (1963). All three were on the other side of the campus, in the Science and Medicine Library: it had clearly been decided that onions could in no way interest someone in "arts" or in "social sciences." (I have just checked the catalogue again, and these are still the University of Toronto Library's entire holdings of books on onions.)

A week later I walked across the campus and looked at *Onions and Their Allies*. (I had doubtless eaten onions several times since the first glance through the catalogue; presumably preparing those dinners jogged my memory.) The work, with its pleasantly punning title, is an excellent and useful one, all about breeding, planting, storing and classifying not only onions but also garlic, leeks, chives and "other alliums." There was, in 1963, no agreement among scientists about how onions make eyes weep. (During the following decade the complex chemistry of this process was to be explored and explained to those whose knowledge of chemistry equips them to understand the explanation.) There is in *Onions and Their Allies* some information, but much less than I wanted, about the great "alliaceous odour." Nothing is said about the various lusts for and prejudices against the eating of onions in our, or in any other, culture. The history and social mythology of onions takes up just three pages of the second chapter of the book. It includes a couple of paragraphs each on ancient Egypt, on India, and on Greek herbalists.

I was soon to find that in order to answer the questions I had about onions, and to clear up all the uncertainties which would subsequently arise, I would have to search in at least eleven different collections of books and read articles in scientific periodicals, journals of anthropology, sociology, and folklore, histories of religion, culinary-historical writings in various journals, business and trade magazines, and so on. There was no such problem with my essay on the battle of Arginousai. All in one section of the library, in a day or two and with relatively little trouble, I had a pad full of notes and a bibliography of books and articles in French, Italian, German, and English going back nearly two centuries, which could have kept a conscientious scholar occupied for years. I am not one of those who despise the study of ancient battles, but I am a child of the twentieth century and surely I had a right to know at least as much about the history of a troublesome but eternally useful vegetable which I personally chopped and fried several times a week? (The French call frying onions "making them come back": I must find out why.)

By the time I was ready to write this book, after years of enjoyment digging for answers to my questions about food and other "ordinary" things, it had become obvious to me how the material, in all its motley variety, should be organized. I would describe a meal, devoting a chapter to each ingredient on the menu. The meal I have chosen is almost as simple and as universally recognizable as could be – nothing "gourmet" about it.

HORS D'OEUVRES:	Corn with salt and butter
ENTRÉE:	Chicken with rice
SALAD:	Lettuce with olive oil and lemon juice
DESSERT:	Ice cream

It will be quickly observed that I have left out bread, cheese, wine or beer, and coffee or tea, milk, and sugar. I have allowed no sauce for the chicken and rice, hoping that my guests would be satisfied with more butter, salt, and perhaps the chicken drippings. I could also have included the wildly improbable saga of pepper. Chapters on the minimal "extras" and the drinks I have mentioned would have produced a book more than twice the size of this one. Each food, of course, deserves book-length treatment. But even concentrating the material into a single chapter per ingredient as I have done, a meal by Escoffier or Carême, or just a modern wedding banquet or Christmas dinner, would require many volumes to do it justice.

A meal is an artistic social construct, ordering the foodstuffs which comprise it into a complex dramatic whole, as a play organizes actions and words into component parts such as acts, scenes, speeches, dialogues, entrances, and exits, all in the sequences designed for them.

However humble it may be, a meal has a definite plot, the intention of which is to intrigue, stimulate, and satisfy. Let us briefly analyse the simple dinner before us.

Firstly, it is a dinner, not a snack or a series of tidbits to be sampled between drinks. It is home-cooking too, for invited guests: there are no multiple choices such as a restaurant would normally offer. It has a messy, dexterity-demanding prologue, a hot central episode, and a dessert which, served in a dish instead of a cone (we do not normally eat ice cream in cones at home), is rich and formal enough fittingly to close a dinner. "The true elements of the idea" of a dinner, De Quincey wrote in "The Casuistry of Roman Meals," are "1. That dinner is that meal, no matter when taken, which is the principal meal; *i.e.*, the meal on which the day's support is thrown. 2. That it is *therefore* the meal of hospitality. 3. That it is the meal (with reference to both Nos. 1 and 2) in which animal food predominates. 4. That it is that meal which, upon a necessity arising for the abolition of all *but* one, would naturally offer itself as that one."

I have chosen a meal which represents the very least I could offer guests who are not intimate friends, that easily-contented group who claim that they would be prepared even to accept what we call "pot luck." This meal, as politeness to friends who are still relative strangers demands, is pre-planned and makes certain gestures towards decorum. Because it is dinner, those eating it will refrain from other pursuits while it is in progress. No one will knit, watch television, or read a newspaper. The possibility of physical violence of any sort will not even cross anyone's mind; and neither will such rudeness as leaving the table before absolutely everyone has finished eating and all agree to rise. During the meal everyone will adhere to a code of behavioural ethics called "table manners" – a set of rules far too complex to discuss in detail here.

The ingredients which make up our dinner have been chosen for their acceptability to people in as many different cultures as possible. The meal itself, nevertheless, has a broadly British structure – although this is a modern, that is, abbreviated, version of it. As David Pocock reports in his introduction to Arnold Palmer's book *Moveable Feasts*, a British dinner in the 1890s might ideally have offered: hors d'oeuvres, soup, fish, entrée, joint, game, sweets and savouries. A modern English hotel typically serves grapefruit or soup, chicken or meat, potatoes or rice, vegetables (often two), and stewed fruit or ice cream or pudding or melon. Our menu clearly keeps to the pattern of the English hotel meal, even though the latter is designed to count as a substantial and fairly ceremonial affair. A recent conference luncheon to which I was invited in Canada offered the following menu: balls of fruit (melon mostly) in a tall coupe, an entrée consisting of chicken, rice, and two vegetables (broccoli and small carrots) all on one plate, with a thin non-coating gravy, and baked Alaska. The construct is palpably a relative of the one I offer here, although there are differences.

Corn is an American vegetable, but eating it at the meal's beginning is more common in England than in the States or Canada. A liking for corn devoured "straight," and especially right off the cob, is thought of in Europe as an Anglo-Saxon idiosyncrasy. The French, for example, still have a tendency to class corn as mainly chicken-feed; the Italians like it ground into something resembling the porridges which were the staple of the ancient Romans. The corn on our menu plays the role of a first course of spaghetti in an Italian dinner: it is filling, so that hunger can be assuaged before we reach the heights represented by the entrée; our appreciation then will depend on more complex responses than simple famished desire. Both corn and spaghetti require dexterity in the eating: many small things have to be dealt with expeditiously. (The fruit shaped into multi-coloured balls at the conference meal I attended, or artichokes requiring to be stripped leaf by leaf and dipped in sauce, are both intended to lift the spirits as well as to whet the appetite.) Corn or spaghetti can provide a stimulating, vivacious, and amusing overture – on condition that the guests are not solemn with hunger, in which case the corn or the spaghetti can equally well be consumed with fierce and silent concentration. (Our meal being, as we shall see, rather on the genteel side, guests in our culture would probably pretend not to be too hungry, even if they were. We prefer, as De Quincey's essay says, "to throw the grace of intellectual enjoyment over an animal necessity.")

Typically Anglo-Saxon, of course, is the butter served with the corn; the dairy theme in our meal will be repeated with the cooking medium for the chicken, and reach its final crescendo in the ice cream. I have removed the traditional two vegetables from the centrepiece and placed them before it (the corn) and after it (the salad). Rice is a starchy staple, and as such does not, in Anglo-Saxon meals, or in Germanic and northern European meals generally, count as a vegetable; rice or potatoes are more important than a vegetable, and an all but indispensable adjunct to meat. My chicken might be roasted or fried, depending on how formal the occasion is to be: roasted is far more prestigious than fried.

The English (and hence the American) tradition with roasts is still to bring in the whole bird or joint and carve it up in front of the guests – an extraordinarily old-fashioned procedure. Ever since the Middle Ages most European cuisines have been moving steadily away from such confrontations with the cutting of carcasses; the kitchen is in most cultures the place for such indelicacies, while the guests are protected by being seated safely in the dining-room. Even in Anglo-Saxon countries, however, modern capitulations to smaller joints, to convenience, and to the custom in hotels, often result in the less grand carving of a joint or a bird into pieces in the kitchen. The meat is then served, like fried portions, already on the plates. Large joints are less popular than they used to be because families are smaller; added to which, North Americans in particular tend to classify "left-overs" with garbage, so that remainders of meat are wasteful. The result has been that joints and whole birds (huge turkeys, for example) have become especially festive in connotation: they are for relatively rare large gatherings, when almost all the meat will probably be consumed at a sitting. (A whole aspect of household management – one hesitates to call it a *cuisine* – has in this process been largely eclipsed: that of What to Do with Left-Overs, how to present them at another meal in a form which the family will accept.)

Whether roasted or fried, my chicken and its accompaniment of rice without gravy would sit clearly differentiated on the plate. This is very American in outlook: it is totally unlike, for example, the famous *poulet basquais*, where the rice can be cooked in the same pot as the chicken, together with tomatoes, onions, garlic, sausages, and paprika, and the whole is served with considerable overlap among ingredients. North Americans usually hate being served several foods mixed together, unless they have consciously chosen to eat an "ethnic" dish. Many will actually eat all of each portion of meat and vegetables one after the other, so keeping the constituents even more obsessively separate, although everything is to be found on the same plate. Some culinary sociologists attribute this to the famous "puritanical" heritage of North America: the desire to be clean and clear. It is a relatively modern taste, however, depending as it does on the household's possessing lots of pots and pans. Huckleberry Finn complained because the widow who adopted him (puritanical as she was) cooked everything by itself: "In a barrel of odds and ends it is different; things get mixed up, and the juice kind of swaps around, and the things go better." Another frequently expressed desire is to "know what it is I am eating." This must have some roots in English tradition: British cuisine has always despised and rejected frivolous, dishonest, or merely confused Continental concoctions; the ideal has always been "the best ingredients, undisguised."

My lettuce salad is placed where the French would put it – after the main course and before the dessert. (Utterly un-French, of course, is my omission of cheese.) Americans traditionally like salad to open a meal; they might even place the salad on the same dish as the chicken and rice (on the "everything on one platter" principle). But in this matter, especially given the overture of corn, Americans might let the lettuce in this position pass. The rationale for it is to provide a pause, to refresh the palate before we launch into the dessert, to get our systems used, after the hot central course, to things at room temperature before we take on something frozen. The ice cream is marvellously modern: a technological feat, rich, formal, and semi-solid in its dish, something which most people in our culture like, but which the host is free either to buy ready-made (this is perfectly acceptable, especially if the host has an absorbing and time-consuming, therefore "important" job) or grandiloquently to make from scratch. In middle-class circles few gifts are as generous or as complimentary these days as the taking, on one's friends' behalf, of time and culinary trouble.

Let us consider the structure of our meal in a little more detail. The core of it is the comfortably traditional schema, M + S + 2V: Meat, Staple, and Two Vegetables. The Meat and Staple are definitely the centre of attraction, the whole point of the meal, the married couple, as it were, at the wedding. The two vegetables (the English like referring to them with cosy familiarity as "two veg") resemble bridesmaids; theirs is a decorative but wholly subordinate and supporting role. This structural principle is foreshadowed by the twin attendants upon the corn (salt and melting butter) and taken up again with the double ornamentation of the salad (more seasoning plus oil and lemon dressing). Subordination, as in the clauses of an English sentence, is still one of our cultural trademarks, in spite of a new tendency to display, in part in order to save time, everything at once on one platter – a whole meal, even, on one TV-dinner tray or airplane dinner package. Equality, plurality, and choice still have to battle with hierarchies of size and value.

Our meal requires several culinary techniques in its creation, for we are not only complex but also competent. We have employed boiling, roasting or frying, tossing raw in a prepared dressing, and freezing. In our meal we use teeth and hands, followed by napkins and perhaps fingerbowls to clean ourselves up (for the corn), a knife for cutting, together with a fork to spear the meat and hold it still (the chicken), the fork held supine, prongs curving up and the knife as a sweeper (the rice), the fork with prongs piercing as primary implement (the salad), and the smooth and comforting, infantile spoon (the ice cream). The use of all these implements, each in the right way at the right time, is something we have had drummed into us since childhood until it has become utterly effortless: a valuable opportunity for a demonstration that we have been Well Brought Up, and are therefore the kind of people who will unquestionably Do.

Again, we should be aware that our meal is almost totally female in connotation. Corn is the American Indian "mother and nourisher"; chicken (pale meat, no red blood, and little fat in evidence) is for us a typically "female" choice; rice, a delicate grain – especially when it is "fluffy," as we like it – white like chicken, and in its mythical origins (though not in our culture) a girl-child; lettuce is light and unfattening, but also cold, green, and (therefore) female; lemons nippled, olive oil virgin, ice cream cold, milky, and served in definitely womanly, rounded shapes. Salt is the one exception, but even it is neuter and not masculine; butter from cream is again female.

Chicken, furthermore, is traditionally festive in overtone, in spite of everything modern factory farming has achieved in making the bird cheap and constantly available. Barbara Pym's novels are full of sly insights into culinary anthropology; in them, "a bird" is for when clergymen are invited for dinner: elevated, not too fleshly, and with a skin "gold-embroidered like a chasuble," as Proust put it. Nowadays chicken and salad are both "chic" for not being fattening and ice cream has prestige because it is luxurious yet democratic and triumphantly modern. Dessert ends the meal on a "high" note, for, notwithstanding our modernity, we are Romantics still, determined to end our works of art with a climax, in spite of the classical centrality of the main course.

My exceedingly simple yet slightly pretentious meal, then, can mean for us a good many things, and entertain us like a well-constructed play in which the partakers are both actors and audience. But equally importantly for my purposes, the construction of a meal requires close attention to variety and contrast among the materials used. All the continents on earth and a good many countries are represented in the ingredients for this particular dinner, and all the types of food: vegetables; staples; meat; raw leaves; fruit; milk and sweetness; vegetable oil; butter, the dairy essence; and the strange, worrisome mineral, salt. (I chose lemon, not vinegar, for my salad dressing for several reasons: I usually prefer it and lemon goes well with chicken; vinegar entails a discussion of wine, which is far too large a subject to undertake in the space available; and finally, I needed a fruit to make my panoply of foods reasonably complete.) The subject matter has also been chosen because it provides appropriate contexts in which to discuss modern social and institutional phenomena such as fast foods, supermarkets, advertising strategies, food fads, and the mythologies on which they batten. Each of the foodstuffs I have chosen has a weird, passionate, often savage history of its own; each has dragged the human race in its wake, constrained us, enticed us, harried, and goaded us in its own particular fashion.

These nine foods among them require the consideration of mighty problems which especially afflict the modern world. Some of these are: the dangers and the triumphs of crop uniformity and genetic engineering; the salting and pollution of the desperately precious fertile areas of the earth; the destruction of cultural tradition and the replacement of it by – what else? – replaceability; democratization being turned into an enemy of culinary excellence; farm mechanization and the loss of human livelihoods; cheap meat versus animal rights; food irradiation, additives, antibiotics, herbicides and pesticides, and the angry distrust they can arouse in us. When I began this book I meant it to be primarily amusing; often, however, I wrote it in outrage and in fear.

Boredom is the twentieth century's version of social *miasma*; we bear in addition, of course, our speciality in natural *miasma*, which is pollution. Boredom arises from the loss of meaning, which in turn comes in part from a failure of *religio* or connectedness with one another and with our past. This book is a modest plea for the realization that absolutely nothing is intrinsically boring, least of all the everyday, ordinary things. These, today, are after all what even we are prepared to admit we have in common. We have recently discovered in ourselves a determination to consider nothing to be beneath consideration, and a willingness to question passionately matters which used to be thought too basic for words. I think the reason for this is that we are fighting back with an altogether healthy urge to recapture ancient but pitifully neglected, thoroughly human responses such as participatory attention, receptivity, and appreciation. We have learned well the lessons about the stupidities of superstition, of misplaced, because ignorant, wonder. It is time now to think about whether we have leaped from the trivial to the vacant. Boredom is an irritable condition, and an exceedingly dangerous one when it is accompanied by enormous destructive power. "The old warnings," W. H. Auden wrote,

> still have power to scare me: Hybris comes to
> an ugly finish, Irreverence
> is a greater oaf than Superstition.

CHAPTER ONE

Corn: Our Mother, Our Life

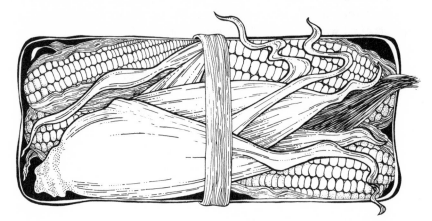

*A*NORTH AMERICAN SUPERMARKET is market place, temple, palace, and parade all rolled into one. It is both the expression and the symbol of the goals and the means of North American civilization, physically embodying the culture's yearnings for size, availability, freedom of choice, uniformity, variety, abundance, convenience, cleanliness, speed, and the reduction of hierarchy to quantity: money and amount. It both tempts and constrains us: lets us loose inside but controls and defines us even as it exacts its toll at the exit. Buying a bag full of groceries at a North American supermarket is as essential for a traveller attempting to understand this culture as taking an evening stroll would be in Spain or Italy, or eating in a popular restaurant in France.

The driving wheel of the supermarket is not always visible: it is not the business of a driving wheel to be ostentatious. But it is there – everywhere. It is American corn, or maize. You cannot buy anything at all in a North American supermarket which has been untouched by corn, with the occasional and single exception of fresh fish – and even that has almost certainly been delivered to the store in cartons or wrappings which are partially created out of corn. Meat *is* largely corn. So is milk: American livestock and poultry is fed and fattened on corn and cornstalks. Frozen meat and fish has a light corn starch coating on it to prevent excessive drying. The brown and golden colouring which constitutes the visual appeal of many soft drinks and puddings comes from corn. All canned foods are bathed in liquid containing corn. Every carton, every wrapping, every plastic container depends on corn products – indeed all modern paper and cardboard, with the exception of newspaper and tissue, is coated in corn.

One primary product of the maize plant is corn oil, which is not only a cooking fat but is important in margarine (butter, remember, is also corn). Corn oil is an essential ingredient in soap, in insecticides (all vegetables and fruits in a supermarket have been treated with insecticides), and of course in such factory-made products as mayonnaise and salad dressings. The taste-bud sensitizer, monosodium glutamate or MSG, is commonly made of corn protein.

Corn syrup – viscous, cheap, not too sweet – is the very basis of candy, ketchup, and commercial ice cream. It is used in processed meats, condensed milk, soft drinks, many modern beers, gin, and vodka. It even goes into the purple marks stamped on meat and other foods. Corn syrup provides body where "body" is lacking, in sauces and soups for instance (the trade says it adds "mouth-feel"). It prevents crystallization and discolouring; it makes foods hold their shape, prevents ingredients from separating, and stabilizes moisture content. It is extremely useful when long shelf-life is the goal.

Corn starch is to be found in baby foods, jams, pickles, vinegar, yeast. It serves as a carrier for the bubbling agents in baking powder; is mixed in with table salt, sugar (especially icing sugar), and many instant coffees in order to promote easy pouring. It is essential in anything dehydrated, such as milk (already corn, of course) or instant potato flakes. Corn starch is white, odourless, tasteless, and easily moulded. It is the invisible coating and the universal neutral carrier for the active ingredients in thousands of products, from headache tablets, toothpastes, and cosmetics to detergents, dog food, match heads, and charcoal briquettes.

All textiles, all leathers are covered in corn. Corn is used when making things stick (adhesives all contain corn) – and also whenever it is necessary that things should *not* stick: candy is dusted or coated with corn, all kinds of metal and plastic moulds use corn. North Americans eat only one-tenth of the corn their countries produce, but that tenth amounts to one and a third kilograms (3 lb.) of corn – in milk, poultry, cheese, meat, butter, and the rest – per person per day.

The supermarket does not by any means represent all the uses of corn in our culture. If you live in North America – and even very possibly if you do not – the house you live in and the furniture in it, the car you drive, even the road you drive on, all depend for their very existence on corn. Modern corn production "grew up" with the industrial and technological revolutions, and the makers of those revolutions were often North Americans. They turned their problem-solving attention to the most readily available raw materials and made whatever they wanted to make – antibiotics or deep-drilling oil-well mud or ceramic spark-plug insulators or embalming fluids – out of the material to hand. And that material was the hardy and obliging fruit of the grass which the Indians called *maïs*.

In English, the word *corn* denotes the staple grain of a country. Wheat is "corn" to the people of a country where wheaten bread is the staple. Oats is "corn" to people who eat oats; rye is "corn" if the staple is rye. When Europeans arrived in America they saw that, for the Indians, maize was the basic food, so the English-speaking newcomers called it "Indian corn." We continue in North America to recognize the primacy of maize in our culture by calling it "corn." In Europe it is called by some form of the Indian word "*maïs*," and it is differentiated from wheat, England's "corn," by being called in England "corn on the cob." The word *maize*, in American usage, refers to the plant as it was when the Indians grew it, before the white men arrived in America – or it is used as a generic, more "botanical" term. American Indians, in their many different languages, always spoke of corn as "Our Mother," "Our Life," "She Who Sustains Us."

The Indians are said – by themselves and by the first outsiders who encountered them – to have lived and died by corn. They measured out their lives by it, used it to build shelters and fences, spent more of their working days at producing it than at any other pursuit, wore it and decorated their bodies with it, ate it as their most substantial food, reverenced it, and offered it to the gods. *Maïs* was omnipresent for them – and now it is every bit as omnipresent in North American life. Without corn, North America – and most particularly modern, technological North America – is inconceivable. Perhaps the relentlessly common-sensical, practical, handy American temperament would have created its lifestyle out of something else if corn had not existed: out of rice perhaps, or potatoes, or even from some other totally unpromoted and therefore "uninteresting" plant. But corn was there, and so corn both founded and spearheaded the triumphant expansion of modern technology. By the same token, the very golden grains which constitute the riches of North America contain within themselves one of the acutest dangers we face: a peril diabolically wedded to our weakness.

HOW THE CORN PLANT WORKS

Maize is a giant grass which bears unusually large seed, even for a giant. Each corn kernel is really a fruit with an oily germ or seed surrounded by its starchy nutrients and enclosed in a skin or hull. The plant is, in fact, a genus all to itself and is the only species in its genus. Its botanical name is *Zea maïs*: *zeia* means "grain" in Greek, and the Haitian Indian term *maïs* may be translated as "the stuff of life."

The Indians observed that different types of corn could cross and produce offspring with characteristics derived from both parents. They believed that the plants' roots mingled underground to produce this effect, and this theory was not proved wrong until 1724, when Judge Paul Dudley of Massachusetts noticed that changes took place in corn when different types were separated by a river, but not when they were separated by a high fence. The "crossing" must therefore take place in the air and not underground. In 1694 the German botanist Camerarius had first startled the world with the news that plants have a sex-life. But James Logan, who worked as an administrator for the Province of Pennsylvania under William Penn, presented in 1727 the first theories about how sex worked in the corn plant. The silks, which hang like bunches of hair from the cobs, are the female element. The male maize flowers are borne on the tassel, and they produce the pollen, 25 million grains per tassel. When the pollen is ripe it is shed and drifts in the wind over the cornfield.

Each time a pollen grain falls on the sticky thread of a corn silk, either on its own plant or on another, a kernel is conceived. The silk develops a tube, and the pollen grain travels through the tube to the embryo at the root of the silk in the cob. There the baby corn kernel takes shape, tightly anchored by a short stem to its place amongst its rows of siblings. Every pollen grain contains two nuclei – one for the oil-germ and one for the starch-endosperm in the kernel. The corn plant adjusts the length of its own cobs according to the likelihood of the amount of grain it will be called upon to house. The factors which the plant mysteriously takes into account include the density of the plant population in a field, weed competition, moisture, the amount of nutrients it is getting, and the availability of light.

The corn cob, together with its progeny, plumps and ripens, and as it does so the silks change colour, from pale greenish white to deep red to brown, so that an expert picker knows just what stage the kernels have reached by the colour of the silks. When the kernels are fully ripe the silks turn into a stiff black fuzz. Corn can be picked and used or eaten at many different stages, and is often preferred when immature. This adds inestimable value to the plant, as long as modern machinery does not dominate the harvest, for it means that the fruit of a single sowing of corn plants can be used over a long period, some ears first as a tender boiled vegetable, some later for roasting, then some for grinding, and some later still as hard feed-grain for animals.

When sweet corn is picked for boiling, it must be rushed at once to the pot; purists claim that you should have the water ready boiling *before* you go out to pick your corn, so that there will be the least delay possible before the heat seizes the sugar in the kernels. The sweetness of sweet corn begins to turn to starch and lose its flavour the moment the cob is snapped from its stalk. Thus sweet corn bought several days old in a shop falls enormously short of its potential flavour. For once the frozen product, if it has been processed correctly, may be gastronomically preferable: modern freezing installations are built as close as possible to the field. The corn is picked, husked, and stripped of its kernels in the field, and should be rushed to the freezer, where the natural process which substitutes starch for sugar is instantly shut off.

The main varieties of maize are popcorn, sweet corn, dent corn, flint corn, and flour corn. Popcorn and flint corn have very hard hulls. When popcorn is heated, the starch inside the skin of the kernel fills with steam until it bursts: steam leaks out of the skins of other types of corn because their hulls are less horny. Popcorn's beautiful cloud and butterfly shapes were greatly prized by the Indians who used them for necklaces and ornaments, just as we string them to decorate Christmas trees today. Many scientists believe that the accidental popping of hard grain in a fire might have first revealed to man the edibility of cereals.

Flint corn, especially Tropical Flint, dominated world markets until the 1920s: flint corn is hardy and resistant to tropical insects, long-lasting and delicious even when eaten daily: the Indians generally liked it best of all types, and most Africans still do. Flour corn is grown little outside of South and Central America, where it is still prized for the ease with which it may be ground by hand. The corn-grinding *metate* stone and the hand-held stone called a *mano* are common sights all over South America, where they are most often placed outside houses, so that the women can work at corn grinding while chatting with their neighbours.

The giant crop among corns all over the world today is dent. It is named after the dimple in the top edge of every kernel, which is formed because of the shrinkage of the soft starch in the endosperm. Dent corn is sweet and starchy – the most prized characteristics for the uses of our civilization. It used to be thought of by the Indians as one of the prime symbols of the female, and it proclaimed the maternal aspects of the divine corn plant.

Sweet corn – the type which we are having to open our meal – must be cooked or frozen immediately. With the exception of this one variety, however, corn which has been successfully dried and correctly stored is one of the longest-lasting foodstuffs known. Ten-year-old corn kernels will germinate. Archaeologists endlessly search for the origins and the time-scale for the development of corn; at one dig made in the pursuit of more knowledge about the history of corn, thousand-year-old corn kernels were uncovered. A donkey happened on the find, and thought it appetizing enough to eat. It has also been found that one-thousand-year-old popcorn can still be successfully popped.

One of corn's main attractions for man has always been its adaptability to storage: corn is the ultimate "long shelf-life" food. Many North American Indian bands kept stocks of kernels under earth-mounds for the winters and times of war, and these fed the earliest European settlers who came upon such hoards during their first cruel winter in 1620–21. It is still customary in Zambia and other maize-growing countries in Africa to save dried corn-kernels underground in covered pits. And as I have mentioned, today corn is the precious material by which modern technology keeps a myriad of other products edible through thousands of miles of travel and months, even years, of storage before they are bought.

The corn cob and its seed is covered entirely with a durable husk.

This is another convenience for man: the green envelope makes the cob easy to harvest, easy to feed to livestock, easy to transport, easy to store. It protects the grain from damage during mechanical harvesting. The corn cob is the original packaged food – again apparently made to suit modern demands.

All this is so miraculous that there has got to be a hitch – and there is. Corn, because of its tight, strong, all-enveloping husk, cannot seed itself. Even if a cob fell to the ground freed from its husk, the resulting seedlings would choke each other because they are so closely set, and so tightly bound to the cob. In fact, if man ceased to take a hand by unwrapping the cob, plucking the seed, and planting it out, *Zea maïs* would become extinct.

Man depends on the corn he has helped to create, but the corn also depends on him. It depends on him for its nutrients; corn is one of the most demanding of food plants in this respect. Corn needs a great deal of water: 370 kilograms of water for each kilogram of dry fodder; 537 litres of water per litre of grain harvested and stripped from the cobs. (That is 4,300 Imperial gallons of water per bushel of grain for those of us whose minds still function in Imperial measurements.) It takes five to twelve years for soil which has once borne maize to return to its former fertility by natural means. When corn is repeatedly sown on one spot, the land has to be artificially fertilized, and this means enormous expenditures of energy and money for the machines, the nutrient chemicals, and their transport. The added fertilizers mean that modern farmers need not leave the land to recover, and can do without rotation of crops. But the fertilizers encourage weeds as well as corn, so that weed-killers have to be assiduously applied.

In a healthy, weed-cleared, and fertilized cornfield, the plants grow extremely quickly. Growth slows down during the day and speeds up in the evening. Under ideal conditions a day's growth can reach eleven and a half centimeters (4 1/2 inches). There are hundreds of accounts of American farmers who say they have *heard* their corn growing. On a warm windless evening during the peak growing time you can sit in a cornfield and hear the earth and the vegetable kingdom at work: a gentle stroke and rasp of leaves unfurling and sweeping along stalk and leaf edge: the hum of the driving wheel of North American civilization.

THE ORIGINS OF CORN

More is known about corn, its demands and its enemies, how it propagates itself and how it grows, than about any other plant on earth. Yet the importance of this vegetable is so enormous that research into corn is being pursued more intensely today than ever. Corn is now known to have originated in Central America. But one great mystery remains: what did the American Indians do to produce corn in the first place? Nothing like this man-sized plant with its huge cobs and succulent kernels exists in uncultivated nature.

In 1953, the earliest known fossil corn pollen was discovered as foundation cores were being drilled for a skyscraper in Mexico City; it was buried deep in what had been the muddy bottom of a lake. There was a great deal of corn pollen in the silt down to a seven-metre (23-ft.) depth, then nothing for sixty-two metres more. At sixty-nine metres, (226 ft.) corn pollen reappeared. It dates from the last interglacial period, and its age is estimated at about eighty thousand years. The corn-like plant which bred this pollen must have been a wild grass with kernels which could fall separately to the ground so that the plant could re-seed itself and so survive without the human intervention necessary in corn as we now know it.

One grass which looks as if it could conceivably have developed into corn, and which still exists in the wild because each of its kernels is enclosed in its own hard self-sufficient shell, is *teosinte*. Teosinte and corn, however, have crucial genetic dissimilarities. In 1978 a botany student called Rafael Guzmán found in the Mexican Jalisco Hills a hitherto unknown type of teosinte grass which could easily crossbreed with corn; the discovery was described as the most important botanical breakthrough of the 1970s. This obliging plant has provided corn not only with what most scientists now think of as a *bona fide* ancestor, the secrets of whose genetic makeup might unlock even more riches from the corn plant, but it has also been made by careful crossbreeding to share with corn its resistance to many diseases and pests. Yet we still do not know what the Indians did to turn the self-seeding teosinte grass, with its small self-contained grains, into a plant with huge podless kernels growing in tight rows on a cob covered with a single sheath.

An archaeological dig at Bat Cave, New Mexico, in the 1940s uncovered seven hundred corn cobs and some tassel fragments, the oldest of which have been dated to fifty-six hundred years ago. These are modern, "man-influenced" corn cobs all right – except for one fact. The cobs (not the kernels, but the cobs) are no longer than a human fingernail. How we do not know, but by the next identifiable stage, three thousand years ago at the latest, the corn cob, presumably because of intervention by Indian farmers, had increased in size to ten centimeters (4 in.) long. At the Coxcatlán cave in the Tehuacán Valley, Mexico, a clear sequence of corn cobs has been found, increasing in length from one to twenty centimeters (1/2 in. to 8 in.) over a span of fifty-five hundred years.

Mexico appears by most accounts to be the heartland, or at least the most fruitful "mixing bowl" for the evolution of corn. But this theory has also been challenged. In 1961 digs were being carried out in Ecuador, on sites which had been inhabited by the Valdivia cultures between about 4000 and 2000 BC. Amongst a heap of pot-sherds left behind by tomb-robbers, archaeologists found pieces of pottery which had been decorated by pressing maize kernels repeatedly into the wet clay in order to produce ornamental designs. One sherd actually had a corn kernel still imbedded in it. The kernel was charred, but its outlines are still clear enough to identify it. Two facts about what is now known as the San Pablo Corn Kernel caused a real shock: the pot-sherd can be securely dated to 2920 BC, and the kernel is the size of a modern one!

If there have been no mistakes made, this find disrupts the whole picture derived from the Bat Cave and other discoveries, in which large kernels do not arrive for at least another thousand years.

When Christopher Columbus arrived in America he immediately noted American corn and its immense importance for the Indians. On November 4, 1492, Columbus disembarked on the island now called Cuba. He was met by Indians who hospitably offered gifts, the most sacred and prodigious substances they knew: tobacco and corn. The word they used for the latter, in the Haitian language spoken on the island, was *maïs*. In this manner, and on a single day, these two fateful plants were introduced to Europe and the rest of the world. Columbus's journal for November 5, 1492, reads in an early translation: "There was a great deal of tilled land sowed with a sort of beans and a sort of grain they call 'Mahiz,' which was well tasted baked or dried, and made into flour."

Over and over again the letters and narratives of the early explorers of America express amazement at the cleanliness, the diligence, and efficiency of Indian farming. In Europe at this time (the fifteenth and sixteenth centuries) seed was sown broadcast, that is in great scattered handfuls, irregularly spaced by the chance fall of the grains. Farmers then waited for the weeds to come up with the crop before any attempt was made to sort through the jumble of growing plants and remove the unwanted growth. The Indians did things differently. Round many of the settlements on the eastern seaboard, fields were laid out with chequerboard accuracy, a mound of earth heaped up in every square. There were no draft animals in North America before the Europeans came; all land-clearance and mound-making was done by hand, with the help of axes and sticks, and with hoes whose blades and points were made of wood, sea-shells, antlers, and the shoulder-blades of large animals.

The women then moved onto the prepared land. They did all the agricultural labour thereafter, up until the harvest, which in some tribes was allotted and stored in quantities decided by the women. At planting time they poked holes into the mounds, and dropped seeds into them: four or six of maize, and, a little while later, a few of beans, a few of squash. Corn, beans, and squash were always eaten together and always planted together: in Iroquois myth they were represented as three in-separable sisters. When the plants emerged from the hill, the corn grew straight and strong, the beans climbed the corn, and the squash plant trailed down the side of the hill and covered the flat land between the mounds. The spreading squash plant helped to keep down weeds. The coastal Indians would plant a fish in every hill as well; to neglect this was sacrilege, and the corn repaid such a sin by refusing to grow properly. The Indians – who can imagine how? – had discovered that maize needs massive doses of fertilizer if it is not completely to drain the soil of nutrients.

Planting was sacred and performed in association with vehement dancing for fertility. In many tribes the women would shake their long hair to encourage the magically similar corn silks to flourish. In Central America, Aztec ceremonies at corn planting included human sacrifice, serpentine dances, skirmishes among priestesses, and a rattle-strewing rite, where the rattle imitated the seed tumbling into the earth. The Green Corn Dance of the Pueblo Indians of the southwestern United States is a survival of ancient customs such as these, and is still performed today.

The right moment for planting was always a matter for extreme caution and meticulous science. "When the young leaves of the oak tree are the size of a squirrel's ear, then plant," the early European settlers were told by the Indians, on whom they depended for any hope of survival. In Guatemala today the descendants of the ancient Maya continue to grow corn by the methods of their ancestors and still there is the anxious scanning of wind and leaf signs, the elaborate preparations and the intensely religious awareness of the right moment to place the seed in the earth. The ancient method for planting is still in favour in Guatemala: poke a hole in the ground with a stick, drop the kernel in, cover, and move on.

The Indian tribes who planted their seed in spaced hills zealously guarded the soil all round each hill from weeds. The first Europeans to see this marvelled at the revelation of this novel neatness, and at so much willing hard work. They were also staggered by the size of the maize plantations: Diego Columbus, Christopher's brother, said he walked twenty-nine kilometers (eighteen miles) through an immaculate field of corn, bean, and squash mounds, and never came to the end of it. The Indians in South and Central America still like to grow beans up their cornstalks, and still they keep down weeds by growing pumpkins and squash between the stalks.

Corn, beans, and squash are as constantly wedded in Indian cooking today as they were in the past. Sometimes meat is added: for the early Indians that meat would often have been puppy. And always they added ash: burnt hickory or the ash of some other wood, or the roasted and crushed shells of mussels they had eaten, or (as in modern Ecuador) the burnt shells of land snails. All this was sheer tradition: corn, beans, and squash, with a pinch of ash in every pot. Only very recently have scientists fully grasped the wisdom of the Indians' behaviour. Corn, we now know, is about 10 per cent protein, but is deficient in the amino acids lysine and tryptophan, which people must get from food. In addition, although corn contains the vitamin niacin, almost all of it occurs in a "bound" form called niacytin, which makes it biologically unavailable to human beings. Corn, in other words, cannot feed people adequately if it is not supplemented by other foods, and beans and squash are excellent complements to corn. The holy threesome, in fact, enabled corn to be consumed as a staple. Wherever the rule has been broken, and corn eaten without the correct supplements, the consequences have been disastrous: outbreaks of pellagra and kwashiorkor, the agonizing diseases of nutrition deficiency.

Pellagra (from the Italian *pelle agra*, "rough skin") causes skin lesions, sore mouth, nausea, and eventually mental disturbances. It was common in the nineteenth century among the poor of the southern United States, who lived typically on a diet of corn in its many versions, gravy, collards, sweet potatoes, rice, and sugar. Joseph Goldberger proved in 1916 that pellagra was induced by the lack of niacin in this corn-centred diet; he was finally forced, in order to make his point, to perform several dramatic experiments on his own person and on those of his wife and friends, to demonstrate that the disease was not caught by infection. The remedy was simply a greater variety of vitamin-rich foods. *Kwashiorkor* is an African word meaning "the disease of the elder child when a new one is born." It occurred when a child was weaned at the birth of a sibling: the disease set in when milk was withdrawn and a diet of corn substituted. Kwashiorkor, caused by deficiency in protein, niacin, and amino acids, is still the main cause of child mortality in many parts of the world.

What about the ash that American Indians added to their corn? They realized that ash (that is, lime or alkali) softens the skins of the corn kernels and makes these easier to grind and to digest. But there is more. Lime, when added to corn, releases the "bound" vitamin niacin, and makes it available to human beings. In fact, if the Indians had not somehow (How?) learned this secret, corn could never have become the main food crop of several civilizations, as it did in pre-Columbian America. The Indians sensed, too, that the ash was for man, to supply his bodily need: when they offered their sacred grain to the gods they never added ash.

The mythology of corn among the American Indians forms a vast and varied tapestry, a revelation of the rich intensity of man's response to nature: his anxiety, his gratitude, his sense of wonder. Since Indian cultures were in many ways founded upon corn, beliefs about the grain express not only its own reign over men, but also much more specific and detailed aspects of human society and institutions. For example, the Indians commonly saw the world as having six directions: north, south, east, and west, and also up and down. Each of the directions was associated with one of the six main colours of corn. For many tribes (colour associations did vary from tribe to tribe) red was for the north, blue the east, black the south, yellow the west; white was for "up" and variegated corn was "down," the underworld. The ancient Mayans of Guatemala, Belize, and the Yucatán placed four corn kernels in each planting mound, one for each of the four Bacabs, the gods who hold up the sky at the four corners of the earth. The fifth day of the Mayan month was named for planting the maize; its pictograph was a ring quartered by a cross, and containing a small circle in each of the quarters: it was a depiction of a planted corn-mound. The first day of the month was Kan, which stood for maize; its pictograph was a stylized corn kernel.

Among the people ruled by the Incas of Peru, no corn could be planted before the supreme Inca himself had announced the spring by turning the earth with a golden plough. He was given a special maize drink concocted by the "chosen virgins" who slept with him alone. This rich fermented brew was used for sacrificial ceremonies and as a drink exclusively for the supreme Inca.

The people of ancient Peru learned ingenious methods of tapping subterranean water for their thirsty maize. They also sailed out to islands in the Pacific to gather guano, the droppings of sea-birds, which they transported to their nutrient-hungry corn on the backs of llamas. They added fertilization to the fields in the form of sardine-heads, one for every planted seed. They dried meat and roasted corn for the long journeys they made through their steep lands – and the Indians of Peru today travel the same routes, with the same provisions. Making their intoxicating maize beer called *chicha* necessitated chewing the kernels slightly first and spitting them out. Human saliva breaks down the starch and converts it into the maltose and glucose necessary to produce alcohol. Many pottery *chicha* vessels have survived, decorated with corn cobs, demon heads, and drunken leaning figures. *Chicha* is still a popular brew.

When the Aztecs of Central America performed human sacrifices the priest cut out the victim's heart with a flint knife, and tossed the warm corpse over the side of the temple terrace. The heart was thought of as having been husked, like a corn cob from its sheath. The head was kept on a special skull rack until its flesh dropped off and only the skull remained, indistinguishable from numerous others like it. Most of the remainder of the body may have been eaten in the form of a "man-stew" – with maize. The Aztecs savagely punished any kind of theft; yet owners of maize fields were expected to allow the hungry travellers who passed by to help themselves to ears from any corn plants that bordered a route.

Corn, for the Indians throughout North, Central, and South America, was a tragic and sacred plant. Every society regards its staple foodstuff in this way: man respects, admires, and may even adore his "stuff of life." He feels sorrow and guilt because he must cut it down in order to live, and he feels joy and gratitude because the plant accepts death and agrees in time to return – if due respect is paid to custom and science – to feed its murderers again. A central myth of the Indians – told with a myriad variations but always essentially the same – may representatively be given in the version of the Ojibways from the region of Lake Superior.

The Ojibways once lived only by hunting and fishing; a hard and precarious life. There arose a young and religiously gifted man with the power of attaining shamanic visions, whose name was Wunzh. Wunzh knew the suffering of the hunter, for his father had no luck and therefore could not feed his family. Wunzh fasted and prayed in order to receive a spirit guide who would tell him what to do to end hunger. At last the spirit guide came: a young man dressed in yellow and green, with a head dress of green feathers. He demanded that Wunzh should wrestle with him, despite the Indian's weakness from fasting. They wrestled until Wunzh was exhausted, and suddenly the spirit disappeared. Twice more he came, and twice more they fought. And then the visitant announced that the Great Spirit was pleased with Wunzh and would grant his prayer. Wunzh must wrestle again till he conquered the spirit and killed him. Then he must strip off his adversary's clothes and throw his corpse down on the ground. This Wunzh did, and in sorrow left the broken body of the wrestler in the forest. When he returned later to the spot the body was gone, but Wunzh saw the tips of the warrior's plumed headdress showing through the earth. Eventually it grew into a plant as tall as a man, and to this cruel but glorious event the Ojibway Indian owed his sustenance, his security, and joy.

Corn for the Indian was both One and Various. Its many colours – orange, white, blue, black, and the rest – seemed to him the many-faceted manifestation of the single and divine sap of *maïs*. There was a deep obligation to preserve its variety. The Hopi Indians allotted to each family in a village one type of corn, and it was that family's responsibility to maintain the purity of that corn type through the generations. In other words, hybridization, the core of the modern development of corn, would have been anathema to the Indians: hybridization confuses categories, refuses priorities, and denies the aspect of Many to what was One.

An eighteenth-century Franciscan missionary wrote of the Mexican

Indians among whom he worked: "Everything they did and said so concerned maize that they almost regarded it as a god. The enchantment and rapture with which they look upon their *milpas* (cornfields) is such that on their account they forget children, wife, and any other pleasures, as though the *milpas* were their final purpose in life and the source of their felicity." Corn must never be wasted, for this was sacrilege: Mexican Indians still say that scattered corn which has not been picked up will complain to God about it. Corn was afraid of being cooked, so a woman must breathe on the corn before throwing it into the pot, to comfort it and accustom it to heat. After the birth of a child, corn cobs must not be burned lest the face of the child should be pitted and blackened like them. Hell, for the Natchez, was a barren waterlogged place where the wicked would eat the flesh of alligators and rotten fish, and where "they will not have any kind of corn." Zuñi Indians thought that corn sprinkled across a doorway should be sufficient to keep an enemy at bay: pathetically, they tried it when the Spaniards came – the people who had no respect for maize.

The Indians had no traction animals and no horses, raised no cattle and drank no milk. When the Europeans came the Indians immediately offered them their maize, as well as the other weird and wonderful vegetables and fruits of the New World, which were soon to change human eating habits the world over. The Europeans brought their great beasts over in ships – and proceeded to feed them on maize, an act which was sacrilege to the Indians, for maize was of the gods, and man alone among creatures could eat it.

The Spanish wasted no time in taking the new grain back to plant at home. American corn has been cultivated in the Iberian peninsula since the sixteenth century. The Indians had shown the Spaniards and Portuguese how corn must be dried before it can be safely stored, and how to safeguard it from predators while it dries. They built wooden platforms in their *milpas*, so constructed that rats and other creatures could not climb up to the grain cache on top. The Spanish version of the early corn cribs were the *horreos* in stone (they are called *espigueiros* in Portugal): wonderful simple structures raised on short fat columns, looking like illustrations from some exotic fairy-tale, and which still are commonly visible, with many regional variations, in Spain and Portugal.

Very soon after Columbus's journey slaves were being brought from Africa to work the new American lands for European colonists from various countries. The British slave-trader Sebastian Cabot used the

Indians' maize to buy slaves from Africa: corn travelled well across the ocean, and it was eagerly received in exchange for men. Those slaves went out to America in the holds that had carried maize, and not a few of them worked corn plantations whose fruits bought more slaves. John Leo visited Africa as early as 1535, and two hundred miles inland on the Niger River he met a tribe who had "a great store of a round and white kind of pulse, the like whereof I never saw in Europe." The Africans called it *manputo*, "Portuguese grain." "This," adds Leo, "is called maiz in the West Indies."

The Portuguese island off the west coast of Africa, São Tomé, was busily importing maize from Equatorial Guinea and Gabon on the mainland in the early sixteenth century. Portuguese ships carried maize to Morocco, Burma, and China and round the coasts of the African continent; South Africans still call the ears of maize "mealies," from the early Portuguese term, *milho grosso*. Holland spread the grain even further afield. The Turkish Empire caused American corn to spread over North Africa and into Hungary and Romania. The Turks themselves never liked maize much: they remained eaters of wheat. But it suited them to let their subject peoples take to maize, because it meant all the more wheat for themselves. For a long time in Europe there was confusion about where the deluge of new foodstuffs was coming from; for many it seemed that the exotic Turkish Empire must be responsible and that the produce came from the East or from Africa. The huge new American chickens were called "turkeys"; and maize was called Guinney wheat, Indian barley, or Turkie wheat in England, *granturco* in Italy, and "Turkish" grain in Germany and Holland.

The very early familiarity of North Africans with maize may have come about through the Moors, who could have carried it with them when many of them were expelled from Spain between 1499 and 1502. Some scholars suggest that Africa had maize much earlier still: the Arabs, who are known to have been navigating the Atlantic as early as 1100 AD, might have encountered it and brought it across the relatively short stretch of ocean from Brazil to Africa. The persistent belief of Europeans that maize came to them from Turkey, and of the Chinese that they received maize from the west (not by sea from the Portuguese as is still most commonly believed) might support the theory that maize spread to the Old World from the New before the journeys of Columbus. Names and dates are less than the tips of the icebergs of history; ideas and commodities can appear to travel faster than people – if the only people we consider are those for whom we have names and dates. After 1492, maize spread over the world with extraordinary alacrity. It was hardy; it travelled; it grew quickly; it provided plenty of food.

HOW CORN IS EATEN

The European settlers in North America survived their first winters because they listened to the Indians and learned fast. They brought wheat seed on the ships with them, and planted it – but owing to different weather and soil conditions or because of bad storage on board, the seed failed, and maize became the mainstay of their lives. They sowed it as the Indians taught them, planting a fish in every mound. On the eastern seaboard the fish were mainly alewives, the herring of the Atlantic which in those days teemed at spawning (and planting) time so copiously that a man had only to lace his fingers in the water and fish would swim into his hands. The Europeans also learned to keep their fields as neat as a "garden bedde" as the Indians did, "not suffering a choaking weede to advance his audacious head above their infant corne." They were taught how much the maize needed water, and when and how to harvest at different times for different purposes.

Then came the cooking lessons. The meal which serves as the structural principle for this book begins with simple boiled immature cobs, buttered and salted. Sweet corn was relatively little prized among most American Indian tribes: sweetness can quickly pall in a food eaten as one's chief sustenance. Boiled young sweet corn was an occasional treat among the bands that raised this particular variety; butter was unknown, and salt in many cases rare. Far more commonly eaten were the kinds of corn that lent themselves to roasting and to grinding into meal. Stoneground corn, as South Americans have traditionally made it and as modern "gourmet" cooks increasingly realize, is far more delicious than machine-ground, because the germ, complete with its fat and nutrients, is left in the grain.

One could have *suppawn*, a corn porridge lightened and slightly sweetened with crushed green corn stalks. *Succotash* was corn and beans stewed together. *Hominy* was flint corn boiled with ash so that the pericarp of the kernels could be washed away; after prolonged boiling the grain emerged greyish white with a smoky flavour. Cornmeal could be cooked on a stone or griddle as a flat cake which was handy to take on journeys, hence its English name, "jonnycake." *Hoecakes* were baked in an oven, spread thinly on a greased iron hoe blade; the name in one Indian language for such a cake was a *nookik*: is it coincidence that this sounds very much like "an hoecake"?

Pone was an Algonquin word for corn cooked as a thin layer of batter on a heated stone, like the hoecake or "journey cake." The method had also been common among the Aztecs, who rationed out corn to every person according to his age, in what was considered an appropriate number per day of thin flat cakes, each at least a foot in diameter. Maize could even be baked into something resembling bread – flat, dense, crumbly (corn lacks the gluten that enables wheaten flour to rise), but filling and delicious. The addition of buttermilk or clabber was a European invention: the Indians had not consumed animals' milk. But the mixture was often cooked in the embers wrapped in husks, which was an Indian method. *Spoon bread* is more elaborate, a baked affair lightened with beaten eggwhites and puffy like a soufflé. *Grits* are coarsely ground white cornmeal with the fine grains sifted out.

In Central and South America, wet hominy is squeezed and kneaded into a dough (*masa*) and fried or baked as tortillas or stuffed and fried as enchiladas. *Masa* ferments quickly in its wet state, so that today it is often dried and ground into flour which is sold as *masa harina. Tamales* have meat or vegetables inside, and are wrapped in corn husks and boiled or steamed. In South America corn is used to make all sorts of drinks as well as food: *atole, pinolillo, chicheme, colada,* and the *chicha* made from chewed corn. Peru prizes its purple corn, which gives colour and flavour to sweet dishes and drinks.

Maize is also precious in Africa – too precious to feed it, as North Americans do, to livestock; cattle in Africa may be given stalks to eat, or the hulls which have been removed from the kernels. The Yorubas of Nigeria eat corn as *ogi*, a mush which requires painstaking soaking, grinding, and washing for several days before it is boiled. The same preparation wrapped in banana leaves and cooked is *agidi*, an important dish in Sierra Leone and the Ivory Coast; a variant is *kenkey*, from Ghana. Often peanuts, red peppers, and palm oil are mixed with the corn; or it is simply cooked and dipped in relish. Corn needs supplementary foodstuffs to complete its nutrient value, and "dipping" is one obvious way to achieve this. The distinctively American habit of dipping food in sauces may well have developed in part from this manner of eating corn.

By the mid-eighteenth century the newcomers to North America had totally accepted Indian corn as their staple food. They had corn for breakfast, lunch, and supper. American soldiers captured in Canada in the War of 1812 and imprisoned at Halifax, Nova Scotia, expressed their deepest need – for the corn they were accustomed to eating daily. "Their cry for '*mush and milk*' was incessant," wrote the superintendant of the camp. "I soon placed before the poor sufferers the object of their long-ings." North Americans did everything they could to induce Europeans to like corn. The dissemination of recipes for cooking the new vegetable was one of the most important means to this end.

Yet in Europe maize has had a chequered history. The Belgians have never accepted corn as part of their national cuisine, and neither have the Germans, the Scandinavians, or the Swiss. The French have always tended to turn up their noses at it, relegating corn to chickenfeed, cooking oil, and the plastics industry. In 1847 the starving Irish refused at first to eat stores of corn brought by the British from America. They called it "Peel's brimstone" after the British prime minister and because it seemed to them to have a sinister colour, yellow like sulphur.

In about 1650, however, Italy suddenly embraced maize, adapting it to the production of the ancient Roman grain porridge, *puls* or *pulmentum*, which was originally made of spelt, millet, or chick-pea flour. Today what the Italians now call *polenta* is popular in the north, cooked much as it is in Africa, and served with squid in its black ink, or tomato sauce. The great nineteenth-century novelist, Alessandro Manzoni, de-scribed steaming yellow *polenta* being poured out onto a wooden board as looking like "a harvest moon in a mist." Byron had a beautiful Venetian mistress who used to float with him in a gondola down the Grand Canal, lazily nibbling bits of *polenta* from a ball of it which she kept warm down the front of her dress, between her breasts.

One of the most assiduously corn-eating nations in Europe is Ro-mania. The Romanians took to the American plant largely because their Turkish overlords did not: they could keep all the maize crop them-selves, while the Turks had access to more Romanian wheat. Maize was thrown as a fertility charm at weddings, much as rice is in other Eu-ropean and American countries. (Maize mixed with rice is still part of wedding rites in Spain.) The Romanians used it in popular medicine to cure colds, burns, and skin diseases. The Romanian poet Lucian Blaga recounts an intoxicating memory:

> As a child I used to love to jump
> naked into the maize barrel,
> drowning up to my neck in golden grain. . . .

CORN FLAKES

A useful cash crop in nineteenth-century America was a special kind of sorghum (*Sorghum vulgare technicum*), grown for the long bristles which sprout from its ears; bristles which created a minor household revolution amidst all the thunderous transformations of housekeeping which occurred in that century. Really efficient brooms were mass-manufactured out of this "broomcorn." Their bristles were densely clustered and evenly trimmed, flexible, and strong.

Selling brooms was the first real employment of a teen-aged Seventh Day Adventist called Will Kellogg. Will's father and mother had become Adventists after the death of their daughter through medical incompetence. When they heard of the medical theories of the Adventist leaders Elder White and Sister White of Battle Creek, Michigan, they sold their broomcorn farm in Connecticut and moved to Battle Creek, where they opened a broom factory.

Water cures were one of the Adventists' healing methods: sponge baths, wrapping patients in wet sheets, sitz baths, foot baths, watersprays, and plunges. Sister White was told in a vision to open hospitals where baths could be administered, and vegetarianism, proper rest, and exercise taught and practised. She opened a sanatorium in Battle Creek and ten years later Will Kellogg's elder brother John Harvey Kellogg, who had prepared himself with a medical degree, took charge of the Battle Creek Sanatorium. The Doctor misspelled the word as "Sanitarium," but stuck to his error when it had been pointed out to him. "Sanitarium," he said, would find its way into dictionaries by the time he was through building up Battle Creek. He was right; it did.

Under John Harvey Kellogg the Sanitarium became one of the largest, richest, and most influential hospitals in the United States. John Harvey himself wrote and argued prolifically about his health philosophy, which he called "biologic living," and about the roles of food, light, water, and exercise in the curing of disease. He wrote over fifty books and was celebrated throughout the United States as a surgeon and a kind of medical guru.

John Harvey was a demonic worker. Only one man could compete with him for sheer energy and concentration on work: his overshadowed, underpaid, unglamorous factotum and younger brother, Will Keith Kellogg. Will did all the organizing of the "San," while his brother was the celebrity and figurehead. He followed wherever his elder brother led. One of these leads was into a series of experiments John Harvey set up in order to find a way of making bread more easily digestible. The Sanitarium had already invented a ground and toasted granular food called Granola.

John Harvey claimed that the idea of flaking wheat by compressing it came to him in a dream in 1894. The rollers already in use for making Granola were set to work to experiment with boiled wheat, and of course a lot of the dull trial-and-error operations which resulted from the flash of inspiration were handled by brother Will. One night the wheat had been left too long after boiling, but the brothers rolled it anyway, and found that each berry turned into an elongated thin flake. They baked the flakes, which turned crisp. It was Will who argued that the flakes – peculiar to look at as they were – should not be ground as Granola grain was ground, but left whole.

Wheat flakes began to be offered to the public, and to catch on, as a breakfast health food. Many companies formed to profit from the new fashion, in spite of the difficulty people had at first with the idea of cold food for breakfast. Three years after the first discovery of the flaking technique, Will began to experiment with corn instead of wheat. "Horse food," the sceptics called it, and the first corn flakes were thick, flavourless and unpopular. But gradually they were improved, flavoured with malt, altered in texture and keeping qualities with chemical additives, thinned, and crisped until corn flakes as we know them were complete. The Kellogg "grain-tempering" process was patented in 1894.

Will Kellogg eventually broke with his brother and the Sanitarium and at last felt capable of striking out on his own. He was forty-six years old. He began to advertise as no one yet had advertised in American – or any other – business practice. He gave away samples of his revolutionary product. He discovered the importance of the package itself as advertising medium: the corn flakes girl, "Sweetheart of the Corn," was dreamed up and then emblazoned on every box. She was an American reincarnation of the mother goddess, of youthfulness and sudden impulse, as with a brilliant smile she embraced a corn-shock. The Sweetheart delivered none of the minatory restrictions Will's brother meted out with his health foods; she *suggested* health and wholesomeness and sound country living (all of them evangelically American values), but advised nothing and promised nothing except pleasure. Early Kellogg slogans included: "Wins its favor through its flavor!" "The breakfast treat that makes you eat!" and "America's Waking Thought." W.K. Kellogg had already discovered the two basic necessities in advertising: recognisability and continuous repetition. He used jingles, famous faces, his own personal signature as endorsement, and insistence that his corn flakes were "the original." Children were perceived almost immediately as a powerful and susceptible means of access to their parents' purses: children were pictured on packages and offered contests, cut-outs, free samples, and rewards for collecting cereal-box tops. Kellogg's also supported corn shows, with prizes for the most uniform ears of maize, in the days before hybrid corn.

When the Depression struck, Will Kellogg surveyed the scenes of despair and catastrophe in the business world all about him. His response was not to cut back, but to redouble his advertising, actually embracing the Depression as his company's biggest break. This was probably his greatest hour as a businessman. For, in fact, it was during the Depression that Americans permanently altered their breakfast habits. The heavy hot early meal became a relic of the past; the reason was partly a lack of money and time, and partly the alternative promulgated by Mr. Kellogg and his imitators and competitors.

From this point on the corn flake enters social history. *Zea maïs*, the divine life-sustainer of the pre-Columbian Indians, the humble underpinning of North American wealth, now enters a new phase of its ancient mythical life. Long ago North Americans had chosen yellow corn and white corn and rejected the rest: blue, black, red, orange, and multi-coloured maize had become so exotic as to be almost indecent – unless used for purely decorative purposes. White, for us, means "pure," and food must look pure, always. Yellow is a little more problematical, but it does suggest sunshine. The xanthophylls present in yellow corn make the skin and legs of the poultry fed on it yellow, and yellow is considered more appetizing than white in a chicken: yellow means "golden," and promises the succulence of roasts and fried meat. Kellogg's and other corn flakes manufacturers work hard to achieve a *golden* flake. It must be toasted, but not too dark, or people will not eat it, no matter what its taste. Kellogg's used to go out of its way to buy white corn in order to achieve just the colour the consumer wants. White corn is not grown much in the Battle Creek area. Now the company has found out how to get the same colour with the more easily available yellow corn: you first bleach the kernels white, then proceed.

Corn flakes' connotations for us are of swiftness, sunshine, youth, and brightness. They are as crisp and snack-like as potato chips, sweetened and salted like junk-food, yet hallowed by Milk, which always says "Mother." In North American culture nothing bathed in fresh milk can be threatening or bad. Corn flakes are light, and therefore can get away with being eaten cold, even for breakfast. They are modern and easy, yet already traditional; a fast-paced bachelor food which still manages to remain associated with childhood and with families. Eating them for breakfast is a habit known to many countries on earth yet universally recognized as typically American. Since the food which it eats provides a nation with its identity, corn flakes thus gains yet another claim to be considered as an institution. There is no great distance between cultural "institutions" in this sense and the reverence and sacrality which characterized the attitude of the Indians to corn in pre-Columbian America.

CORN AND GENETICS

The ubiquity of the corn plant in Colonial America had made it standard material for a thousand uses which had nothing to do with food. One device, which united tobacco and corn, was the corncob smoking pipe. This became an institution in the United States when it began to be manufactured commercially in 1869 at Washington, Missouri, still the corncob-pipe capital of the world. A University of Missouri professor has even provided the business recently with its own specially developed hard cob, corn hybrid MO Pipe 12. The cobs are aged seven years before being carved. They are light, strong, and plentiful, so that the pipes are disposable and replaceable: traditional and rustic, yet convenient and modern. Corn cobs have also done service as fuel, fishing corks, bottle-stoppers, mousehole plugs, back-scratchers, scrubbing brushes, hair curlers, and toilet paper. Stalks piled up outside the walls of a house provided insulation for the winter. Husks were shredded to stuff mattresses and woven into chair-seats or hats.

The colonists moved westward only as fast as corn-lands could be cleared and planted. And as modern American society invented itself, more and more uses were found for corn.

The corn embryo in its kernel is surrounded with a copious sugary food supply, which changes in time to starch. Starch is insoluble in cold water, but in warm its granules burst and form a viscous, jelly-like liquid which becomes firm when it cools; a high temperature produces a gum-like substance called *dextrin*, which is extremely useful for its adhesive properties.

Dextrin, used in the manufacture of porcelain, has to be treated first with sulphurous acid to prevent discolouration in the ovens. In the first decade of the nineteenth century a Russian chemist called G. S. C. Kirchoff mistakenly overdid the treatment, and found to his amazement that he had turned his dextrin into a sweet sticky stuff which (coloured and treated) we now call corn syrup. And so man found that he could convert starch, readily available in the familiar corn kernel, back into the magical substance for which he had been prepared for so long to kill and enslave: sugar. Sugar was to become as limitlessly available as corn starch, and as cheap.

The several spectacular metamorphoses of which starch is capable make it one of the most versatile materials on earth. The ancient Egyptians had obtained it from wheat and used it to coat and stiffen papyrus. The Romans used it in medicines, cosmetics, foods, and fabrics. Wheat was the source of starch in early America also: a company called Colgate and Co. of Jersey City produced starch from wheat. In 1841, an Englishman, Orlando Jones, showed how starch could be extracted from corn, thereby doing a great deal to change the course of American history. In 1844, Colgate dropped wheat for corn as their source of starch.

Today only one-third of the corn starch produced is used in food. The rest goes into thousands of commodities, from latex paint and toothpaste to core binders for the moulding of iron, steel, and aluminium. The Starch Round Table of the American Corn Industries Research Foundation is an annual conference of scientists from all over the world who review the latest research on starch in the service of mankind. They discuss water-resistant (hydrophobic) starch, adhesive starch and anti-adhesive starch, starch in textiles, rubber, woodworking, leather, metallurgy, paper-making, cosmetics, and plastics. They also discuss how to reduce the constituents of starch which absorb oxygen and kill fish when starchy waste waters are discharged into rivers. The Board watches constantly for new mutants of corn. One famous mutant of maize was the previously unknown waxy corn, which was discovered by J. M. W. Farnham, an American Presbyterian missionary in China, and was later found in North and South America as well. Its starch is nearly 100 per cent amylopectin, which makes waxy corn an important commercial crop for the glue and instant pudding industries.

The scientists also discuss genetics. Corn grows very fast and responds extremely well to hybridization. Add to these facts the huge economic importance of the corn crop, the centrality of corn to what is techno-logically the most advanced society on earth, and it becomes clear why it is that corn is genetically the most tinkered-with plant in existence. Gregor Mendel, the Austrian monk who discovered the laws of genetics, used peas in his little garden for his experiments. Very soon after Men-del's forgotten discoveries had been brought to light again by a Dutch botanist in 1900, an American named George Harrison Shull began Mendelian researches into corn.

Eventually the secret of control over corn breeding was found. The rule, once formulated, is very simple: first you produce four inbred lines of maize. Then you cross, and cross again. The pathetic stunted little cobs with twisted rows of kernels which result from inbreeding resume and then multiply their vigour when they are allowed to cross with other similarly inbred plants. Desirable traits triumph over un-desirable; quantity is enormously increased; there are no disappoint-ments from controlled seed, and no nasty surprises. Since the 1920s, hybrid corn has revolutionized American farming, and hybridization has been called the greatest agricultural accomplishment since agricul-ture itself was invented ten thousand years ago.

The Indians had relied on spiritual qualities in themselves – prepa-ration, attitude, and intent – to produce good crops. They insisted on variety, and they knew that maintaining variety meant preventing dif-ferent types of corn from mixing. The European newcomers had adapted Indian beliefs and methods to their own empirical ways. They set about perfecting types of corn, learning by the look and feel of a cob whether it was producing good healthy seed, then choosing the best kernels to plant. The idea was to improve the crop gradually by always planting the best of every batch. Increased yields were the goal: bigger cobs and more ears per plant wherever possible.

In 1893 a farmer called James Reid won a prize for his spectacular corn. He had inherited the strain from his father Robert, improved and perfected it for many years, and finally showed it at the Chicago World's Fair. It was called Reid's Yellow Dent, and it was the result of a failure and an accident. Back in 1847, Robert Reid's crop of reddish corn had failed in patches, so he planted the bald spots in his fields with a flint corn called Little Yellow. One type fertilized the other, and Reid's Yellow Dent was the prize-winning result. The cobs were heavy with golden yellow kernels, all of them plump and evenly spaced from cob tip to beautifully rounded butt. Reid's Yellow Dent was snatched up and planted by whoever could get it; it spread across the United States.

A corollary of all the jubilation and success was hardly noticed then, but for the first time the bell tolled, enunciating the theme of one of the twentieth century's nightmares. Reid's Yellow Dent was so good, so obviously preferable, that other corns were forgotten, simply not planted. And "not planted," when we speak of "man-created" *Zea maïs*, means nonexistent forever after. Thousands of kinds of corn, varieties reverently preserved and kept separate and distinct by the Indians, as well as many carefully improved by American farmers, disappeared off the face of the earth.

The years between 1900 and 1920 in the United States and Canada were the years of the corn shows. Farmers were educated in farming methods and modernization. There were corn trains which travelled across the continent disseminating information, teaching farmers how to recognize good seed corn, and how to test it to make sure it would grow before planting it. Corn-shucking contests became a spectator sport. At the annual corn shows, farmers exhibited their best cobs and won prizes for the beauty of the ears. One of the great American myths was being created and accepted with ever-increasing confidence and fervour: that beauty – in corn as in anything else – is largely a matter of uniformity. *Straight* rows of kernels were admired, truly *cylindrical* cobs, absolute uniformity of colour, yellow or white. (Red corn, black, blue, and the rest had long ago been eliminated as unacceptable for North Americans.) Curiously enough, beauty was allowed to overshadow performance in these years: a farmer showed only a few perfect ears; the amount of the yield was not taken into consideration in awarding the prizes.

In 1922 hybrid corn began to become commercially available. By 1950 the corn shows and the corn judges had been swept away: hybrid corns (based largely on germ-plasm from Reid's Yellow Dent) became available which were absolutely reliable, predictable, and capable of yields previously undreamed of. Farm machinery was invented, and once it appeared it had to be bought if a farmer wanted to stay in business. Corn genetics enabled farm machinery to operate, because it produced plants to order which the machines could handle.

As mentioned earlier, a corn plant is both male (its tassels) and female (its silks). Hybrid corn seed is achieved by removing the tassels of the inbred line of corn which is to bear the grain, so that the plant cannot seed itself but will receive pollen from the other inbred parent chosen to be planted in the same field. "Tasselling" (removing the tassels, which has to be done by hand so that the rest of the plant suffers no damage) is still an enormous summer task in many countries, demanding waves of temporary labour at the appropriate times. Poor tasselling can mean an undesirable mixture of hybrid and non-hybrid seed. Ultra-modern seed farms in the United States and Canada, and increasingly in Europe, have adopted a new technique which does away with this human labour: male sterile plants have been designed, by genetic manipulation, to produce no pollen.

Corn has been bred for "standability": stalks stiff enough that ears can be mechanically harvested without the plants collapsing. "Standability" is placed above "yield" in many lists of the desirable features of corn for the farmer. Other priorities in hybrid corn are: yield, maturation at a time when the least possible drying is required, disease and insect resistance, machine suitability (not too many cobs, a plant which does not grow too high or too low, relative weakness of ear-attachment to the stalk), uniformity and quality of grain.

Geneticists have also tackled corn's protein deficiency in an effort to make grain capable in itself of supplying all nutritional needs. They have come up with Opaque 11, named after a corn gene which increases available lysine in the kernels. Opaque 11 has so far proved most useful in feeding pigs, which have nutritional needs very similar to man's. But Opaque 11 "buys" its uncommon protein strength with what geneticists call "garbage traits": low yield, and a soft kernel susceptible to moulds and damage in harvesting.

The world now grows 500 million metric tons of corn a year, nearly half of it in the United States. Eighty per cent of the American maize crop is produced in the Corn Belt, an area 350,000 miles square, which stretches from western Ohio to eastern Nebraska, with the largest corn tonnage of all coming from Iowa and Illinois. The hungry mouths of the world and the tireless wheels of industry depend upon this modern hybrid wonder, the answer to thousands of years of human fears, hopes, and endeavours. American corn is a spearhead of the modern "Green Revolution," one of the proudest answers of scientists to the threat of world hunger.

"And he gave it for his opinion," Jonathan Swift wrote in *Gulliver's Travels*, "that whoever could make two ears of corn or two blades of grass to grow upon a spot of ground where only one grew before, would deserve better of mankind, and do more essential service to his country than the whole race of politicians put together." What would he have thought of the scientists who gave us American corn, a single grain of which in four months flat can multiply itself eight hundred times over?

NOW THE BAD NEWS

In the 1930s, farms in the United States, and soon after in Canada, began to be mechanized. The arduous labour of farming was lifted from man's shoulders for the first time since he had learned to make vegetation grow for him instead of having to hunt for it. Today's corn farmer prepares his soil with machines. Maize drains the soil of nitrogen and this must constantly be replaced, so anhydrous ammonia – a stable gas created when atmospheric nitrogen is flared under pressure with methane – is sold in huge metal cylinders to farmers. They literally inject the soil with gas, drawing a system of knives behind tractors mounted with pressurized tanks of ammonia.

Machines then move in to plant the seed by means of calibrated plates or air pressure. Next phosphorus, often in liquid form which permits direct contact with the seed, and potassium and other nutrients are added in proportions ascertained by scientific analysis of the soil. Insecticides are applied – the seed already having received treatment with insecticides before planting. Weed-killers are essential, because soils artificially nourished with nitrogen and other chemicals make weeds grow as fast as corn. Herbicides, like insecticides, are, in the language of the sales catalogues, "preplant incorporated, preemergence or post-emergence in application."

But weeds and insects are learning to adapt to these poison doses: insects resistant to insecticides and "new" weeds immune to herbicides constantly appear, and ever more complex programmes of poisons must be developed. More and more farmers are arming themselves with computers to analyse soil and correct plant populations.

The growing corn needs huge quantities of water, which nearly always has to be piped in and sprayed over the plants. This water seeps through a soil soaked in chemicals, and inevitably leaches the chemicals into the region's groundwater system: the nitrite levels of groundwater in the Corn Belt are often twice as high as what is thought to be the upper limit of potability. Phosphate runoff from these soils fills rivers and ponds with algae.

The harvest is done mechanically: the kernels are even stripped from the cobs in the field. Human labour is reduced to driving the tractors and sorting, and even the latter is scarcely necessary for corn, so high is the predictable uniformity of the hybrid product. And then the corn must be speed-dried with hot air to improve its keeping qualities, and carefully cooled to prevent cracking. Natural drying is very difficult if quantities are very large, as they are on a modern farm.

With corn, as with so many crops, machines replacing people means more food, but fewer people working. In the early twentieth century over 90 per cent of North Americans lived on the land; now 97 per cent of them live in towns and cities. That is quite a transformation – a shifting of population on an unprecedentedly huge scale. Just over 3 per cent of the citizens of the United States now feed the entire population. Decline in the number of people living in the countryside means huge farms, and far fewer of them. Few indeed can afford the capital investment in machinery and in chemicals that are needed to begin, or even to continue, a farm. The wonder-corn seed must be constantly created anew: it does not keep its vigour. Therefore seed companies create hybrid grain, and farmers must buy their seed every year.

Small towns have disappeared by the hundreds in North America, and with them rural social institutions, customs, traditions. Farmers now must travel huge distances to get off their own farms – to transport their children to school for example, or to get to a doctor. Even on successful working farms with all their battle array of heavy equipment, farmers find that they need non-farm income: increasingly they take other jobs – bus driving, teaching, selling insurance, even working in factories – with all the travel involved in getting to the extra employment. The truth is that farmers are not often rich, or even particularly well off. The machines certainly produce plenty of corn and other farm crops, but prices to the consumer are extraordinarily low, and the machines are extremely expensive to run and repair as well as to buy.

Less is paid for food, in terms of percentage of income, in North America than anywhere else on earth since the history of universal "incomes" began. North Americans keep their money for other things – mainly for other machines. Low food costs, brought about by machines, permit people to buy themselves more machines. It seems simple, and quite delightful; as long as hidden costs (loss of water for example, or loss of alternatives) are kept out of sight.

Vast quantities of the corn crop are consumed by people in the form of beef, pork, and chicken. Corn-fattening animals for market is a hugely profitable process. Beef calves are kept, after weaning, for six months on three meals a day of hay, oats, corn, and cornstalks. When they weigh 365 kilograms (800 lbs.) they are sold to a feedlot operator, who gives them an unvarying diet of ground corn till they clock in at 550 kilograms (1,200 lbs.), the agreed market weight. The animals are kept in large numbers and in very close confinement: movement, by building up muscle, inhibits fat. Feed is carted in to them automatically and the manure is trundled out. But even granted modern transport and disposal technology the pollution resulting from the endless massive tonnages of manure which result from beef fattening is a horror which has hardly begun to be understood, let alone treated. Water, both underground and in surrounding streams, is poisoned and wasted – irreparably, so far.

In Guatemala today live the descendants of the ancient Mayans. Like many Indian tribes, they practise agricultural methods a thousand and more years old. Every farmer first chooses his corn patch or *milpa* with enormous care, having regard to the site and the soil. He prepares his land by slashing the underbrush and cutting down the trees. Next, he waits, watching clouds and leaves, moon and wind, leaving his plot to dry out until the perfect day arrives.

Then comes the exultant moment when the dry vegetation is set on fire. The Indians report that the firing causes them "immense joy." The fire, they say, kills the insects noxious to corn and makes the soil "sweat," which is extremely good for it, especially if rain occurs immediately after firing. The moment the ash has cooled, and not a day later, the planting is done, right into the ash. The farmers poke sticks into the ground, drop in a few kernels and cover them roughly. They leave tree stumps standing; they make holes not in rows but wherever seems right in the spaces between stumps.

As the corn grows, they double the stalks over to protect the cobs from rainwater, and watch it carefully, scaring off swarms of parrots and other predators. Often a family moves into a hut in the corn patch – which might be quite far from the village – and lives there while the corn grows, tending it and enjoying the hunt for animals which the growing maize draws to itself like fish after bait. Living in the *milpa* for a few months is regarded as a restful, recreative time, full of stimulating fun and profit. Finally the harvest is culled, by hand. After this the *milpa* is abandoned: left for nature to re-instal itself, and for the land to become "young and strong" again. A *milpa* cannot be slashed and burned for at least seven years after a harvest, for the corn has "sucked dry" or "withered" the soil.

Now all this slash-and-burn or "swidden" agriculture (the method is typical of that of many societies which still exist) is not nearly productive enough. It is far too much work, wasteful and slow and unaware of the power man now has of controlling the plant and its predators. Besides, populations are growing and hungry: they need to be fed. Once hybrid corn was established in the United States, it was not long before a movement began to carry the new knowledge and its successful progeny to the Third World. HYVs (High Yielding Varieties) of corn were introduced to people long used to much less, and much slower production. The "Green Revolution" had begun. It was enthusiastically and gratefully accepted. There is no doubt that large numbers of people owe their lives to its benefits.

Yet – once again – there has been a heartbreaking price to pay. It was discovered (too late) that the sudden introduction of modern agriculture into traditional societies very often benefited the rich, destroying the small farmers' livelihoods and all their independence. Expensive machines are available to few, and instantly crush competition. Mechanization always reduces employment, forcing people to leave the land for the crowded and often desperately poor cities. "Green Revolution" methods cost a great deal in water and in money for chemicals and seed, even when the machines have been installed. Technological prowess has so far maintained its prestige almost intact, because its benefits are so swift and so obvious. The risks it takes are only intermittently perceived to be risks, and then only when the damage has been done.

A well-meaning team of agriculturalists moves in to a swidden system not unlike the Guatemalan example we looked at. The untidiness, the wastage of the slash-and-burn method are swiftly gauged. In goes the heavy equipment. No more tree stumps, slashed undergrowth, ash. Parrots are so heavily discouraged that they will never trouble this region – or any other – again. For a year or two, an unbelievable amount of cylindrical yellow straight-rowed corn is triumphantly grown on ground pumped full of nitrogen and phosphate. But finally truth is revealed and tragic knowledge achieved: it becomes apparent that the forest's topsoil – that topsoil which had been preserved, waited on, and respected by generation upon generation of Indian slash-and-burn farmers – has been destroyed. And that top-soil can never be restored. The damage is done and irreparable.

It will not be long before dependence on artificial fertilizers will be so intense that it will be counterproductive in terms of cost and further destruction. By this time, many traditional crops will also have been lost to modern streamlining and size: vast, fragile corn monocultures with surpluses to sell for cash will have replaced a whole gamut of nutritious, home-grown foods. The fossil fuels and the phosphate upon which the "Green Revolution" relies have often to be imported at considerable and unending cost. It has been estimated that by the new methods it takes the equivalent in fossil fuels of seven hundred and fifty litres of petroleum to produce one hectare of corn (67 Imperial gallons to produce 1 acre).

Worst of all, varieties of corn are disappearing by the dozen even as these words are being written. A corn not being planted is a corn which ceases to exist; man alone can keep *Zea maïs* alive. Hybrid corns have been created, and continue to be crossed and improved and adapted to various circumstances, but hybrids are *combinations* only. Their ancestral lines are germ-plasm from corn varieties. Which lines are used is in fact largely a matter of chance. Reid's Yellow Dent was itself an accident. And often corn types which have extraordinarily valuable traits have come to light in obscure traditional corn cultures. Who knows what possibilities lay in the genetic material of the thousands of corns we have rejected and therefore lost in the last hundred years?

In 1970 an epidemic of corn leaf blight struck the United States: oblong lesions appeared on the leaves, stalks weakened and fell, yield was greatly reduced. This new mutant strain of an ancient scourge victimized only one type of corn – but that type had been planted by almost every farmer in the country. This corn variety contained Texas cytoplasm, the secret of the new way to prevent the labour of tasselling. Scientists hurriedly replaced the Texas with normal cytoplasm, thousands of people suddenly found temporary tasselling jobs again, and the danger was soon averted. This was possible only because alternative genes existed. One of the most popular traits of the labour-saving corn hybrids with Texas cytoplasm in their parentage had been the built-in resistance of these plants to corn leaf blight – the corn leaf blight people were used to, that is. It took only a slight mutation in the same blight to cancel out this scientific advance. Meanwhile confidence in the latest technology had led to intense standardization and therefore to a terrifying vulnerability to the disease. Yet even now, with the lesson of 1970 behind us, only six main strains make up the gene stock of nearly 50 per cent of all corn grown in the United States.

Sheer variety in the plant kingdom turns out to be a fact of inestimable value for man. The Indians, as we recall, had revered variety. The war which modern North Americans have waged against the necessity to work has benefited from what seems at first sight a tactical triumph: uniformity. Uniform crops are easy to sow, easy to harvest, easy to sell. Machines like, demand, and produce uniformity. But nature loathes it: her strength lies in multiplicity and in differences. Sameness, in biology, means fewer possibilities and, therefore, weakness.

Awareness of the fragility of huge monocultures of corn (or of wheat, rice, or anything else) has spurred efforts to preserve examples of threatened plant types, even if they do not seem for the moment to be useful. The trouble with these collections, however, is that they are even more dependent on man than corn is in the field. Plant libraries must be artificially operated and maintained; mistakes or interruptions in the servicing of these institutions – a simple electric power cut for example – can, of course, mean disastrous and perhaps permanent losses.

And who is to own the plant collections? The people from whose countries the germ-plasm was taken in the first place? Or the people who found and saved the germ-plasm, built the new preserving facilities when the dangers were first realized, and who now take most responsibility for the upkeep of the holdings? The United States and Canada, Japan and Europe have hardly any natural resources of germ-plasm for the major food crops of the world, most of which originated in Latin America, Asia, and Africa. Central America gave corn to the world, yet North American and European-owned multi-national corporations control the creation of hybrid corns and sell the seeds to the Third

World. The same corporations produce the whole array of products without which "Green Revolution" farming cannot continue: fertilizers, pesticides, herbicides, and heavy machinery. Some Third World representatives even complain that they are not getting the very best hybrid seed, that the United States and other powerful countries keep the best grain for themselves, and that they limit access by poorer countries to the germ-plasm holdings.

So the wrangling and hard feelings continue, even as genetic erosion goes on almost unabated. Uniformity, disguise itself as it may behind the multiplicity of cans, boxes, bottles, and cartons in our supermarkets, is a peculiarly modern curse. Everything on the shelves contains corn. We therefore depend on corn. But corn depends increasingly, because of our wanton wastefulness, on us. Our own demonstrations of our incapacity to manage have placed us more and more exclusively and inescapably in charge.

CHAPTER TWO

Salt: The Edible Rock

*T*HE FIRST OF THE SALT MEN on record was found in 1573. He
was bearded and fully clothed in a woollen jacket and trousers,
leather shoes, and a conical cap. His flesh was yellow and hard as a
rock, but perfectly preserved because he was buried in salt. After the
people of the village had had a good look at him, spread out in church
"like a salted codfish," he was given a Christian burial in the mountain,
"to get him out of men's thoughts." At least three other bodies in a
similar state have been found in the shafts of salt-mines in the same
region near Salzburg (Salt Town), Austria. They were all victims of
mine accidents between two and three thousand years ago.

In 1836 a cemetery dating back to the age of the Salt Men was found
in the vicinity of the nearby village of Hallstatt (which also means Salt
Town). So far, well over two thousand graves have been excavated at
this site, many of them royal burials equipped with gold jewellery,
chariots, iron weapons, and joints of salt beef for the journey to the

other world. Tiny Hallstatt has given its name to a whole civilization whose confines stretched from Spain to Yugoslavia during the First Millennium BC. These were the early Celts, who made the transition from the Bronze to the Iron Age in Europe. Hallstatt princes could import the finest art works from ancient Greece. They traded with the Etruscans, the Egyptians, and the Romans, and their merchant subjects continually travelled back and forth for distances as great as that between southern France and Cornwall.

Neither the riches nor the travel would have been possible without these people's knowledge of salt deposits, salt mining, and the properties of salt. Hallstatt miners knew exactly how and at what angle best to sink a shaft through surface layers of soil to the richest salt seams in the mountains. As they walked down into the tunnel they had made, they would grip their "lamps" in their teeth: long pine sticks soaked in resin and lighted at the end. Down below, roped bunches of burning pine lit the work-face. Remains of these torches have been found, together with many miners' tools, the goatskin sacks they strapped to their backs for hauling back precious lumps of salt, wooden buckets, water bags – even a Wagnerian-looking musical instrument made of horn, used, perhaps, to signal a miner's whereabouts in case of mishap.

These Iron-Age men used old-fashioned bronze in the mines, for they had found out that bronze resists salt corrosion better than iron does. They were prepared to live and work high in the cold and dangerous mountains in order to get salt, even though contemporary settlements are almost invariably to be found in sheltered valleys. The miners knew how and where to find salt, and this gave the Hallstatt Celts an endlessly useful headstart in trading relations with other people less fortunate, less energetic, or less informed than themselves.

"God has distributed His benefits in such a manner that there is no area on the earth so rich that it does not lack all sorts of goods," wrote the French political theorist Jean Bodin in 1568. "It appears that God did this in order to induce all the subjects of His Republic to entertain friendly relations with one another." For many thousands of years human beings have longed for salt. Until one hundred years ago, salt was to be had only from great distances; at the cost of long, skilled, and watchful labour; or with the aid of enormous courage and technological expertise. Salt has forced man to explore, to think, to work, to travel. To obtain salt he has erected whole political and economic systems; he has fought, built, destroyed, extorted, and haggled.

Like corn, salt has received the full blast of modern man's scientific attention, but until recently salt has been available only in relatively tiny amounts: its historic importance has been a direct function of its rarity. Salt has never been thought of as motherly or bountiful like maize. On the contrary, its mythical character is habitually dry and sterile. Salt is clever and sly and hard to get; a little of it goes a very long way. It is a thing of fate and malediction, both necessary and absolutely irreplaceable.

SALT MINES

In the earliest times, men usually let animals find salt for them. An outcrop of rock salt was called a salt-"lick" because animals went there to lick it. When the Europeans came to North America they did not find it trackless, for buffalo trails had been worn for centuries to the salt-licks, and it was along these smoothed short-cuts through and round natural obstacles that the first explorers began to move across the continent. Amazingly early in human history, men began to dig into the earth to find salt. All over the world, people like the Hallstatt miners have tunnelled along salt seams, braving floods, the collapse of roofs and walls, exhaustion, salt-burn, suffocation, and accidents with their light-source, fire.

Modern salt-mining has become, in comparison, almost miraculously safe and productive. In many cases, mining engineers take advantage of what has always been considered one of the eeriest of the attributes of salt: the rock is not only edible but it also dissolves, and can be returned to its solid state again. Water is injected into the salt seams through tunnels bored from the surface; the brine is pumped out and then evaporated to produce salt again.

This method, like the digging of rock-salt mines, leaves empty spaces under the earth where the salt has been removed. A quarter of the city of Detroit, Michigan, stands over the hollow warrens of a salt mine. Gigantic glittering vaults, salt pillars, and passages can make awesome sites for tourists to visit today, and satisfy man's ancient craving for caves and grottos in the earth. The salt mines of Wieliczka, near Krakow, Poland, are over a thousand years old. They contain huge toothed wheels, vast wooden staircases, and support structures worthy of the imagination of Piranesi. Dance halls have been installed in the mines;

elaborate bas-reliefs in salt decorate the walls, and there are also chapels, with statues and altars carved in granite-grey sodium chloride. Part of the mine has become a hospital for sufferers from respiratory ailments because the temperature and the humidity in the vaults is ideal and constant. An old salt mine near Erivan in Soviet Armenia has also become a clinic: the sulfates and other microelements remaining in its salt walls are considered beneficial in the treatment of allergies.

For over a hundred and fifty years after the Europeans' arrival in North America, their increasingly determined hunt for underground salt deposits was bedevilled by the irritating fact that a discovery of salt was very often accompanied by a gush of filthy black pitch. A salt-dome is a vast, seemingly bottomless, column of salt squeezed up from the earth's depths, often "billowing" near the surface into a dome shape. In 1901, drilling at a salt-dome in Texas produced the largest spurt of the black stuff yet seen. But by this time scientists understood the properties of petroleum, and Spindletop, as the gusher was called, showed that it was possible to find oil in sufficient quantities to use it as fuel. So the petroleum industry was born. From this time onwards, the discovery of salt became precious as one useful pointer to the possible presence of oil-wells.

Most of the salt-domes in and around the Gulf of Mexico in the United States have now been explored and a good deal of their associated oil extracted. Many of the old salt-works, both there and elsewhere in the United States, are being used as storage facilities, for oil reserves mostly: old mines are hidden, easily guarded, and use no surface space. The Underground Vaults and Storage Company of Hutchinson, Kansas, owns an old salt-mine which it rents out as a depot to anyone who wants to use it. The survivors of a nuclear war will be able, if they can make their way to Hutchinson, Kansas, and get 200 metres (650 feet) down into the salt-shafts, to retrieve an assortment of objects which have been chosen partly with them in mind. There are seeds of hybrid plants, the files of various commercial enterprises, secret formulae for making brand-name products, food for the treasure-finders, and even folding cots, just in case they bring their babies with them. There is a film library which includes *Gone with the Wind*, *Polly of the Circus*, and lots of Buster Keaton.

A further use for salt-dome cavities has been suggested recently. Could we not use these spaces – deepened, or even especially created – to store the ever-mounting quantities of nuclear waste which our energy-hungry age keeps producing? Nuclear waste (which is at present being, we hope temporarily, stored in steel and concrete tanks) can remain a radioactive threat for ten thousand years; perhaps we could safely bury it in a salt-dome, fill the cavity up with salt, and somehow keep memory of the spot green for thousands of years, so that no one in future ages will accidentally find their way into a lethal waste-dump. Salt beds have the advantage of dryness, and tend not to be present in earthquake-prone areas.

The idea has been seriously considered. One snag is a recent finding that gamma radiation and heat from waste canisters creates corrosive acid in salt, and this in turn attacks the protective packaging and increases radiation leakage. American government regulations say that the packaging around nuclear waste must remain intact for three hundred to a thousand of the ten thousand dangerous years, so (for the moment) the idea is in limbo. There is also, unfortunately, a danger of water leaking into a salt dome: in November 1980 a good deal of a lake drained away into the shaft of a salt mine under Jefferson Island, Louisiana, when an oil drill punctured it by mistake. Even keeping reserves of petroleum in salt cavities is dangerous: in 1980, for instance, the population of a small town in Texas fled as fumes began to leak out of the ground. The town was built over a salt-dome which was being used for storing oil and natural gas products.

SALT GARDENS

Salt is an edible rock – a contradiction in terms. Not only is it mined, but it is also harvested – and this is another of the ways in which salt slips out of our net of categories, which customarily pits Hunters and Gatherers against Agriculturists, and Miners (industrial workers) against Peasants. Those who make gardens in order to win salt from the sea must prepare their land with intimate knowledge of its position and properties, watch the climate with unceasing vigilance, wait for the crop, remove obstacles in the way of its growth, and bring it in at precisely the right moment. They must have the shrewdness, the know-how, and the patience of farmers, and must run many of the same risks.

A salt garden is a chequerboard of wide shallow basins or "saltings" created at a place which the sea tide covers in a manageable measure. Incoming sea water has to be shut out when the ponds contain exactly the right amount of water. They must be kept clean and whole, and the sea water has to be guided where it ought to go, from basin to basin as the sun evaporates it to a thickly concentrated "pickle" or "mother-liquor" from which the salt will crystallize out. Passage through lime ponds for the deposition of calcium sulfate is followed by more draining, waiting, washing, storing, and cleaning of salt-ponds so that the process can begin again.

Rain is a grave set-back for a salt garden: the ponds should, if possible, be covered before rain comes, and rainwater must be carefully skimmed off if it falls onto the carefully acquired brine concentrations. Sun is needed – a great deal of it. Salt, said Pythagoras, is born of the purest of parents: the sun and the sea. The end-product of this process is known to the trade as solar salt. This, probably the oldest of salt-winning techniques, is the one often preferred where salt is used in religious observance. Ecologically, the solar method is by far the least damaging way of winning salt, but it takes time and human labour, and so the practice is gradually dying out.

Salt is an exceptionally heavy commodity; in the past, people who lived far from the sea or a salt mine, or on a coast with not enough sunshine, had to pay high transport costs or find other ways to get salt. They might burn plants which contained salt, or char brine-soaked wood and sprinkle the black ash or the powdered burnt wood over their food. They might leach salt-impregnated peat or sea sand, or, in very cold climates, concentrate brines by removing ice from them. A very early method was *briquetage*. Clay cups of brine were fired until the water evaporated and the salt hardened; the clay was then broken off and discarded. Many archaeological sites, from the Second Millennium BC to quite recent times, are laden with the débris of *briquetage*.

When Julius Caesar arrived in Britain he was disgusted to find the natives of Cheshire flinging heated stones into the brine of their salt springs, and scraping off the resultant salt crusts. He sent for "salinators" from Rome, and these men taught the Britons to boil their brine in shallow lead pans over fires – a method which slowly improved, survived, and is still used today.

If brine is swiftly boiled it produces cubic salt crystals; if it is gently heated just enough for surface evaporation to take place the crystals are pyramidal, and to the naked eye look flaky rather than granular. Surface-evaporated salt, as opposed to salt evaporated mechanically and chemically from the brine, is called "grainer" salt in North America, and has survived as a specialty product: it is close enough to the pure solar salt to be accepted as kosher by Orthodox Jews. It is also highly sought after by gastronomes, because it is not treated with additives. "Unrefined," in the perversity of modern language and practice, has come to be synonymous with "pure."

Most salt used for culinary purposes today is the result of evaporation of brines by means of sophisticated heating machines. The first multiple-effect salt evaporator was built in the United States in 1899. The salt is separated from the brine, heated, cleaned, spun and sucked dry, then mechanically packed and labelled. The process is fast, and the salt is fine-grained and extremely free from impurities. Unprocessed sea salt, on the other hand, is grey, with coarse and irregular grains, and often damp. It is loaded with calcium and magnesium chlorides which deliquesce and give a slightly bitter, faster, and sharper taste sensation which is much prized by gourmets.

Salt is hygroscopic: it attracts moisture. This is why the holes in salt shakers can clog up in damp weather. In the past most salt was served frankly damp in a dish, and it was taken with the fingers or in a spoon. Erasmus said it was very impolite to take it with a knife which had not been cleaned off first on a hunk of bread. But people would much rather it ran free, so that "When it rains, it pours," which is the (justified) claim of one of the most successful advertising slogans ever devised, that for Morton's Salt (1910). For this reason salt grains are marketed with a coating of chemicals to keep them separate. A tiny percentage of potassium iodide is also added in areas such as the Swiss Alps and the North American Great Lakes region, where there is a deficiency of iodine in the soil and therefore in people's diet. Iodine deficiency leads to goitre, a swelling of the thyroid glands at the base of the throat. The iodide is accompanied by a stabilizing mixture of sodium thiosulfate and calcium hydrate. To sensitive palates, the result of all the subtractions and additives is a condiment depleted in complexity as well as in sheer salty taste.

The arts of salt-winning are various, and they are all ancient. Even modern heating machines serve merely to evaporate, which is a variant on the old solar or salt-boiling method. Japan is today the only major industrialized country which has no underground salt beds in its territory, although Scandinavia is also chronically short of salt. The lack is serious, and only partly alleviated by solar salt gardens, which are annoyingly slow for modern industrialists. Brine-boiling uses enormous amounts of fuel, which the Japanese do not have. Instead they have come up with the first really new idea for retrieving salt since prehistory. This is electro-dialysis; sea water is concentrated into brine by means of electrically charged membranes. These collect and separate the positively and negatively charged ions of sodium and chloride, the components of common salt; the salt-cleared water is then drained away from the concentrated brine. The method has been in successful operation, both to obtain salt and to desalinate sea water, since 1965.

THE MYSTERIES OF SALINITY

Most people sitting down to a meal such as the one we are considering will reach for the salt-cellar, knowing that its contents can enhance the taste of the corn, the rice, the lettuce, and probably the chicken as well. Those of us who seem to want more salt than others do were especially relieved to be told recently that salt is not really as dangerous as we had been led to believe. For some years we had been loudly exhorted to curb our appetite for salt and even to cut out salt altogether, because it raised our blood pressures and caused us to retain fluids. Which of these claims is true?

The fact is that our desire for salt is little understood; so is our need for it, and so is the reason for the saltiness of our bodies. It is usually thought that we are salty – our blood, our sweat, our tears, our urine, our saliva (the word derives from *sal*, Latin for "salt"), are salty – because life began in the sea. We are walking marine environments, and the appeal of the taste of salt for us is in our natures.

Consuming salt nevertheless makes us thirsty. It has only recently been established that the hypothalamus at the base of the brain is what arouses our desire to drink. This organ measures the concentrations of sodium and potassium ions in our body's fluids, and when these become too high because of a loss of water, or if we take in an excess of sodium as a component of salt, we feel thirst.

Sodium and chloride ions have electrical charges which enable them to carry current: together they keep the liquids in our cells and their surroundings in balance, drawing water molecules through membranes when necessary to hold them in steady quantities. If blood cells were surrounded by a saltless liquid, water would seep into them through the membranes and they would burst. The amount of salt itself in the body is governed by many co-ordinated mechanisms: the kidneys, for instance, which get rid of excess salt through urination; and sweat which throws off varying amounts of salt, whatever will suffice to keep the balance.

A sufficient salt intake for a normal human being is between 1.1 and 3.3 grams a day. But the average European or American customarily eats as much as ten times that amount; we leave it to our bodies to deal with the overdose. When "modern" diseases make us worried and we look round for a "modern" cause, salt is easily pounced upon as the culprit. Hypertension, and consequent heart and kidney disease and stroke, have recently been blamed on salt: there must, we feel, be a cost for our grossly excessive behaviour. Now scientists are saying that merely cutting back on salt is far too simplistic a solution to hypertension, and that eating too little calcium or potassium is just as likely to be harmful to the body. And yet salted foods like cheese (which provides both calcium and potassium) are often just the things people do without when they give up salt.

Why is the earth full of salt? We now know that it *is* full of salt, in spite of the apparent rarity of the substance which has tantalized mankind for so many thousands of years. Almost every country on earth possesses vast resources of underground salt in seams and domes and layers often hundreds of metres thick and hundreds of kilometres in extent. Where did it come from? Many scientists have believed that it came from the sea. In eons of geological time, oceans have spread then evaporated, and the salt they left has been folded and rolled, squeezed and kneaded deep into the earth, or extruded above it as salt mountains and salt glaciers.

Where did the sea get its salt then?

The sea varies in its salinity, but is, on average, 3.5 per cent salt; that is enough salt, if it were powdered, to cover the whole earth thirty-six centimetres (14 ins.) deep. Aristotle's explanation for the presence of salt was the opposite of the one mentioned previously: the sea, he thought, began as fresh water, but became salty from rain and rivers washing salt into it from the earth. Even allowing for the fact that the sea is constantly depositing some of its salt on the land, this would mean that the sea would get saltier all the time, and we now know, from the evidence of tiny pools of sea-water trapped in sedimentary rock, that the salinity of the oceans has not increased since at least Cambrian times; it was if anything greater then. And the fossils of marine life in those rocks are similar to the creatures living in the sea today; their environment must, therefore, have been not unlike our ocean. Moreover, rock salt does not contain marine fossils, and this throws doubt upon its oceanic origin.

Another of salt's mysteries is this: if our bodies need so little, why do we crave it so much? Unlike the human "sweet tooth," our salt hunger is shared by animals: cows, for instance, love salt, and will lick a hole in a wall they find pleasantly salty. Our tongues are well supplied with salt-tasting buds, and to compound our frailty, saltiness enhances the taste of sweet things and disguises bitterness. It also helps make stale or spoiled food edible.

But many peoples have simply never known that salt existed and have lived perfectly healthy lives without it. Australian aborigines and American Indians and Inuit often knew no salt. Early human settlements were apparently not built to be near salt-springs. Human beings, it seems, learn about salt (and become addicted to it) at a very precise moment in their history: when they cease being almost exclusively carnivorous and learn to eat vegetables in quantities usually available only when they grow them themselves. When people begin not only to eat a lot of vegetables, but to reduce the salt content in their food by boiling it – a cooking method which presupposes the ability to make metal pots that can be set directly over a fire – then salt becomes more desirable still.

Carnivorous animals and meat-hunting men find enough salt in blood to satisfy them. Certain African tribes who have never been able to assure themselves of a salt supply, prick the necks of their living cattle and drink their blood. There is no immediate need to slaughter a cow for meat since, alive, she is a sort of walking larder, providing protein and salt.

It is herbivorous animals that love salt. One theory about the origin of the domestication of cattle by man is inspired by the "salt tie" which still operates between reindeer herders and their animals. Cattle may originally have been taught when very young that they could get their salt from men. They would then range freely in search of pasture. Their "owners" needed only to visit them occasionally in the field with gifts of salt to remind them that they were no longer wild. Men could then proceed to take advantage of the relationship.

Salt, in myths all over the world, is seen as a "newcomer," an addition whose necessity is not perceived before it arrives, but which is intensely attractive, indeed irresistible, once it is tried. Here, for example, is a North American Indian myth about the presence of a salt-lick near the home of the Indian who told it:

> Salt used to be far away. He was a man and was travelling through the country. The Indians never used salt then. He looked ugly all over, and the people did not like him. He came to a camp and said, "Let me put my hand in there, then the food will taste well."
>
> "No," said the cook, "I want to eat this, you look too ugly."
>
> He went off to another band and said, "Let me put my hand in here, it will taste well."
>
> "No, your hand is too dirty."
>
> He came to another band and said the same thing, but people declined his offer. At last he came to a single man, and he was a cook. He said, "I want to put my hand into the food, then it will taste better." And the cook allowed him to do so, and he put in his hand.
>
> "Now taste it." The Indian tasted it and it was good. Salt settled there and stayed forever, about ten or twelve miles from St. Thomas.

Notice in this story that people are suspicious about salt. For one thing, eating it is eating earth, and that in itself is peculiar behaviour. You add it to your food, it disappears, yet it indescribably alters the taste of everything you eat. Salt is weird, powerful, dangerous, and "extra." In religious symbolism it is always linked with "strong," power-ful substances like iron or blood. We feel that a little of it is all we need, that this little has made all the difference, and that we ought not to abuse the privilege of having it. Furthermore, adding salt is being clever, and getting salt has always taxed human intelligence. By the same token we feel that we could easily be tricked by someone who cunningly adds salt without our knowing it, thus imparting a sinister attraction to something we ought not to want. When someone "salts" a mine he wishes to sell, he plants nuggets of gold in his worthless property for dupes to find.

All these ancient symbolic notes are struck in our modern, apparently "scientific" distrust of salt in our food. Our readiness to feel uneasy about the hand of processors in what we innocently buy and ingest is encouraged by revelations about the salt content of common packaged foods. We did not know until the alarm was raised recently that instant chocolate pudding has more salt in it than potato chips, that canned vegetables always receive a mechanically-supplied salt tablet (How large?) before the can is sealed, that tomato ketchup is a bottled battlefield for the forces of salt and sugar. Our response is to demand explanations, to insist on better labelling – and in many cases to switch to saltless food. And instantly the challenge is accepted by a business community alert to what it is that people will pay for. A whole new market has been created, where the sophisticated prestige of "No Salt Added" replaces the primitive seduction of hidden seasonings.

Salt is both "farmed" like wheat, and "searched for" like game or wild berries. Bread (grown, harvested, ground, leavened, and baked) and salt (found, won, collected and efficiently transported) together cover the field: they represent man as Farmer, patiently and wisely nurturing his crops, but also as Hunter, Scientist, Adventurer, and Organizer. Bread and salt are customarily offered in Russia (where the word for "hospitality" means literally "bread-salt") and in other coun-tries, as a sign of welcome to a guest: bread and salt symbolize the precious stores of the house, the fruits of the host's labour, his patience, his ingenuity, his civilized foresight and preparedness.

Oath-taking, in many cultures, is a ceremony involving salt, just as the act of swearing may employ blood or iron as a sign denoting a person's unbreakable word. Salt is shared at table, in a context of order and contentment. Traditional Bedouin will never fight a man with whom they have once eaten salt. When the Lord God of Israel made a covenant with the Jews, it was a Covenant of Salt, denoting an unalterable bond of friendship. It also meant that the Jews had settled down in the Promised Land, had ceased to be sheep-herding nomads, and would now eat the fruit of their harvests, cooked and seasoned with salt.

KEEPING AND MOVING

Soon after the Arabian camel reached Africa in the fourth century AD, the peoples of the Mediterranean found a way to reach a new world. Gold, the immortal metal of kings, was becoming ever scarcer in Europe and more prized. The Africans away to the south, beyond the Sahara, had plenty of gold, and apparently thought it nothing special. There was one thing they did want and could not find for themselves, and the Arabs and later the Europeans soon found out what it was. And so the salt caravans began to cross the desert to the salt deposits of Teghaza in northern Mali. From the eighth century onwards, the three to four thousand camels in each of these caravans were loaded up by their Moslem owners with copper pots, woven rugs and clothing, grains and dried fruit, all of which would later be exchanged for slabs of salt at Ouadane (Mauritania), Teghaza, and later Taoudeni (Mali). Then they plodded on, bearing their cargo of salt, to Timbuktu, a place whose whereabouts was kept secret from the infidels. Timbuktu gradually became to the European imagination a city of magnificence and mystery. Explorers dreamed of finding it for hundreds of years; the Frenchman René Caillié finally did in 1828 – and was bitterly disappointed.

Timbuktu was a trading post founded by Tuareg nomads in about 1000 AD, on a branch of the Niger River. It has no gold, and no salt; it merely served as a stopping-place for the caravans, a place where guides could be found for the most secret part of the whole journey. Many days' travelling out of Timbuktu a place was reached where the Mute Exchange with the mysterious Africans could begin. First the seller would beat drums to show he had arrived, leave a heap of salt-slabs out, and retire. In time the buyer would venture forward and leave gold, or ivory, or sometimes a slave, next to the salt, and then disappear. The seller looked over the offering and would leave without touching anything if he was not satisfied. His unseen client would then raise the offering or remove it. When the seller took the African's offering he beat his drums again, and the deal was sealed: they never saw each other or exchanged a word.

When all the trading was done the caravan returned to the sea coast of Morocco. There the goods it carried (gold dust, ivory, slaves, and goat skins to be sold as "Morocco" leather) were shipped to the Near East and to Italy or Spain. The caravan journey had taken about six months. In this manner, from the eighth to the sixteenth centuries AD, Europe alone received six metric tons of African gold per year. The gold/salt trade finally ceased at the end of the nineteenth century, but to this day caravans from Taoudeni carry salt to Timbuktu.

The Danakil Depression in Ethiopia is a weird moonscape 193 kilometres (120 miles) long, covered with brilliantly coloured salt hills and chemically green warm lakes. It bubbles with sulphur springs, geysers, and volcanic activity. Five thousand Danakil nomads hold traditional rights to exploit the salt plain. They cut and load salt bricks in the boiling sun and live for the season in houses made of salt. An ancient trail still leads camels, donkeys, and mules many kilometres up into the hills for trade with the Ethiopian highlands and beyond. The salt they carry is used as money; it passes from hand to hand in exchange for other goods; it increases in value in proportion to its distance from the salt plain of Danakil. The Aksum Empire of Ethiopia traded this rich asset with Egyptians, Romans, Arabs, and Indians before the third century AD, but the exchange is certainly far older. The incredible exertions of all these people and animals, the intricate systems of relationship and value, and the vast distances travelled, are typical effects of the human desire for salt.

Salt towns have always been rich and busy places, and proud of their special status. The Greek word for salt is *hals*. Derivatives from this word often substitute *s* for *h*, which is why the Romans called it *sal* and we say "salt." Salt names abound for western European towns, rivers, and hills, and these may be clues to the history of their occupation: Halle, Hallein, Reichenhall, Hallstatt; Alès, Alesia (the French drop their *h*'s); Salies, Salins, La Salle, Moselle, Salzburg, Salcott, Salsomaggiore. Salina was the original name of Syracuse, New York. Malaga is Phoenician for "salt."

At least by the date of the Domesday Book, the Anglo-Saxon term *wich* meant "a place where there is salt," so we get Droitwich, Nantwich, Northwich, Sandwich. Sodom, in the neighbourhood of which Lot's wife turned into a pillar of salt (petrification, turning into stone, is a common story-punishment for looking back when you shouldn't – but then, salt is "rock"), was near to the Dead Sea and to numerous salt mines. Its name is probably a contraction of *Sadeh Adom*, meaning "red field" or "field of blood." The reason may be that when solar salt is evaporated from brine springs and lakes, the concentrate often turns bright red because of bacterial action.

Salt towns were often centres for the salting of meat (if inland) or of fish (by the sea), for salt was man's most useful preservative: without it he would have suffered greatly during the winters. Until recently, unless a farmer had enough land to grow his own hay, he had no means of keeping his cattle alive during the cold months, and thus the feast of St. Martin, November 11, was the day on which farmers traditionally slaughtered their animals, salted the meat, and packed it in barrels to keep. On that day the innards, ground and enclosed in sausage-skins, were consumed in vast quantities, together with the first of the new wine. Martinmas was known as the Feast of Sausages and Black Puddings. Brined pork-in-the-barrel was a precious source of meat and fat for soups, *garbures*, sauerkrauts, and *cassoulets* through the winter. The pork-barrel was also to become a North American institution, together with "pork barrelling," which meant doling out tasty morsels of jobs or patronage to one's friends. Beef was often "corned," or covered with large salt crystals. (The Old Norse word *korn* meant a grain-sized lump of anything.)

Ocean fish was salted as soon as it was caught. Fresh sea fish was not available to anyone who lived away from the coast until the arrival of modern transport and refrigeration. Salted foods were big business – so big that not even wars interrupted trade. The northern Protestant countries of Europe supplied a great deal of salted fish to the Catholic southern countries for consumption during Lent and the rest of the year, all through the sixteenth, seventeenth, and eighteenth centuries. But the north (where the fishing was excellent and efficient) needed solar salt from the warm south in order to send back their herring and haddock (both words may derive from *hals*, and mean "salted"), and cod. And the south – mainly the western coasts of France, Spain, and Portugal – supplied salt through all the long wars of those centuries, to the profit and satisfaction of everybody involved.

The chemistry of salt's preservative action is still not completely explained. It prevents spoiling microbes from living where it is present, but, used in the correct amounts, it also promotes the growth of lactic acid bacteria, and this helps products like salted cabbage to ferment into sauerkraut. Salt penetrates moisture-filled meat, fish, or vegetables. It also causes blood and water to run out (in this role salt renders meat kosher in Jewish observance), and in sufficient quantities it will dry flesh and skin completely. Blood extraction and the prevention of decomposition make salt vital in the curing and tanning of leather – just as it was an important ingredient in the Egyptian recipe for mummification.

Its role in seasoning and food preservation made salt so necessary that people were willing to travel punishing distances to get it. But without salt, and its ability to keep food, long journeys would themselves have been impossible. People carried hard nutritious cheese and salted beef – dry, light, delicious, and edible without cooking – when they had to travel lightly and did not know where the next meal was available. Salting made food exportable. The fish of faraway Newfoundland was worth catching for consumption in Europe because, with a certain amount of careful organization, it could be salted.

From the end of the fifteenth century, Basque, French, Dutch, and English fishermen were hauling in Newfoundland cod, the most bountiful catch mankind has ever recorded. (From the sixteenth to the eighteenth centuries cod made up 60 per cent of all fish eaten in Europe.) Fishing fleets called in and loaded up with salt at Spanish and Portuguese ports before sailing across the Atlantic. Once caught, the fish was cut up, cleaned, and salted right in the fishing boats, which were filled to the brim with their load. This "green" cod was often dried as *bacalao*, either when the ship returned to Europe or at facilities set up on the Newfoundland coast itself. Some of the fish was taken to the Caribbean, where it fed slaves on cotton and sugar plantations. The boats, emptied first of their salt, then of their cod, now took molasses on board, and cotton and rum, for the journey back to Europe. Salt caused travel, used trade channels, and simultaneously facilitated both travel and trade. Caribbean people still have a taste for salt cod. And Portuguese fishing-boats still arrive in Newfoundland ports loaded with salt to preserve their cod-catch from the Grand Banks.

Salting food is now a relatively minor industry: Parma ham, *brandade de morue*, conserved goose have become gourmet treats where once they were peasants' standbys. The modern method of keeping food is by refrigeration, which means that not only can we keep perishable goods, but we can supply them for sale far away from their place of origin. But salt has not been dislodged from its central role in the keeping and moving of food, for the freezing process itself depends on sodium chloride. Salt's combined melting and temperature-lowering action upon ice and water has the effect of removing latent heat from adjacent substances. It is mixed with crushed ice in refrigerated railroad cars, and later in our meal we will see that it is used in the same way in the old-fashioned method of making ice-cream. In fact, ice itself is manufactured by salt brines, cooled through alternately compressed and expanded ammonia or other gases. Liquid sodium, one of the two main ingredients of common salt, is what is used to cool nuclear reactors.

Even the roads travelled on in cold climates depend these days upon salt to clear them of ice and snow and keep traffic moving. When salt is thrown onto snow, some salt dissolves and some ice melts to produce brine. Each salt grain melts a path downward through the ice for itself, forming brine on the way. When the brine hits the pavement it spreads out and melts the bond between the pavement surface and the ice over it, making it easy to break the ice and throw it aside.

Finally, as the Hallstatt miners knew, the presence of salt makes metals rust. Our cars are attacked by the salt laid down to clear a way for them, because salt increases the solubility and therefore the availability of the cause of corrosion, which is oxygen.

TAXES

Salt was one of the first articles traded by man. Ever since the earliest pact was reached, many thousands of years ago, between people who had salt and people who had none, salt has been one of the most manipulated, most politicized substances on earth. The world's oldest trade routes often had the principal aim of connecting salt resources to human habitations. One of these is the *Via Salaria* or Salt Road, which connected the saltings of the port of Ostia with Rome and the far Adriatic; it is one of the oldest roads in Italy. Salt has been sold in lumps, loaves, tablets, bricks, and grains. It has helped make the fortunes of towns, countries, and whole civilizations. The word "salary" dates from the Roman distribution of salt as part of their soldiers' pay; an inadequate person, we still say, is "not worth their salt." Marco Polo saw salt, moulded into cakes and stamped with the imperial seal of the Great Khan, used as money in Tibet.

Many wars have been waged over salt. Morocco fought Mali in the sixteenth century for the mines of Taoudeni; the Venetians, whose salt interests are an historical study in themselves, destroyed Comacchio in the tenth century and the salt gardens of Cervia in the fourteenth; pirates throughout the centuries ambushed and raided the slow heavy convoys of salt ships. Cortés and his Spaniards found important allies for their conquest of Mexico in the Tlaxcalan people, to whom they offered access to salt and cotton. The Tlaxcalans hated Montezuma and the Aztecs, says a sixteenth-century source, because "they ate no salt, since there was none in their country, nor were they allowed to buy it anywhere else, nor did they wear any cotton clothing. . . ." It was the Aztecs who kept these people from salt and from their favourite clothing material; even tyrannical foreigners seemed to them useful allies against their oppressive neighbours.

One of the ways in which governments have made themselves useful is in assuring all their subjects sufficient salt from a common store and at a standard price by monopolizing all salt sources and their distributing mechanisms. The ancient Egyptians had a salt monopoly, as did China from the seventh century BC. Salt was also one of the first commodities to be taxed.

"The art of taxation," said the seventeenth-century French statesman Jean Baptiste Colbert, "consists of plucking the goose so as to obtain the most feathers with the least hissing." Colbert could not have spoken of taxation without an implied reference to the Gabelle, the famous French salt tax. He could not, perhaps, have guessed that his particular goose would one day do a great deal more than hiss.

The Gabelle was instituted in 1259 by Charles of Anjou in Provence, in imitation of the Arabs, who were the first since the fall of Rome to re-introduce the concept of salt monopoly and salt taxing. (*Al quábala*, "tax" in Arabic, is the origin of the word *Gabelle*.) The French kings began to use the system in the fourteenth century, and it spread all over Europe. France kept on using it in spite of inefficiencies, irritations, abuses, and riots, even despite its status as one of the causes of the French Revolution, until 1945. (Its abolition by the Revolution lasted only fifteen years.)

Taxing salt had definite advantages. Salt sources were always well known, and salt transportation a cumbrous business which could easily be regulated: salt was taxed at frontiers and on entry to provinces and towns. Everybody ate salt in more or less equal amounts, so everyone paid the tax equally. (This is repugnant to our concept of taxing according to income; we should recall, however, that in the fourteenth century very few people had what we would call an income, and not everyone "without an income" was poor.) Honey can take the place of sugar, and margarine may be used instead of butter; but there is no substitute for salt. Demand for it, in the economic jargon of our own day, was "inelastic": taxation could therefore realize dependable sums without changing people's buying habits.

The salt tax was never accepted with docility. If the theory of the Gabelle is a lesson in crude economics, the history of it is also a lesson in tax evasion. People pretended to have lost their stores of salt in rain storms and household accidents, they clandestinely made their own salt by digging for it or by evaporating brine, they sold inferior salt at superior prices, smuggled it, and passed it to each other in secret. In England and Scotland, "every year 10,000 people are seized for salt smuggling," wrote the Earl of Dundonald in 1785, "and 300 sent to the gallows for contraband trade in salt and tobacco." He thought civilized people should tax hearths (as England had once done) instead of salt, for a hearth did not move around, and its owner was rich enough to own a house. A salt tax was almost as thorough as a census: everyone paid, rich and poor alike. The principle was thought important enough to warrant forcing each person to buy a certain amount of salt. And when the government needed more money, people were simply required to buy more salt. (We recall that originally salt monopolies were invented to assure each person's supply.) Enforcement of a salt tax cannot be achieved without violation of privacy: inspectors would search people's houses, peer into families' cooking-pots, and haul offenders away from their dinner tables.

In 1825, after four hundred years of resentment, England abolished her salt tax. She was the first country to do so. The impetus was the growth of her empire, the Industrial Revolution, and the advancement of technology which was to reverse totally the role of salt in human history. Not much earlier, however, Britain had monopolized salt in India; in 1863 she abandoned the monopoly (already very unpopular in the colony) and imposed a salt tax. She simultaneously began exporting Cheshire salt to India, to sell it there at the same price as India's own product.

Home salt-making – even looking for salt – now became a crime in India; the *malangis* or salt evaporators became almost extinct as a class. For many years unrest and real suffering grew in intensity. Poor Indian peasants, with their vegetarian and frequently monotonous diet, had a great hunger for salt. In 1923, almost a century after Britain had abolished the tax in her own country, the British government, with singular callousness, doubled India's salt tax. Many British parliamentarians protested, with no result.

When Mahatma Gandhi was asked by the All India Congress Committee to initiate a "call to action," he made a theatrically brilliant decision. He began a three-week pilgrimage to the sea, gathering followers as he went. On April 6, 1930, Gandhi reached Dandi Beach in Gujarat. After a ceremonial sea bath (salt water, like salt itself, means purity), Gandhi began to pick up salt incrustations which lay free for the taking on the beach. India's fight for independence had begun.

Satyagrahis (non-violent activists) undertook to get India's salt and sell it free of tax. They carried it from the beaches in their fists; police had no other way of confiscating it than to snatch it from them, handful by handful. Many were beaten and imprisoned; many more kept taking their place. The movement grew; *satyagrahi* salt, people said, was "as pure as blood." Valuable jewellery was given away in exchange for a lump of salt wrapped in a leaf. Women came out of *purdah* to violate the salt laws; foreign salt was dumped into the sea; there were strikes, pickets, and giant meetings.

Finally Lord Irwin, Viceroy of India, made a pact with Gandhi in March 1931. People living near the salt sands and solar salt ponds could, as a result of this agreement, collect salt, or make their own, and sell it in local villages. The most irritating aspect of the salt tax – the prevention of free domestic use – was thus alleviated, although the commercial tax remained. At the signing of the pact, Irwin drank Gandhi's health with a cup of tea, but the Mahatma asked for a glass of lemon juice and water, and added a pinch of salt. With superb timing and his instinct for the perfect symbol, he had tested his theory of non-violent resistance, and he now judged that the Indian people were ready and able to embark on the process of making the British leave India.

SYMBOLIC SALT

Salt is the only rock directly consumed by man. It corrodes but preserves, desiccates but is wrested from the water. It has fascinated man for thousands of years not only as a substance he prized and was willing to labour to obtain, but also as a generator of poetic and of mythic meaning. The contradictions it embodies only intensify its power and its links with experience of the sacred.

Salt brings flavour to life, and people accustomed to salt find their food tasteless, flat, and dull without it. This is the point of the folktale from which Shakespeare derived *King Lear*. In the original story, the youngest daughter of the king, unlike her articulate and dishonest sisters, tells her father that her love for him is not like silver or gold, as they had claimed, but "like salt." Enraged, he throws her out of the palace. She eventually is to be married, and invites the king (who does not know who she is or recognize her under her veil) to the wedding feast. She has ordered all the food to be prepared without salt. The king, finding the dinner inedible, weeps for his youngest daughter and finally understands how important a pinch of humble salt is to man's happiness. She identifies herself, the two are reconciled – and presumably the salt-cellars are produced with a flourish. The story shows that a daughter's sincere love is unassertive and may be taken for granted, but it is dependable and irreplaceable. In refusing or in losing it, a father is left without the kind of thing that gives zest to life.

When Jesus called his followers "the salt of the earth," he was telling them that they were irreplaceable, and that their mission was to give people what makes life worth living. There were few of them, but they were sufficient to season the whole earth, as a very little salt or a tiny bit of leaven is enough. They and their message would persevere and endure, as salt is the great conserver, the image of permanence. Jesus went on immediately, in Matthew's Gospel, to use an image of light. The two metaphors are connected both by opposition (salt is in the earth, light must be raised on high; salt is tasted while light is seen), and by similarity, for salt has always been associated with fire and brightness.

Salt, once isolated, is white and glittering. It is the opposite of wet. You win it by freeing it from water with the help of fire and the sun, and it dries out flesh. Eating salt causes thirst. Dryness, in the pre-Socratic cosmic system which still informs our imagery, is always connected with fire, heat, and light.

For the alchemists, common salt (one of the elements of matter) was neither masculine nor feminine but neuter: the edible rock always has something a little inhuman about it; it disconcertingly sits astride categories. Salt does have to do with sex, however, because it is a dynamic substance which both alters itself and causes change. Like sex, it is exciting and dangerous and gives pleasure. Salt comes out of the sea like the goddess of sex, Aphrodite, whose name the ancient Greeks thought meant "sea-foam-born." In European folk custom, impotence has traditionally been cured by a hilarious, bawdy salting of the disobliging member by a crowd of women.

Often priests or mourners or people who are in a state of crisis — those whom society has marginalized, for whatever reason — must observe a taboo on salt. Eating no salt, which is often accompanied by sexual continence, means a fight to maintain equilibrium at a time of turbulence and difficulty, when one has no need of the dynamic. It also means that one has left society, rejecting the enticements and the comforts of civilization, or that one intends to dramatize a profound discontent with the way society is conducting itself.

Salt represents the civilized: it requires know-how to get it, and a sophisticated combination of cooking and spoilt, jaded appetites to need it. Its sharp taste suggests sharpness of intellect and liveliness of mind.

Salt (bright, dry, titillating, and dynamic) is synonymous in several languages with wit and wisdom.

It preserves things from corruption – even as it corrodes other things with its bite. A little of it fertilizes the land; a lot sterilizes it. Because salt stops rot and because it is fiery, salt is intrinsically pure. It is the child of the sun and the sea, two basic symbols of cleanliness and purity. Salt keeps meat safe for the winter and so feeds man; it is, therefore, a blessing. Salt also means barrenness, and it is, therefore, used for cursing. Its imperishable rock-nature, and its purity and wisdom make it the material of oaths and covenants, which guarantee, if the swearer breaks his oath, that malediction will fall upon him.

Salt as covenant-sealer signifies friendship and hospitality. The silver salt-cellar was a central and often highly decorative ornament on the banquet tables of all rich European families: it marked off the close friends of the family from those "below the salt," who were not considered worthy of such intimacy. When someone inadvertently spills salt, it is considered unlucky because it signifies enmity and malediction. Leonardo da Vinci followed this tradition in his fresco of the Last Supper when he depicted Judas as upsetting the salt-cellar.

Here as before, however, salt is powerfully contradictory: because it is pure and strong, it *counteracts* malediction. Witches hate salt. They never served it at their sabbaths, and if you put some under a witch's cushion she could not sit down: this was considered a sure-fire method of finding out whether someone was a witch or not. Devils also detest it. Therefore, if you are unlucky enough to spill salt, all you have to do is throw some over your left shoulder (where all bad spirits congregate) and the evil will be undone. An owl's cry is a malediction: to neutralize it, one has to sprinkle salt on the bird's tail.

Until recently, salt was part of the Roman Catholic baptismal ceremony (Luther banned it as Popish superstition). A few grains were placed on the baby's tongue to signify purity, endurance, wisdom, power, uniqueness ("You are the salt of the earth"), and protection from evil. It was a sign of God's friendship and his power over Satan.

SALT AND MODERN TECHNOLOGY

Humphry Davy succeeded in separating the components of common salt in 1810. There was chlorine, a poisonous greenish gas; and sodium, a silvery quasi-liquid metal which burst into flame when it touched water, was corrosive for inorganic matter, and absolutely lethal to anything living. No conceivable use could be imagined for either ingredient, and each was so violently reactive that it could barely be contained or stored under laboratory conditions. People marvelled that the contents of their dinner-table salt-cellars should be shown to be so dreadful. Humphry himself was to inspire, in a bored sixteen-year-old chemistry student called E. Clerihew Bentley, the very first clerihew (the verse form has since become traditional, like the limerick):

> Sir Humphry Davy
> Abominated gravy.
> He lived in the odium
> Of having discovered Sodium.

It took many decades for the effects of the splitting of salt to take hold, but the truth was that salt would never look the same again, and the earth has never recovered from the shift in human perception; maybe it never will.

The power of chlorine was found to be applicable as a textile bleach, and this was to remain its principle function for a hundred years. The production of this chlorine from salt entailed, of course, the piling up of the noxious left-over sodium. Scientists began to search for a use for sodium.

Potash had been an ingredient since ancient times in the making of soap and glass. But in the eighteenth century a new function for potash was found in the creation of saltpetre for gunpowder. Whole forests were burned in Europe and her colonies to obtain potash for military use; glass and soap had increasingly to depend on natural soda to replace potash. This led to a shortage of soda – just at a time when soap, rather than lye, was increasingly in demand for household laundry: people living in cities had no access to wood, and lye cannot be made of coal ashes. The French chemist Michel-Eugène Chevreul discovered the nature of the action of alkali upon fat in the making of soap, and his compatriot Nicolas Leblanc developed a method of making soda (alkali) out of the previously maligned sodium. Waste had been turned to gold.

Artificial soda factories in Manchester by the 1850s were pouring out hydrochloric acid fumes and the "rotten egg" gas, hydrogen sulphide. These, combined with smoke from two million tons of coal burned per year, provoked the earliest dazed realization that perhaps a problem was being born. A use was urgently sought for the unfortunate by-product of artificial soda, hydrochloric acid. It was found at last in the dye industry.

Meanwhile, research into further uses for sodium went on. Soda or sodium hydroxide were found to be effective in extracting aluminium from its ore – the first new major metal extracted from the earth in two thousand years. Then sodium hydroxide was applied to cellulose to create rayon, the first artificial textile. From this time on, sodium was admitted to be a highly productive chemical. Chlorine became a side-effect of sodium hydroxide production, and a use had now to be sought for the mounting quantities of it.

In the early twentieth century, chlorine's bleaching properties were applied not only to textiles but also to wood-pulp for the paper-making industry. Then it was found that chlorine could disinfect water. But chlorine finally burst into stardom when it became indispensable in the making of vinyls and other plastics, solvents, pesticides and herbicides, and in the cooling, braking, and "anti-knock" fluids used in automobiles.

Chlorine is the basis of various defoliants and poisons for gas warfare; its compound chloroform was considered a miraculous pain-killer (until it was found to be more dangerous than ether). It is part of carbon tetrachloride, which was extensively used as a dry-cleaning spirit until other chemicals replaced it. Refrigerant fluids now depend upon chlorine as does the gas in aerosol cans. Plastic, pesticides, the aerosol can: all are the progeny of chlorine – and therefore of common salt.

We met pesticides and herbicides in the history of corn, as the miracle-workers of the modern "Green Revolution." They are chlorinated hydrocarbons, man-made substances which have not so far been found in nature. They are not, therefore, *unmade* by nature either: they are "non-biodegradable" substances which, after use, add to the ever-growing quantity of wastes we cannot get rid of. In addition, the huge amount of chlorine required to make plastics, pesticides, aerosol cans, solvents, and other things leaves behind the rest of the salt from which it has been derived. The disposal problem, in other words, has reversed itself and reappeared: since 1970, sodium hydroxide (from which chlorine had been the unfortunate refuse) has become an excessive waste product of chlorine. What now shall we do with the unused sodium hydroxide. . . ?

Because of the salting of our roads, and the necessity for "automotive fluids," for aluminium, and for plastics in every car, the automobile is the world's largest consumer of salt. (We recall that the history of petroleum, the fuel of the automobile, is also part of the history of salt.) Road-salting, which in the United States meant the sprinkling of thirty-three kilograms of salt per head of population in 1974, has now become so extravagant and widespread that it amounts to an actual redistribution of terrestrial salt. Fresh-water lakes receive hundreds of tons of salt run-off annually. The saline content of Lake Erie, for instance, increased five times between 1939 and 1971, mostly because of road salting.

Some of the richest farmland on earth is to be found in California. Two spectacularly fertile areas, the Imperial and the San Joaquin valleys, were once the possessors of deep dry soils with no water supply. They have been brought to life by vast artificial irrigation schemes. In 1901, the Imperial Valley began to be watered from the Colorado River, which had deposited its silts to create the rich soil in the first place, then changed its course. Thousands of miles of canals now carry water to every corner of the Valley, which produces feed-lots of grass for fattening cattle, and billions of vegetables of every kind, which are transported in refrigerated rail-cars for sale in every state in the United States and all over Canada. Because the Colorado River is a turbulent flooder, it has twice been dammed – by the Hoover Dam and the Imperial Dam – so that the water can be further controlled.

But the Colorado, because of the salty desert lands through which it flows, is also an unusually salty river. It carries with it the salt-laden run-off from other irrigated areas on its route, and evaporation from the huge dammed lakes concentrates its salinity further. A sixty-five hectare (160-acre) cotton field in one growing season receives about 1,800 metric tonnes (2,000 tons) of salt with the water of the Colorado, and the amount is steadily increasing in spite of vast funds being poured into desalination projects. The story of the San Joaquin Valley is similar, although on an even larger scale. When two huge new water projects are complete, nearly two million metric tonnes of salt will be deposited in the Valley, along with the water, every year.

Holland has a comparable problem: its underground soils are already salted by sea water, and its fresh-water source is the salty and chemical-laden Rhine. Egypt's Aswan Dam has eliminated the periodic flooding of the Nile, which used to wash salts out of the region's topsoil. A vast new drainage system to combat salt build-up is now being constructed at a cost of a billion dollars. It will be able to correct salt damage to part of one small valley only. It is estimated that salt spread by irrigated agriculture will have destroyed between 50 and 65 per cent of all artificially watered land on earth before the end of this century.

The only remedies seem to be better drainage, and the leaching of the excess salt from the soil by pouring millions of gallons of fresh water over and through it. But the drainage schemes cost more than the original irrigation systems did; and unpolluted water is swiftly becoming a precious commodity, not to be wasted as a mere washing facility for salty soil. Scientists are fighting to find salt-resistant hybrid strains of cotton, of lettuce, of tomatoes, and the rest – so far without success. Salt-tolerant strains of food plants simply produce too little, and no one yet has found a way out of what appears to be nature's rule: the higher the growth rate, the more salt-sensitive a plant will be. The most promising work being done at the moment is in juggling high-saline and less-saline water with the periods of plant life-cycles. For instance, low-salt water is kept for the germination of seedlings, high-salt water being permitted when the plant reaches six inches high, and so on. Relatively salt-resistant plants which remove some of the salt from the soil, are rotated with sensitive ones, and sloped beds are furrowed with salt-collecting depressions which are later flushed out to help cleanse the soil of salt. The organization and the technological cunning required to work all this out and to balance the whole panoply of strategies and varying conditions become more complex and expensive year by year.

Before 1850, everyone knew what salt was for: men ate it, shared it with their cattle, and used it to preserve food. It was complicated and often dangerous to get it and to supply it; most people received it in very limited quantities at the end of a long and hard journey. Ever since 1850, there has been a universal and continuous increase in human consumption of salt. The salt industry has been called "perhaps the most tangible realization of the ideology of perpetual growth."

From time to time the public becomes aware of a strange new word, the name of a pollutant which is scarcely known outside laboratories and chemical catalogues until something nasty leaks onto a highway or spills into drinking water or poisons the air and forces its way into everyday human conversation. Most of these chemical pollutants (efficient in their place but lethal anywhere else) are in some way or other salt-derived, with chlorine or sodium designated in their unwieldy names. Examples are chlorinated phenols and the notorious poly-chlorinated biphenyls (PCBs).

The use of salt for culinary purposes has become "statistically insignificant" in relation to the quantities in demand for industry. The making of solar salt has declined dramatically because modern mining methods are increasingly fast, efficient, and similar all over the world. The ancient, almost esoteric arts of salt-winning have become completely inadequate to produce the huge tonnages of salt now required for industry. Trade in salt has dwindled, for with modern boring and geological expertise, any country can find its own salt deposits, which we now know to exist in or near most regions in the world.

The earth contains almost inconceivable quantities of salt: here is one resource we need never fear using up. However, getting salt and using it requires energy. Even primitive salt-boiling uses vast amounts of fuel: in its time the practice has caused timber shortages, wood- and coal-smoke pollution, and even human migrations. The principle fuel for modern chemical industries is oil rather than wood, and the main raw material for many chlorinated chemicals is also petroleum – but petroleum, unlike salt, is not inexhaustible, and unlike wood, is not renewable.

Salt, whose strangeness has always awed men's minds, has never been less understood by ordinary people. Its secrets have become the preserve of chemists, whose complex and arcane skills cut them severely off from the comprehension of most of us. At the same time, never has common salt more effectively ruled human behaviour. The familiar salt-cellar appears at times to have unleashed a double demon with whose dance we Sorcerer's Apprentices can barely keep up. If we are ever to gain the upper hand, we shall have to exorcize him, salt his tail with sodium chloride, the ancient symbol of wisdom itself.

CHAPTER THREE

Butter
–and Something
"Just as Good"

*F*RESH SWEET CORN, boiled and eaten straight off the cob, is a dish so simple that it is scarcely appropriate to call it a "dish" at all. Because of this, and because we are allowed to dispense almost entirely with utensils in the process, eating corn off the cob makes us feel robust, earthy, and in touch with nature and basic rock-bottom reality. But the delicious, simple, honest corn cob is in fact the crowning achievement of enormous human efforts of will, imagination, foresight, drive, and relentless, obsessive selectivity – to say nothing of the inconceivable complexities of "simple" nature. The pinch of salt we sprinkle over the corn is an ancient symbol of creative ingenuity, and today more than ever representative of human technological ambition.

Finally, with a lordly gesture, we douse our corn in butter. The rows of kernels, rounded and yellow like little butter pats themselves, are anointed with a golden semi-solid fat which melts and trickles over the corn, lubricating it, rounding out its flavour, and completing its appeal.

It is exceedingly difficult for us to achieve opportunities to revel in the experience of extreme simplicity. And it is not easy either to describe or to account for our own culture's particular predilection for butter – a loyalty so fierce and so unreasoning that it is called, by those opposed to it, the "butter mystique."

Butter is the *crème de la crème*, the quintessence of the risen richness of milk itself, and as such has traditionally belonged to the exclusive category of "best" things: "top," "opulent," "pure" things. Even for cultures that almost never eat it, butter often achieves an aura of medicinal and cosmetic power; among the butter-eaters, that minority of people who originate in the steppes and the cold north, it has always had regal status as a substance both unique and splendidly filling.

In some respects butter has only one peer among foodstuffs, and that is honey. Milk and honey are the only substances people commonly eat which are created by animals specifically to feed their young. Butter is thick and golden. So is honey, which in many religions is the nearest thing to the food of the gods themselves. Butter and honey are delicious together: they complement each other, and harmonize with each other. They are the ultimate fat and the original sugar, products of land which is rich and fertile (and may be said to "flow with milk and honey"). Our enjoyment of them demonstrates human domination over the animal kingdom. At the same time, neither butter-making nor honey-collecting necessarily entails the guilt which men have sometimes, in their more thoughtful moments, suffered when they killed animals to feed themselves.

Butter has it both ways: not only is it a fat, and as such broadly delectable; it also comes haloed with all the complexities and perversities of status. The immediate appeal of grease resembles that of sugar: it is so easy to like it that "good taste" (that ineffable and therefore unattackable bastion of the élite) is always very quick to find it disgusting. The German word *Schmalz* usually means lard, but includes the very finest fat, which is butter; in Yiddish it means most commonly chicken fat. The term in English now denotes (as it can in German and Yiddish) a far-too-easy and therefore repulsive sentimentality, of the kind we also describe as "sugary." Too many people like it; they pile it on; it is offensive to the superior few who have plenty available and are therefore sickened by excess. But the Germans still have an expression which most aptly describes the other side of the coin: something *ohne Salz und Schmalz*, without salt and grease, is boring and wishy-washy.

In spite of modern struggles against obesity and the consequent revulsion of people of taste from most fats wherever they are detectable, butter still maintains the "high" connotations which it has inherited from the past. Butter has always seemed magical because of the mystery of its solidification out of milk. Absolutely nothing else is made like this, or from such a noble substance as milk. Butter is irreproachable, unique, and irreplaceable. In this it is like salt, except that salt, as earth, is strange in being edible, whereas milk's prime function is to feed. Corn, as we now normally eat it, is either white or yellow. Salt is white. Milk is white, butter yellow, honey gold. For us the colours white and gold have distinct meanings, but they both signify purity, delectableness, even heavenliness.

Industrialized modern civilizations, whether capitalist or communist, find it extremely difficult to accept that anything is either unique or irreplaceable. The myth is egalitarian, and the ostensible goal is either universal availability of everything, or absolute interchangeability, or both. This means that the claims of anything either to rarity or to having no substitute must instantly be questioned. Salt has remained irreplaceable, but it has been found to be anything but scarce – indeed we risk being salted to death if we do not take care: the battle against the rarity of salt is definitely over.

The "butter mystique" is challenged by margarine, a substance born of the industrial age, expressive of technological claims and methods, and one which relentlessly contests the notion that the quality of butter is inimitable. But the old monarch refuses to be dislodged, and has not been above using some thoroughly disreputable tactics in the battle. The ferocity in itself should alert us to the fact that there is a great deal more going on here than a simple scrap for a market between butter and margarine.

BUTTER MAKING

The first cooking pots were containers found in nature: pods, husks, gourds, shells, and animal skins. Since butter as it separates from milk is a highly perishable commodity, the extensive use of it is usually found in cold countries, and among people who herd animals for a living. It is perfectly possible that butter was first discovered by travellers carrying whole milk in animal-skin containers, who opened their pouches after a long bumpy trip to find the miracle had occurred: the milk had spontaneously turned into butter and a thin, still drinkable liquid, buttermilk. People had only to reproduce the jouncing and agitating of milk to create butter whenever they wanted it. Until very recently in the Middle East, butter churning was often done by street vendors, squatting before a paunch full of milk suspended on cords from a stick tripod, which the milkman shook and jiggled till he could hear that the butter had "come" inside.

It takes about twenty litres of milk to churn out one kilogram of butter. Exactly how churning works is still unclear. The process involves breaking down the foam produced by the incorporation of air into whipped cream by continuing to beat the mass at a temperature between 12° and 18°C. (53° and 64°F.). Membranes which keep globules of fat apart in the cream are first softened then broken; the fat begins to coagulate, and emulsifiers such as lecithin from the ruptured membranes help burst bubble walls in the foam, so allowing all the fat to mass together. The finished butter, separated from its buttermilk, is an immensely complex system of water droplets, air bubbles, milk fat crystals and free (non-crystalline) fat. Butters can vary a good deal, because of the churning, in density and spreadability (that is, in the ordering of their molecular composition) as well as in taste.

The Celts, whom we have already met mining their salt at Hallstatt in modern Austria, are thought to have had much to do with introducing the technology of butter-churning to the areas of modern Europe, such as modern Germany, France, and Britain, which they influenced for over a millennium before Christ. They were expert barrel and churn makers, and their access to salt must early on have given them the means of preserving butter.

Hand churning always called for both strength and discernment. The simplest of the European butter churns, invented early in the Middle Ages and commonly in use well into the nineteenth century, was a narrow upright wooden tub with a lid, through the centre of which ran a long wooden rod fitted with a perforated attachment at the bottom. The dairymaid stood over the tub and pounded this plunger or dasher up and down in the cream till the sound and the feel of the contents told her the butter had formed in globules of the correct size.

The regularity, the precise speed, and the length of the strokes were important. Churning had to be done at the right time of the morning or evening to ensure that the temperature was correct; the process could take hours in hot or stormy weather.

The butter when ready was collected, kneaded, and pummelled to expel any beads of buttermilk still enclosed in the fat. Then it was "flung" into pots for home use, or salted and packed into firkins or barrels for sale. When people made their own butter, every town and every household provided a different product. Each region preferred a distinctive traditional shape – round, rectangular, or cubed; and every farm had a carved wooden stamp for marking its merchandise. In Cambridgeshire, butter was cylindrical, passed through a ring gauge and sold by the yard. Butter also came in pieces the size and shape of an egg, which is why old-fashioned recipes often awkwardly demand that you should "take a piece of butter the size [sometimes this is changed to the "weight"] of an egg. . . ."

After the butter had been made, the buttermilk could be heated and its remaining solid content strained off to make hard cheese. Those who could afford to feed buttermilk to their pigs produced prime quality pork. (The "buttermilk" sold in North American supermarkets today is an entirely different product, made of pasteurized skim milk with a culture added to thicken it and increase its lactic acid content.)

Dairy work included milking, making cream and butter, and also the sophisticated art of making cheese. In Europe it was always done by women. The word "dairy" is from Middle English *dey* – a female servant. The dairy was associated with the house as opposed to the lands; "inside" has always been female in the Western imagination, and "outside" male, so that the man's place was in the public eye while the woman's was at home. Also, milk was perhaps considered self-evidently a woman's affair.

A "cool hand" was the term used for giftedness in butter-making: kneading butter required swift, firm movements and a low temperature. When a farmer from an English county like Cheshire, famous for its dairy produce, sought a wife, he chose brawn over delicacy every time. In one village it was traditional for a young girl to lift the immensely heavy lid of the parish chest with one hand, to show how desirable she was.

People often claimed that they could tell from the taste of the butter which of their cows had produced it. Differences stemmed from the physical constitution of the cow, what she had eaten, and what season of the year it was, as well as from variations in the treatment of the milk itself. The milk was left to stand while the cream rose to the top. Fine butter was made from the first cream skimmed from the milk. The second skimming produced lower-quality "after-butter," while "whey butter," the cheapest, was made from curds remaining in the whey after cheese had been made from whole milk. The best butter of all was made from the "strokings," the cow's richest milk which arrived, with the aid of the milkmaid's careful stroking, only at the end of each milking session.

The length of time the cream was allowed to stand was of enormous importance to the taste of butter. People used generally to like a strong lactic flavour, so that cream was left to ripen before churning for at least three and as long as seven days. Most factory butter sold today is from "sweet," very newly risen and pasteurized cream, with a mild lactic acid added. The method discourages bacteria and also satisfies the increasing modern demand for mildness of flavour in everything. Ripe-butter enthusiasts in North America can buy a product which is given the added strength of dried bacillic cultures imported from one of the European countries which still produce strong-tasting butter: Germany, Austria, Holland, Belgium, or Switzerland. This butter, labelled with the happy epithet "cultured," is sold at "luxury" prices in specialty stores; a minority of people are willing to pay more for something resembling the original heady taste. Butter made from newly risen cream requires more salt for keeping than does ripe butter, and this has until quite recently resulted in taste preferences: salt for mild butter lovers, and saltless for those who like butter ripe.

At least four hundred volatile compounds have been detected in the aroma of butter. The alteration or lack of even one of these is liable to be noticed immediately, so sensitive and fastidious are our bodily mechanisms for responding to milk. "Rancid" derives from the Latin *rancidus*, "rank" or "stinking": it is a term reserved exclusively for fats. There are two main kinds of rancidity: hydrolytic (change caused by the absorption of flavours from food or micro-organisms) and oxidative (reaction with oxygen in the air). People can learn actively to like some forms of the first type, acquiring a taste for soured cream, ripened butter, and the various rotten properties in the great cheeses, such as Stilton, Pont l'Evèque, and Roquefort. Aroma scientists sadly concede that people's reactions to "off flavours" are "subjectively organoleptic": different people like different things. Hydrolysis is our own body's method of digesting fat.

Oxidative rancidity, on the other hand, is totally unacceptable; reaction to it is always immediate revulsion. We are, it seems, biologically primed not to eat oxidated fat, for doing so can cause diarrhoea, poor growth, loss of hair, skin lesions, anorexia, emaciation, and intestinal haemorrhages. Oxidation begins with exposure to air, and for this reason butter should be kept covered. Supermarket fluorescent light – indeed light of any kind – promotes rancidity, which is why good-quality butter is now sold wrapped in foil.

Butter varies in colour from pale cream to yellow, depending largely on what the cow eats. Winter butter has always been pale, and summer butter yellow. It was believed for centuries that eating buttercups made the cow give yellow butter; this, indeed, is the origin of the flower's common name. (In fact, of course, all kinds of plant pigments, not merely yellow flowers, give butter its colour.) Children still hold a buttercup under a friend's chin, and if a golden colour is reflected, they say, "You love butter." People have always liked the idea of butter being yellow: the colour distinguished butter from lard, and since the essential richness of the milk was the dominating idea, gold is naturally the desired colour.

From the Middle Ages onwards we have records of people colouring butter which they did not consider yellow enough. A law was passed in Paris in 1396 forbidding the tinting of butter with "saucy flowers," herbs, or drugs. Marigolds (that is, pot marigolds or calendulas, not the originally American plant of the same name) were traditionally stored salted in earthenware pots, taken out when needed and beaten with a small iron ball to extract juice for colouring winter butter. Carrot juice, saffron, and later annatto, an orange-red dye extracted from the fruit of a South American tree, were other agents. Today annatto and other oil-soluble dyes are used for the same purpose, but in the United States the powerful dairy lobby has seen to it that the colouring of butter does not have to be confessed on the wrapping. Our distrust of modern chemical additives makes it worth disguising an ancient practice.

"Butter is made from crayme," wrote Andrew Boorde in 1542. "It is good to eat in the mornyng – a lytell porcyon is good for every man in the mornyng if it be newe made." People commonly believed that butter was bad for the stomach unless eaten first thing in the day: it was thought to lie in a layer at the top of the stomach's contents "as the fatness doth swim above in a boiling pot." Everyone agreed, too, that butter should be eaten as soon as possible after it was churned – the ideal being to own your cow and churn your butter daily. The reason was gastronomic as well as hygienic, and the ideal was possible only if you lived in the country.

Most city people today seldom see rotten food, but taste fresh food more rarely still. As far as butter goes, we have almost conquered rancidity by means of cold storage, careful packaging, and sterilization. But milk is now factory produced (the trade still calls it "creamery" milk because of the clean and delicious ring of the word), which means that it is mixed from the yield of hundreds of cows raised on standard feed. It is often weeks or even months old before we get it. We are not provided with a choice of different levels of cream-ripening. The product we buy is therefore always the same, and we have almost forgotten what freshly churned butter is like.

UNACCEPTABLE, COSMETIC, AND MEDICINAL BUTTER

A Greek poem satyrizing a Thracian wedding in the fourth century BC describes the guests as "butterophagous gentry" with unkempt hair. The two attributes amount to the same thing: untidy hair and butter-eating were equally outlandish. Greeks in their own estimation had better coiffeurs than anything available to Thracians; Greeks preferred olive oil to barbarous butter.

The word *butter* comes from *bou-tyron*, which seems to mean "cow-cheese" in Greek. Some scholars think, however, that the word was borrowed from the language of the northern and butterophagous Scythians, who herded cattle; Greeks lived mostly from sheep and goats whose milk, which they consumed mainly as cheese, was relatively low in butter (or butyric) fat. Butter divides the people of northern Europe as radically from the oil-loving southerners as beer and cider distinguish them from wine-drinkers. People from Mediterranean lands believed until at least the eighteenth century that butter was a cause of the leprosy which seemed to be so prevalent in the north. The Cardinal of Aragon took his own cook and plenty of olive oil when he visited Holland in 1516.

Most people, aside from Caucasian northern Europeans and their descendants and a few nomadic African tribes, are biologically lactose-intolerant after their milk-drinking, mammalian infancy. This means that they are simply unable to stomach raw milk. Human babies are born with provisions of the enzyme lactase which enables them to digest lactose or milk sugar. Ability to manufacture the enzyme is soon lost in lactose-intolerant people, who thereafter cannot drink more than a cup or so of raw milk without suffering nausea and diarrhoea. The reason for this is thought to be the evolutionary undesirability of having adults compete with their own offspring for the milk-source. The people who began to domesticate cattle about ten thousand years ago developed lactose tolerance into adulthood: those who could take milk, on occasion using it as their major food source, survived and handed on the trait to their children. Lactose helps in the absorption of calcium; it is, therefore, extra-desirable for the populations who live in the cold, relatively sunless north, where little vitamin D is created in the human skin. This may be why the development of the capacity to keep ingesting plenty of milk is an especially northern trait. It has been found that cultural acceptance of milk eventually produces a sufficiency of the enzyme in the population – although an estimated 16 per cent of people will never be able to take raw milk, even in our own unprecedentedly milk-loving society.

Greeks, Arabs, and Near-Eastern Jews, whose cultures are resistant to raw milk, dislike drinking it in spite of a long dairying history. The indigenous millions of Oceania, the Americas, China, and Japan remain largely milk intolerant. Butter, cheese, yoghurt, and soured milk like *laban* are all low in lactose because the fermenting bacteria use it up as fuel; these foods are therefore biologically acceptable by everybody, although non-milk-drinking people may eat them very seldom. Butter is more extravagant to make, and in its solid form more difficult to keep, than the other low-lactose milk products, and may therefore become a rarity and as such either precious or abominable, depending on the circumstances of the encounter with it.

In the oil-loving European south, butter, being expensive and relatively rare, tends to be perceived as a luxury. In the Middle Ages it was one of the foods banned during Lent. This was a minor inconvenience in the south where the normal cooking medium was olive or walnut oil; it was however a great hardship in the north, where butter was an everyday necessity. Clever southern businessmen cashed in on Lent by selling oil to the north during this time. The more cynical northerners would simply pay their way out of the ban; the magnificent Butter

Tower of Rouen Cathedral was built with money which the Church received from people who preferred to pay rather than forgo their daily butter. Not being allowed to eat butter especially enraged the idealistic Martin Luther. "For at Rome they themselves laugh at the fasts," he wrote in 1520, "making us foreigners eat the oil with which they would not grease their shoes, and afterwards selling us liberty to eat butter. . . ."

In the days before the Japanese came systematically into contact with the west, butter was practically unknown to them. Those who did meet Europeans were appalled by their stench: people who seldom touch animal products are extremely sensitive to the body-odour exuded by eaters of animal fat. It was butter, the Japanese thought, which made Europeans so peculiarly rank: *bata-kusai* they called them (using the English word for the foul substance): "butter-stinkers."

Fat discourages insects and fat keeps you warm. Many travellers who have lived among pastoral societies in cold climates, like the Mongols and Tibetans, have described how these people spent their lives coated in grease, usually butter, which might turn black and rancid before anyone seemed to mind. People have always enjoyed oiling their bodies, and hot water for washing was not commonly available until very recently. Our own fanatical obsession with washing is mostly new and largely a matter of our own self-esteem: it is a habit which would have astounded most of our ancestors, including the fastidious and supercilious Greeks.

Another very luxurious practice, often available only to the rich, was coating one's hair in butter or lard. It kept down vermin, helped preserve order in an elaborate hair-do, and added a gleam for which even we occasionally yearn, with our "structuring" hair-gel, brilliantine, and other hair oils. In many societies, including ancient Egypt and modern Ethiopia, a lump of fatty incense or of perfumed butter was placed on the head and allowed to melt and drizzle voluptuously down one's face and body. The connotations of "greasy" were with "shiny" – richness, lubrication, brightness – and not, as we have it, with nausea, dirt, and "foreigners."

Butter has always been considered to have medicinal properties. Lubrication was the key here. Butter was the finest fat for softening the skin. It was said to relieve burns and babies' rashes, and was often thought to help children's growing pains and stiffness of the joints in the old. Pliny wrote that butter "has the properties of oil, and is used for anointing by all the barbarians – and by us [Romans] in the case of children." Wounded elephants in first-century India were treated by being made to swallow butter, or by having their wounds anointed with it. The Celtic word for butter is from the Indo-European for "ointment," and the Vikings called butter "cow-smear."

One strange but widely used sixteenth-century European medicine against pain in the joints was made from butter left to liquefy in the sun for several days and then drunk; it is thought that the method might have increased the vitamin D in this rancid concoction, which could thus have developed anti-rachitic properties (despite the nasty side-effects which must also have been produced). Butter's "lubricating" effect when drunk rancid also made it a useful laxative.

THE SECRET NAME OF BUTTER

Butter can be kept from going rancid by melting it and removing the milk solids which separate out of it. First the whey proteins, which gather as froth on the top of hot melted butter, are skimmed off, and then the middle layer of clarified oil is carefully poured away from the casein and salt which have sunk to the bottom of the pan. Clarified butter, the golden liquid which results, will last a year or longer without refrigeration if no air comes in contact with it, and it possesses the further advantage of not burning easily when used as a cooking medium.

In India, clarified butter is called *ghee*. It is the most precious substance provided by the most sacred beast on earth, the cow. In Hindu mythology, Prajápati, Lord of Creatures, created *ghee* by rubbing or "churning" his hands together and then poured it into fire to engender his progeny; whenever the Vedic ritual was performed of pouring *ghee* into fire, it was a re-enactment of creation. (Butter in mythologies the world over is a symbol of semen: churning represents the sexual act, and also the formation of a child in its mother's womb.)

Later, during the Deluge, continues the Indian myth, the honey-like elixir of immortality called *amrita* got lost in the cosmic ocean of milk. The gods and the demons joined forces to save it by churning the ocean until various gods and sacred objects solidified out like butter from the milk: the cow of plenty, the goddess of wine, the moon, the terrible poison which is twin-liquor to *amrita*, the coral tree which perfumes the world, the goddess of beauty holding a lotus; finally the physician of the gods stepped carefully forward, carrying a milk-white bowl full of *amrita*.

One of the hymns of the Rg Veda (*circa* 1500 BC) is in praise of *ghee*, and is intended to be accompanied by ritual libations of the golden substance into fire. These are some of the words:

This is the secret name of Butter:
"Tongue of the gods," "navel of immortality."
We will proclaim the name of Butter;
We will sustain it in this sacrifice by bowing low . . .
These waves of Butter flow like gazelles before the hunter . . .
Streams of Butter caress the burning wood.
Agni, the fire, loves them and is satisfied.

Here butter is fertilizing seed, a regenerator of riches: its sputtering and crackling reawaken Agni himself. It also represents the pure energy of communal prayer and the inspiration to mysticism and poetry.

Statues of Vishnu and Krishna are ritually anointed with two intensely sacred mixtures of five substances, one called *pançamrita*: milk, curds, *ghee*, honey, and sugar, and the other "the five products of the cow": milk, curds, *ghee*, urine, and dung. Both of these can be used to purify people who have committed temporarily polluting offenses, or as antidotes to poison and disease. The lamps that light the holiest places in Hindu temples are wicks burning in *ghee* – as are the lamps swung in circular motions before the images of various deities, or lit at the great Festival of Lights in honour of Lakshmi and Rama.

Hindus rank food (high to low) as raw, superior cooked, inferior cooked, and garbage. No one may eat "inferior" foods, like rice and lentils, which have been touched by someone of a lower caste than himself; but anything "superior" may be taken from any caste except the lowest of all. Inferior food cooked in irreproachable *ghee* instantly becomes *pakka*, "complete" or "superior," and edible even by a Brahmin. A travelling Brahmin who does not know who has been touching the food available to him, must receive everything he eats raw and still unpeeled, unless food vendors can demonstrate that their wares are cooked in *ghee*.

Ghee is expensive and much in demand, because of its exalted status, at Hindu weddings. Male guests are expected to compete with each other to see who can eat the most of it: consuming a kilo or more at a sitting is considered a proof of virility. The occasion and the sexual connotations of *ghee* turn the contest into a kind of fertility ritual.

In 1948, one of the last descriptions was made of the Festival of the

Butter Gods in Tibet. What Harrison Forman, writing for the *Canadian Geographic*, saw was one of the world's most magnificent religious celebrations, a particularly splendid example of which took place annually at the monastery he visited, Kum Bum Gomba. Half a million pilgrims, representative of the Buddhist world from Siberia to modern Sri Lanka, and from the Russian Pamirs to the Pacific, took part in the festival and were themselves part of the pageantry. It continued for many days, with songs and dancing, masked theatre, a huge market, the Questioning of the Lamas, chanted prayers, and music accompanied by cymbals, drums, gongs, flutes, oboes, and brass trumpets up to twenty feet long. The climax of the whole celebration was the night-long display of the Butter Gods.

Immense panels of bas-reliefs representing Buddhist deities and mythical subjects had been carved in yak butter by scores of lamas, supervised by a guild of artists acclaimed as among the finest in the Buddhist world. They had taken months to make the figures, which were multicoloured, as much as three metres (10 ft.) tall, and amazingly intricate, with every hair, every realistic detail of the design on their "silken" clothes, every bead in their elaborate jewellery meticulously carved and moulded in butter. Some of the tableaux included hundreds of lively figures in action. The monks had had to work in the cold, and often suffered from frozen hands and feet during the winter weeks of work. Every year the sculptures were entirely different.

The crowd surged forward to gaze at the butter figures in the flickering light of thousands of yak-butter lamps. As the night passed the butter began to melt in the heat. By dawn it was all over: the temporary is intrinsic to the nature of festivals. The sacred occasion had passed, and the special manifestation of the gods was finished for that year.

THE BUTTER CULTURES

Tibetan life still revolves around the yak, which this people has herded and placed at the centre of its culture for at least two thousand years. Tibetans are warmed by yak-dung fires and lit by yak-butter lamps; they eat yak meat and yak blood, butter, cheese, and yoghurt; they use yaks for transport and weave clothing, blankets, shelters, and even boats out of yak hair. Their staple dish is *tsampa*, made of salted tea pounded together with yak butter, to which toasted barley flour is added and mixed by hand before eating. The dependence in so many ways upon their particular animal herd is typical of pastoralists, the original "butter-eaters," the world over.

Russians in the regions of Uzbek, Bashkir, and Kirgiz still drink mares' and donkeys' milk and turn it into *kumyss*, a powerful fermented liquor or spirit, often served with lumps of butter in it. *Kumyss* is mentioned in reports from Christian missionaries in central Siberia in 1253; Marco Polo wrote in 1298 that Genghis Khan kept a stable of ten thousand white horses for the production of *kumyss*. This is probably the same drink as the *oxygala* ("sharp milk") which the ancient Greeks knew from the horse-riding and "butterophagous" Scythians. Hero-dotus had reported that the Scythians used to blind their slaves and then make them sit round wooden barrels full of mares' milk and "stir them round and round; the stuff that rises to the top is skimmed, and considered more valuable than what sinks to the bottom." The Scythians ate horse meat and horse butter and drank horse buttermilk and *oxygala*, using strainers to remove the scum; many of these strainers of bone, and *kumyss* or *oxygala* jars with sieves built into them, have been found in Scythian tombs, together, sometimes, with the tattooed bodies of the Scythians themselves, preserved in the icy soil of central Russia.

In T'ang China, *kumyss*, clotted cream, and clarified butter were three stages in a hierarchy of products derived from milk. In Buddhist religious imagery, each of them symbolized a stage in the transformation of the soul. Clarified butter represented the ultimate development of the Buddha spirit.

The descendants of the Caucasian pastoralists who now people northern Europe have long been the world's largest consumers of butter. The Dutch used to be called by the English "buttermouths" and "butterboxes" after their insistence on carrying their own butter supply with them in boxes when they travelled. The Irish, it is said, may still eat more butter than any population on earth. They have always spread and dolloped it onto their staple foods: porridge, then potatoes and bread. When poverty forced people to do without butter, the substance simply became more symbolic than ever of riches and plenty. Giving butter to a guest or a stranger was Christian hospitality. The obituary of a miser in 1486 reads "Neidh O'Mulconry, head of the inhospitality of Ireland, died. It was he who solemnly swore that he would never give bread and butter together to guests." And the medieval Vision of MacConglinne, which is supposed to cause the mouth of the Devil himself to drool with greed, places butter squarely into its landscape of custards, bacon, and glistening fat.

Some of the commonest archaeological finds in Ireland are barrels of ancient butter, buried in the bogs. The Norsemen, the Finns, the Icelanders, and the Scots had done the same: they flavoured butter heavily with garlic, knuckled it into a wooden firkin, and buried it for years in the bogs – for so long that people were known to plant trees to mark the butter's burial site. The longer it was left, the more delicious it became. A further advantage was doubtless the safety of supplies from robbers, or enemies in wartime. Most of the Irish archaeological specimens date from the seventeenth and early eighteenth centuries. Although some of our sources imply that bog butter turned red, the firkins in the Irish National Museum contain "a greyish cheese-like substance, partially hardened, not much like butter, and quite free from putrefaction" because of the cool, antiseptic, anaerobic, and acidic properties of peat bogs.

In Morocco, *smen* is still a delicacy. It is made by kneading butter with various decoctions of herbs, cinnamon, and other spices; the mixture is then cooked, salted, and strained like *ghee*. It is poured into jugs, tightly stoppered, and buried in the ground for months, sometimes years. Stores of the precious stuff are saved for special feasts. The smell is considered especially magnificent: a particularly aged pot of the family *smen* may be brought out of the cellars for honoured guests to sniff. The *smen* represents the riches of the house. The necessity of "doctoring" a perishable substance in order to save it in hot weather is in this manner turned into a gastronomic triumph, and hedged about with tradition and prestige. Other versions of clarified butter, called *samna* by non-Moroccan Arabs, are to be found throughout the Middle East.

We ourselves, in the modern industrial system created by Europe and America, might legitimately lament that "no surprises" is the nearest we seem to have come to an ideal in consumer satisfaction, and that there is very little variety in the butter offered for sale. Yet we cannot forget either that the provision of butter to European cities in the past was always a chancy and often a criminal enterprise; if you did not live in the country your butter could be very nasty indeed.

Butter was heavily salted for preservation on its long journey by boat or cart into town, or in order to last through the winter. One record, dating to 1305, tells us that one pound of salt was added to every ten pounds of butter or cheese. Not surprisingly, people usually washed their butter, kneading it with water then pummelling the liquid out, in order to remove most of the salt before eating it. Butter was often sold in a half-liquid state, or was available only rancid; Tobias Smollett complained in 1748 of some "that tasted of train-oil thickened with salt." Sometimes butter came from cows which were led through the cities by vendors and milked in the street. There was no hygiene control; storage places were often smelly and unventilated, and produced in butter what was known as a "cowhouse" odour. Butter was frequently adulterated with lard; if rancid, washed with milk and water and salted again for sale; or falsely said to be from districts famous for good butter. A favourite trick was incorporating as much water as the butter would hold. The cheap nineteenth-century Dutch butter Londoners called "Bosh," and which may or may not have come from Holland, contained up to 33 per cent water.

Butter has not always enjoyed the same prestige among the affluent in western Europe. Medieval recipe books, written mainly for the nobility, call for relatively little butter. Since supplies of it were plentiful until late winter in English cities until the seventeenth century, butter (like oysters) was eaten mainly by the poor, much of it with bread and cheese or herbs. The little consumed by the rich was used mostly in cooking. One result of this was vitamin A deficiency in the richer classes, who suffered commonly from bladder and kidney stones. People noticed that the Dutch, famous for the quantity of butter they ate, were less afflicted by such stones than other nations. An old Dutch proverb went: "Eat butter first, and eat it last, and live till a hundred years be past." It is not easy to obtain historical information on the eye disease called xerophthalmia, but during the First World War we know that the Danes developed this eye disease from vitamin A deficiency because they were selling most of their butter to the Germans, who were prepared to pay high prices for it. When a low price for butter was enforced, more Danes could afford to eat it, and the number of cases of xerophthalmia became negligible within one year.

Butter and cheese fed the navies of England and Holland from the sixteenth century onward, on the new long sea voyages. An Elizabethan seaman's ration was 115 grams (1/4 lb.) of butter per day, in addition to a bottle of beer, 450 grams (1 lb.) of ship's biscuit, and 225 grams (1/2 lb.) of cheese. By 1730 the figures for supplies of butter to London show 225 grams (1/2 lb.) of butter being consumed per person per week. The gradual emergence of the middle class from Tudor times onward meant an increasing consumption of butter by wealthier people: butter slowly rose from the category of "food for the poor." By the eighteenth century the rich had acquired the habit of eating plenty of it. England, first into the Industrial Revolution with its attendant rise in the population and desertion of the country for cities, soon had to import large amounts of butter from the Continent.

What we now know as French cuisine was one of the great social and artistic achievements of the nineteenth century. It was based upon olive oil in the south and butter in the north; and since prestige and power lay mostly in the north, butter became one of the foundations of the art and science of the great French chefs – of what is known as *cuisine classique*. To this day southern French cooking tends to be called "hearty" or "robust," and other rustic epithets, even by its greatest admirers: delicacy and *finesse* generally involve the use of butter.

By 1902, English upper-class families were eating three times as much butter as the rest of the population; it had become one of the ways in which they demonstrated their superiority. Margarine had already begun seriously to undermine butter sales, but the passion for butter (in part because it remained the first choice and the luxury of the rich, living literally off the fat of the land) was if anything greater than ever.

Ever since the early years of this century the trend has been gradually reversing itself. Increasingly, people in wealthy countries, like the upper classes in pre-seventeenth-century Europe, feel it behoves them to reduce their intake of visible fat. Then, butter was poor men's food and despised as such. Now, eating little fat although plenty of it is available, and managing – through an aristocratic combination of expense, pride, and self control – not to *be* fat, has attained the kind of ineffable prestige which once accrued to soft hands and clean linen. Our sedentary lives and access to various alternative sources of calories have induced in us a shudder at the thought of the unctuous and quivering lumps of fat for which Homer's gods lusted. Most of us do eat a lot of grease, but less than a third of it is actually seen and tasted as fat; compound and processed foods effectively disguise the rest.

Yet the *idea* of butter, and words like "buttery," "deep-buttered," or "butterball," retain their enticing power in North American language. The reason is partly traditional. The English and the Dutch who emigrated to the States in the seventeenth, eighteenth, and nineteenth centuries took the butter habit with them. Foreign travellers commonly noted that Americans ate absolutely everything – porridge, soup, meat, vegetables, and puddings – swimming in butter. On extended journeys a cow was often taken along and its milk allowed to churn itself in the barrels with the lurching of the wagons. The butter was removed, washed, and salted at night.

When Catharine Beecher and Harriet Beecher Stowe wrote *The American Woman's Home*, they complained bitterly about the low standard and the rancidity of much American butter: they had to "taste 20 firkins" of it before finding one that was edible. But they incidentally demonstrate for us how all-pervasively buttery the American diet was. Bad butter, they wrote, "stands sentinel at the door to bar your way to every other kind of food. You turn from your dreadful half-slice of bread, which fills your mouth with bitterness, to your beef-steak, which proves virulent with the same poison; you think to take refuge in vegetable diet, and find the butter in the string-beans, and polluting the innocence of early peas; it is in the corn, in the succotash, in the squash; the beets swim in it, the onions have it poured over them. Hungry and miserable, you think to solace yourself in the dessert; but the pastry is cursed, the cake is acrid with the same plague." The date was 1869. A French chemist, that very year, was busy inventing margarine.

SOME BUTTER BELIEFS AND EXPRESSIONS

Right up until the early twentieth century in Europe and America, many farmers believed that butter, being a magic and mystical substance, was especially at risk through witchcraft. When cows "went dry" and gave no milk, or when their milk provided little butter, or when churning simply did not cause the butter to coagulate, sorcery was at work. A witch could come into your dairy, cry, "Give no milk!" and the damage was done; the power and the butter-fat were in all probability transferred to the witch's own cow. She could bewitch your cream so that churning was useless.

You could counter-attack by plunging a crooked sixpence or a piece of red-hot iron, such as a poker or a horse-shoe, into the cream, whip the tub or tie it up, or fling anti-maledictory salt both into the churn and into the fire. Prevention of sorcery was achieved by always keeping handy a piece of the magic mountain ash, rowan, either tied to the churn or used as a stirring implement; many churns were bought with rowan-wood handles already provided. In Germany you asked for help

in churning from the butter saint, Azeca or Haseka, who had changed
rancid butter into sweet by praying over it. Or you could invoke St.
Brigit of Ireland, whose loving generosity enabled her to feed strangers
on magically renewed stores of butter. The most common English
charm, still used in 1929 and sung as the plunger was thrust up and
down, went:

> Come, butter, come,
> Come, butter, come,
> Peter stands at the gate
> Waiting for a buttered cake,
> Come, butter, come.

Butter, as we have already seen, often symbolizes sperm or the growth
of a child in the womb. The thrusting of the churn plunger, the in-
vocation to butter to "come," the cosmic creativity of *ghee* – uses of the
metaphor range from the superstitious to the sublime. The word *butter*
is often a euphemism for "excrement" as well, since it too is formed
inside and ejected from the body. Butter is riches, and can therefore
represent very specifically "profit" or "money." An interesting confirmation, all this, of Freud's claim that we tend to dream money, excrement, and sperm interchangeably, for butter represents, as we have
seen, all three.

The money-wise "know on which side their bread is buttered," and
the wasteful "butter their bread on both sides." In the Old Testament
butter is used as a hyperbole for luxury, when a rich man "washes his
feet in butter" or "sees torrents of honey and butter." Flattering words,
fine and over-lavish, are used to "butter us up." "Churning" is working
hard and "butter" is the reward, in Jewish, Coptic, and probably many
other proverbs. An English wedding custom was to present the couple,
on their arrival at their new home, with a pot of butter to presage
prosperity and fertility for the future. "Guns will make us powerful";
said Goering in 1936, "butter will only make us fat": the statement
equates guns with war, and butter with peace.

The French sell butter in a special shop, a *crémerie*, where one also
buys milk, cream, cheese, and eggs. These are the vital but "innocent"
foodstuffs: animal products, but those not obtained by spilling blood.
Purity is stressed in *crémeries*, where all is customarily white and shiny.
Most of them employ women servers: the female association with the
idea of a dairy lives on. Butter appears packaged in the now-usual silver

or gold foil, but often the very best of it is still served from the *motte* – a huge shameless tower of unwrapped voluptuousness, with gleaming facets where chunks of butter have been cut off with a wire to the specifications of the customer. It is copious and rich, rural and nostalgic, with charms to be resisted only by the extremely hygiene-bound or the fat-hating. Butter in a *motte* is not squared-off, brand-named, labelled, and "industrialized": it constitutes a monumental snub to the concept of margarine.

MARGARINE: A MELODRAMA IN SEVERAL ACTS

First you took beef fat chopped with sheep's stomachs and cows' udders, soaked them in milk, and suspended the mixture in water and potash, at blood heat. (The idea was to "digest" the fat as a cow seems to turn her body fat into the materials from which butter is derived; the udders were meant to add the indefinable something which is lacking in fats which have not passed through a cow's teats.) Next, you pressed the amalgamation between warmed plates so that liquid fat separated from solid. The runny part was called "oleine," and what was left, being hard and white, was "margarine." (*Margaron* and *margarites* mean "pearl" in Greek.) The "oleine," which had roughly the same melting point as butter, was churned and then squeezed, gritty and oleaginous, into containers and marketed. The product soon received in English the composite name, "oleomargarine."

The substance was invented on the Imperial Farm at Vincennes, outside Paris, in 1869. Europe had recently suffered a devastating cattle plague. Butter was difficult to get, and expensive. The French Emperor Napoleon III had offered a prize for the invention of something cheap to take the place of butter. Hippolyte Mège-Mouriès, a food chemist who had already earned two gold medals for making more bread with less flour, undertook his research with the personal support of the emperor and won the prize for his new spread. The addition of milk to the suet was what in fact gave margarine a taste with some chance of acceptability: the udders and stomachs were soon rejected as un- necessary. Almost immediately the Franco-Prussian War broke out and Mège, unable to begin producing his invention, sold the patent to the Dutch in 1871, and to the Americans and the Prussians soon after the war. It was Holland, already a world leader in butter production, which first developed the French invention.

Holland's best customers for dairy products were the English, now more deeply enmeshed than any other society on earth in the Industrial Revolution. England's population was exploding, and the swiftly emptying countryside could supply less and less of the nutritional needs of the vast urban conglomerates being created by the factories. The Dutch soon found that margarine was more durable than butter and therefore simpler to hold for sale and to transport. Margarine was born from, through, and for the new industrial age.

The substitute spread began as a meat product tied directly to the beef and dairy industries. In the United States, after the first margarine plant had opened in the mid 1870s in Manhattan, margarine production soon became a minor adjunct (for Americans had no trouble getting enough butter) to the giant meat-packing companies centred in Chicago. In Europe, where by the late nineteenth century the poor had increasingly to forgo butter and eat beef tallow and lard instead, the new industry found it difficult to obtain enough fat, largely because so many people were eating it "straight." Soon beef suet had to be imported from the United States. But the market for margarine was among the poor, and buying fat made it more and more difficult to keep the price of margarine low enough so that the people who ate it could afford it.

A second dawn for the fortunes of margarine occurred between 1902 and 1915, when a method was discovered and perfected for hardening oil. The reason why animal fats congeal to spreadable (and harder) consistencies is that they have sufficient hydrogen molecules in them: they are "saturated" with hydrogen. Add hydrogen to oil – any oil – and it turns solid.

Liquid vegetable and fish oils, which until then had been unsuitable for spreading on bread, began to be perceived as raw materials for margarine. The possibilities were endless, and no time was lost in developing plantations of oil-bearing crops: oil and coconut palms, cottonseed, sunflowers, soy beans, maize, peanuts, sesame, rapeseed, even shea butter (the fruit of an African tree), babassu palms from Brazil, and olive trees. Marine oils came from whales, and from oily fish like herring, pilchards, and anchovies.

It makes no difference, as far as taste goes, which oil is used, for all individual properties of the raw materials are automatically removed in the processing. Oil seeds are crushed, heated, moistened, pressed, and filtered with the help of petroleum-based solvents so that all the meal, husks, and so on are eliminated. (These are often pressed into cakes and sold as cattle feed.) The oil is then degummed, and treated with caustic soda so that unwanted fatty acids are turned into a soapy substance and drained off. Next the oil is bleached of all colour and deodorized. It is then hydrogenated with pure hydrogen and a copper (formerly a nickel) catalyst, filtered, and refined a second time. By now the medium for the making of margarine has the same tasteless, colourless, uniform consistency no matter where the process began: at this point the milk bacteria, the aromas, and the colouring are added to make it as much like butter as possible.

Nearly all of the vegetable oils for margarine came at first from tropical countries: from places like Nigeria, the Philippines, India, and Brazil. Welcome sources of income opened up, as the rich industrialized northern populations began to eat margarine in ever-increasing amounts. Margarine is a butter substitute, invented by northern butter-eaters; it has never even tried to taste like anything except butter. People whose habits do not include the eating of butter spread on bread do not consume it themselves, but many non-butter cultures happen to be in tropical zones, precisely the areas where oil-seed crops grow best.

As aroma scientists enthusiastically got to work unlocking the secrets of butter's attractions and trying to apply this knowledge to improvements in the palatability of margarine, more and more tropical lands were turned over to raising lucrative crops for sale to the north. As time went on, plantations began to crush their own seed, and at least partly refine the oil before selling it to the margarine factories, which always remained close to their customers in Europe and North America.

The trump cards, however, remained securely in the hands of the buyers. For margarine oils are entirely interchangeable: there is nothing infuriatingly unique about any one of them, as there is with butter-fat. Any oil will do—and therefore the margarine corporations could buy whatever oil was cheapest. Shortages, special qualities, colour, taste— none of these made the slightest difference; and alternatives were always available.

As giant food corporations formed and expanded, tropical plantations fell more and more under their control. Unilever (which began as a butter- and then a margarine-selling business) is now the world's largest food-processing company; its revenues reached $20 billion in 1983. Unilever decides in large measure what crops will be grown, and in what quantities, in many Third World countries, particularly in Africa. International corporations like Unilever now do their own advertising (to create and sustain demand), and provide their own transportation, importing, exporting, research, and development of ideas and products. They see to it that people who can pay get what they want. The invention of margarine, where raw materials are reduced to complete neutrality and then given character by means of additives, was a major factor in the creation of the giant modern systems of food production and profit.

Meanwhile, back among the people whom margarine was designed to please, and near the beginning of this century, the battle with butter had begun in earnest. The ties of the new industrial product with meat and dairying had snapped, and now margarine began seriously to threaten butter sales. The reason was mostly that margarine was cheaper than butter. Butter producers were unwilling to lower prices since they were selling what they themselves made; margarine producers could cheapen their wares because the people who actually grew the oil seeds (as opposed to those who marketed them) could be paid little. But as prosperity mounted in the industrialized countries, Ernst Engel's law came into force: expenditure on food does not increase in the same ratio as income, but becomes relatively lower. People learn to expect that food will be cheap; money is for spending on other things.

The butter industry had in the beginning two main advantages over margarine. One was that it was already in place, not struggling for a foothold. The other was that butter is central to the mythologies of our culture, bathed as it is in tradition, in prestige, in folklore. The taste of butter is the ideal which margarine is trying, even now, to attain. Butter is so entrenched as a basic and preferred food that margarine never turned aside to become something different from the original, but has coveted butter's domain all along. Being a child of our times, however, margarine never accepted that the ancient mystique pertained to butter alone, and could not believe that butter was irreplaceable.

On the whole, the producers of butter fought a very dirty fight. The butter lobby sought to shut out margarine by forcing governments to tax the rival product till its price was as close as possible to butter's. Several intensively butter-producing countries, such as Canada and New

Zealand, simply forbade margarine production. (New Zealand still makes no margarine, although recently, because of margarine's new "health" weapon, sales of it have been permitted. Canada rescinded its law in 1948, even later in some of the provinces.) Other countries insisted that no margarine be sold without an admixture of butter, to protect their dairy farmers.

The fact that poor people bought most margarine was often used insidiously to shame those who were trying not to be perceived as poor. In German towns with more than five thousand inhabitants, buyers had to go into a food shop by a separate entrance in order to get margarine, or into a partitioned-off section of the shop which everyone knew was for those who ate the cheaper stuff. The official reason for this was that butter sellers might be tempted to "adulterate" their produce with margarine if the two substances were allowed shelf contact. Margarine was packaged differently from butter – in cubes rather than bricks – and bore a tell-tale red stripe to distinguish it, in addition to the demeaning word *margarine* on the box.

From the very beginning, nowhere was margarine allowed to be called by a name remotely resembling the word *butter*. Fear of the consumers being fooled was the reason, as well as the jealous guarding by dairy interests of butter's semi-sacred status. The United States had 180 applications for butter-substitute patents after margarine first arrived in the 1870s. The names of some of these were "oleoid," "creamine," "butteroid," and "butterine." "Butterine" was the name by which the product was first known in England. Legislation was passed in the United States in 1886 forbidding every echo of "butter," and making "oleomargarine" the generic name – which it remained for sixty-four years. The British changed "butterine" to "margarine" by law in 1887.

Margarine, being factory made, has always been a brand-name product in the west, with fierce competition between the brands for the best, that is the most butter-like, taste. These names like to suggest nostalgia (Blue Bonnet), the regal (Imperial), the childlike and natural (Stork, Flora, Country Crock) – whatever might participate in something of the prestige of butter. Relatively rarely is the modernity of margarine stressed, as in *L'Avenir* (The Future) in France.

Handcuffed as it is to the concept of butteriness, margarine launched in the twenties a long-lasting series of advertisements in many languages, which showed blindfolded people trying both spreads and pronouncing,

"You can't tell the difference," a judgement which no one who heard it at the time would have thought himself sufficiently insensitive to make. Butter, forced into publicity which has insisted more and more neurotically on its own ineffable singularity, has ended up with slogans as lame as "Only butter is butter." In Russia, where state-controlled margarine production has grown to surpass butter production in volume as the country becomes industrialized, there are two kinds available: kitchen, and better-quality table margarine. The latter is marked with a cow on its wrapper, "to indicate the product's uses."

Butter's meanest punches in the battle with the upstart began as early as 1902 in the United States, even before hydrogenation technology became available. Margarine was called a "harmful drug," and stores had to be licensed to sell it. Butter producers primly and cunningly insisted that, since margarine was not butter, it should be prevented by every means from resembling butter. Above all, it should be denied the golden colour which, as butter had good reason to know, proves irresistible to buyers, no matter what the substance actually tastes like. Unless it wanted to bear a heavy tax, margarine had to be sold lard-white. Five of the states went so far as to have all margarine dyed pink, presumably so that no one could take it seriously, let alone eat it as a daily basic food or cook anything in it without turning the stomachs of their family and guests.

Margarine countered first of all by including in packages a tube, bag, or tablet with yellow colouring matter in it. You kneaded the dye into the white fat by hand – often imperfectly, so that the finished product had a streaky look. The job was accepted as something a man could do in the kitchen without endangering his self-esteem – like emptying garbage and sharpening knives. Presumably it did not drag him too inextricably into the "female" activity of actual cooking.

By the 1920s, when hydrogenated vegetable oil had become almost exclusively the raw material of American margarine, yellow oils had become available; if not deprived of all their colour, these could make margarine "naturally yellow," and the tax had been circumvented. But the American dairy industry kept fighting, and in 1931 a tax was slapped on all margarine containing yellow oils; in 1934 it became illegal to use any kind of unbleached oil in margarine. Meanwhile, the role of "purity" in the butter myth was turned against it in 1923, when Congress forbade the addition to butter of any other ingredients, including those enhancing spreadability; margarine, less "pure," rushed to embrace spreadability, which has remained perhaps its greatest advantage (apart from cost and the cholesterol scare) in consumer preference over butter.

Further good fortune arrived for the margarine industry when the Second World War began: war is always bad for butter. During the war millions of people in Europe were forced to eat margarine rather than butter. They grumbled, but made the substitution. A butterless world was seen to be possible.

In 1950 the discriminatory taxes against margarine were lifted in the United States and the long and greasy word *oleomargarine* was officially changed to *margarine*. (Pronunciation of the *g* had long been softened in popular practice – presumably on an analogy with the way in which a hard *g* becomes soft in the name *Marjorie*, a derivative of *Margaret*. The British shorten the word to *marge*, with connotations which include familiarity, boredom, and contempt.) Margarine, allowed to "float" freely on the market, swiftly caught up with butter in sales, especially when the "quality" and higher-priced margarines were first introduced in 1956.

The taste of margarine began soon after the war to be improved, by leaps and bounds. Sales grew internationally. Intensive research by Unilever in the 1950s discovered hundreds of the flavour components of butter, and ways were found of synthesizing these and adding them to margarine. Lecithin, which increased plasticity, was added originally as egg yolk; later, cheaper chemicals were substituted for the egg. Margarine can now be provided with spreadability at almost any temperature, to order.

All the manipulations to which margarine is subjected make it very prone to flavour reversion. Soy bean oil, for instance, may quickly develop an interesting, but in margarine undesirable, smell of freshly cut green beans. Autoxidation because of exposure to air and light is common. The precursors of a host of persistent "off-flavours" had to be pinned down, and anti-oxidant additives devised to block them. This extraordinarily complex process of analysis and correction is known as hydro-refining.

Deprivation of butter, in the populations of the north, has always been known as one of the causes of eye problems, skin diseases, kidney stones, and rickets. The reason is butter's richness in vitamin A, which is in short supply if few fresh vegetables and little sun are available. Vitamins A and D are now added, by law in many countries, to margarine.

The colour of butter was endlessly studied, until it was found that the addition to margarine of an orange-yellow dye with a pink tinge gave a good approximation. Margarine was often provided in North America with a pronounced yellow hue – much yellower even than coloured butter. This is usually the case where the law still prevents margarine from looking like butter – in Ontario, for instance. When margarine is permitted to resemble butter it tries to do so – and greatly gains in sales as a result. Butter generally sticks to paleness, denoting thereby the fastidious restraint of the Real Thing, which does not need to strive for effect. Margarine is not entirely defenceless, however, with its carefully cultivated shiny appearance and the obvious and immediate consumer-appeal of gold. Many aroma scientists say they are convinced that margarine is now in no respect inferior to butter, and even that it surpasses butter in colour, in plasticity, in "lustre," and in taste. It keeps longer, and it still costs less.

Within the last five years "lightness" has become a gigantic food fad. Being thin, as we saw earlier, is a status symbol, trailing connotations of youth, modernity, health, education, and money. Just as facile and sugary art is "schmalzy" (literally, "fatty"), so *being* fat has come to be regarded as too easy, and as in poor taste. A thin body suggests discipline and competence in the face of a world which is perceived as ever more complicated and dangerous. The sufferings undergone by slimmers, the hours of jogging and lifting weights, the self-denial, and the acquisition of know-how required to "think thin," are gladly undergone by the privileged classes: it is aristocratic and self-centred austerity – an entirely different matter from abstemiousness imposed by necessity. Those members of the poorer classes who want to escape their image find that being thin can be an essential first step.

"One can never be too rich or too thin" is an aphorism attributed to the Duchess of Windsor. Being both rich and thin is a difficult enterprise, indeed almost unprecedented as an ideal. Into the paradoxical gap between the capacity to spend money and the need to eat less steps a brilliant solution: "light" food. In buying "light" food we can pay more for what costs less to produce in the first place, eat less and so measure up to the desired norm, and receive as an added bonus the suggestion that our behaviour is "enlightened."

So a multi-million dollar business is born: "light" beer, "slimming" fast-foods and snacks, "diet" pop – and "light-tasting" margarine. Eyeing always the cost of butter, which must continue to exceed that of its rival, the "quality" light-tasting product could increase its price as consumer demand grew. Only giant corporations with their technology and machinery for subtracting calories, changing flavours, substituting materials, and, above all, publicizing the results, can manage the trick. A cow is incapable of changing its ways to conform to fashion. Margarine, on the other hand, is versatility itself.

The dairy industry, especially in Europe, has in recent years received massive support from agricultural programmes. Farmers have been assured of their livelihoods by being given a guaranteed buyer and a minimum price for their milk. In this scheme of things butter had played a large part, since butter uses a great deal of milk and can now be refrigerated and kept for months on end while some use is being sought for it. The ludicrous image of vast tonnages of luxury fat going begging – the "butter mountain" as it is called – has been the result. Margarine has, of course, played its role in the problem, but margarine producers can primly point out that margarine is much more adaptable in every way than butter is – who has heard yet of a margarine mountain? (Since 1984, the European Economic Community has imposed quotas to limit the quantity of milk produced; in the United States farmers are being encouraged to sell their herds to be killed and sold as beef.)

A growing public awareness of the role played by cholesterol in heart attacks and strokes has given margarine a further boost. Cholesterol has been studied by chemists and medical researchers for a hundred years, but only in the last decade has the name become a household word – with quite a lot of help from the margarine industry. Cholesterol, a complex alcohol compound, is necessary to the health of all our body cells. But in atherosclerosis, or hardening of the arteries, cholesterol from excess low-density lipo-proteins in the blood forms mushy plaques which fill up the arteries, eventually block the flow of blood, and cause heart attacks or strokes. Diet is obviously an important reason for the original proclivity to the disease – although since two people may eat the same diet and only one suffer atherosclerosis, diet is not the only consideration. The condition appears to arise mainly from high consumption of animal products, including eggs, milk, and butter. Animal fats, including butter, contain cholesterol. In addition they are saturated fats, and saturated fats assist cholesterol formation by the body itself.

Margarine made from vegetable oil does not actually carry cholesterol, as butter does. Its oils may be saturated, but they may equally well (once the public has been shown that it ought to prefer unsaturated oils) be chosen for their polyunsaturated or mono-unsaturated character. Margarine would be liquid were it not hydrogenated. This process produces saturated-fat-like substances called trans-fatty acids, and these tend (like saturated fats) to cause the body itself to produce cholesterol. These are exceedingly complex chemical biological reactions, and scientists understand as yet little of their nature, let alone of their ultimate effects. In order that they may be used as a marketing ploy, however, considerable simplification must occur in the language used to describe them. Nowadays, margarine loudly proclaims its polyunsaturatedness, even though, as we shall see in the chapter on olive oil, polyunsaturatedness may soon become less sought after than mono-unsaturatedness. The dairy lobby has so far seen to it that wherever the presence of polyunsaturated oils is announced, the percentage of saturated oils must be mentioned also. What is still not included on margarine labels is notification of the presence of trans-fatty acids (whose effects are similar to those of saturated fats) in the margarine.

The very latest technology in margarine, immensely complex as it is, and having been achieved after enormous effort and expense, involves the thickening of vegetable oils without hydrogenation. The result is a reduction (though not yet an elimination) of saturated fats in the mix. The product is advertised as being utterly medicinal in character ("originally sold by doctor's prescription") yet "simply" delicious. It tries but fails to taste like butter.

The corn oil, the soy bean oil, and the sunflower oil industries (all of these oils are polyunsaturated) have moved massively into the production of margarine, and the public is being assiduously reminded of the terrors of cholesterol and of saturated fats (but not of trans-fatty acids), to the extreme discomfiture of the arch-rival, butter. Palm-kernel oil and coconut oil (both saturated) have suffered heavily: margarine packages admit only with embarrassment that they "may contain" one of them. It may be not without significance that palm kernels and coconuts are tropical Third World produce, whereas corn, soy beans, and sunflowers are three of the largest crops in the United States.

In North America, people now eat four times as much margarine as they eat butter. Most, if forced to consider taste alone, would probably admit they still prefer butter, but margarine, being more economical, is used in cooking processes where the fat flavour is least discernible. Wherever "gourmet" food remains or becomes the ideal, butter eclipses margarine with ease. There still exists an anti-margarine prejudice in the absolute sense: in Ontario, for example, restaurants are permitted by law to serve margarine provided they clearly publicize the fact. Under this threat, almost all of them back down and serve butter. Some people are prepared to forgo butter because of the cholesterol, although merely substituting margarine for butter would, of course, be useless unless the whole nature of one's diet were changed as well; and if one's diet were healthy a reasonable amount of butter would do most people no harm.

Too much cholesterol is a condition prevalent in western industrialized societies where our traditional lust for the luxury of butter plays only one note in a cacophony of strident and constant calls to consume. Margarine, butter's fabricated image, is a wonderful mirror of certain aspects of ourselves. It was invented because we had decided to leave the countryside and live in cities, with the result that food supplies, which had to be brought to us from a distance, spoiled and became expensive. Yet we continued to yearn for butter, which had long been one of the indisputable marks of well-being. Margarine, factory-made and longer lasting than butter, was one of the earliest examples of a food artificially formulated for city living, mass production, long shelf life, nationwide distribution, and centralized warehousing. Very few people need to be employed in the manufacture of margarine.

All these characteristics made it impossible for butter to compete in price. It was forced into the category of "gourmet" eating, and threatened with losing its status as the staple. The price of butter, except for the special "cultured" variety, is kept low by margarine's competition; there is very little money to be made these days from the marketing of butter. Meanwhile, a new élitism is being enthroned: the market for natural products (butter being only one of these) has begun to limit itself to those who are able to pay more. A new puzzle has arisen for those who can afford to be torn, this time between being Thin and Healthy (eating margarine) and being a Gourmet (eating butter). Margarine, even in North America, still lacks "class." In addition, those who want to be Thin and Healthy usually wish to eat what is Natural, and butter is more "natural" than machine-made margarine.

The vicious, even ridiculous desperation with which butter has fought margarine in our own society is in part an index of the anxiety we experience as we watch ways of life we have loved being killed off, apparently inexorably. The struggle was – and is – theatrically symbolic.

It represents the great oppositions articulated in our culture: the land versus the city, the farm (despite the extent to which dairy farming has become mechanized) versus the factory, independent versus corporately-controlled business, tradition versus not-necessarily-preferable novelty, nature versus human manipulation, labour-intensive versus machine-operated industry, uniqueness versus interchangeability.

The idea of neutralizing oil before "turning it into" something else had arrived as early as 1883, when Mark Twain, travelling down the Mississippi, overheard two "oily villains" plotting to kill butter with margarine and sell the world "cottonseed olive oil." "'You can't tell it from butter,' said the margarine man, 'by George, an *expert* can't. . . . Butter's had its *day* – and from this out, butter goes to the wall.'" Twain described the two as "brisk men, energetic of movement and speech; the dollar their god, how to get it their religion."

Twain enunciated a distaste which has grown increasingly prevalent in the century since he wrote. We are afraid of the irreparable damage constantly being wrought by "brisk, energetic" go-getters with narrow self-interest their only concern and the lowering of standards never entering their calculations. It is not that the dairy industry is poor or innocent: it is now largely "agribusiness" just as corn is, and its steel fist has given it away time and again. But a shiver goes down our spine, just the same, at the thought of butter "going to the wall." We are aware, as Twain was not, that it actually could happen. We respect and admire the expertise that has gone into the making and improving of margarine; we are grateful because it is cheaper than butter; but it remains hard to *love* margarine. To describe pastry, for instance, as "margariny" still manages to add nothing to its attraction.

Widespread information on the role of cholesterol in heart disease and the health- and status-conscious preference for "light" food, have both been used brilliantly by margarine in its battle with butter. Margarine has already achieved universal (though partial) acceptance in the kitchens of all industrialized countries, and gone a long way to closing the flavour gap with its rival. The new cholesterol weapon has cloaked margarine with much greater stature as the next act in the drama gets under way. On the other hand, a rising demand in the west for the epicurean dimensions of eating is a shot in the arm for butter, the original, the traditional, the natural and "finest." So the drama continues, intense, unpredictable, and filled with incident. Like the very best theatre, the struggle is not only formidably balanced, but archetypal.

One recent incident in the saga has been the introduction, so far mainly for restaurant use, of "butter-flavoured" vegetable oil for cooking: margarine, in other words, but unsolidified. The advertisements righteously proclaim: "No Cholesterol." One brand of this product praises its own "honest-to-butter" flavour. "Honesty," to be sure, is a concept which has been stretched a long way; but the substitution of *butter* for *God* or for *goodness* in the slogan is hyperbolic homage indeed – as though imitation were not flattery enough.

CHAPTER FOUR

Chicken: From Jungle Fowl to Patties

*C*ARVING UP a whole animal, whether a chicken or an ox, has from time immemorial expressed not only family feeling and cohesion among the people sharing that animal, but also hierarchy and difference. In ancient Greece, for example, an animal eaten in common was a symbol of the organization of the group, and indeed of society itself, in its diversity as well as its wholeness. A pig or an ox has only four legs, one liver, two haunches, and so on: it is impossible for everyone to receive the same cut of meat. Many traditions have assigned status to various cuts; it mattered deeply which piece you got, and it usually fell to the head man to be the carver, who "did the honours" and assigned to each person his "portion," which could be broadly representative of his kinship or friendship status, and of his lot in life. Our society will have none of that – and nothing more directly expresses our loathing of hierarchy than the pre-cut, pre-coated, ground-and-reconstituted portions, often computer-calculated to be equal, which we get as fast food.

At our meal, which is an old-fashioned home-cooked affair with a whole roast chicken as the meat portion of its main course, each guest will state his preference, for drumstick or breast, white or dark meat. We shall murmur our choices, yet almost always assent to what we are offered. Older women and men will be consulted first; but a good carver (the role still tends to be played by a male) will endeavour to save at least a little breast for everyone.

European settlers brought to North America the tradition that eating fowl was special – behaviour both ceremonial and festive. Rich families ate roast chicken, shared out by the knife-wielding chief male of the family, on Sundays. King Henri IV of France had in the sixteenth century pronounced the ideal of extending this universally desired luxury to everybody: "I hope to make France so prosperous that every peasant will have a chicken in his pot on Sundays." Americans worked hard to turn the occasional treat into an everyday occurrence, as well as to make it available to all. In 1928 the Republican Party won an election in the United States with the help of the slogan, "A chicken in every pot": even the limitation to periodicity had been broken. As chicken became increasingly common, the role of the roasted festive fowl fell more often to the turkey, which was winged, feathered, and fattened, and could be roasted to an elaborate gold like a chicken, but which was much more impressive in size, with a larger capacity for special stuffings. A whole roast chicken can still exude some of its former stylish glory, however. Indeed, the facts that it is pale meat and perceived as "light" have recently added to its prestige.

The knife-and-fork revolution which swept Europe in the sixteenth and seventeenth centuries never entirely conquered the eating of fowl. Bird meat is much easier to disengage from the bone with the teeth than with a knife and fork; drumsticks and wings seem almost made to be held. So the paradox arose that chicken, which for a long time was made the centrepiece of meals on special occasions, was quite often the only meat people were commonly allowed to treat with the utter informality of handling it at table.

In North America, especially in the southern United States, there arose a strong preference for fried chicken: fowl cut up in advance instead of being ceremonially carved before the assembled group. Chicken in pieces became one of the original American "finger foods," eaten on occasions where formality is sacrificed to relaxed conviviality, together with sandwiched food, corn on the cob, and food hand-dipped in sauces. Modern fast foods greatly encourage the banishment of knives and forks: informality as well as speed require it. (An important secondary consideration, one which is more frequently expressed by fast-food managers, is that removing cutlery means there is nothing to steal.)

Fried and crumbed chicken pieces have been marketed as fast foods with huge success, for poultry, especially modern fast-grown chicken meat, is bland and acceptable to almost every palate. It can even claim to be unfattening and a "low-cholesterol" food, because fowl fat (except in capons) does not marble the meat, but lines the body immediately under the skin and is contained in pockets, so that it is easily removed. Yet, in spite of chicken's many strong points in modern schemes of taste, the poultry industry has produced such enormous amounts of meat that new ways of eating chicken have been urgently sought in order to whet demand.

The fact is that the chicken, in order to become absolutely malleable and modern, has had to escape its intractable shape. What used to be the source of its symbolism – the differentiation embodied by a whole trussed fowl – has become an anachronistic defect. Even pre-cut, fried chicken pieces constitute a somewhat limited answer: choices still have to be made and distinctions drawn. A deboning process has now been perfected, and this has opened up a vast new future for the chicken. Boneless meat is available for chicken sticks, chicken rolls, chicken frank-furters, and chicken chunks. The beef hamburger, which is still the centre and focus of the fast-food industry, is being challenged by a new technological feat: the cheap, light, springy (the word is that of poultry scientists) chicken pattie with its machine-tooled shape, square, circular, or oblong. Scientific articles commonly call it "restructured steak."

Fast-food outlets are cultural institutions dedicated not only to deal-ing swiftly with mankind's compulsion to eat and drink regularly, but also to doing battle with his twin and fatal limitations of space and time. The campaign is waged with the weapons of the industrial and technological age; its driving force is our own particular and paradoxical blend of obsessive rationality and relaxed asceticism.

Fast foods are processed and sold by giant industrial complexes which control every detail of their operations, from the smallest ingredient to the carefully calculated appearance of every eating place. The goal is to give an impression of the omnipresence and the invariability of

McDonald's or of Kentucky Fried: travel as far as you like, and it will always be as though you were still at home, in the arms of the parent company. Space loses its ancient association with change and surprise. You can without difficulty seek out the identical ambience, the very same taste you knew and liked before you set out.

These parent companies are called "chains." When you travel (and mobility is another of our cultural institutions), they provide links which render your route as predictable and as secure, as protective and as limiting as swaddling bands. It is no accident that both the kind of food they sell and their marketing methods make a direct appeal to the infantile in all of us. "Chains" stretch out along the highways, where they supply food as efficiently and as swiftly as gas from a fuel pump. They also, by means of their repetitiveness, bind and homogenize city neighbourhoods. They supply in large measure modern man's apparent need to obliterate the difference between "this place" and "that," and to make as irrelevant as possible the distinction between "now" and "then."

Uniformity, as every chain retailer is aware, makes good economic sense. Mass sales and ease of packaging and handling merchandise demand predictability – standard quality being, in the end, only one aspect of the sameness required. But the uniformity and the sheer volume of food supplied by fast-food chains are also expressions of our democratic aspirations. Everybody gets the same list of choices, everywhere. Nothing is served to which anyone could take exception, unless élitist notions, such as distaste for sweetness or demands for the personal touch, intrude. The aim is to please most people, and not to truckle to the difficult or pretentious few. The tastes of children are catered to especially. Grown-ups simply eat – and enjoy – what their children like. Abundant wrappings and boxes proclaim technologically perfected hygiene and simultaneously suggest a child's party with presents. Taste blandness also flattens out differences among adults: there are no strong "weird" flavours creating exclusive group preferences and societal distinctions.

Speed of service not only attacks the time limitation, it forestalls an increasingly widespread incapacity to be kept waiting, even if waiting might be a prerequisite for superior food. Speed also helps make certain that hierarchical formality cannot arise. Formality stratifies by organizing space and relationship, and to do this it takes time. It is true that we are "served" from behind the counter, and that the preparation and "further processing" which any single food item has undergone is achieved only through the expertise of an army of scientists and marketing agents and the toil of a host of machine operators – but we never see any of this. We witness only the swiftly and smartly performed final step as the food is handed to us, cartoned and wrapped, crumbed and sand-wiched. There is no involvement with the personnel of the restaurant. Everything is impersonal; the very language used in ordering and serv-ing may be pre-learned, almost ritualized. The method prevents time-wasting and possibly complex exchanges, and irrelevant chat. It is all so honed-down, rational, and predictable that it is difficult to imagine how we could further mechanize the process.

GALLUS GALLUS

In the forests of northern India, through Burma, Thailand, Kampuchea, and down to Sumatra, there lives a wild, shy, and easily angered bird. It is about one kilogram (2 lb.) in weight when fully grown, with dark olive-to-bluish legs, a black breast, and shining reddish-brown back and tail feathers. It has a distinctive fleshy crest on its head, and an unnerving cackle and scream. *Gallus gallus*, the Red Jungle Fowl, was identified by Charles Darwin as the originator of the modern domestic chicken. Other jungle fowl are now thought to have contributed to the gene stock. But the Red Jungle Fowl, which is still abundant in its region of origin, looks very like a small and streamlined version of our own farm poultry.

It is commonly believed that domestication of the chicken occurred long after human beings had learned to tame and systematically exploit many other kinds of animals. This is because the shy jungle fowl would never have voluntarily associated itself with man or scavenged from him as did the other beasts we first learned to live with and to subjugate: animals like the dog, the goat, and the sheep. In fact, the earliest use of the cock for man appears to have been as a focus of religiously oriented sport. The people of the Indus Valley had domesticated the jungle fowl by 2000 BC. A seal from Mohenjo Daro, one of the Indus Valley's twin capital cities, depicts two cocks fighting.

Neither domestic fowl nor hens' eggs became fundamentally impor-tant in human diet until Roman times; indeed for half their recorded history, and in many places to this day, it has been the male of the species which was most valued – for cock-fighting, as a pet alarm clock, or as a provider of beautiful long tail feathers for sartorial adornment. The hens' eggs were eaten in small quantities by some and regarded as abominations by others. Actually eating chicken meat was usually thought barely worthwhile. The wild jungle fowl does not have a great deal of flesh on it, and once the aforementioned purposes of the domesticated chicken had been served for long enough and the bird was killed, it was tough, dry, and generally unrewarding. Meat-lovers, until recent times, could easily hunt flesh which was more delicious as well as more copious.

Throughout the countries of the jungle fowl's origin, and including the Pacific Islands, Tibet, and Mongolia, the chicken is thought to be a prophetic bird: divination by means of its bones, and sometimes through inspection of its intestines or liver, has been a matter of solemn human concern. Chicken bones have fine perforations in them which vary from fowl to fowl. Bamboo splinters are inserted into the holes and project at different angles; directions and distances between splinters are then measured and made the basis of chicken-bone divination. (The bones of intensively bred modern chickens exhibit far smaller variations in the number and position of the perforations; they make a much less satisfactory medium for magic than those of birds closer to the wild.)

Chicken divination has an intense following still among tribes in upper Burma and in Thailand, and a long history among the tribal populations of southern China. It is a fascinating fact that in Africa, where chickens spread sporadically (until a hundred years ago many tribes had never seen them, but others had cultivated them for centuries), divination by chicken blood and bones is also practised. Some African tribes keep cocks to wake them up in the morning, others keep them for their feathers. Others again use chickens in various sacrificial rituals. Many refuse on any account to eat chickens or their eggs, or both, and regard the birds as sacred messengers between us and the world beyond. These attitudes are extraordinarily similar to those held in south-east Asia and in ancient Iran. Following the trail of these customs, we can perhaps see how the Indian fowl reached and then travelled through Africa, via the chicken-divining regions of Ethiopia, the Sudan, and Uganda.

The reasons why Africans from many tribes refuse to eat chicken flesh, or deny it to sections of their societal groups, are various. Hens, for instance, may be considered promiscuous and careless about family structures ("they lay their eggs here and there"), and generally incapable of important distinctions ("they eat whatever they come across: worms, bugs, excrement, anything"). African women may therefore be warned against eating them, for fear of taking on the characteristics of what they consume. In much the same way chickens are thought unclean by high-caste Indian Hindus because the creatures show no discrimination in their eating habits: a Brahmin should take a purificatory bath after touching a chicken. Loathing of chickens serves also to distinguish Hindus from Moslems, who eat a great deal of poultry. Buddhists are nauseated by domestic fowl because they eat living worms and bugs; in Tibet, chickens are loathed for their claws which resemble those of the vultures which pick at corpses. Food always symbolically underpins societal categories; foods are often forbidden because they are perceived as violations of the system. It is not necessary to be consciously aware of a structural violation; one reacts simply and directly with avoidance and abhorrence.

Eggs, the world over, are symbols of fertility and of pure and un-differentiated power, of a force which is as yet unharnessed and un-directed. In the nineteenth century a German explorer in Africa was murdered because he horrified his hosts by devouring unspeakable eggs. In Pakistan, south-east Asia, the Pacific Islands, and in parts of Africa (again that insistent and surprising similarity) eggs are often thought to be delicacies – provided that the inside has turned visibly and palpably into a chicken fetus: potentiality must have committed itself before it can be found delectable. Eggs, for women, are sexy and therefore dan-gerous, or fertility-replacing (eating them might fool her body into not producing offspring itself), and strictly forbidden. Eggs may be thought of as hens' excrement and rejected as unclean.

When the Aryans invaded northern India in the second millennium BC, they quickly learned to admire the jungle fowl and decided that it was sacred; by about 1000 BC they had forbidden the eating of its flesh. Meanwhile the Sumerians had come into contact with domestic fowl through their distant trade with the Indus Valley. Chickens, from 2000 BC onward, have been exceedingly useful on long sea voyages: they lay eggs on board, perpetuate themselves, and grow quickly to an edible size. The Chinese have cultivated chickens since the second millennium BC. They bred huge fowl with dark heavy bones, black skin, thickly feathered legs, pink combs, and almost no ability to fly. The first of these Cochin or Shanghai chickens to reach Britain arrived as a present for the royal family in 1835; they caused a sensation, with tens of thousands of people fighting to get a glimpse of them. The event started a century-long devotion to the hobby and business of breeding different varieties of chickens in Europe and America.

For a long time it was thought that the ancient Egyptians had no knowledge of the chicken until Hellenistic times. That idea was shattered in 1923, when a limestone sherd from 1350 BC was found in a tomb in the Valley of the Kings near Thebes. It bears a swiftly but confidently drawn cock. The Egyptians appear not to have been concerned thereafter with chickens in their art and writing, until their incubators became the wonder of the Mediterranean world a thousand years later. Maybe they kept a very few chickens for mere amusement. Perhaps cocks were associated with the sun-religion of Akhnaton, and exterminated after the death of Tutankhamen. (Akhnaton's Hymn to the Sun of the fourteenth century BC celebrates a chick breaking out of its shell; but we do not know whether the bird is of the species *Gallus gallus* or not.) What is certain is that for food the Egyptians, as their art abundantly shows us, raised quails, as well as ducks, geese, and other non-gallinaceous birds.

The Theban pot-sherd ruins a previously clear and obvious picture of a Mediterranean world ignorant of chickens until Greeks encountered Persians. There are no chickens in the Old Testament, and none in Homer or Hesiod. An eighth century BC Assyrian cylinder seal does depict a cock-fight, but Assyria was next door to Iran. After the Persian Wars, Greek literature begins to abound in references to chickens (which the Greeks often called "Persian birds"), and Greek art pours out representations of them on coins, sculpture, and pottery.

The Persians had been obsessed with chickens, and especially with cocks, from the moment they began to import domestic fowl from India. The two sacred animals in Zoroastrian religion were the dog and the cock. The dog guarded households and flocks; the cock had a special relationship with fire and light which made his cry a terror to darkness and evil. Persians, who so honoured the light of the sun that they prayed and ritually bathed themselves at every sunrise, never permitted themselves to be separated from the sacred power of the cock. The long-fingered yellow demon of sleep, Bashyacta, would overcome everything if it were not for the challenge he daily receives from the cock.

Chickens spread north from Persia as well as west: they were taken up by the Scythians who adorned their coffins with images of cocks; they became favourites of the Celts, the Gauls, and the ancient Britons. When Julius Caesar arrived in Britain in the first century BC the natives were already breeding cocks and hens. "They think it unlawful to feed upon hares, chickens or geese," he wrote, "yet they breed them up for their amusement and pleasures": once more we find the fowl being reared for sport and its flesh forbidden as food. Cocks' powerfully spurred leg-bones have been found at sites of the Roman period in Britain; they confirm that cock-fighting, for which Britain was to be famous many centuries later, had already become popular.

The Romans, adopting and perfecting the technology of the Hellenistic Greeks, raised domestic fowl for eating, and especially for their eggs. The Romans learned the science of incubation from the Greeks and the Egyptians, and from the Greeks they learned how to castrate cocks to produce fat capons. They kept capons, which they called "half-males," *semimares*, in battery cages as they did dormice and other table delicacies, and they sometimes forbade killing chickens for meat, not as the result of a taboo but because their eggs were too valuable. Roman writers on agriculture devote long passages to the correct raising and care of fowl; descriptions of Roman dinner-parties include among the courses gargantuan quantities of chicken and eggs.

The Romans had their own version of chicken-divination, which they called *auspicium ex tripudiis*. They took the auspices by throwing chicken-feed to a flock of sacred fowls. If the birds ate so greedily that the grain fell to the ground from their beaks and rhythmically bounced (the *tripudium* was a triple-step in a warlike dance), then the battle would be won; if not, it should not be undertaken. On one famous occasion during the First Punic War an exasperated Roman admiral named P. Claudius Pulcher, who wanted badly to attack the Carthaginians even though the chickens refused their feed, seized the sacred fowl and threw them overboard. "If they will not eat," he cried, "let them drink!" – and lost the battle.

Gallus is the Roman word for the bird; some have thought that the name refers to France, *Gallia*, which may have been one early introducer of chickens to the Italian peninsula, Greek Sicily being the other. It is much more likely, however, that *gallus* comes from the same root as the word "poultry." This root is the Hindu word *pil*, which becomes *pullus* and *gallus* (Latin), *pollo* (Italian), *poulet* (French), and *pullet* (English). Another widely-used stem for words designating chickens is thought also to originate in India: it is *kuk*, Sanskrit *kukata*, Latin *cucurio*, *kuku* in many African languages, *Küchlein* (German), *coq* (French), *kieken* (Dutch), *cock* and *chicken* in English.

The Portuguese first landed in Brazil on April 22, 1500. Within thirty years of that date chickens were described as common in South America. The newcomers would probably have brought some chickens on board ship with them, since sailors usually did this, but a thirty-year period seems unprecedentedly short for the extensive spreading of knowledgeable acquaintance with an entirely new domestic creature. Was there some kind of indigenous South American Jungle Fowl? Did the indefatigable Polynesians, who undoubtedly got their chickens originally from Asia, carry the domestic fowl across the ocean long before the Europeans arrived?

The Indians of South America are described by the early European settlers as keeping their chickens for their feathers and for cockfighting; they would seldom eat either the birds or their eggs. This behaviour did not follow European example, except for the pleasure in cockfighting; indeed it seems strangely reminiscent of Asian practice, and of that of the African tribes who are believed to have received chickens ultimately from Asia. Another strange fact is that the last supreme Inca of Peru was named Atahualpa, and his uncle was called Hualpa. *Hualpa*, in the Quechua language, means "chicken." Did the Incas call chickens (newly arrived from Europe) after their ruler, or were the supreme Inca and his uncle named after chickens (already well known in Peru)?

There exists in South America today a race of chicken which looks very similar to certain Asiatic breeds. They are called Araucanas, after the Chilean Indian mountain tribe which raised them, and which had almost no contact with Europeans until the end of the nineteenth century. Pure-bred Araucanas are black-skinned and rumpless (lacking the final segments of the spinal column), with ear puffs, pea combs, and "silky" or hair-like feathers; all of these are characteristics of Asian fowl rather than of European breeds. They also, uniquely in the poultry world, lay green and blue eggs. If the Polynesians brought chickens to South America from the east before the Europeans arrived, it means that the voyagers travelled fast, because chickens need water, and could not have survived a long, slow, drifting journey.

THE FIGHTING COCK

Ever since the first domestication of the jungle fowl, cocks have been raised and appreciated for a great deal more than their final fate in the family cooking pot. They were potent expressions of power and paradox, and symbols of masculine courage and prestige.

The domestic cock greets light with sound. This daily miracle has led him to be considered a sacred bird, a boundary marker, both link and distinction between sight and sound, light and dark, life and death, here and the beyond. The weird association of light with the cock's crow made him a chaser of darkness and, with that, of evil; he awoke men from the death of sleep and so symbolized the Messianic Age for Jews and the Resurrection for Christians. The steeples of many churches are topped for this reason with the figure of a cock.

The crowing cock frightened away ghosts, as Horatio in *Hamlet* explains he has heard it said; and the fourth-century hymn of St. Ambrose greets the singing dawn rooster who returns hope to the sick and to travellers, releases them from the fear of robbers, and restores faith to doubters. An Italian boy-child born with the crowing of the cock was often named Galeazzo, so that he would remember this lucky concurrence of events all his life. Among the Germans, the cock was associated in folklore and magic with fire; his comb in particular was symbolic of flames.

Gods associated with light loved the cock: Helios, Ahura Mazda, Mithras, and Osiris, to whom, in Hellenistic times, black or variegated cocks and white cocks were sacrificed, because he was a dying-and-rising god, one who knew both the underworld and the light of the sun. The cock has been called upon symbolically to participate in mysteries concerned with immortality. He was sacred to Asclepius, the Greek god of healing, whose mythology concerned dying and restoring to life. The philosopher Socrates asked on his deathbed for a cock to be sacrificed on his behalf in honour of Asclepius, for he believed he was not dying but recovering and awakening to a more abundant life. In Mohammedan legend, the Prophet saw in the First Heaven a vast cock whose crest brushed the boundary of the Second Heaven. It is the crowing of this cosmic fowl which awakens every living creature except man; and when it ceases to crow the Day of Judgement will be at hand.

A cooked cock, in several medieval stories, stood up and crowed in his dish, thereby revealing a crime which till then had remained hidden; a living hen and cock are still kept in memory of such a legend in a church on the pilgrimage route to Compostela in northern Spain. Sometimes people have avoided keeping cocks because of their crowing: the Kikuyu of Kenya because they did not want their whereabouts given away to their enemies or their victims, the ancient Greek Sybarites (allegedly) because they liked sleeping late in the mornings.

The magnificent cocks on the silver coins of Himera, a Greek city in Sicily, are puns on the city's name: *Himera* suggests both "day" and "sexual desire." The cock has always been a byword for its lust – to the point where, in many languages besides English, *cock* is synonymous with the male sexual organ itself. It was for this reason that in Victorian, and especially in nineteenth-century North American usage the word *rooster* was substituted as the bird's name. Cocks' combs and cocks' testicles have seemed from time immemorial powerful aphrodisiacs. In ancient Greece a cock was a gift with specific sexual connotations from an older male to a young boy. The cock expressed the sheer maleness of the couple, their virile aggressivity and energy. (The alternative gift, a hare, referred to the joys of the chase: the boy's unwillingness and flight being considered to be as erotically enticing as a woman's "playing hard to get.")

Men have always found in the cock a model of pugnacity and courage. It is the bird's instinct to be easily aroused to rage, to fly at his opponent, and to fight till one or both of them drop dead; while a cock can crawl – no matter how battered and mutilated he is – he will fight on. The sight of cock facing cock has inspired men with battle-lust (the Greek general Themistocles was said to have roused his men to emulate fighting cocks), has urged them to fling themselves into competitive exploits (the goddess Athene appears together with a cock on vases won as prizes for athletic victories), and has encouraged them to strut in the panoplies of male pride. Does not the cock wear a crested "helmet," spurs and plumes, and wattles which in many languages are known as "beards"? The hybristic swagger of the cock has found its way into many English expressions. A *coxcomb* means an insolent upstart; a man may be as *cocky* as a rooster with crest erect and looking for trouble. The *cocksure* are bound someday to get what is coming to them, and when they do they must expect to be *crestfallen*.

Cockfighting is thought by some to be the oldest living sport. The joy men took in watching cockfights almost certainly led to the domestication of the bird in the first place; and the sacred status of cocks from earliest times must have meant that this sport, like so many others, was imbued in the beginning with religious significance. There is no doubt that cockfighting even today is profoundly theatrical; the audience invest the combatants with symbolic roles, so that they act out the aggressions and struggles for power of the gamblers and betters standing (or rather, "shouting, bawling, pounding, and vociferating like a very Babel") in a ring around the padded cockpit. The process can have a complex societal role, letting off emotional steam in a manner harmless to the spectators.

In the first century BC, cockfights were held annually in the Athenian theatre sacred to the phallic, orgiastic, and gorgeously costumed god Dionysus; a cockfight is carved on the marble throne of the god's priest, with the winged boy Agon, the personification of contest, setting the cocks ready to fight. In Aristophanes' comedy, *Clouds*, where "Right" and "Wrong" do battle with words, the two actors may well have been dressed as fighting cocks. An early use for the sport may have been as a decision-making device: an impossibly difficult choice found dramatic resolution through the impersonation by fighting cocks of the two possibilities, one being "killed off" by the other. Cocks are equals and alike; from earliest times a fighting pair of them has been made to represent the relentless savagery of civil war. The cocks' wounds and death may on occasion have constituted a kind of ritual scapegoats' sacrifice to avert man's own violence and prevent it from destroying his society. In any event, it was commonly felt that a cockfight was not only simple fun to watch, but also a drama with several messages, and that the lessons needed to be drawn, witnessed, and endlessly repeated.

Cocks, like men, are armed for battle with lethal metal swords. The cock's natural spurs are removed from its legs and on to the stumps are bound one of two kinds of metal spur: sword-like slashing blades are traditional in the east, and sharp points in the west. The method helps to equalize the combatants since natural spurs vary a good deal in length and strength. The metal weapons are designed to draw blood and so increase the excitement, and, in fact, a single blow from one of these weapons often kills. "Naked-heel" fighting, with natural spurs and no metal weapons, is preferred in India and in some other eastern countries; in this form of the sport endurance is valued more highly than speed or agility. A naked-heel fight can last a whole day. This devotion to taking one's time over one's pleasures is completely different from the typical western enjoyment of short and violent sensations, timed by the stop-watch. Cocks in some places are "dubbed" before a fight: their wattles and crest are cut off, much as a soldier used to remove his beard before battle in case an enemy snatched and held it. The birds may wear hoods into the fray, like fighting airplane pilots.

Before the fight, cocks live a glorious life. They are massaged, exercised, petted, and admired: bathed, shampooed, and fed on delicacies. Exercising one's rooster meant jogging behind him to keep him running, and every now and then presenting him with an ordinary cock (which had to be carried under the owner's arm for protection) to encourage his irritability and aggression. In ancient Greece and Egypt, garlic or bread sopped in wine was considered especially fortifying for cocks; South Americans like to give them hot chili-peppers; in eighteenth-century England we hear of them being given pastries made of wheaten flour, eggs, and large quantities of butter. An owner had personally to find and supply the varieties of living grubs and insects which his game cock particularly fancied. A man "fed like a fighting cock" was uncommonly sleek.

The master of a cock, in many societies, has been found to identify himself, and especially his sexual prowess, closely with his bird. Clifford Geertz, the anthropologist, can describe fighting cocks as being for the Balinese "ambulant genitals with a life of their own." In ancient Greek art the cock was often made explicitly to resemble a male's sexual organs. All kinds of more or less overt sexual symbolism surrounds the care given to cocks before and during the fight. They are caressed, fed sexually stimulating food, ceremonially bathed in scented water or in urine. During the fight, a bleeding cock has its wounds licked by his master – who might be moved actually to put the chicken's whole head into his mouth, sucking and blowing, in order to revive it. The method is used all over the world, although it is often considered a rather affected gesture. Spurs may be dramatically licked before the fight begins, to prove that they have not been poisoned. Cockfighting is like wrestling: a celebration of rampant virility, with melodramatic flourishes, extravagant displays of resolution, honour, arrogance, and excess, huge stylized gestures, and a violent climax where inseparably interwoven Chance and Design are seen irresistibly to have taken effect.

Men from widely different social backgrounds have always met and mixed at cockfighting bouts. It seems clear that the discovery of a common base-line fellowship among lords, workers, peasants, and bourgeois males is part of the essence of the exercise. The outlawing of cockfighting, which began to be effected in England in 1834, was a symptom of deep-seated changes in society. A general increase in social equality would reduce society's need dramatically to express the natural similarity among men in a system where class rules were rigid and waived only on special occasions. There would be less flaunting of bloodlust from then on; cruelty was to take a new, less colourful and individualistic, more concealed and more efficient turn, as human beings conceived and perfected factory farming.

Yet the ancient sport lives on. It is widespread in South and Central America and in the Caribbean countries, and it also exists in spite of the non-violence of religions like Buddhism and Hinduism in India and south-east Asia, the lands where the birds originated. Today the Philippine Islands are probably the world centre for cocking; international "mains" (large cockfighting contests) take place there from time to time. In the United States and Europe, where it is forbidden by law, cockfighting continues to flourish illegally. All the traditions, the lore, the breeds, and the intricate rules are maintained and handed on, a furtive survival of an ancient passion in a world which, officially at least, has little room and less sympathy for strutting and flamboyant masculinity or for violence accorded gaudy enjoyment and studied respect.

MOTHER HEN

Light rouses the cock to crow, and it is light which passes through the hen's eye, activates the pituitary gland at the base of her skull to secrete certain hormones in her body, and starts her ovary working to lay eggs. Every baby hen hatches with five or six thousand microscopic egg-germs already awaiting completion in her body. She is ready to begin creating and laying from this vast store when she is about six months old.

The hen's ovary is a very large organ, because although she is a big bird, her eggs are enormous in relation to her body size – they are so big that she can carry only one egg to completion in her body at a time. Hens, like all female vertebrates, begin with paired ovaries; but in her case the right ovary withers away so that only one egg needs to be given space. Only a tiny fraction of the egg-germs she carries will eventually end up as eggs; what it is that makes these privileged few do so is unknown. Quite naturally, scientists would dearly like to understand and then draw profit from knowledge of the mechanism.

The female hormone estrogen is partly responsible for the hen's behaviour both in making her submissive to the cock at coition, and in causing her to seek and prepare a nest in which to lay her eggs. It apparently even causes her to emit a pre-laying call. Nest-preparation is so biologically necessary as part of the laying process that caged battery hens will often cry out and struggle to obey this part of nature's demand.

Hens lay according to the length of daylight; when days are short (in winter when it is too cold to raise chicks) there is not enough light, under natural conditions, to rouse the hen's ovary to mature eggs within her body. Once light has triggered intense hormonal activity in the hen, ovulation occurs about six or eight hours later. She will now begin laying eggs, usually one every twenty-five hours. In ovulation, the yolk erupts from the ovary's constraining membranes and is drawn down the oviduct into the hen's infundibulum. At this point the yolk rests for fifteen minutes in its journey, and it is during this pause that fertilization may occur, whether directly or by male sperm stored in the hen's body. After these fifteen minutes the yolk will move on and then begin to be surrounded by white, by its two membranes, and by the shell: sperm penetration is rendered impossible. It is a common misapprehension that fertilization is required for an egg to be produced; this is not the case. The vast majority of hens' eggs are now marketed unfertilized so that they will not develop into chicks. Even the presence of a minute blood spot such as occurs in fertilized eggs (without harming them nutritionally in any way), revolts many people in our culture, and such eggs are not kosher in the Jewish tradition. A tiny haemorrhage sometimes occurs at ovulation, producing a little blood on the surface of the yolk, again harmlessly.

The yolk is moved from the hen's infundibulum, again by muscular contractions, into the magnum, where it rotates and is swathed in egg-white, which twists at the long ends like a candy wrapper: the white's end-knots are easily found when an egg is cracked open. The membranes are added during the hour the egg takes to pass down the isthmus of the oviduct; the two membranes are in contact with each other over the whole surface of the egg white, except at the egg's blunt end, where they part company to form the air sac. In the uterus or shell gland the egg waits eighteen to twenty hours as calcium salts from the tissue of this cavity create the shell, and the hen's body gently kneads the egg into its oval (literally, "eggy") shape. Again, what it is that prompts the hen to lay her egg is not completely understood. The act takes only a few seconds and it is often greeted by the hen with a cackle of triumph.

When she has laid a number of eggs, another hormonal change takes place in her body. One of the hormones involved is prolactin, a substance named after its effect in mammals, which is to make the female breast produce milk. It causes instinctual maternal behaviour in all vertebrate creatures: amphibians return to water in order to lay eggs, the female fowl anxiously gathers her chicks together when night falls. Prolactin also makes hens "broody," that is, intent upon setting on the eggs they have laid and keeping them warm till they hatch. (Broodiness is a thorough nuisance in battery or factory layers: one reason for the preference for White Leghorns over all others in factory farming is that, with the help of careful breeding, they are chickens lacking an intense brooding instinct.)

A broody hen fluffs up her feathers until she is almost twice her normal size. Her tail feathers rise and spread. She stays that way all through brooding, hatching, and raising her young. The reason for the physical change is that with these feathers she keeps her eggs warm, and also finds room under them for the hatched chicks. As soon as her chicks are ready for independence, the hen's feathers subside, she suddenly and totally ignores her offspring, and they just as unconcernedly abandon her. Part of this transformation is due to the subsidence of the hen's feathers: the chicks have known her by her ballooning size and shape, by her maternal clucks, and her general motherly concern. Her diminished size as her feathers lie down, and her loss of the mothering urge, combine to make her simply unrecognizable to her chickens – and out of sight is out of mind. So nature, at precisely the right moment, painlessly severs the close and vital tie between mother and babies.

During the three weeks it takes a hen to hatch her eggs, her temperature rises and she needs very little to eat. She sits tight on the nest and refuses to move, except for about fifteen minutes a day when she rushes off to grab enough food and drink for survival, before hurrying back to her duty. (So closely calculated is nature's provision for the welfare of hen and eggs that artificial incubators have regularly to be cooled for fifteen minutes to allow for this rest-period in a hen's day.) Three times daily the hen must turn every egg in her nest with her beak, in order to ensure that they are warmed all over, and to prevent the embryos inside from sticking to the shells.

Although the eggs were laid over a period of up to three weeks before the hen began to brood over them, all the chicks hatch, after an incubation period of approximately twenty-one days, within forty-eight hours of each other. Forty-eight hours is the amount of time a hen can stay on her nest without leaving and the length of time a chick just out of its shell can survive without food or water. (The latter fact is of enormous importance for modern hatcheries, which use the bonus in time for the transport of baby chicks from incubating firms to fatteners.) The first-born chick begins peeping in its shell twenty-four hours before it hatches; the others soon take up the cry, thus notifying each other and their mother that zero-hour is approaching. Experiments with turkeys have shown that a chick's cheeping is a matter of life and death to it. If a mother turkey hears no sound from her nestling (the experimenters deafened a turkey hen to see what would happen), she immediately pecks it to death, taking it for a nest enemy. In a turkey's brain the sight of a chick is not enough; the sound must complete the picture.

When its time comes, the chick saws its way out of the shell with a rough piece of its bill which is called an "egg tooth"; this specialized piece of anatomy disappears after use. The mother hen has to concentrate as, one by one, underneath her and out of her sight, the chicks struggle out of their shells and lie down, exhausted and faintly cheeping, to recover from their ordeal. One false move and the hen may trample some of her brood to death, or smother them. Once the chick's down is dry, it begins peeping loudly, largely to help the mother know where it is. The muffled cheeps in the shells also keep her informed of how much longer she needs to stay on the nest.

When the whole brood is hatched, the hen sallies forth with her chickens, who are ready immediately to feed themselves. What they continue to need is their mother's warmth and it is again through their cheeps that the chicks let her know their need. The hen will suddenly (without any warning discernible to us) squat down on the ground, and the chicks will rush under her outspread wings and feathers and stay there until they are warmed through, after which they will set off again on their perpetually exciting quest for bugs, grubs, and seeds.

MAN'S EYE VIEW

In spite of the fact that chickens have seldom roused people's affections – they are too scratchy, self-absorbed, un-mammalian, and, above all, too edible for that – the cock, the hen, and their chicks have always lived close to their owners' houses. They need protection, especially at night, from the predators which are constantly after their eggs and their flesh; they are kept close by for feeding purposes; and their nests need constantly to be checked for their contents. The care of barnyard animals – rabbits, chickens, ducks, and the rest – has always been women's work, "house" work, along with everything concerned with milk and dairying. Constantly under the eye of their human owners, chickens have been in all societies the subjects of speculation, moralizing, fable-telling, and mythologizing.

Cocks have always delighted us with their pride, their dignified and angry flamboyance, their sexual vigour, and their courage. A cock may almost achieve the status of a pet, not only because of his useful crow, but also because he is perceived as the walking achievement of a swaggering and self-confident *macho* ideal. We have already remarked that men may see cocks as actually embodying their own sexual prowess, and allow the sight of a bloody cockfight to spur them to battle.

The Greek god Hermes had a great deal in common with cocks. Similarities include his winged, intensely masculine and phallic nature; his role as psychopomp or leader of the souls across the boundary separating life from death; and his patronage of eloquence. The cock crows, and people listen: this was conclusive proof that public eloquence was a quintessentially male virtue. The hen's modest cluck showed that women should keep their words short and low, and attuned to domestic concerns. The rooster was thought to symbolize the church preacher, warning and rousing his flock; it followed that holding forth, in women and hens, was inappropriate and ridiculous. The cock "rules the roost," and protects his womenfolk from other cocks and from foreign marauders. His manner of "possessing" a hen sexually is violent and imperious; she simply, silently, and apparently without pleasure, submits. The cock has provided a richly suggestive model for the maintenance of masculine prestige. It was not a model meant to be a Christian ideal, however. The only time chickens get into the New Testament, aside from the dawn crow of the cock when Peter had denied knowing Jesus three times, is when Jesus compared himself not to a rooster but to a mother hen, longing to gather the children of Jerusalem like chickens under his wings.

Barnyard fowl (not game-cocks and their cock-breeding spouses, whose symbolism is entirely different) have in our own culture, and until our own day, been thought the easiest of creatures to feed. There was nothing "scientific" about it; hens foraged for food and were grateful for scraps. People marvelled at how generously productive the homely and easily pleased hen could be. (In different cultures, the hen, as mentioned earlier, is an abomination precisely because she eats anything: her behaviour denotes promiscuity and lack of discrimination in the female, whose role is to embody the idea of purity itself.)

Chickens have one of the toughest digestive tracts on earth; if they habitually eat hard objects they solve the problem simply by swallowing stones which lodge in their gizzards and help in the grinding process. The "corn cycle," which used to operate on many American farms, began with the feeding of whole kernels to cattle. Unchewed corn passed through the cows and into their excrement. Hogs scavenged in the dung, and ate the corn they found in it; sharp-eyed chickens were then allowed to hunt through the pigs' manure for particles of undigested corn. European visitors were amazed at American ingenuity and at the saving of waste and labour. There was no grinding of corn and no need for feed containers. The hen took refuse and turned it into gold. She was a modest, hard-working, and submissive wife, as irreproachably fecund and maternally devoted as she was thrifty. She was a model for nineteenth-century Protestant womanhood.

Her mate the cock (or rather, rooster) was a gentleman, and punctual with his crowing. He looked after his family; it was his duty, because he was stronger and cleverer than they, to show them where they could find food, and people often claimed they had witnessed his fatherly concern. Because he was a bird he could afford openly to have many wives whereas a modicum of discretion was required when a Victorian gentleman kept mistresses or pursued his female servants. The cock made quite certain, of course, that he alone was in charge of his household by keeping upstart roosters fiercely at bay. His womenfolk could be very difficult at times – but he kept them in order through his patience and his effortless masculine prestige. "It belongs to their very nature," wrote a nineteenth-century authority on hens, "to be marshalled by one of the stronger sex, who is a kind, though a strict master, and a considerate, though stern disciplinarian."

In 1922, a Norwegian psychologist called T. Schjelderup-Ebbe officially demonstrated that hens themselves observed what he called a "pecking order." One hen dominates the rest and demands signs of submission, in particular a cowering demeanour and lowered head; she pecks any insufficiently humble hen into subordination. The hens lower in prestige than herself similarly browbeat others, and so on down until one poor creature is constantly set upon by the rest, being pecked by all the others and having no one herself to peck. Especially fierce battles result if newcomers are introduced into an established order. Cocks easily rule over all hens; it is a very sorry specimen of rooster that allows himself to be "hen-pecked."

The discovery of the pecking order in chickens was received less as a revelation than as confirmation of what everyone knew to be the case. Some chickens (and people, of course) are better and stronger than others; it is sensible – and it was now "proved" to be natural as well – to reinforce this state of affairs with any means at our disposal. It was considered especially fascinating to discover that women (that is, hens) are guilty of this behaviour among themselves, with the extremely poignant proviso that any male could impose his authority over his womenfolk at any time. Fewer reflections have been inspired by the fact that pecking order develops only when chickens are kept in confinement; the fierce territorial instinct of the birds, ensuring as it does that each family has enough land on which to feed, has positive value and less violent effects when they live uncaged.

Sex roles, after all, had been confirmed by chickendom since ancient times. Aelian tells us that cocks were kept in the temple of Herakles, while his wife Hebe had hens. Between the temples flowed "a never-failing channel of clear water." Hens absolutely never went into the temple of Herakles, whereas cocks at mating time flew over the stream to choose their mates. When, after fertilizing the hens, they returned to their home, they were "cleansed by the water that separates the sexes." A cock sometimes helps a hen to hatch eggs, Aelian avers elsewhere, and when he does so he ceases to be able to crow: "I fancy he is conscious that he is then doing the work of a female and not of a male."

When a hen produced a small malformed egg, as happens sometimes at a first laying, the unsuccessful object used to be called a "cock's egg" or "cokeney" in early English. The word was often used of a foolish or spoilt child, the pride of its doting mother; and then by country people to put down soft and ignorant city-dwellers. The expression was taken over by Londoners and used with pride: it is the origin of the name *Cockney*.

A hen sometimes develops spurs, a masculine trait. Such a bird has always been destined for the pot, or at any rate for death, because people believed she could not be a good layer and in any case was liable to pierce any eggs she produced with her spurs. It is a fact which cannot escape the notice of even the most unwilling witness that hens quite often crow. Such an event has always been considered sinister – an omen of war, of a death in the family, of a breakdown in society. The separation of male and female roles has until recently formed the basis of societal structure, to the extent that any tampering with the categories suggested the collapse of order. Cocks and hens had to conform to the roles we projected onto them, and to confirm for us the moulds we forced upon each other.

"The barnyard rooster," according to a recent history of European and American food economics, "is now a figment of the urbanite's imagination." As increasing equality between men and women gives us entirely new spectacles through which to view the social scene, the cock and his mate automatically lose their secondary and literary use as an Aesopian representation of our sexual roles and a proof of wisdom in our organization of human relationships. At almost the same moment, the whole flock of barnyard fowl has disappeared from our view, to be locked away, forced to conform to a utilitarian scheme, deprived of as many of their natural behavioral patterns as are thought inconvenient, and pressured ever more relentlessly to produce. Let us hope that the suspicion does not become even more insistent that once again we might be thrusting upon chickens a role which is a kind of prophetic model, a metaphor for the general direction of present human goals, and for the price we are prepared to pay, and to make others pay, in order to satisfy what we perceive to be our needs.

MODERN METHODS OF KEEPING AND KILLING POULTRY

In 1934, a Californian businessman called John Kimber seized upon the growing realization among chicken farmers that eggs were one thing and chicken meat another, and that the production of each would be more profitable if undertaken separately. He put this insight into practice, and revolutionized modern chicken farming.

From this time on chickens were intensively bred for egg-laying power, an effort which culminated, in North America, in the hybrid White Leghorn hen and chickens related to her. She lays white eggs, and most North Americans prefer eggs white; there are pockets of brown-egg fanciers in the eastern United States and Canada, and most Europeans respond more warmly to brown eggs. The colour of the shell bears no relation to the quality of the egg, but consumers are adamant on this point. The White Leghorn is the world's most prolific egg-layer: she will give 230 to 300 eggs during her most fertile two-year laying period – after which she is slaughtered. This compares with the very few and sporadic clutches, about thirty eggs a year, laid by chickens in the wild, before men began selecting and breeding them.

It was also in the 1930s that systematic use began to be made of the ancient farmers' lore that hens lay more eggs when there is more light: more during long summer days, for example, than in winter. As we now know, light stimulates the pituitary gland at the base of a hen's brain, and this causes a greater flow of the hormone which in turn rouses the hen's ovary to activity. Nature's built-in rest-period for the hen, the months after her fall moulting during which she would nor-mally lay no eggs, was now brought to an unceremonious end. It was found that depriving a hen of food and water for four or five days could induce moulting, and that after a much briefer time than is naturally provided she could be made to start laying eggs again.

Laying chickens, kept in what is called in England the battery system, live in small cages made of wire so that their droppings fall through the cage floor and can be removed from below with little difficulty; chicken-manure can cause disease to spread among chickens in con-finement. They live under bright light for up to seventeen or sometimes more hours out of every twenty-four, depending on the amount of light the hens can bear and still keep laying eggs. They poke their heads out of their cages in order to feed on grain, heavily dosed with egg-en-couraging additives and antibiotics, moving by them on conveyor belts. Cage floors are slanted so that the eggs, as they are laid, roll down onto another conveyor belt passing in front of them. On this the eggs are carried to machines which grade, clean, and pack them. If a hen's eggs are constantly removed so that she never manages to provide herself with a clutch of eggs to brood on, she will be further stimulated to keep laying.

Shell-thickness is a difficult problem for poultrymen: hens which produce eggs non-stop all their lives often manage to supply only thin-shelled eggs, and mechanical collection and packaging requires shell strength. A great deal of research is continually done on feed and additives to increase calcium delivery and its conversion into tougher shells.

Hens are caged in groups of about four, to economize on the high heat which encourages egg-laying; they can sit or stand, but never run about – or even turn round. Each bird has only ten centimetres (4 ins.) of cage width to spare, though its wing span is about seventy-six centimetres (30 ins.). The British *Protection of Birds Act* reads:

> If any person keeps or confines any bird whatsoever in any cage or other receptacle which is not sufficient in height, length or breadth to permit the bird to stretch its wings freely, he shall be guilty of an offense against the Act, and be liable to a special penalty. . . . Provided that this subsection shall not apply to poultry.

In close confinement, chickens often peck and worry each other; they are therefore routinely declawed and debeaked. More than half the upper beak and some of the lower is cut off; this leaves enough beak for feeding, but it is more difficult for the hen to peck at feathers. The pecking order which naturally operates among hens can still mean that a chicken helplessly caged with enemies may be tortured to death by them. The response of scientists has been to breed more docile hens. But cannibalism, even with debeaking, continues to kill off battery chickens. The economics of chicken factory farming simply takes losses into account: mortality must threaten profitability before concern is aroused.

Hens only are required in hatcheries, for laying; cocks are retained merely to breed replacements for "spent" hens. Cocks are allowed to keep their beaks, because holding a hen by the nape of her neck with his beak is indispensable to a cock's mating performance. New batches of chickens are regularly hatched and sexed; nine out of ten baby cocks are suffocated or incinerated, or crushed to death and then fed to hogs. Thousands of male chicks may be destroyed on a single day in a large hatchery. Sexing tiny chickens is a highly skilled job, and one of the few in the field which have not been mechanized. (Another is the impregnating of turkeys: the huge modern breeds of turkey have almost no sexual prowess left; coition has to be replaced by human intervention.)

Raising and slaughtering chickens for their meat is an entirely different business enterprise, though it too begins, of course, with the laying of hens' eggs. Chickens especially bred to lay eggs for human consumption do not make good enough eating to be considered marketable. Fowls have therefore been bred by modern geneticists especially for meat production. These birds must grow as fast as possible on the least feed feasible. They must have the largest conceivable ratio of flesh to bone and muscle. Many broilers these days are crosses of White Cornish cocks and white Plymouth Rock hens. (Specialization is such that a firm may produce only males which are used to cross with females produced by another company.) Whiteness is important because dark feathers may leave a speckled appearance in a chicken's skin when it has been plucked. Feathering must be plentiful, since crowded conditions mean, as one poultry scientist says, that "poorly feathered birds are subject to tears and scratches" which downgrade the product in the eyes of the consumer.

In order to keep down costs, scientists wage perpetual war on characteristics which may be natural in chickens, but which are poorly adapted to the business scene. Broodiness and fierceness are redundant in a battery cage: these traits are as far as possible genetically excised. Chickens take up space, and "scientifically fortified" chickenfeed is expensive. The undaunted ingenuity of the geneticists has come up with an answer: the Mini Mother. This is a specially bred dwarf female chicken, to be used for breeding broiler fowl; she does not hand on her small size to her offspring. Mini Mothers eat less and take up less space than normal hens. They may even be kept in cages, whereas up till now hens which breed broilers have lived relatively free lives on deep litter.

The deep-litter method is used not only to breed broilers but also to raise them for the table. Concrete flooring is covered with dried rice hulls, peanut shells, and maize cobs to soak up moisture from droppings. Chickens raised by modern methods produce enormous quantities of droppings – 200 million tons a year in the United States alone; seven and a half kilograms (17 lb.) per broiler chicken (each of which is dead at the age of eight weeks), and forty-one kilograms (90 lb.) per year per laying fowl. As each flock of birds is killed and before the replacements arrive, the litter is removed and living quarters fumigated.

In the past, chicken manure was considered a highly valuable fertilizer. As late as 1948 in England, laying fowl were kept in portable hen-houses with fenced runs attached. These were moved daily over grassland so that the hens manured the ground. In these days of petroleum-based soil additives, however, there is no use for the manure which is created in such vast quantities by confining and fattening processes. This is true not only for chickens but for other animals as well. Chicken manure has become a troublesome noxious waste.

One ray of hope for this problem lies in recent research, being carried out mainly in Third World countries. It is suggested that deep litter from intensive chicken-farming might become a component of cattle feed. The litter – droppings, bedding, and all – is disinfected of all pathogenic organisms, dehydrated, and then provided as 15 per cent of the fodder for cattle and goats. Chicken droppings and litter provide fibre, crude protein, calcium, and phosphorus for cows, and in this manner it is converted into human food. The rest of the nitrogen-rich litter can be used as fertilizer, and the problem of poultry waste is reduced. One of the remaining problems is the heavily chemical composition of chickenfeed: all the additives and antibiotics, which are accepted now as normal in chicken meat, would pass in uncontrollable amounts into the cows' milk. It is being suggested that, where litter is re-used, chickenfeed might have to be modified.

The antibiotics which all factory-farmed creatures must consume in large quantities in order to curb the disease and stress arising from their confinement, have turned out simultaneously to accelerate flesh production. The reason for this is not fully known, but it is thought that killing off bacteria in the gut of an animal leaves more food energy to go into weight gain. Offsetting this bonus to the business is the necessity to keep up research into disease control, as bacteria keep breeding resistance to each successive antibiotic treatment. These antibiotics are ingested by people eating chicken. The consequences could include human immunity to antibiotic treatment of our own diseases.

A hen's laying time, even when she is producing meat-chickens, is considered far too valuable for her to spend it hatching eggs and raising her brood. Incubators, which hatch and warm baby chicks artificially, were known in Ptolemaic Egypt, but the knowledge appears to have been lost in the west after the fall of Rome. The technique did survive, however, until the eighteenth century in a small Egyptian village called Berma in the Nile Delta, where thirty thousand chickens were raised at a time – a huge number by pre-Industrial Revolution standards. Most extraordinary of all, the birds were hatched in all seasons of the year.

Berma's methods were fiercely kept secrets, handed down with strict rules from fathers to sons in the village.

At the beginning of the eighteenth century the Grand Duke of Tuscany organized a *coup* whereby a native of this village was brought (by bribery or force?) to Florence, and he divulged the secret to the Duke's entourage. The news reached the ears of the brilliant and versatile French scientist, Antoine Ferchault de Réaumur, who in 1747 addressed the Paris Academy on the subject of chicken incubators. He claimed that a lamb's fleece, together with artificial heat, could warm chickens as effectively as a hen could with her protective wings. Two years later he published a book on the subject which was quickly translated into English. For the first time since antiquity, Europeans could eat the same amount of chicken and eggs, and pay the same price for them, all year round.

In the fattening process meat fowl are crowded together in close confinement, for running about encourages muscle where tenderness is all. They are kept very warm and in semi-darkness because light and cool air makes chickens lively, and they are fed as much as they will eat with the aid of appetite-stimulating additives. The allotment of space is so finely calculated that by the time they are fat enough for slaughter the broilerhouse is one tight mass of chickens; movement is almost impossible. Light is further dimmed to reduce the birds' energy levels to the absolute minimum.

The combination of breeding for fast growth and of the production and mixing of quick-fattening feed has resulted in what is called a "feed-conversion ratio" which is regarded as an economic triumph by the chicken industry. About 2.2 kilograms (5 lb.) of grain are needed to achieve each kilogram (2.2 lb.) of chicken in the seven weeks of what the business calls "grow-out"; in the 1950s it took 6 kilograms (13 lb.) of feed and sixteen weeks to produce a 1.5 kilogram (3.3 lb.) bird. It is a fact much less stressed by the industry that a chicken must be bled, gutted, defeathered, decapitated, and have its feet cut off; only 44 per cent of it is, in fact, edible. This means that it takes more like 9 to 10 kilograms (20 to 22 lb.) of grain to produce 1 kilogram of chicken meat. We should bear in mind that poultry farming is the most efficient way of converting grain into flesh; other meat industries consume much more agricultural produce. A new growth-hormone to be added to chickenfeed can speed up the growth-rate by a further 15 per cent. The only problem with its application is fear of the public revulsion which occasionally manifests itself against hormones injected into foods. Chicken has a special problem because, as we shall see, its attraction as food involves connotations of mildness, innocence, and healing power.

It is the feed companies which continue to call the economic shots: chicken prices are so low (because poultry farmers can now fatten birds for the required size without feeding them long), and feed so expensive that poultry keepers may consider even a few days' delay in their operations a disaster; a million or more chickens can quickly consume a fattening company's profits. And studies have shown that the public simply will not buy chickens which are larger (and therefore older and with a stronger taste) than expected. Today's North American and British consumer has been found to require tenderness and pale flesh above every other consideration, and swift growth and early killing provide both at a low cost. Nigeria, which now imports dressed poultry from North America, still prefers a pronounced chicken taste. The industry has to keep broilers longer than the usual seven or eight weeks, especially for a market prepared to pay more because of its quirk in taste.

At exactly the right date, then, the chicken "catchers" go out from the meat-packing company to bring in the birds for slaughter. They do this at night, since, as chicken-raisers have known for thousands of years, drowsy fowl are easier to handle than cackling, flapping, awake ones; absence of light renders chickens very easy to manage. The trucks, each bearing several thousand chickens, return to the slaughterhouse with the greatest dispatch, to minimize "shrinkage." This is the trade's name for the loss of weight and the death of some of the chickens, which takes place between collecting and loading fowl and slaughtering them. Factors which cause "shrinkage" are cages even more crowded on the trucks than in the chicken sheds, lack of air (chickens need three times as much air as human beings do, yet they are commonly crated for transport as though they needed none), rough handling, struggle, and excretion during the change. Chickens are given heavy fibre diets to discourage diarrhoea just before they are collected. They are customarily starved for some hours before slaughter.

When the working day begins at the slaughterhouse, the birds are hung upside down by their feet on moving conveyor belts and passed through a vat full of an electrically charged salt solution, where most – though not all – are shocked senseless. (The electric voltage could be turned up to ensure the death of all the fowl, but the aim is only to relax them, since killing them before their throats are cut makes bleeding less satisfactory.) In the past, the chickens' heads were pierced instead with a needle to paralyse the brain; this made feathers easier to remove. The automatic picker or plucker has made this practice obsolete.

The line moves without stopping to the Kill Room where automatic blades slit throats. A human "back-up killer" has the job of finishing off any chickens that the automatic blades fail to dispatch completely. The file of bodies passes into the Bleed Tunnel, where most of the blood is vacuum-sucked out of the birds in fifty seconds or less. This step ensures the keeping quality of the meat; furthermore, an insufficiently bled fowl will have a blotchy appearance which is unacceptable to shoppers. As we shall see, blood is not part of the chicken-meat myth.

Next, the procession moves on to the Scalding Tank, where hot water loosens the feathers. Plucking is done mechanically. Rubber fingers protrude from the sides of a tunnel through which the chickens travel. The fingers revolve and vibrate over the bodies as they pass slowly by. The chickens are singed to remove any remaining body hair; their heads are jerked away and their feet chopped off, automatically; and polyphosphates are then injected to prolong shelf life.

After mechanical drawing – removal of the viscera – hearts, gizzards, livers, and necks are sorted from the rest, packaged in paper and replaced inside the chickens' bodies. Government inspectors pass and grade each "finished" bird, and finally the chickens are packaged and frozen, or taken in chilled trucks to supermarkets to be sold fresh. Frozen birds have to be checked for "freezer burn," which causes unattractive discolouration of the skin together with desiccation and loss of tenderness. The chickens which have not made the grade – because of skin bruises, tears, or blisters, broken bones, or bluish flesh owing to insufficient fat beneath the skin – are turned over for use in pet food, canned chicken soup and bouillon cubes, or are emulsified in such products as frankfurters, bologna, and summer sausage. The feet are exported in huge numbers to the Orient, where chicken feet are considered delicious, not sinister or too reminiscent of a living creature, as they are for many of us. Feathers are processed and included in chicken feed mixes.

WHO CARES?

Human beings are touchy about cannibalism. For one thing, they are nauseated by the thought of eating (or, of course, being eaten by) anyone they know. For this reason, and also because it seems to confirm our potential for empathy and kindness, we carefully dissociate ourselves from animals we want to eat: many of us prefer not to be acquainted with them beforehand. When we give a pet a name – especially a human name – we automatically confer upon it immunity from being killed by us and eaten. We go to considerable lengths to assure ourselves that animals are very different from us, and that they therefore do not suffer from treatment we would hate. We generally avoid actually killing what we eat ourselves, and do everything we can to prevent ourselves from realizing that a death has occurred at all.

Of all edible creatures (with the exception of insects, which are still nutritious and popular complements to the diets of many people) domestic fowl are probably least likely to arouse affection in us. Chickens are almost without exception mean-tempered, cowardly, and stupid in our folk-tales and idioms. We rarely give them pet names. We think of them as slightly demonic (demons in folklore often have chickens' feet) and often downright eerie (they run around when their heads are chopped off – which shows how inadequate their brains are, and how different from ours).

All of which is extremely useful to us, since chickens make delicious, versatile, and delicate meat, which we can easily eat without a shred of compunction to mar our pleasure. A cow has melting brown eyes with lashes, a pig is hairless and curvaceous like a human being (and, largely for this reason, has been popular for thousands of years as a substitute for human sacrifices), a sheep is woolly, and lambs are innocent. All of them are mammals, and the death of any one of them has at least some chance of evoking human sympathy. People have never been able to drum up much of that for chickens. Poultry scientists go so far as to think of chickens less as bird-life than as vegetable matter or as manufactured goods: they habitually speak of chicken meat as a "crop" which, with the help of machinery, they "harvest," and they call the cutting up of chickens by factory workers "the disassembly line."

Yet today there is an increasing – though not overwhelming – revulsion being expressed about the lot of battery and broiler chickens, as well as about factory-farming methods in general. One reason is the inhuman nature of this treatment of animals. People have almost no physical contact at all with factory-farmed creatures. They just push buttons most of the time: one man can look after tens of thousands of birds. Factory farming inevitably smells quite infernally bad, and people today are particularly disgusted by the idea of anything stinking.

There is another uncomfortable point. Overcrowded conditions, imprisonment, and being subjected to mechanical, bureaucratic, and anonymous controls are peculiarly twentieth-century nightmares. We suffer these ourselves and we force other people to suffer them. Modern chicken farming reminds us of penitentiaries and concentration camps. The ruthless efficiency, the relegation to a place out of sight, the sordid and undramatic lining up for mass slaughter; these are things we recognize only too well – when we think of them. And we prefer not to think of them for long.

Meanwhile, the spread of factory farming is accelerating. We are selling our expertise everywhere, and Third World countries – India, Bangladesh, Africa, the Middle East, Malaysia – are buying it with enthusiasm. It is part of "becoming modern"; the technology glitters with prestige. Chicken, in many of these countries once the food of feasts and the privilege of the rich, can now be mass-produced. The promise is enticing – who would be untempted? Yet battery- and broiler-chicken farming does not arrive free from conditions and hidden hooks. Countries which do not grow large surpluses of grain for human consumption embark on schemes to feed what little they have to chickens – nine or ten kilos of grain for each kilo of meat. Even more ominously, they engage to pay for and import "scientific" chickenfeed. The initial capital outlay for the machinery and plant can be huge; and almost no extra work is provided for the unemployed. In fact, concentrating chickens into huge batteries and fattening sheds destroys small marketing initiatives, earns money for those who already have it, and in poor countries uses grain which could feed the poor in order to produce food only for the rich.

Not all Third World countries are taken in; they frequently refuse the full mechanical package and try methods somewhat less "rationalized" and more sensibly adapted to existing conditions. A group of American agricultural scientists on a recent tour of China expressed surprise at how "technologically far behind" the Chinese are; farmed flocks are small (a few hundred to sixteen thousand birds), and chickens there still have "access to outdoor runs." The backwardness was attributed partly to the "insufficient" and "unscientific" feed supplies made available for chickens, and to a resistance to change which was explained by "a relative abundance of labor" in China.

In some places attempts are being made to find more humane methods of raising chickens. Dr. Agostino Volanti's poultry houses, which allow natural ventilation and light, are being tried on a small scale in France, England, Spain, Belgium, Iraq, and Saudi Arabia. Some people are prepared, in Canada and the United States, to seek out operations allowing chickens free range, and to pay slightly more for their eggs if they come from free-ranging chickens. ("Free range," though, turns out seldom to mean any longer that the chickens have been kept at night in a henhouse, allowed out in the daytime to roam in a fenced-in area, and fed no chemicals whatever. It is much more likely to designate birds raised indoors on corn or soy, with either no antibiotics and colorants, or only those which remain in the chickens' intestines and are removed when the birds are eviscerated.) In England and West Germany there are increasingly vocal movements to fight chicken batteries, and factory farming of all kinds. But on the whole, imprisonment of animals and cruel disregard for their happiness is enormously on the increase world-wide.

When people actually confront the facts about their treatment of animals in order to provide themselves with cheap meat, they are often shocked and concerned. Those facts are not faced often, partly because the facts are not insistently publicized, but partly also because people are happier not knowing and not thinking. Battery and broiler farming is treated, of course, as a *fait accompli,* and therefore a permanent necessity. The cholesterol scare, for instance, has made the public in rich countries think that they might now be eating too many eggs. As a result, egg markets are falling. The reaction is not to stop or decrease battery farming but rather to institute expensive research into removing cholesterol from eggs, so that, with the help of even more technological manipulation, we may keep battery farming afloat.

In the end, claim what we may about the innocence of our motives and the humanity of our intentions, the only things which protect factory farm animals from being subjected to greater and greater degrees of cruelty are the limits of necessity and the extent of our own self-interest. Broilers are raised on deep litter and not in batteries because wire causes fowls' breasts to blister, and we like to sit down at table to unblistered breast. A laying fowl may not survive twenty-four hours a day of bright lights forcing her to keep producing eggs. Consumers do not like the look of bruised flesh and torn skin, broken bones or deformed backs: they just will not buy those chickens, so trouble is taken to keep the fowl whole until they are slaughtered. Recent experiments on poultry have involved scientists screaming at chickens and otherwise irritating them. It has in this manner been discovered that chickens which are gently sung and spoken to and touched daily are more resistant to diseases than birds which are ignored, harrassed, or shouted at. This kind of demonstration might seem to the layman proof positive of the obvious, but for the moment it is a chicken's only hope.

THE FLEXIBLE CHICKEN

The nature of modern chicken farming has made several instructions which are customarily found in old recipes obsolete. We no longer need to truss our chickens closely for roasting, protecting the breast with the legs: modern chickens are bred for huge breasts which are in little danger of drying out. (Turkey breasts became so large at one point that the birds could hardly stand without toppling over, and the genetics of the thing had to be readjusted.) Modern chickens are very young when slaughtered and, therefore, cook very quickly. Part of the reason for trussing a bird (aside from a desire to reduce the leggy, winged shape of the creature to something more like a chaste football form) was that chickens killed when old would take a long time to cook and needed to conserve their juices. It is now more sensible to let the chicken's legs spread in the oven (perhaps tying them loosely so that the skin does not tear) in order to allow the upper inner thighs to cook through by the time the rest of the chicken is ready. Factory-farmed chickens have plenty of fat, so French recipes which demand slathers of butter, to moisten the flesh of lean free-range chickens, need to be adapted to altered circumstance: much less butter – though enough to flavour and lubricate the bird – is required. Basting a factory broiler is largely a waste of time.

Four hundred million battery broilers are raised and slaughtered in Britain every year. The figure for the United States is five billion. The industry's phenomenal growth has created problems of its own. Market analysts speak of an inexplicable "chicken fatigue" which overtakes people who eat chicken several times a week – the very same people who will happily eat beef every day of the year. Chicken farming, in spite of its expertise, remains a risky business because of fierce competition and the fact that it "mass-produces a perishable item." In other words, chickens kept in concentration-camp confinement can easily catch diseases; may die *en masse* if mistakes, such as incorrect changes in temperature, are made; may turn into a vast economic liability if calculations in timing and volume of demand fail, or if a new virus suddenly strikes. As one chicken tycoon recently put it: "Sell 'em or smell 'em." Everything humanly possible is done to avoid these dangers, but the risks remain, and the threat of overproduction is constant. Chicken saturation at home (a human being eats only a certain amount of chicken) naturally causes businessmen to look abroad to untapped Third World markets for their machinery, their know-how, and their formula feed.

One way out of problems is onward and upward. The ingenuity being expended on making chicken meat ever more enticing, and on fitting it ever more closely into people's "lifestyles," is awe-inspiring. Chickens now come "self-basting" (liquid, fats, and stabilizers are injected under the skin so that they ooze outwards as the birds roast), pre-marinated (with injections of flavours and tenderizers), ready-coated in various batters, pre-cooked in pieces (needing heat for three minutes only before eating), stuffed or rolled, either whole or in parts.

Much fast-food chicken is broiled at the slaughterers'. The trick is in the timing. *Rigor mortis* sets in twenty to thirty minutes after a chicken dies – much faster than in a beef animal. After that, the bird must wait at least eight and preferably twenty-four hours before its muscles relax and it can be cooked or frozen. Otherwise the bird will be formidably and irredeemably tough. Given the extremely tight schedule of meat production ("time is money"), even eight hours is far too long to wait. There is only one alternative: the birds must be plucked, singed, drawn, cooked, and stripped from the bone within twenty minutes (some say that should be six minutes) of death.

Deboned meat, including the millions of breasts required for fast foods, now accounts for huge tonnages of chicken – as much as 70 per cent of what is sold in some parts of the United States. In the deboning process, after breasts, wings, and drumstick meat have been removed, the chicken's carcass is crushed and the bones extruded. Tiny bits of bone are then sucked and screened out. What is left is a paste, which can be added to frankfurters, bologna, or canned soup. This paste has to be further processed or frozen very quickly; it cannot be stored long without losing its flavour and having its colour darken. Redness from the haemoglobin which escapes from cracked bones intensifies the latter effect. Textured soybean protein is often added to make up for the loss of protein when the meat is heated for serving.

One of the most impressive achievements of deboning is that it returns utility to parts of the chicken that are devalued by many consumers. Nearly a billion pounds of necks and giblets reach American kitchens every year. Research has shown that half the buyers take out of the cavity of their chicken the carefully wrapped heart, gizzard, and liver and simply feed it to the cat; they usually throw the neck away. When chicken meat is reduced to a homogeneous paste, however, hearts and gizzards can be used, and the boniness of the neck is simply eliminated. Unfortunately, North Americans in general dislike the taste of liver, so that the makers of sausages and other processed meats feel they cannot use the livers. Some of these are sold to the minority of liver-lovers in a breaded "finger-food" form, as are wings, pre-cooked to deep-fry or bake in three minutes, and marketed under such appellations as "Wing Dings."

Most North Americans want nothing but breast, although there is a strong following for drumsticks in the southern States. Fast-food chunks and "planks" are mostly breast. What do we do with thighs, backs, and the rest? Deboning provides the answer. Thigh meat is a darker colour than breast, and this relatively unpopular trait can be used actually to improve the appearance of turkey and poultry "ham" rolls. Furthermore, there is the question of what to do with the egg-laying hens, two and a half years old when they die – nearly twenty times as old as the broilers we buy whole in our supermarkets. These, too, can now be turned to good account, particularly since the chicken-taste of a fowl's flesh increases with age, and the flavour of a broiler, which is light to begin with, does suffer in the crushing and bone-screening process. Adding older fowl is called "improving the chicken note."

A market researcher said recently about chicken: "People don't want the bones. They just want to take it out of the package, plunk it in the microwave and serve it." The restructured chicken steak (paste, bits, soy, and additives) supplies this dream – but at a price. A further-processed equivalent of a whole chicken can cost three times the price of a raw dressed bird. The cost in taste lies of course at the discretion of the buyer; and the billions of chickens slaughtered every year will not complain. The only conceivable saving for us is in time and effort. We have apparently not yet discovered whether there are any limits to what we will do, pay, and put up with in order not to have to wait and not to have to cook.

EATING WHITE, EATING GOLD

Blancmange, the original medieval French invention, was a "standing" pottage (you could stand your spoon up in it) made of capon flesh "teased small with a pin," whole boiled rice, almond milk, and plenty of sweetening. (Meat and sweet things were not habitually separated in European cooking until recent times.) Blancmange could also be made with fish, and a meatless version (milk, almonds, egg whites, sugar, and hartshorn jelly) appeared in the seventeenth century. When arrowroot starch began to be imported into Britain in the 1820s it was used to thicken the opaque, white, and unquestionably meatless confection we now know as "blancmange"; this was the precursor of all our modern cornstarch instant puddings. But the original blancmange consisted of almonds, chicken-flesh, and sugar, with various white additions.

Chicken is pale meat, and this fact has always sharply differentiated it in men's minds from the red and bloody flesh of mammals. Chicken blancmange was a light, fortifying pudding which was eaten as a first or second course at a large dinner party to set off the heavy meat courses. White food in general, associated as it is in our minds with mildness and soothing innocence, has often been thought especially appropriate for sick people, children, and women.

Chicken soup is an almost universal panacea. It is "Jewish penicillin," dished out in hot loving bowlfuls to people with colds or fevers. A scientific experiment has actually established that the aroma of chicken soup speeds the flow of mucous through nasal passages; the velocity of the passage of mucous increased 33 per cent in the noses of the volunteers. In China, women in childbed are given a diet of chicken soup, chicken, and eggs; a customary gift to the family of a new-born baby is a chicken, to feed the mother. Old people and the sick in China are also thought to digest eggs and chicken best. In Italy or France people who suffer from their "livers" are told by their doctors to "eat white" until they recover: apples and rice, and chicken as their condition begins to improve. Chicken, according to the seventeenth-century English writer on health, Thomas Muffett, is a meat of "thin and light substance, engendering thin and fine blood, fit for fine complexions, idle citizens, tender persons, and such as are upon recovery out of some great sickness."

People today often categorize what they eat on a scale which ranges from the impossibly "strong" (each other, or named pets like dogs or horses, or carnivores because they themselves eat meat) to the "weakest" and most generally acceptable (fruit, cereals, leaf and root vegetables.) The strictest vegetarians will eat only the "weakest," least "aggressive" foods. They differentiate themselves by name (calling themselves *vegans*) from vegetarians who, although they refuse to eat meat, will permit themselves to consume animal products: eggs, milk, and cheese.

Meat is nearly always eaten cooked, whereas cheese, milk, and vegetables do not necessarily require the mediation of fire (that masculine, powerful, and technological element) to make them acceptable to "civilized" people. Methods of cooking meat have a hierarchy of their own, which in our culture ranges from boiling and steaming (low), through stewing, frying, grilling or broiling, and finally roasting (the highest). Meats themselves are placed on a ladder of power ranging from fish (the lowest rung and the most "female" of meats), through poultry, to the "strongest," red meat. (Pork is less "masculine" than beef partly because it is pinker when raw and cooks to a pale colour.)

The meat eaten by the heroes of ancient Greece was spitted, roasted, and red, with plenty of glistening fat. Homer does not picture his heroes eating vegetables, fish, or fowl, says the second/third-century scholar Athenaeus, "because eating these is a sign of greed, and also because it was judged unseemly, and beneath the level of heroic and godlike deeds, to spend time preparing these for table." The shish-kebabs preferred by the Greek heroes were fast foods, far removed from lowly simmered pottages and stews, and from small bony fish and fowl.

The "white meats," fish and poultry, are mild and non-aggressive within the overall category of flesh. Certain kinds of fish may, however, be granted special prestige because of their scarcity. Today, for example, shellfish has become expensive and relatively rare. Oysters and lobsters, poor men's fare till the late nineteenth century, have now become exceedingly *chic*. But fish has traditionally been so low on the scale that it was commonly permitted in such religious strategies as Lenten abstinence or the Catholic institution of "fish on Fridays." Lowering one's sights from meat to fish was an exercise in humility, and designed to raise consciousness by elected self-restraint, and by forcing oneself to remember.

Chicken was not much higher on this scale than fish; it was commonly considered to be a compromise abstention from meat during Lent for children and invalids. Birds are classified with fish in the Book of Genesis, where both are born from the waters on a different day from the earth-born four-footed beasts. The widely influential text of St. Benedict's Rule (sixth century) laid down that monks should be vegetarians except during illness, with fish permitted where available. In Chapter 39, however, Benedict mentions abstention by all except the very weak and the sick from "the flesh of quadrupeds." It did not take long for the monks to interpret these words as allowing them to eat chicken.

Poultry is still thought fit for restrained and mild eating. It is for people who eat lightly and have "refined" tastes (Muffett, we recall, said it was for "fine" blood): it is delicate enough to give pleasure to those who can afford to keep food in proper perspective. Chicken may be seen as offering the opposite of what Roland Barthes called the "bull-like strength" believed to be imparted by full-blooded beefsteak. A Frenchman may justify almost any aggressive human behaviour by saying that a man is "defending his beefsteak"; no one would be silly enough to make huge gestures in order to save his chicken. Traditionally, women in our society would tend to choose chicken, white wine, and salad from a restaurant menu, whereas men would go for steak, red wine, and potatoes.

Today's further-processed chicken, such as chunks and fried parts, often comes heavily crumbed. The pieces are thus rounded out and cloaked, turned into abstract shapes (the advertisements like to borrow the mystique of modern architecture and call them "functional forms") which effectively distance us from the idea of animals, carving, and slaughter. Many companies selling crumbed and frozen chicken and fish openly claim that they have "created" fish or "invented" chicken: we are being offered, not cod or poultry, but something else again, a thing utterly reshaped and "refined." Steak, on the other hand, even the circular hamburger pattie, comes seared with the marks of fire, and is nakedly meaty. Anglo-Saxons generally prefer meat cooked brown all through, but a gesture towards the bloodiness so dear to the French is made with gouts of tomato sauce in a thick, sweet, and stagey red.

Since chicken is "light" eating, its flesh must be as pale as possible; this is an important reason for the careful de-blooding of the factory-dressed chicken and for the public's overwhelming preference for breast meat. As we saw with "light-tasting" margarine, our heavily-fed civilization grants special prestige to eating "light." Most fish has been much neglected in North America because of traditional eating habits: bones are considered a nuisance, and the relatively affluent North Americans have been able to confine themselves to eating prestigious foods only. But since fish and chicken are "light," low in cholesterol, and relatively non-fattening, they are set to achieve a new kind of allure – they are now beginning to denote health, slimness, and the social aura which goes with them. Chicken flesh has traditionally been classified as "restrained": now that restraint in one's eating habits has acquired socially admired consequences, this meat is obviously changing its "lowly" image.

But paleness has always in some degree mitigated the humble status of chicken, in spite of the power denoted by red meat. In fact, as mentioned earlier, a whole roast fowl carved before the guests has long been a first choice for festive occasions in our culture. If properly treated, chicken obligingly turns golden. For centuries Europeans adored gold for festive dishes. From the Middle Ages on they doused food in saffron and marigold sauces, daubed egg-yolks over meats, yellowed their pastries, and even gilded joints of meat and large pieces of confectionary. Gold is still high in our mythology; its appeal has been brilliantly harnessed by the marketing of crumbed chicken chunks under the word *nuggets*. Many modern factory-farmers use xanthophyll additives in order to induce in poultry flesh and legs the desired yellowish hue. Where chickens are sold with the feet still attached, the public insists that they should be a definite yellow, in spite of the fact that customers will almost invariably discard the feet or ask the butcher to remove them before the sale.

Our reactions to the chicken still range from contempt to reverence. Nothing could express the contradiction more neatly than Proust's description of his narrator's servant Françoise killing and serving a chicken:

When I went in, I saw her in the scullery which opened on to the back yard, in the process of killing a chicken which, by its desperate and quite natural resistance, accompanied by Françoise, beside herself with rage as she attempted to slit its throat beneath the ear, with shrill cries of "Filthy creature! Filthy creature!" made the saintly meekness and unction of our servant rather less prominent than it would do, next day at dinner, when it made its appearance in a skin gold-embroidered like a chasuble, and its precious juice was poured out drop by drop as from a pyx. When it was dead, Françoise collected its streaming blood, which did not, however, drown her rancour, for she gave vent to another burst of rage, and gazing down at the carcass of her enemy, uttered a final "Filthy creature!"

CHAPTER FIVE

Rice: The Tyrant with a Soul

R ICE, as the starchy staple of our dinner, is a comforting partner to chicken: filling, fat-and-juice absorbing, bland enough not to overwhelm the delicate flavour of the meat. Rice, in our own world view, is usually perceived as a simple, useful, unassuming cereal. It is something for which we feel grateful if we think about it at all, but it is nothing to arouse the passions. If our supplies of it were cut off for one reason or another, we should be irritated, but we could eat potatoes instead, or pasta, or more bread, or some of the many other grains available, such as millet and barley, or leguminous seeds like lentils or white beans: all of these alternatives, even the relatively recently introduced potato, are more traditional staples in the European diet than is rice.

It is easy, therefore, for us to forget the enormous importance of rice to the human race. This grain is the main sustenance of half the population of the earth. If at this minute some catastrophe were to kill off all the rice crops of the world, at least a billion and a half human beings would suffer acute hunger, and millions would die of starvation before anything could be done to save them. Growing rice occupies the entire lives of over a billion people; it constitutes the only source of buying power for as many millions. Sixty-five kilos (145 lb.) of rice are milled annually for every person on earth, although eating habits vary enormously: a Frenchman, for example, eats an average of 2 kilos (4 lb.) of rice per year, while an inhabitant of a country like Burma, Bangladesh, or Malagasy happily consumes 150 kilos (330 lb.) of rice annually, and more if circumstances allow or require it.

Even if one could comprehend the quantity of rice which people grow and eat and the centrality of its place in the biological welfare of the race, it still remains to conceive the extent of a second role of rice, as a creator and controller of human society. Where rice reigns, it governs power structures, technological prowess, population figures, interpersonal relationships, religious custom. Once human beings agree to grow rice as a staple crop, they are caught in a web of consequences from which they cannot escape – if only because from that moment on rice dictates to them not only what they must do, but also what they prefer.

PADDY

Paddy is a Malaysian word meaning rice growing in deep water; it may also refer to rice grains in the husk, harvested but as yet unmilled. A paddy field is surrounded by dykes and designed so that it can be flooded and drained at appropriate times, and so that water levels may be controlled as closely as possible. Much rice still depends entirely on monsoon rain water and on the seasonal flooding of rivers; but over millennia man has learned to channel water to rice, at the cost of enormous and never-ending labour. Flooded rice produces far more grains than rice grown on dry land or gathered in the wild, and the yield of artificially irrigated rice can increase by more than a third again. Watered paddies make rice grow so fast that two crops can be harvested each year from the same soil – with one, two, or even three vegetable crops added between rice harvests in some circumstances. Water-borne nutrients are constantly replenished as fields are flooded, and dykes or "bunds" prevent soil erosion. In tropical lands a paddy field can be producing food all year round, and it need never lie fallow.

But rice began as a dry-land plant (it is still often grown in dry fields), and it retains the characteristics of any cereal: rice, like wheat, is a grass, and it evolved in the same dry valleys of central Asia as wheat did. Rice grains grow from the top of the plant on an inflorescence called a panicle, which has five or more radiating ribs, with grains hanging along each rib. These grains are edible fruit with tough brown husks, like the fruit of wheat or oats. In common with all grasses, rice has stems with nodes, and long narrow leaves with parallel, not branched, veins.

Unlike other cereals, rice has the capacity, which it must have evolved in tropical flood plains, to grow in water: it takes advantage of the nutrients which come with water, but is not drowned by it. (Only the tuber taro, among major food crops, can also flourish in water; another exception is the American barley which is called "wild rice" because of this characteristic.) Once a rice seed which is submerged in water germinates, the plant shoots up quickly: it needs to break through the water's surface into the air. The roots of rice, because of its dry-land origin, require plenty of oxygen, and that is available only from the air and, to a certain extent, from even slightly moving water. Rice, unlike other dry-land plants, does not drown because it has evolved a "breathing" mechanism. It sucks in air through pores in its above-surface leaves; a cushion of air soon covers the plant's stalks and leaves under water, and this provides a second source of air. Carbon dioxide emitted by the plant dissolves in water much more quickly than oxygen does; this causes a lowering of pressure which drags in more air to feed the plant.

In some kinds of rice the stalks between the nodes can elongate at an astonishing rate – up to twenty-five centimetres (10 in.) per day – when flood waters are rising. The plant keeps pace with the water's depth, holding its top leaves above the surface and receiving air. The stalk can reach as much as five metres (16 ft.) in length if it is required to do so, but what causes it to "judge" how long it needs to grow is little understood. Emergency roots at the top of the plant are provided so that if the moving waters uproot it the rice can float and live by its adventitious roots until it touches bottom again as the waters recede, and simply reestablishes itself in its new home. If the rice ripens before the waters recede, farmers may harvest it from the water's surface by boat.

Most varieties of rice do best in water ten centimetres (4 in.) deep. The seed sends its primary shoot straight up, after which branches, called *tillers*, grow from the base. Each tiller can produce a panicle of rice. The plant's topmost leaf, its "flag," is largely responsible for re-acting to sunlight by photosynthesis, a process which governs the total number of rice grains the plant will bear.

Paddy rice can be grown in widely differing climatic conditions: from ten thousand feet high in the Himalayas to river deltas and mangrove swamps by the sea; from as far north as Czechoslovakia to as far south as Argentina and New Zealand; and in temperatures dropping from those of Egypt and Australia to those of France and Hungary.

Tens of thousands of kinds of rice have been officially counted. They vary in taste, scent, size, and colour (pink rice, blue rice, purple, yellow, and striped, as well as gradations from cream to white). A traditional rice farmer is expected to use the accumulated lore handed down to him by his ancestors in order to juggle types and times, light and rainfall, soil and the slope of the ground, tastes and market prices, in order to know what to plant, when and where.

As the plant grows and its fruit ripens, predators must be kept at bay. Just as traditional maize growers have always had to contend with rats and parrots, rice farmers must frighten rodents and birds from the paddy with slingshots and mud pellets or noisemakers and twirlers. Crabs must be hunted and caught before they devastate the rice-stalks under water. Elephants were once, in south-east Asia, a major fear: a passing herd unless headed off could crush an entire farm in five minutes, houses and all.

When the rice is ready the paddy must be drained and left to dry, while the grain goes on ripening, until the ground is easy to walk on. The moment for harvesting is critical: rice which is too dry may crack in the husking. The stalks are cut, traditionally with a knife or snapped off by hand; in parts of Africa a certain type of snail shell makes a sharp harvest tool. The cut rice is often stacked for further drying, and then the grain must be removed. Traditional threshing methods include treading the stalks, beating them with flails, whipping them against a stationary object, drawing bundles of panicles across forked spikes, and walking water-buffaloes in a circle over the heap, sometimes dragging heavy wooden platforms behind them: the grains fall through the stalks to the bottom while the straws protect the grain from the animal's hoofs. Today small gasoline-powered threshers are practical, reasonably priced, and becoming common.

Next the grain is husked, and typically winnowed by being shaken in flat trays; this is usually a woman's job. It takes years of practice to learn how to toss the rice correctly, so that the light husks separate out from the grains; they must then be jerked over to the edge of the tray and lifted to the wind so that the clean grains fall to a mat on the ground and the chaff is carried off into the air. The feat is commonly accompanied by songs and yodelled entreaties to encourage the wind.

Almost immediately after the harvest, dykes have to be repaired and strengthened and the paddy field cleared, levelled, ploughed, and fertilized in readiness for a new crop. If there is to be a second round of rice, the farmer (or rather, his wife and children: planting is usually "female" work) may plant seed in holes drilled in the dry ground; the field is flooded only when plants have reached a secure height. Alternatively, forty-day-old seedlings from a nursery are transplanted to the flooded paddy. This is labour-intensive and back-breaking work, but it usually gives much better yields than other methods. It saves precious time and even more precious space during the first stages of growth, and the young plants can be boosted in advance with fertilizing manure to make them grow faster. The earth has to be watered and smoothed or "puddled" till it is in a soupy mud condition before transplanting takes place. This layer of mud seals the ground surface and prevents water percolating through the soil. The other traditional method of planting is to broadcast seed, scattering it into the dust of the field before the rains come or the nearby river floods.

RICE AND CIVILIZATION

None of this brief description of rice cultivation has taken into account the intricacies and the heavy discipline of water. Water has to be found, collected, guided, and channelled to the paddies. Fields must be meticulously levelled and slightly graded for water flow and retention behind low dykes. The presence of water in mountainous areas may give rise to the growing of rice on terraces so that the water can be made to descend from field to field down the mountainside. This involves gigantic earthworks and walls, all the labour of cutting away the slopes, and chiselling the mountain into flat fields with walls to hold water. The two-thousand-year-old terraces of the Ifugao of Luzon in the northern Philippines are one of the world's wonders. They cover an area over four hundred kilometers (250 miles) square, and reach, in undulating levelled sections, from the floor of the valley to a height of over a thousand metres (1,100 yds.). More than twenty thousand kilometers (12,500 miles) of stone walls retain the paddy waters; they were built without the aid of either machinery or draft animals.

Aqueducts, bamboo pipes, drains, pumps, and sluices have all to be devised. Water may have to be raised from wells or from reservoirs, or lifted to paddies on higher ground by means of pedal-pumps and hydraulic systems of different kinds. People dependent on flooding rivers and monsoon rains have to understand seasons and weather, and be able to dam floodwaters, divert them, or adapt to their flow.

In other words, paddy rice requires hard and incessant work, and a fiendishly difficult combination of both flexibility and organization. It succeeds only if it is controlled by a society of people ready to pull together, to synchronize with nature, to obey the rules they have invented, and above all to keep at it: everything must be in good repair and in good supply, always. Large-scale works (canals, terraces, reservoirs) have to be planned with the future in mind and with technological expertise. Then they must be built with labour freed, through the co-operation of everyone, from day-to-day farming. Everything has subsequently to be maintained in good order. Intensive rice cultivation needs many hands.

But an assurance of a constant, good food supply in turn gives rise to a concentration of people. The earliest Chinese civilization did not grow rice, but founded its prosperity on wheat, millet, and sorghum – and to this day northern China is not fixated on rice. Aquatic rice farming reached southern China from India or from the "Golden Triangle" (an area which includes Burma, Thailand, Laos, southern China, and Vietnam) probably in the early second millennium BC. The practice of artificial irrigation was established much later, from the fifth to the first centuries BC (the first extant mention of it is in the Book of Poetry of the Chou Dynasty, about 780 BC). Intensive rice cultivation was fully in place south of the Yangtze River only when early-maturing rice, imported from the Champa people of what is now Vietnam, had been mastered and spread, enabling the Chinese to grow two crops a year on a single plot. The date was as late as the eleventh century AD. By the fourteenth century there were three times as many people in the south as in the north of China, whereas the T'ang Census of 754 AD had shown 75 per cent of the Chinese living north of the Yangtze.

Rice, in short, is a major cause of the crowding together of huge populations – for which reason damage to rice farming can result in human catastrophe. And any dislocation in society means that rice growing will surely suffer. When people decide to take upon themselves the discipline of raising paddy rice, they commit themselves to nothing less than life-long labour, and also to unending control both internalized and political.

But rice, as we recall, does not have to grow in water at all. On dry land it behaves like any cereal. The slash-and-burn method which is still used for maize in the forests of South America will work very well for rice in the mountains of Thailand or Vietnam. Paddy rice is raised in the valleys where water gathers and on terraces carved out on well-watered hill slopes; dry rice, which will grow anywhere, feeds the people who are prepared to live frugally but lazily, up in the mountains. (Dry rice is frequently called "upland" rice, even though it can be grown at low altitudes.) Dry-land rice is also the only small-grained cereal which can be grown in low-lying tropical rain forests, which are too humid for the proper ripening of other cereals.

Dry-rice people need to move on every year in order to find unused land, leaving the clearing they have made gradually to return to the forest; it cannot be used for rice again for between three and ten, and sometimes as much as twenty years. But aside from this nuisance and anxiety, life for them is relatively easy: no standing knee-deep in mud, bent and steaming in the sun, no ploughing and dyke-repairing, no hierarchy dispensing rules and management, no hydraulics. And also, no crowds: upland rice growers have to be few, for the land cannot support many like them, even though their cultures are delicate and complex, and they maintain themselves by living lightly on the earth. Depending on soil and climatic conditions, slash-and-burn rice can support only between 13 and 52 people per square kilometer (35 to 130 per square mile).

Water for the paddy-fields and their enormous hard-working populations brings with it organic matter and minerals from the soil it has passed over, nutrients which the leaves of the forests supply for upland rice. Water, with the help of various micro-organisms, also fixes nitrogen for the plants. It keeps temperature and environment steady in regions where extreme conditions often succeed one another. A great many weeds, as rampant as rice in the tropics but unable to survive in water, are eliminated. Water-weeds thrive, however, and have still to be rooted out. In traditional China this was done by hand, the farmer simultaneously smoothing and stirring the soil as he worked. Weeds were never wasted, but kept and fermented for fertilizer, or pushed back under the soil as soon as they were found, to provide precious "green manure" – phosphorus, nitrogen, and potassium for the rice. Hands were often armed with metal or bamboo claws to help in this work.

Green manure is supplemented with animal dung wherever possible. In China, where there is no taboo against using human waste on the fields, and where animal dung is scarce, a close symbiosis grew up between town and country: the town not only bought rice and sold the farmer his tools, wood, and oil, but it also provided the needed fertilizer. The relationship is utterly different from the fierce differentiation which we ourselves make between city and rural life. The Chinese had their own opposition which they used in categorizing the world: there were the many paddy-rice men settled in the narrow, spatially constricted valleys, and there were the few dry-rice nomads in the mountains. Dry-land cereal growers also lived in the broad and comparatively empty northern plains.

The considerable advantages of irrigated rice are gained only through the human energy expended in controlling nature's cycle. Brute force is rarely the kind of energy that is required: alert sensitivity, co-operation, precision, and persistence are far more valuable. A household cannot manage without at least sporadic help from neighbours, and water supplies must eventually depend on laws to ensure equitable distribution, and on the structure of society as a whole.

A spectacular modern example of such a structure is on the island of Bali, where a network of temples co-ordinates farming activities. All the farmers using water from a common canal form a group called a *tempek*. They are neighbours who know each other well and help each other out; they regularly perform religious rice rituals together at a small shrine in the fields. All the *tempeks* using a common dam form one *subak*; a *subak* has two temples, one near the dam and one in the fields. The temples house a ritual calendar which regulates planting and harvesting for all the *tempeks*, keeping time-tables staggered but regular. One mountain temple co-ordinates all *subak* temple rituals (there are about thirteen hundred *subaks* in all), while two lake temples near the centre of the island govern farming for the whole area, one for western Bali and the other for northern, southern, and eastern Bali. Every 210 days a festival is held at the lake temples when delegations from the *subak* temples meet each other. Theatrical performances and religious ceremonies support and enliven the whole orderly and highly sophisticated system, where time and space are made constantly to reflect each other, and society is simultaneously knit closely together and made aware of its own independent parts.

In general, leaving the uplands for the valleys and for paddy rice means a change in diet: far more rice but also far less meat, and (until a degree of extreme sophistication is reached) far less variety. Technology and control result in increasing dependence upon the product controlled. In the uplands, people can hunt all kinds of animals and birds and collect wild fruits and berries in addition to their crops of vegetables and dry-land rice. Down among the paddies there are very soon hardly any trees at all, and wild animals other than rats become rare. Every inch of space is used to grow rice; animal herding is far too wasteful of land. In traditional China, peasants raised chickens and pigs, but space was so scarce even for these barnyard scavengers, that methods of confining animals were invented which prefigure factory farming. The water buffalo, which can thrive in mud and wet, was used for ploughing and transport – both of which were, however, commonly achieved by human effort alone. Paddy rice growers eat rice with vegetables and a little fish. This is not to say that they are sorry. On the contrary, rice has a weird drawing power: the more people eat it the more they like it.

Rice paddies largely denude the land of wood and even of bamboo, making fuel scarce and precious. One brilliant southern Chinese adaptation to this restriction was the invention of the cuisine of the wok, where a minute or two of fierce heat was all that was required to cook the vegetables, eels, fish, frogs, edible rats, and dried oysters which accompanied the main dish of rice. True, the rice still needed to be boiled, but large quantities of rice can be cooked at a time: rice reheats well and can be eaten cold. Often it would be prepared in the village and brought out in lots every two or three days to the fields, where workers lived in temporary huts from the spring to the fall. Again we notice the typically Chinese interaction between town and country.

Chopping things small helped the Chinese to use as little fuel as possible, even when they boiled, stewed, steamed, or roasted their food;

and bite-sized pieces made knives at table unnecessary. The Italian traveller Francesco Carletti wrote at the beginning of the seventeenth century that the Chinese ate with "two slim sticks made in a round shape and blunted, the length of a man's hand and as thick as a quill for writing. . . ." Europeans at this date still usually ate with their fingers and their knives; the fork had become common only in a few upper-class circles. "They can pick up anything, no matter how tiny it is, very cleanly and without soiling their hands. For that reason they do not use tablecloths or napkins or even knives, as everything comes to the table minutely cut up. . . . When they want to eat it, they bring the bowl it is in close to their mouth and then, with those two sticks, are able to fill their mouth with marvellous agility and swiftness." Chopsticks had been in use in China since artificially irrigated rice had made its way there around the fourth century BC.

"The meat [of a man who wants to sacrifice to the ancestors]," Confucius counselled in about 500 BC, "must at the very most not be enough to make his breath smell of meat rather than of rice." Rice was really the food one ate: the rest was merely relish. There are innumerable proverbs still working to instil the important principle in children's minds: it is rude, shameful, and unacceptable to expect a quantity of relish disproportionate to the amount of rice in one's bowl. Relish is *ts'ai* in modern Chinese; rice is *fan* – a word which can be synonymous with food in general. No meal is considered filling unless it includes rice – in fact, no eating-session counts as a meal unless rice is part of it. For a greeting equivalent to "How do you do?" the Chinese ask, "Have you eaten until you feel you have had enough?" – a question which implies a hope that the addressee has had plenty of rice. A well-wisher at the Chinese New Year will pray "that your rice may never burn." In China, upsetting one's rice-bowl – like upsetting the salt-cellar in our own society – was an extremely bad omen, and wilfully to invert a fellow-guest's rice bowl was an insult so deadly that it could lead to bloodshed. An "iron rice bowl" is a modern Chinese expression for job security, while being unemployed is "breaking the rice bowl."

Fan is part of the ancient and elaborate system of *yang* versus *yin* by which traditional Chinese thinking divides up the universe. *Yin* (drink) nourishes its opposite in man, the *yang* in him; eating, which is *yang*, feeds the *yin*, perceived as the other great Opposite which helps constitute the cosmos in general and man in particular. *Fan* is the most important example of things eaten (*shih*). Among the Five Elements which make up the physical world (Metal, Wood, Water, Fire, and Earth), *fan* is related to Earth. *Ts'ai* or relish, on the other hand, is associated with Fire. But Earth and Fire, within the overall category of things nourishing the *yin*, are as different as could be. This perception, coloured by different cooking methods for *fan* and *ts'ai*, once went so far as to govern the kinds of pots from which one could serve one's food. *Ts'ai* dishes could not be made of bronze because Fire and Metal are never harmonious; relish had to be served in wood, basketry, or pottery. Metal containers were used only for "earthy" *fan*, and for drinks made of rice or other grains.

The Chinese, like people everywhere, have always used food to make societal distinctions. The rich gourmet was endlessly finicky about rice types, provenances, aromas, and cooking styles; the poor had to be content with brown rice or gruel (*conjee*). The Chinese of the south could disparage the northerners for eating dry-land grains instead of prestigious rice. The north retaliated by mocking the southerners' partiality for frogs from the paddies; the Anglo-Saxon dismissal of Frenchmen by calling them *frogs* is very similar.

Foreigners ate differently from Chinese; but in Chinese minds there were degrees of savagery, just as there were more and less horrible deviations from the norm. Meat, for instance, had always to be cooked with Fire; and all Chinese had to eat at least some grain food. There were stories in China of barbarians who ate raw meat with *fan*, and of others who ate cooked meat but no *fan*. These luckless people were utterly un-Chinese. And then there were monsters who, men said, ate raw meat and no rice or grain at all; they proved by this that they were scarcely human. In all cases, rice was most distinctive of Chinese culture. Only relatively recently had the Chinese learned intensive rice-growing in paddy fields, and pride in the technological mastery which this represented made any other staple look primitive in comparison.

The intoxicating joy which the Chinese felt in preparing and cooking *shih* and *fan* is captured for us in a poem, "Sheng Min," from the Book of Poetry of the Chou period (eighth century BC):

> We pound the grain, we bale it out.
> We sift, we tread,
> We wash it – soak, soak;
> We boil it all steamy . . .
> As soon as the smell rises

God on high is very pleased:
"What smell is this, so strong and good?"

THE SOUL OF RICE

The god Anta was a poor little god: he had no arms and no legs. He was long but narrow, like a snake. One day the great god Batara Guru built a magnificent new temple for himself, and asked all the other gods for offerings. Every one of them was proud to bring something to show his or her worth – all except Anta, who had nothing to bring, and could not even get himself to the celebration. Anta in his loneliness wept three tears, and each of them turned into an egg; Anta was delighted. But an eagle swept down and, cruelly mocking Anta's weakness, forced him to break the eggs, one by one. Before he could be made to crack the third egg, however (for Anta put up a heroic fight against his persecutor), it hatched, and out of it came a beautiful female baby.

Her name was Samyam Sri, and she was so lovely that Uma, Batara Guru's wife, agreed to breast-feed her since Anta had no woman. When she grew up Batara desired intensely to sleep with her – but this would have been incest, because of the breast-feeding. Batara was furious with his wife for having unwittingly foiled his lust, and tried every means to rape Samyam Sri. The other gods were horrified, and eventually found no other recourse but to kill Sri, in order to save her from Batara. They buried her, lamenting dreadfully. But in a very short time a miracle occurred: out of the body of the dead maiden grew rice (from her eyes), sticky rice (from her chest), the palm-tree (from her vulva), and many other trees and grasses. All these Batara gave to man to nourish him. For this reason we often say that rice is Samyam Sri.

This story is the Indonesian version of a myth common in its essentials throughout the islands of the Indochina seas, including Japan. Rice in this part of the world is everywhere a woman. She is tender, beautiful, and timid, and she dislikes being handled by men. The inviolability of sex roles is heavily underlined by the preferences of rice: men can prepare the land, level it, plough it, repair dykes, and attend to irrigation, but women should plant rice, especially if the planting is done from the nursery when the seedlings are already quite big. Women also should weed, winnow, and cook.

Never is rice to be more carefully treated than at budding time. The Thais say that at this stage she is like a pregnant woman, with a craving for bitter and sour tastes like limes or lemons. She likes offerings to be brought to her in the fields – mirrors, perfumes, and scented powders as well as food, for she is very vain. Men must keep well away at this time, because a man would not be able to withstand the attraction of her beauty, and would be tempted to ravish her – which would, of course, ruin the crop.

When reaping time comes rice will lose her soul. For this reason a woman of the house must go secretly into the fields before the harvest and gather rice panicles in a special ceremonial manner, and make them into a rice doll. The tiny figure – about a hand's span in length – is laid in a basket, and the soul of rice is invoked and asked to inhabit the doll. Carried home and installed in the family's granary, the rice soul will ensure that fertile seed is available for the coming year. It is still good manners for a purchaser of rice to give back to the farmer a handful of grain: the plant's soul, to impregnate next year's crop. The act is an elegant sign of co-operation and good will.

It is very important that any crushing, threshing, and cooking should be done well away from a standing paddy: rice must be protected as long as possible from the knowledge that one day she must be done to death in order to feed people. The theme is common wherever grain is raised as a staple food. People feel grief that the grain must die; a tragedy, inevitable and cruel, takes place with every harvest.

Rice is like mother's milk, white and pure nourishment from maternal womanhood. Every grain of it is part of the body of the Thai Rice Goddess, Maeae Posop, and it contains a bit of her *khwan* or indestructible reincarnated soul-stuff. The *khwan* in a person is nourished by his or her mother before birth, by her milk after birth, and by rice thereafter; there is in this way no break in female nurture throughout human life.

The Thai, Malay, and Burmese myths all insist on the delicate nature of rice. Whether it is a baby or a shy young girl, it is always easily offended or hurt. It must be treated, the Malays say, "as though one were carrying a flat-bottomed shallow tray brimful of cooking oil." Rice, in other words, displays what is considered acceptable public demeanour by the people themselves. The ideal is to be unassuming, gentle, and sensitive. They feel deep shame when harsh words are used, and their feelings are easily offended by inconsiderate or ill-mannered behaviour. They concentrate on not letting unwanted violence erupt: there is no room for emotions getting out of hand. Rice is like themselves – and they have taken on these characteristics through their age-long devotion to rice and their adaptation to the crowded conditions which rice creates. The people have needed to cultivate the co-operative traits which suit rice best: sensitivity to wind, water, and weather, reciprocal neighbourliness, amenability to authority, patience, endurance, and the capacity to deal intelligently but ruthlessly with their own violent propensities. Cockfighting, as we saw, is a ritual dear to the rice-growing Balinese and the Philippine islanders: men can project onto the cocks their own aggression and let the cocks, not the men, bleed for it.

Once upon a time, the Malaysians say, rice never had to be harvested from the fields: it is man's own fault that he now has to eat rice, as he eats bread, by the sweat of his brow. Every day, the story goes, a single rice grain would appear in the farmer's house and make its way into the cooking pot. The housewife knew that she had to cook the grain without ever opening the lid; if she kept the taboo intact the pot would be ready by the afternoon, full of cooked rice. But one of her children ignored her warnings one day, and peeked into the pot. It is said that what the child saw was a small girl crouching inside – and the damage was done. The girl was angry at having been seen, and from that day onward, rice for man has meant back-breaking labour and careful propitiations of the offended sensibilities of the goddess. This tale resembles the Greek story of Pandora's Box, where curiosity, which was also part of the crime of Eve in the Biblical story, brought misery to the human race.

Another common series of rice myths expresses the pride and fear which are apparently indissociable from technological prowess. A human being (a male this time) undertakes a heroic quest when people are starving: he travels to heaven, steals rice from the gods, and carries it back to plant in the paddies. The Indonesian version of this story has the culture-hero hide the seed in a wound in his leg. Man was a hopeless creature – ill-adapted to the earth and weak, unlike the animals who manifestly know what they are and how to look after themselves. A Promethean hero has saved man: fitted him with a god-like intelligence and the knowledge of how to raise rice. Man can now live, forever infected with divinity, in spite of the will of the gods. The price is heavy: toil, self-control, endless vigilance, and – if he is wise – humility even in the face of his success. Above all, he must never let slip his respect and his gratitude for rice.

Use is commonly made of some pivotally important food crop as a timing and measuring device. Like beer in many African cultures, rice (*vary*) on the island of Madagascar expresses man's understanding of time and space. "The time it takes to cook rice" (*indray mahamasa-vary* in Malagasy) means "about half an hour." A distance may be given as "twice the time it takes to cook rice," meaning that it is about an hour's walk. Instead of months, they have the seasons at which rice is different heights and at different stages: *mena vary*, "when the rice is gold," is an especially significant time-referent. All measures of volume and weight use rice-measures as a standard, the basic unit being called *vary iray*, "a rice." Rice was money in the time before Madagascar came into contact with Europeans. When the Malagasis first got metal money, they simply chopped up the coins and made the value of the pieces equivalent to their weight in rice.

Everywhere rice is a symbol of fecundity. In Hindu marriage ceremonies the couple have to stand in a shallow basket while rice is poured over their heads – a blessing for the pourer as well as for the married pair. In our own society, a long way outside the area where rice reigns, the white grains (pure as well as plentiful) are traditionally flung at newly wed couples as they leave church. (*Confetti* means sugar-coated candies or "comfits" which Italians substituted for rice; confetti made of paper punched into circles has become for us a technologically produced and lighter version of rice.) A great length of time and many happy events are imagined by the guests throwing rice, in addition to fertility. Fortune (in this case good fortune) has always, in the west, been pictured as bouncing particles, random and plentiful.

In Sri Lanka, geomancers (earth-magicians) and astrologers are consulted when rice is planted. Everything is meticulously prescribed by the seers, down to the clothing that must be worn by the sower. When droughts or pests devour the rice, the goddess Pattini must be propitiated. The men of the village stand in lines about thirty metres (100 ft.) apart; they toss coconuts back and forth, and try to smash them with coconuts held in their hands. The coconut fights go on for days, and are followed by a feast. One purpose of the ritual game is in a highly controlled fashion to release frustrations, and in so doing to encourage fertility; the rain of colliding rice-grains flung by the crowd at our weddings may have a similar aggressive aspect. Our own ancestors many centuries ago felt it was worth stoning a specially designated victim in order to help the crops to grow.

A Japanese saying makes rice the most sacred thing on earth, second only to the Emperor. In Buddhism, the world is categorized into ten parts, the first of which is Buddha and the tenth Hell; Rice is second. (The name of Buddha's father was Suddhodana, "Pure Rice.") In China, *Tou*, the Rice Measure, was the eighth of the twenty-eight constellations. It symbolized the "full measure" of justice, mercy, and virtue which every human being should receive from others regardless of his station. The character *Tou*, originally a simple square like the four-sided rice measure, represented the Chinese Empire. The Taoist goddess Tou Mu, "Mother of the Rice Measure," was a virgin and a deity of the sea. Her image was carried on every Chinese junk, sometimes together with those of her useful twin attendants, Thousand Mile Eyes and Fair Wind Ears.

Just as every year the supreme Inca of Peru ceremonially ploughed the earth with gold and so began the planting of corn, the Chinese Emperor had to use an ancient ornamental plough annually to prepare a sacred field so that his empire could receive the blessing of rice. The immensely complex ritual of the emperor's First Ploughing, every February fifth, ended when earth from the field was distributed for scattering on the plots of the farmers attending the festival. Good crops were inconceivable without this rite. Animal sacrifice has until recent times been widely used to induce fertility in the rice fields: blood is more powerful even than the paddy waters. There was a time when the sacrificial victim had been human, and perhaps that victim was once the king himself. The Inca and the Chinese Emperor, with their power for ensuring good crops, were perhaps recalling by their actions the more desperate and violent methods of their ancestors.

For centuries the rice paddies of Indochina have been yielding the kind of abundance which only modern chemically fertilized fields are able to surpass. The miracle of the paddies is now known to have been caused in large part by a tiny floating water fern which lives in symbiotic relationship with assorted blue-green algae. These work together to convert atmospheric nitrogen into ammonia and soluble nitrates, and so to "fix" it in a form that the plant can use to boost its growth. The blue-green algae and their ferns, named *azolla* after *azote*, the French chemist Lavoisier's term for nitrogen, are at present the subject of intense research at the world's most advanced centres for rice science. Understanding the minute snake-like alga *anabaena azollae*, and azolla itself, might eventually enable rice farmers in Asia to cut down on the increasingly expensive and often dangerous chemical fertilizers they are now using in order to augment their crops. Azolla gets its energy from sunlight and is ecologically safe.

Once, sometime in the eleventh century AD, in North Vietnam, a giant Buddhist monk called Khong Minh Khong was carrying a yoke on his shoulders as he travelled through the rice paddies of the Red River Delta. From each end of his yoke hung enormous baskets full of azolla, and as the giant monk jogged along, clumps of the tiny ferns fell out of the baskets and onto the paddies of the three villages of La Van, Bung, and Bich Du. The rice prospered amazingly, but the three villages told no one the secret of their miraculous harvests. By the seventeenth century, however, the inhabitants of the three villages were busy raising azolla in nurseries during the summer; they collected the fern's spores and sold them to other farmers, who would scatter them every January over their transplanted winter rice seedlings. To this day a temple stands in the Delta, honouring Khong Minh Khong as the founder of the azolla technique.

RICE AND MODERN MIRACLES

Rice in North America is raised by methods utterly different from anything we have looked at so far; and the methods are indissociable from attitudes of mind. First the enormous fields are levelled with the aid of laser beams, which are intercepted and processed by computers mounted on mechanical earthmoving machines drawn by tractors. The land is flattened to a very slight slope (one or two parts per thousand) to facilitate water dispersal. Dykes, called "levees" in the United States, are constructed by special twin-disk ploughs which as they move forward automatically pile up earth behind them into continuous mounds two to three feet high. One man can very quickly bank up soil around a field hundreds of metres wide. The land is then gone over again with another precision leveller.

The next step is the mechanical injection of nitrogen fertilizer, whether liquid or solid, at precisely three inches below the surface, which is the depth most accessible to rice roots, and also below the zone of soil which will oxidize in contact with the water. Rice seeds are soaked first in fungicide, then in water for twenty-four hours. The fields are flooded and then sown by airplanes, which scatter the rice over the water's surface; the heavy water-sodden seed quickly sinks and germinates. One man can sow 500 kilograms (1,200 lb.) of presoaked rice in an hour, or 200 hectares (500 acres) in an eight-hour day. Water levels are automatically controlled. Weeds are killed off by several types of herbicides sprayed from planes; government regulations attempt to control the amount of poisons used, because the water is recycled when the fields are drained for the harvest. The mature rice is gathered by huge combines fitted with tracks to help them move through the mud. The rest of the drying, threshing, milling and packaging is done mechanically. Another method of rice-growing used in the United States involves drilling the seed into the prepared dry fields, which are subsequently dyked and flooded; always the system is wholly mechanized.

The United States grows less than 2 per cent of the world's total rice crop. Yet it is also the largest exporter of rice on earth; it sells up to 60 per cent of its yield abroad. Few hands are needed to grow the rice, and Americans consume very little of it – a mere five kilos (11 lb.) per head per year, one-thirtieth of the amount which the poor in southeast Asia eat when they can get it. In North America, rice is even less tyrannical than it is soulful.

On one matter Americans are adamant, however: rice must be long-grained, very white, and what English-speaking people call "fluffy." That is, every grain must be separate and rather dry. The sticky and the glutinous in this culture are held for the most part in abhorrence: these properties attack our socially-conditioned preferences for what is clear and clean, free, equal, and individually self-contained. Even rice pudding revolts some of us because of its glutinous quality, especially when it emerges as a compact mass; we all know the answer to the question in A. A. Milne's poem:

> And it's lovely rice pudding for dinner again!
> What *is* the matter with Mary Jane?

The Japanese and others, on the other hand, actually prefer their rice to stick together in lumps; they like the consistency and sweetish taste of sticky rice. Eating it with chopsticks is easy. When it is white, the Japanese want rice to be as white and glossy as it can be – a thin coating of glucose is spread over the grains with the aid of what is called a trumble machine, which also dusts talc over the sticky surface. There have been fears expressed that this practice may cause cancer, but most people now think that whiting rice is harmless.

Americans and most Europeans prefer the kind of rice which is grown in tropical heat; it is typically sensitive to temperature but not to light, and it is native to the Indian subcontinent – whence its name, *indica*. The most prestigious of indica rices, and a great favourite in the west, is Basmati, grown in northern India and Pakistan; its aromatic, long, and slender grains double in length with the cooking, a process which is still a subject of scientific puzzlement. Sticky rice, on the other hand, called *japonica* outside China (where it is known as *sinica*), has short wide grains which stick together during cooking, is relatively resistant to temperature changes while growing, but responsive to the duration of sunlight. It has a sweeter and altogether stronger taste than most indica, which tends to blandness. The softest and stickiest type of japonica, the true "glutinous rice," is especially prized in Laos and northeastern Thailand; in other countries it is reserved for making cakes, soups, and sauces. *Congee*, sticky rice boiled for three hours in about twelve times as much water as rice, is turned, in China and Japan, into sweet and savoury snacks, or eaten sugared for breakfast as the equivalent of porridge in northern Europe. In most poor countries of the world, the water in which rice is cooked is cooled, often fermented slightly, and drunk, so that the nutrients which escape into rice water are not wasted.

The different characteristics of the two main types of rice, japonica and indica, form the basis of modern genetics in riziculture. Indica rice grows very tall (160 to 200 centimetres, or over 5 ft. in height) and has a tendency to "lodge," or fall over with its heavy head of grains in the mud. Lodging is always undesirable, but not a very great problem when harvesting is done by hand. When mechanized farming takes over, indica (despite western taste preference for it) is a very difficult crop indeed. Indica has excellent drought tolerance, however, and better resistance to insects and diseases than glutinous varieties display. Japonica rice is shorter and therefore less liable to lodge. It has a further advantage which makes it extremely acceptable to modern farming methods, in spite of its stickiness and attraction for diseases and pests: japonica loves chemical fertilizers, whereas indica dies if too many of them are applied.

The trick, then, for rice geneticists was to marry the two types in such a way as to combine the desirable traits and eliminate the difficult ones. In 1959 the Rockefeller and the Ford foundations united to fund the International Rice Research Institute, with headquarters at Los Baños, sixty-seven kilometres (42 miles) south of Manila in the Philippines. The IRRI (with initials which neatly recall the triumphs possible through irrigation) was founded in order to do for rice what scientists had already achieved for wheat: the great food staple of the western world had seen its yield increase vastly, thanks to "genetic engineering" coupled with the application of petroleum-based fertilizers.

It did not take long – a mere seven years – for the International Rice Research Institute to present the world with what was quickly nicknamed "Miracle Rice," IR8, the eighth hybrid to come out of IRRI, and the instigator of a revolution in world riziculture. IR8 had a short stature, thanks to japonica genes reinforced by those of a strange semi-dwarf wild variety from Taiwan. This unique and once highly localized Taiwanese rice, named Dee Geo Woo Gen, has in consequence of this "Green Revolution" provided some of the most widely used rice genes in existence.

Short stems made the new rice resistant to lodging, even when powerful fertilizers caused the plant to shoot up quickly; IR8 took only 125 days to grow instead of the previous record of 150 days. (The newest hybrids grow in 100 days or less.) Shortness also ensured that energy went into grain-production and not into stem height. The new rice had stiff strong straws and large ears which detached themselves easily from the plant, rendering it perfect for machine harvesting. Sensitivity to length of daylight was bred out so that it could be used for off-season cropping anywhere; but it was also amenable, like japonica, to heavy doses of yield-increasing fertilizer.

The new rice was disseminated extremely quickly throughout the world; more than eighty countries planted it. Average yields of rice rose about 30 per cent between 1968 and 1981, beginning with the arrival of IR8. Organizing the "Green Revolution" in rice meant education for new techniques of sowing and irrigating, the introduction of fertilizers and heavy machinery, the building of all the paraphernalia required to harvest, transport, and mill the new crops. Dry-land rice is not amenable to the modern techniques, with the result that about 10 per cent more land than formerly was brought under irrigation.

After the first euphoria (and far more quickly in the case of rice than for the other cereals), certain unpleasant side-effects of the "Green

Revolution" began to haunt the rice-eating populations of the world, who nevertheless continued gratefully to plant "high-yield" rice. The enormous cost of importing chemical fertilizers hit hard, in spite of all the crop gains, in poor countries. Heavy machinery involved the destruction of tiny fields: what had been an economizing skill came, overnight, to be considered antiquated and not economically viable.

Everyone planted the same rice everywhere, and used the same pesticides. Since people eat so much rice where rice is the staple, there is a great danger of pesticide build-up in human bodies. Rice-protecting poisons immediately kill the denizens of rice paddies: fish, often the main source of protein, died off, with the sadly ironic result that "more rice" could mean "worse nutrition." "Miracle rice has led to miracle locusts," became a gloomy aphorism in Pakistan as insects swiftly adapted themselves and overcame the poisons designed to control them. In traditional cultures, the periodic drying of the rice paddies and the planting of garden vegetables had served to interrupt the reproductive cycle of the brown plant-hopper, one of the most devastating plagues of rice; but "miracle" rice now filled the paddies non-stop. The pests rejoiced and vastly multiplied.

And when all was said and done people did not *like* IR8 much: it was chalky, tended to break easily in the milling, and there were complaints that it tasted odd. It was also always the same. Rice eaters are intensely knowledgeable about varieties of flavour and aroma in their favourite food; they may be used to eating little, but they care a great deal whether that little is good. Scientists bemoaned the ingratitude of those who, far more easily than ever before, could fill their stomachs with rice; why couldn't they just eat up and forget the taste?

There is always a way out of these kinds of dilemmas – back to the drawing-board. A new kind of rice was devised, then another, then another. IR20 was armed against a disease called *tungro*, but was vanquished by grassy-stunt virus and brown plant-hoppers. (The heavy and compact tillering of the new semi-dwarf rices modifies the microclimate around the plants and actually increases their attraction for insects.) IR26 finally overcame the disease and the new wave of pests, but was easily flattened by wind. Researchers went to Taiwan for a special type of wind-resistant rice, but found it had vanished: the Taiwanese had not thought that kind of rice was worth growing any more, since everyone was raising "miracles." (All wild rices on Taiwan have now been officially declared extinct.) When IR36 came out, 65 per cent of Philippine and 60 per cent of Indonesian paddy fields were sown with the new marvel. The brown plant-hopper was nonplussed for four whole years. It finally did rise to the challenge, however, and destroyed the hopes of IR36. By 1982, IRRI was ready to throw IR56 into the breach. And so the dance goes on. No "new rice" can hope to last more than four years; most are useless in less than two.

Many scientists are now saying that hybrid rice, grown uniformly on millions of hectares, presents too great a risk from pest hordes; a wide variety of rice-types should be grown in order to keep depradations down. The rice farmers of Thailand, for instance, have grown modern hybrids only in the dry season on 10 per cent of their planted land; hundreds of traditional varieties were raised in the rainy season on most of the fields. As a result Thailand has suffered no major epidemics during the past twenty years, and has also managed to maintain its position as part of what is called "the rice-bowl of Asia." Many rice-growing countries have found that their soil and water becomes contaminated by the new pesticides. Ever since 1976, work has been done on finding easily degradable versions of pest-killers, and many now realize that even these should be used only when crops are actually in danger.

Another most important realization is that everything must be done to save rice varieties which are being threatened with replacement and extinction because of the very success of the "high-yield" hybrids. The example of the disappearance of the wind-resistant Taiwanese rice shows how serious the loss of a rice variety can be. Another wild Taiwanese rice was incorporated into hybrid stock and helped save "miracle" rice from a flare-up of ragged stunt virus in India in 1977. This genetic material, completely lost to its natural habitat because of concentration by the Taiwanese on "miracle" rice, was available only because it had been artificially preserved at the International Rice Germplasm Centre (associated with IRRI) in the Philippines.

This, the largest of the word's germ-plasm "libraries," was established in 1961. It brought together samples of rice types from national collections all over the world; for the first time there was money and technology available to keep seeds alive and in storage for up to fifty years. Before that, plant stocks had to be grown every year or so in order to survive; mixtures, duplications, mislabelling, and irreparable losses had become increasingly common. Today, repeatedly renewed exploration campaigns send botanists out to find previously uncollected samples of rice varieties. It is estimated that about half the world's living range of rice varieties is now packaged and stored at the IRGC at Los Baños, and at other rice "banks." Organization and emergency action has saved rice from possible genetic disaster. Also, concentrating varieties in these centres has facilitated further genetic experimentation.

Yet, for the less optimistic among us, half a dozen public institutions seem perilously slender threads on which to hang the future of half the world's food staple. Absolutely nothing must ever go wrong with a giant modern plant "library." A war, power failures, lack of funding, incompetence, or plain laziness could at any point destroy forever whole expanses of nature's abundance. Man's first decision, many centuries ago, to take control of rice made him endlessly dependent, for his cultural as well as his biological well-being, on rice. Today we have to learn to control our own prowess before the devices we have cleverly invented turn into traps. The extent to which we hold the power of rice genetics in our hands is the extent to which we must respect it. The word "hybrid," after all, is commonly thought to derive from the idea of vigour contained in the Greek term "hybris." The word has other connotations, more tragic and maybe even more germane.

THE ORIGINS AND SPREAD OF RICE

Bulu is a cousin of japonica rice with wider, hairy leaves and hair-like awns on the grains (*bulu* means "bearded"). It is a rapidly disappearing species and has never been found anywhere but in the very ancient Philippine rice terraces, Java and Bali, and the mountains of Madagascar. *Bulu* is a rare clue to one route which rice took as it spread over the world; it is a living proof of early historical connections between these far-flung islands. A few centuries before Christ, at the latest, canoes from Java made the fifty-six-hundred-kilometre (3,500-mile) journey to Madagascar bearing rice and bananas. The Malagasy still use outrigger canoes and Javanese musical instruments such as the marimba; they also cultivate paddy rice on terraces with intensive irrigation – a method which seems never to have crossed the three-hundred-kilometre (200-mile) distance which separates the island from mainland Africa.

The earliest origins of rice are so ancient and so little understood that scientists become lyrical in their speculations. One theory has rice beginning on the ancient supercontinent of Gondwanaland, before it split up to form Africa, Antarctica, Australia, South America, and south and south-east Asia. For rice has been found in what appears to be an indigenous state in all parts of the earth except Europe, North America, northern Asia, and the Arctic.

The earliest wild-rice gatherers known to us were the negroid Hoabinhians who lived in southern China and North Vietnam (they are named after a North Vietnamese archaeological site) about ten to four thousand years before Christ. Theirs was a Neolithic culture older than that of the Middle East. The race is now confined to the Melanesian islands; but their ancestral home, lying between the two great rice centres of India and China, is usually believed to be where the cultivation of rice began.

Irrigated rice came relatively very late to India, China, and southeast Asia. That is because a high degree of civilization is presupposed by the necessary technology. The easy-going tubers, such as taro and yams, provide adequate nourishment for people with one-third or less of the labour which rice requires. In Luzon in the northern Philippines tubers are still planted, largely symbolically, among the rice; this is perhaps a traditional memory of the relatively recent arrival of rice cultivation, and of the time before rice supplanted the older crops. Many scientists believe that rice agriculture really only arrives when stocks of wild animals have been depleted to such an extent that there are not enough left to complement a diet of tubers. Others think that the original systematic cultivation of rice was triggered off in the early second millennium BC by contact with the margins of the ancient wheat- and barley-growing cultures which lay to the west of India; complex historical reasons were responsible for the spread of rice to the rest of the world.

Our word *rice* derives from the Aramaic term *ourouzza*; it was probably from its usage at Babylon, in modern Iraq, that both Greek (*oryzon*) and Arabic (*arozz*) took their names for rice, and these two languages handed on the term to the various tongues of Europe. It was the Persians, yet again, who had bridged east and west, carrying rice cultivation from India to the Euphrates. For the Greeks and Romans the plant remained fairly rare, and was therefore used semi-medicinally. The Arabs, and the Turks when they settled in Asia Minor, took rice very seriously indeed. The Arabs called rice *aish* ("life") just like wheat, because for them it often rivals bread in importance, and they planted it widely in their Spanish territories. The Spanish word for "rice" is taken directly from Arabic *arozz*, and the international word *pilaf* (denoting boiled rice with meat), derived from Persian, became the Spanish *paella.*

Rice took many centuries to induce Europeans other than Spaniards to be interested in it. During the Middle Ages rice would arrive in England on spice ships from the Orient, and was stored carefully away in the locked spice-cupboards of British mansions. The grains were precious, and thought of in the plural. "Take rice," say the early recipes, "and wash them clean. . . ." Rice was nearly everywhere considered an ingredient for puddings, and eaten very sparingly, with sugar and powdered spice. (Four tablespoons of rice are enough to make an excellent rice pudding for a modern family.) "If you boyle rice in milk adding thereto sugar and cinnamon, it will provouke into venerie," says a late-Elizabethan profferer of good advice. As late as 1873, Alexandre Dumas's *Dictionnaire* of cuisine lists almost nothing but desserts under the entry *riz.*

Rice was soft, sugary, eaten with milk and cream, fed to babies, and easily thought of as infantile; it sustained racial prejudices as well. Nietzsche thought that eating rice caused one to become addicted to opium; the gourmet Brillat-Savarin warned that eating such food made people soft and cowardly, like the rice-eating Indians who could be conquered by anyone who thought it worth the effort. Montesquieu, on the other hand (*De l'ésprit des lois*, 1748), had noted that rice induces hard work, the co-operative virtues, and justice.

When Vasco da Gama returned from India in 1499, the spices and other food discoveries which he presented to King Manoel the Fortunate of Portugal set off a new interest in rice cultivation in his native country. From Portugal the fashion spread to Piedmont in Italy, where rice had been grown on a small scale since the tenth century. Intensive rice farming in the Po Valley began in 1522, with the aid of water diverted from mountain streams and the building of a complex canal system. The consequences for Italian cuisine were immense. Excellent fish were raised in rice irrigation water, and *rane dorate*, skinned frogs dipped in flour and fried in olive oil, became a famous delicacy. Italian rice is round, with an opaque pearly middle; alone among western cooking traditions, the Italian preference is for short-grained rice eaten sticky, with a binding of sauce and cheese. "Rice," the Italians say, "is born in water and dies in wine."

Thomas Jefferson was visiting Italy in 1787, having been sent to Europe as America's first Ambassador to France. During the American

Revolution, the British in South Carolina had depleted both the crops of America's rice and the seed which was needed for replanting. In spite of Italian laws jealously guarding Piedmont rice seed, Jefferson managed to get his hands on a few sacks of it, and smuggled it out of the country, breaking the Italian monopoly and replenishing the North American rice-fields. Long-grain rice took over from the round variety, and rice itself was supplanted by cotton in the Carolinas in the nineteenth century, but the name "Carolina rice" survives as the appellation for a crop now grown mostly in California, Texas, and Arkansas.

South Carolina rice farming had begun with seed brought on ships from Madagascar in the 1680s and '90s. Slaves from north-west Africa were soon being shipped in to work the rice fields; they came with ancient expertise in the technology of rice, knowledge which their English masters mostly lacked. Many North American practices in the early years of rice cultivation were similar to those used in Africa. Threshing, for instance, was done with flails, and husking with mortars and pestles.

Many of the slaves for North America's cotton and sugar-cane plantations came from the south-west African coast. On the long journey out, American ships called in at the Windward Coast (stretching from Sierra Leone to the Ivory Coast) where they loaded up with African rice for the rest of the trip; payment was largely in Brazilian tobacco and New England rum. On the Windward and Gold coasts they also found slaves who could work rice plantations back home. There is increasing evidence that slave traders were choosy about their merchandise: they knew that Africans could supply not only brawn but specific know-how, so they looked for men with the skills required.

Most varieties of rice eaten in the world today, including both indica and japonica, are of the species *Oryza sativa*. There are other kinds of rice, however, and many of them survive in Africa. The most important of these is *Oryza glaberrima*, which may be indigenous to north Africa, or may have been introduced there from the Orient by the Arabs. *Oryza glaberrima* was central to the prosperity of an African rice kingdom which flourished on the flood-plains of the Niger River, near Timbuktu in modern Mali, in the sixteenth century. Rice is still grown in traditional ways in Mali, where weeds are suffocated by being cut off below the water's surface by workers standing waist- and even neck-deep in water. Seedlings are grown in calabashes, then transplanted into the river beds, or seeds are sown broadcast over the water. It is necessary to protect the rice from phytophagous (plant-eating) fish, seed-eating birds, and locust swarms.

Rice is also grown intensively in the tropical rain forests of the Guinea Coast, and in mangrove swamps on the seaboard of Guinea-Conakry. When the Portuguese introduced *Oryza sativa* to the Guinea Coast in the early sixteenth century, they found the Africans there already practising complex rice-irrigation methods, and dealing with the salinity of the seaside soil. They had built dykes to keep out the sea-water, and sluice-gates of hollowed tree-trunks to allow rain and river water to leach out the salt. Where the salination was most serious, they grew their rice on raised soil ridges.

Oryza sativa grows very successfully in Africa: it caught on and spread quickly after its introduction by the Arabs down Africa's east coast, and by the Portuguese who called in at the north-west seaboard on their return journeys from expeditions to India. The rice which the Portuguese ships carried may have been taken on board at East African landing points and transported by them to the west, via the toe of the African continent.

Today the populations of Africa demand more and more rice. The cereal very easily becomes a top favourite wherever people are accustomed to designing their meals around one main staple. Rice is easily digestible and easily stored. People never tire of eating it, even as a daily food and often at consecutive meals, over a lifetime: rice is one of the most consistently palatable items of the human diet. Almost nobody is constitutionally incapable of assimilating it.

Vast irrigation projects are under way in Africa to increase rice yields. The Chinese are naturally in the forefront of the supply of expertise in the field. The upheaval in African eating habits is profound. Millet and sorghum, the ancient African staples, and cassava, yams, and even maize seem increasingly less prestigious and "modern" as items for human consumption, especially in large African cities. Rice is particularly amenable to the large-scale agricultural engineering projects which are thought necessary for the raising of all the food so urgently needed in Africa. Modern technology, in turn, makes rice seem *chic* and alluring.

With rice, the "Green Revolution" arrives. Its attendant problems can be particularly exacerbated and dangerous in Africa. Rice phases out the traditional crops which respond poorly to petroleum-based fertilizers: in any case, none of them can compete in yield with irrigated rice. The result can be, as we have seen in previous discussions of technological agriculture, loss of alternatives, loss of traditional know-how, and far-reaching changes in taste and social custom. Expensive heavy machinery must be imported, and fuel costs are high. Mechanized ploughing needs extremely careful controls if it is not to ruin the precarious balance of Africa's fragile soil surfaces. Erosion, and the leaching of nutrients where rainfall is heavy, are common results of overdoing cultivation, especially where the long labour of terracing and walling fields (which incidentally prevents soil erosion) is not part of the strategy. Living lightly on the land and taking advantage of wide space and wild animal life are characteristic of many African traditions; the close, tight, intensely regimented life of rice growers is often foreign indeed. The consequences of adapting to it must be immense, if unforeseeable.

SICKNESS AND HEALTH

Standing water has always been known mysteriously to cause disease: agues and the recurring sickness called *quartan* or *tertian fever*. The cause seemed to be bad air (which is the literal meaning of the word *malaria*) exhaled from certain bodies of water – and some of these were undoubtedly rice paddies. The problem was particularly bad in southern Europe. In the fourteenth century the Crown of Aragon forbade rice cultivation altogether in Valencia, and as late as 1860 a Spanish decree ordered that no trees were to be grown in areas planted to rice, so that the "bad air" could easily blow away.

When rice paddies were abandoned, malaria could strike with particular malevolence. The Siamese attacked the Cambodian capital, Angkor, in the fifteenth century. The damage they did was great, but its most devastating effect was the interruption of irrigation schemes in the rice fields. Water stood still, paddies were not properly drained, and malaria struck, wiping out a whole civilization.

Virulent malaria became rife in South Carolina in the eighteenth century, partly because African slaves were imported in large numbers to work the rice fields, and with them arrived a new species of malaria-carrying mosquito. It is believed that the American Indians knew that foreigners could bring fever with them, and that this accounts for some of their ferocity in fighting off newcomers in swampy south-eastern North America. It is certainly true that where populations are sedentary and visitors few, people suffer relatively little from malaria. A great deal also depends on the type of the local mosquito and its breeding habits: Malaysia, for instance, in spite of its fields of standing water, has never suffered from malarial fever as southern Europe or parts of Africa have done, because Malaysian mosquitoes do not breed freely in muddy, sediment-carrying rice paddies.

The anopheles mosquito (the blood-drinking female of which is the vector for malaria) depends on stagnant water for breeding; therefore the constantly recurring drainage of rice fields, and a slight movement of the water through the paddies, act as important controls on malaria. This explains why it is that malaria can become epidemic as soon as incessant work on rice-paddies stops for whatever reason. Larvicide oils spread over the water's surface or poisons dissolved in paddy water have been quite successful in reducing the mosquito population. The "miracle drug," DDT, which did a great deal to fight mosquitoes after its launching world-wide in 1946, was banned in 1964 because it is so dangerous to birds, fish, and insects beneficial to man, and because people were consuming it in their food. In any case, mosquitoes evolved resistance to it.

One ecologically safe method of fighting mosquitoes in rice paddies is the propagation in them of the tiny North American fish called *gambusia*. It loves eating mosquito larvae, and adapts easily to different kinds of water conditions. *Gambusia* was introduced with success into paddy waters in Spain, Greece, Italy, and Russia in the 1920s and '30s. The fish, which reduced but could not eradicate malaria (fish populations, unlike human populations, never destroy a useful food source), was mostly dropped as a malaria fighter after the introduction of DDT.

Malaria has never been eradicated from the earth, as scientists until quite recently believed it could be; in fact the incidence of the disease has increased world-wide. Human travel and the upheavals of war are the reasons, as is also the spread of rice cultivation in previously non-rice-eating countries. Now scientists think that the most we can hope to do is control malarial outbreaks as best we can with drugs, routine checks, and general health measures. The price is constant (that is, often tedious and repetitive) vigilance, and a preparedness to spend money protecting people.

"Polishing" rice – removing its bran and germ entirely – gives the grain long shelf-life, whereas rice encased in fat-containing bran may turn rancid, especially in hot humid weather. Milled rice is quick-cooking, soft, and easily digestible; in addition, polishing (the very word suggests refinement) brings out the prized colour, white. Eating brown rice often has a social stigma attached to it, much as brown bread once had in the west: brown rice has not been treated to the extra trouble and expense of milling. Also, if rice with a lot of bran is eaten as almost all one's nourishment, it can cause serious digestive problems.

Polishing rice, however, rids the grain of its protein and nearly all of its vitamins, which are mostly of the B-complex and reside in the bran. The rice grain is naturally wrinkled, and the tight bran skin espouses its scored surface; for this reason it has hardly ever been possible, until recent times, to remove absolutely all of the bran. Modern machinery, of course, can handle the most deeply imbedded bran with no difficulty. Undermilling is still frequent in the tropics, however, and this insufficiency has been an enormous aid to nutrition. The "brown" rice available in health-food stores in Europe and North America is lightly milled; it retains 8 per cent of the protein, plus a little fat, and a few vitamins and minerals. It takes longer to cook than white rice, and retains a chewy consistency.

In 1886, the Dutch colonial service sent a commission of inquiry out to Indonesia to find the cause of an epidemic of beri-beri which was devastating the native population. A germ was discovered which the commissioned professors thought must be the culprit. A young Army doctor called Christian Eijkman was left behind in Indonesia to continue researches into the new "find." After making little progress for two years, Eijkman happened to notice that his hospital laboratory's chickens, which were kept for experimental purposes, appeared to be showing some of the symptoms of beri-beri: general muscular weakness and an inability to walk. The doctor thought they had caught his "germ" — until suddenly the chickens recovered their health.

The essential insight came with Eijkman's realization that the recovery coincided with a change in the birds' diet. The chickens were discovered to have been temporarily fed on left-over rice from the bowls of the hospital staff and patients: it was white rice which had given the chickens beri-beri, and a return to their customary brown rice cured them. Beri-beri, as Eijkman and his successor Gerrit Grijns saw, was caused by deficiency and not germs; there was something in the bran which polished rice lacked; without it, people and animals living largely on rice became seriously debilitated. Beri-beri had been a rare disease until the mid-nineteenth century, when the super-efficient truncated-cone rice mill was invented.

In 1912, Frederick Hopkins demonstrated that what he called "accessory factors of the diet" were absolutely essential to human health, but that these factors were something entirely different from fats, carbohydrates, or minerals. Casimir Funk coined a word for the mysterious life-enhancing substances: he called them "vitamines" from *vita*, meaning "life"; and once they were given a name (the "e" was eventually dropped) research began in earnest. The anti-beri-beri factor was finally isolated by Robert R. Williams in the United States; it was vitamin B_1, now commonly called *thiamine*. Williams and his team of assistants managed, after years of hard work, to find the components and chemical connections which comprise the substance, and, in 1936, thiamine was artificially synthesized. It is now routinely added to commercially processed rice and wheat products.

For thousands of years the peoples of India have been parboiling their rice. It has recently been found that this preparation in fact preserves vitamins in the grain: it makes possible the removal of the bran without destroying most of the nutritional value of rice. Parboiled rice is cleaned and soaked, steamed, dried, and only then it is milled. In the process it becomes yellowish in colour and hardens. This increases its imperviousness to insects, and also renders later overmilling unlikely. Foreign matter is washed and steamed away so that storage becomes safer; cracks and stresses in the grain are repaired in the steaming process, making the rice less likely to break. Most importantly of all, parboiling drives the vitamins in rice bran into the core of the grain and so stores them for human consumption. The process avoids the problem of "enriched" rice, where vitamins are coated onto the grains and a lot of the goodness tends to wash off in the cooking.

The word *parboiled* often confuses shoppers: it sounds as if the product is pre-cooked or "quick-cooking," whereas parboiled rice in fact takes about ten minutes longer to cook than raw white rice does. (Strictly speaking, parboiled rice "hydrates.") The American product, converted rice, is usually a modification of the method which includes freezing the rice slowly so that ice crystals create a porous and "quick-cooking" structure for the gelatinized starch. The precooked "instant" rices on the market may have been puffed so that holes are introduced into the grain into which hot water can readily penetrate.

INNOCENCE AND EXPERIENCE

In the 1890s a group of German physicists discovered a method of making starch easier to study under a microscope: they heated rice in a test tube until the grains expanded. Publication of these experiments attracted the attention of an American biochemist named Alexander P. Anderson, who was looking for ways of increasing the digestibility of starch. He travelled to Munich in 1895, to see the new technique for himself. His German colleagues warned him not to seal the end of the test tube during the heating process, or the steam pressure would explode it.

Anderson, still in Munich, could hardly wait to try heating rice in a sealed tube. The tube shattered, sprayed glass all over the laboratory, and out came puffed rice more than eight times the size of the raw grain – "as good a puffed rice as was ever puffed anywhere," Anderson declared. After his return to America, he began years of exceedingly dangerous experiments. "It's a wonder that he didn't blow himself up," his friends said, and in 1902 workers refused to go near his workshop after a huge blast had torn out the floor. He eventually tried stuffing his rice into an old cannon left over from the Spanish-American War –and a modern brainwave was born.

The public first got a view of Quaker Puffed Rice at the World's Fair of 1904, when eight bronze cannons exploded rice over the heads of a huge crowd. A cousin of the Mikado of Japan was present, to report back home on a possible new market for rice. Today, puffed rice and puffed wheat are still exploded in a machine which, in spite of safety devices and its huge size, is still essentially a gun, from which puffed grain erupts with a roar. The steam pressure causes an estimated 125 million explosions within each grain of rice.

In the early days, puffed rice was coated in caramel and sold like popcorn. It was a long time before the product was marketed as a breakfast cereal, with the slogan "Shot from Guns" and a picture in the publicity material of "Prof. A. P. Anderson," whose craggy professorial face, broad forehead, and octogon-shaped rimless glasses turned out to be an ad-man's dream: the combination of Science and the Spectacular proved one of the great winners in advertising history. At the New York World's Fair in 1965 a man-and-wife circus team had themselves shot out of a cannon four times daily to provide publicity for Puffed Rice and its brother-product, Puffed Wheat.

Oven-crisped puffed rice is much more popular than the plain type these days. Breakfast cereals, which now quite often mix rice with other grains, constitute a large proportion of the market for rice in North America. The American brewing industry increasingly uses rice and corn instead of malted barley for making beer, especially since "light" food has begun to be promoted as healthy. Rice and corn are, of course, much cheaper and easier to mechanize than barley malt; and manufacturers say they are good for "stability and uniformity in the product." They also give beer the bland taste and the pale colour which the concept of "lightness" suggests.

But by far the most important use for rice in the western world is as baby food. There is hardly one of us alive who has not depended on rice during the months in which we were weaned from milk to solids. As we have seen, rice is mild, bland, easily-digestible, and non-allergenic. Ever since baby foods began to be prepared commercially in the United States in 1921, rice has been an ingredient of almost every package and jar of them. In fact, rice is thought to have been the very first infant food on earth: women may have learned to shorten their two-to-four-year nursing period by inventing rice gruel and feeding it to their babies.

It was women, too, almost certainly who discovered how to turn rice into alcohol, probably by chewing slightly and spitting out the grains, as is still commonly done to induce the fermentation of cereals in many parts of the world. Since cereals can be used to make alcohol while tubers like taro cannot, the arrival of a taste for strong drinks is another of the momentous societal changes which take place when there is a switch from root to cereal crops.

Rice wine, some form of which is drunk wherever rice is grown, is called *sake* in Japan. The word is an abbreviation of *sakae*, "prosperity," which is associated in men's minds with the "merry feeling" induced by the brew. Sake is the object of extremely careful handling, as are alcoholic drinks in most cultures. At the gate of every Zen Buddhist temple in Japan, inscriptions on a stone pillar warn that garlic and wine are never to be admitted over the threshold; Eison, the great pioneer of Zen, did everything he could to spread tea-drinking as an alternative to taking sake in Japan. Sake has, however, been called the sacramental wine of the much older Shinto religion. Shinto has a number of sake gods, and most weddings in Japan are celebrated according to Shinto rites, where the exchange and drinking of cups of sake seal the marriage contract. Many kinds of occasion require the drinking of sake in Japan, from the Dolls' Festival every March third to the solemn Viewing of the Full Moon in autumn, which is accompanied by the consumption of pale gold sake and moon-shaped white dumplings, together with the recital of one's own specially-composed poetry.

Rice wine is really a still beer. The first step in making it is the creation of a starter for sake yeast. A carefully mixed culture of yellow-green *Aspergillus oryzae* spores is scattered onto steamed rice, and this creates *koji*, the equivalent of malt for beer. This is added to more steamed rice and fermented for about twenty days. What types and blends of rice are used, when and at what stages to add the *koji*, and at what temperature, are all crucial elements of the art of sake brewing, where various fragrances and complex tastes can be created by skilful practitioners. Pale yellow or white liquid sake is then filtered out of the dense mash and put away, carefully shielded from sunlight, to mature. Sake does not improve with keeping beyond a year, and light can darken the liquid and ruin its taste. It is best drunk warm, as close as possible to 50° C.(122° F.) – a circumstance which reduces the drink's original alcohol level, which is between 14 and 18 per cent.

The alcoholic powers of sake, however, in addition to the bottles made of opaque porcelain for the exclusion of light, and even the tiny cups in which the drink is customarily served, are all pressed into service in the sophisticated and intense social exercise of the Japanese Business Dinner. The Japanese anthropologist Harumi Befu has explained, from the inside, one of the rituals which Japan has evolved in order to enact and celebrate this society's insistence both on close communal interaction, and on clearly marked, formal assignations of hierarchy, obligation, and honour.

Japanese business dinners must take place outside the sacrosanct privacy of the home. By preference, however, the restaurant chosen should be a traditional Japanese one, which offers several advantages over a western-style eating place: a separate room can be booked in advance especially for a "business group"; a professional female overseer of dinners undertakes to keep the conversation bubbling and everyone's spirits high; the possibility of ordering everything in advance means that there is no menu and that therefore no distinct and separate choices need be made; and, above all, no money need change hands in front of the company. In this manner as much as possible of the character of home entertainment is preserved, and the impersonality of a restaurant *venue* is turned into a carefully orchestrated opportunity for human contact and interaction.

During dinner everyone must drink copious draughts of sake and enter into the spirit of things by allowing himself to come quickly under its influence; the professional dinner-overseer, who drinks very little, encourages the guests by appearing herself to become merrier and more jocular as the meal proceeds. Warm sake is not enormously alcoholic, but Japanese dinner guests seem to succumb to it surprisingly quickly. Certainly the Japanese, who eat a lot less fat than westerners do, are more easily affected by alcohol – but the main point is that getting tight is part of playing the game. Those who do not get completely drunk and go to sleep will suddenly become quite sober and capable of looking after themselves and their weaker friends when it is time to go home. There are rules about when and where one may get drunk, and *looking* as if one is drunk may in certain circumstances be an urbane and con-siderate social ploy. The behaviour of people drinking alcohol shows enormous variation from culture to culture; societal pressures almost always control it, and solo drinking bouts are for this reason almost universally dangerous and deliberately discouraged.

At a Japanese dinner one never pours sake for oneself. Pouring is done by guests for each other, as a sign of social awareness and good will. Sake cups for dinner parties are tiny, so that the service must be constantly repeated, and everyone must be on the watch for the chance to be neigh-bourly and fill somebody else's cup. Secondly, one who is being served sake must not leave the cup on the table, but must lift it in his hand towards the bottle. This obliges the receiver of the service to notice the action, and to thank his benefactor both during and after it.

The opaque bottle with its large mouth is rather difficult to manage, because it is impossible to know how much sake is inside, and how far it has to be tipped in order to pour it. The tiny cup held in someone else's hand is hard to fill with no spills – and spilling is very bad manners. Add to this difficulty the fact that all the guests become tighter and more fuddled as the party progresses, and the action of constantly pouring sake for others becomes quite a feat. The intense concentration and co-operation required is, of course, the object of the exercise. Con-versation, laughing, joking, and also precisely timed and elaborate social scoring and impression-making continue all the while. Manoeuvres with sake cups include the feigned refusal: the receiver of a neighbour's attentions raises his cup to prevent its being filled yet again; the pourer retaliates by raising his bottle at the same moment and pouring nonetheless. "Too much" must be ceremoniously refused; cups must however be filled; and above all, no matter how drunk the contestants, nothing must be spilled.

People of lower status often ask for the privilege of pouring for people of higher status and may move from their positions to do so. This makes it possible for converse and contact to occur between lower and higher stations; otherwise the seating arrangements might keep the various ranks apart throughout the meal. When one has drunk a cupful of sake he offers the empty cup to someone else. While pouring is often from lower to higher in status, cup-offering begins from higher to lower. The response is to offer a cup back to the powerful one – either the same cup or that of another person. The action symbolizes the reaffirmation of a pact between the two and a salute across the boundary separating social ranks.

The upshot of a whole sequence of such moves and counter-moves is that cups travel up and down among the company, "binding" them together; and those who have received the most homage end up with the largest number of cups standing before them, while people of the lowest status have none. The amount of honour offered a man is thus given tangible and visible expression. Cups are provided in the centre of the group for this stage of the proceedings, to be taken by the cupless so that drinking may continue.

The whole dinner party is an improvised drama, with roles of varying importance, elaborate stage business, props, and theatrical conventions. At the same time it is a deadly serious affair where tremendous decisions may be made, well camouflaged by the decorative façade, but understood by all. Everyone knows the rules, is made to participate, and indeed contributes to the script, and everyone is both actor and audience.

The Japanese often say that having a western businessman present at one of their dinner parties is utterly exhausting. Hospitality decrees that the foreign guest, after all, has the principal role. But he is precisely the one who has no idea of how to play his part – often no idea, even, that he is actually on stage. The others have to make-believe that his *faux pas* are charming improvised variations on the agreed scenario. They have to "carry" the clumsy westerner and simultaneously prevent him from finding out that he is an utterly inept performer. He probably does not know how to negotiate a deal without making appalling errors of taste – or even how to get drunk in the prescribed and courteous manner. He has not been brought up, trained, sensitized, toned and strengthened, beautified and polished by the complex social exigencies of rice.

CHAPTER SIX

Lettuce: The Vicissitudes of Salad

*I*N THE COURSE of the year 1984, the food industry in the United States launched 3,340 new products; another several thousand bright ideas and cunning new methods for preparing, combining, preserving, and packaging foods were patented and awaiting buyers and promoters. Novelties included Pizza in a Cone (bought frozen, to be heated in one's microwave: obviates crusts and bending slices when eaten in the hand; flanges on the cone are provided to catch drips), Snack Pellets (long-lasting, compact, and amenable to any flavouring; can be shipped anywhere; need only to be fried and they puff up into a "finger food"), and many artificial flavourings such as Condensed Milk Taste (for fudge) and new varieties of liquid wood smokes (lending a barbecued taste and red-brown colour to anything: one factory already produces eight hundred thousand gallons of liquid smokes a year).

"New products are to a business enterprise what raindrops are to a parched lawn." The principle, according to modern processing tycoons, applies to food as much as to anything else. A few ancient foodstuffs remain intractable to modern inventiveness, however. These are mostly vegetables which require, annoyingly, to be eaten "fresh." Many vegetables respond, it is true, to dehydration, preservation in liquid, or freezing. But lettuce, one of the most popular foods in the modern western diet, remains so far difficult to change or to treat. Something has been achieved in the direction of toughness and staving off rot: modern hard crisp lettuce heads can survive much mechanized handling and achieve shelf-lives as long as three weeks. But on the farm, workers are, for the time being, still needed for supplementary weeding of the lettuce rows and to inspect the growing plants for harvest readiness, because lettuces in the field refuse, in spite of every attention, to mature simultaneously. Attempts genetically to square the spherical lettuce, such as have already given us the tough and boxy tomato, have failed: the lettuce head remains round and therefore awkward to wrap by machine. Even the search for a flat-bottomed lettuce has so far been in vain. Lettuces, especially leaf lettuces, still last a disappointingly short time after they have been harvested; and freezing one can quickly turn it into a limp and slimy rag.

But everybody in the western world loves lettuce, and regularly, even ritually, eats it. Lettuce is often the only green vegetable on the menu (as it is on ours), and for many people, it may be the only greenstuff commonly found in their diet. It provides an easy and pleasant way to alleviate any guilt arising from the realization that meat and carbohydrates have yet again dominated the meal. Curly lettuce leaves are a universally acceptable device for decorating other foods, and sandwiches rely heavily upon them for freshness, juiciness, and crunch. The leaf is non-fattening and usually eaten raw, and eating it is therefore virtuous for the body-conscious. *Vitamins* and *minerals* are at present such prestigious words that the advisers of food businessmen openly urge that the terms be used in ads and on packages wherever feasible; and lettuce, apart from water, contains almost nothing but vitamins and minerals.

Lettuce, in other words, has modern mythologies very much on its side. It merits respect from the food industry even though relatively little can be done to "enhance" it or to "move" sales of it. The nickname for lettuce in the trade is "green gold." Iceberg lettuce, as grown in California for a mass market, is the basis of a vast and specialized industry, requiring enormous amounts of capital, complex organization for optimum speed of delivery, and detailed co-ordination with dealers and supermarkets across the North American continent. The Californian lettuce head has recently begun to reach international markets as well. If the irradiation of vegetables becomes an acceptable method of preserving them, lettuce might even begin a new phase in its long, unassuming, but doggedly successful economic history.

FOR AND AGAINST SEX

The word *lettuce* is from the plural of the French *laitue* (early French *laictue*), a derivative of the Latin *lactuca*, meaning "milky." The sap of lettuce looks very much like milk, especially in wild varieties. Lettuce is one of 12,500 species of plants with milky sap or latex. When rubber supplies were low during the Second World War, *Lactuca virosa*, or the strong-smelling prickly lettuce, was investigated to see if its latex could partially replace that of the Brazilian *hevea* or rubber tree. The rubber yield of lettuce was unfortunately too low to be useful.

For thousands of years people have speculated on the powers and uses of lettuce sap. The earliest known meaning attached to the substance is its association in the mythology of ancient Egypt with semen. The lettuce of the Egyptians was tall and pointed, with leaves flattened against a central phallic stem. It was sacred to the god Min, in whose processions growing tubs or "gardens" of lettuce were ceremonially carried. Min's main jurisdictions were over vegetation and procreation. His sacred animal was a white bull fed copiously on lettuces to increase his sexual potency.

The beginning of the annual Egyptian harvest festival was the Coming Forth of Min, when the god's statues were carried out of his temples. Min was a stiff hieratic figure, with legs bound tightly together like those of a mummy. He was one of the oldest gods in the Egyptian pantheon, and his representation reflects a very early sculptural style. He had an erect phallus, long, thin, and elegant. He wore a skullcap with two tall feathers and two streamers hanging down his back, and wielded a flail in his raised hand. Min was repeatedly painted by his priests with a black bituminous substance, to symbolize the fertile soil of Egypt and the promise of vegetable regeneration to come. The Pharoah ceremonially reaped grain at the harvest festival and then solemnly approached the god with an offering of two large lettuces, holding one in each hand. This scene is the subject of carved reliefs from Egyptian tombs of many periods; the earliest known example is about forty-five hundred years old. Pharoah ritually begot his heir at Min's festival, probably identifying himself with the god as he did so. Later Min was returned to his shrine, which was quite small and surmounted by a tall leaf-shaped fan sacred to the god. Min's house was surrounded by a garden full of lettuces.

There is still a popular belief in the Nile Valley that lettuce promotes fertility in males. This idea appears to have been preserved from the time of the ancient Egyptians, because for well over twenty-five hundred years a completely different opinion about lettuce has obtained in the rest of the Mediterranean region where the lettuce plant originated. A minor tradition makes lettuce an emblem for female sexuality (Alciati's *Emblemata libellus*, 1546 and 1551, calls lettuce an *amuletum Veneris*), and the same idea is to be found in Sumerian texts of the third millennium BC, where the goddess Inanna's pubic hair is compared to lettuce leaves. But on the whole, there has been staunch agreement for a long time that lettuce is cold, soporific, and the very opposite of aphrodisiac. "Lettuse," as Andrew Boorde put it in 1542, "doth extynct veneryous [*i.e.*, sexual] actes."

Modern chemists confirm that lettuce juice, in particular the milky sap of the wild *Lactuca virosa*, does contain a hypnotic (inducer of sleep) or narcotic similar to opium. When lettuce runs prematurely to seed a chemical reaction takes place which increases the soporific effect. *Lactucarium*, or lettuce juice, has been used for centuries as a calmant in cases of insomnia, nervous disorders, rheumatism, coughs, colic, and seasickness. It was thickened and then dried into white cakes, to be prescribed to patients, together with poppy seed, before surgery and to alleviate pain. Crops of *Lactuca virosa* are still grown, notably in France, for making tinctures which are prescribed for coughs, and for bronchial and asthmatic conditions. The calming effect may also inhibit sexual desire.

Since sex in human beings is not merely a mechanical matter, the beliefs surrounding both aphrodisiacs and anaphrodisiacs help to determine our response to them. People have always tended to attribute to vegetation medicinal properties which correspond to the appearance of the plant in question. Plants with lung-shaped leaves, for instance, were eaten for bronchial complaints; consuming twinned fruit was thought to give rise to the birth of twins; and walnut-kernels look like little brains nestling in their nuts, which made them appropriate medicine for brain-fevers. The medieval version of this kind of thinking was called the Doctrine of Signatures. It held that the medicinal qualities in plants were made visible as "signatures of Natures owne impression," and writers quite commonly express the wish that human beings bore similar imprints so that one could tell a person's worth by some sign on his person.

The ancient Greeks knew a lettuce which they considered to be especially useful for inhibiting sex. It was squat and round (without a head however, for heads were bred later), and with very short roots. It was the opposite, that is, of the tall phallus-shaped lettuce. Pythagoras especially recommended this plant to his ascetic disciples, calling it *eunuch,* a word which literally means "keeping seductive women under control." (The Persians had castrated male servants – eunuchs – to perform this office in the King's harem.) Women, we are told, preferred to call the plant *astutis,* "incapable of an erection."

If one had unwittingly eaten an aphrodisiac and wished to escape its spell, a lettuce was always the obvious antidote. On the other hand, a character in an ancient Greek comedy, the *Impotents* (*Astutoi*) of Euboulos, warns his wife that she has "only herself to blame" if she serves him lettuce for supper. Lettuce in mixed salads could be counterbalanced by herbs which promoted sexual libido, in order to achieve a balanced after-effect. Rocket or *arugula* has for centuries been thought a powerful aphrodisiac and therefore appropriate to be eaten with lettuce. "Eat cress" was an ancient Greek rebuke in the guise of advice to dull and sluggish people – and watercress was another complement to salads based on lettuce. The Romans called watercress *nasturtium.* (The flower we now call by this name is the Peruvian cress, both the leaves and the flowers of which are excellent in salads.) The word *nasturtium* derives from the Latin for "nostril-torment," which describes the action of pungent watercress; prickly nostrils were thought to portend a general influx of vigour.

Another "signature" may have strengthened the reputation of lettuce as a plant which induced sterility: the milk in lettuce was associated with women's milk. Wet-nurses kept up their milk supply by drinking plenty of lettuce soup. The plant was often given in order to help a mother's milk come after giving birth; interestingly enough, the American prickly lettuce was called "milk leaf" by the Meskwaki Indians and prescribed by them for the same purpose. The calming effect of lettuce latex may indeed have helped the mother's milk supply. Breast-feeding is a form of natural birth-control, and milk can therefore be perceived as an inhibitor of fertility. Young wives who habitually ate lettuce were warned that it might prevent them from becoming pregnant. Also milk, even vegetable "milk," is easily perceived as "female" and not, therefore, a promoter of male sexual urges.

Lettuce is 90-95 per cent water, and is for this reason greatly prized in desert climates. Along the roads leading out of the city of Baghdad are many stalls selling lettuces. People stop their cars, buy lettuces, and consume them whole, just as they are. It is said that eating unsalted lettuce quenches thirst for much longer than drinking water does. (Lettuce has been known as a vegetable in Iraq since at least the third millennium BC; and the scribes of King Merodach-Baladan in the seventh century BC recorded lettuces growing on the terraces of the Hanging Gardens of Babylon.)

Yet another reason for the anaphrodisiac qualities of lettuce is to be found in the system of humoral medicine, where lettuce is classed as cold, largely because of its liquid character. Humoral medicine dates back – in the west at least – to what is called the "hippocratic complex" of the ancient Greeks; the Arabs inherited it from the Greeks and Romans and taught it to the Spaniards, who carried it with them to Central and South America in the sixteenth century. There the "hippocratic complex" was accepted without any difficulty by the Aztecs and other Indian cultures because they already had extraordinarily similar sets of beliefs of their own. In China and Malaysia people have come, apparently independently, to the very same kinds of conclusions: the *yang-yin* system was discussed in the chapter on rice.

The world, according to this system, is divided into a series of diametrically opposing principles: up and down, light and dark, male and female, hot and cold, dry and wet, and so on. Harmony and balance must be found between these opposites, or turbulence and pain will be the result. Human health is, like everything else in the universe, a question of balance; sickness is the body out of kilter, and medicine a matter of compensating for excess and deficiency, chiefly by means of diet.

Some diseases and conditions of the body are "hot": among these are fevers, burns, and pregnancy. A wise person will help his body by eating "cold" things to counteract his "hot" condition. Everything edible has a value: for instance, in the system prevailing among Nahuatl Indians in the southern valley of Mexico, all vegetables are "fresh," that is, cold (because they are juicy and grow in well-watered ground and anything that has to do with water is preeminently cold), yet slightly warmed by the sun (obviously hot). Vegetables, then, are cold but not overwhelmingly so, and can be used to cool an over-warmed body. Exceptions to the rule about vegetables include peas, which are considered entirely cold, and chilis and onions, which are clearly hot. Hot soup is classified as "cold" because it is liquid; whereas ice is "hot" because it is hard, burns to the touch, and contact with it turns vegetation brown. Methods of cooking (boiling versus frying, for example) can temper the heat or the cold of foods.

Within this system, lettuce is invariably cold: juicy, eaten raw, a "cool" green in colour, requiring plenty of moisture in order to grow. Because it is cold, it goes with "female" in the schema of opposites, together with "wet," "dark," and so on: it is diametrically opposed to all that is hot, dry, bright, and masculine. Lettuce is "fresh" rather than dangerously cold, however: as John Gerard wrote in his *Herball* (1633), "Lettuce is a cold and moist pot-herbe, yet not in the extream degree of cold or moisture, but altogether moderately, for otherwise it were not to be eaten." Even lettuce seeds were cold; pharmaceutical books of the seventeenth and eighteenth centuries constantly call for the Four Lesser Cold Seeds, of endive, succory, purslane, and lettuce. ("Lesser" meant smaller than the Four Greater Cold Seeds, of cucumber, gourds, melons, and citruls or yellow melons.)

Insomnia (making one sweaty and giving rise to thrashing movements) is very hot – so lettuce is the obvious cooling remedy.

> If you need rest,
> Lettuce and cowslip wine *probatum est*

wrote Alexander Pope. Lettuce, therefore, is "sedative" from one medical point of view, and "cold," therefore sleep-inducing, from another. But then, "cold" and "still" can easily be seen as homogeneous. "A dish of lettice and a clear Fountain," wrote Jeremy Taylor in 1651, "can cool all my Heat." Passion is fiery, and cooling lettuce will dampen the flame.

In the Greek myth of Adonis, the young hunting hero is born of the incestuous union of Myrrha with her father. After giving birth to Adonis, Myrrha was metamorphosed into the tree which gives the heady perfume, myrrh. The myrrh tree and its scent were thought of as hot, dry, and incorruptible – the food of gods, not men. Adonis died after being gored by a wild boar in a lettuce bed, where his lover, the goddess Aphrodite, had hidden him. (Phaon, in a different story, was a ferryman who was made young and beautiful by Aphrodite, and who made himself irresistibly seductive by rubbing himself with perfume. He was hidden by the goddess from the husbands he had cuckolded in a lettuce bed, and there among the herbs of impotency he died.)

The story of Adonis, according to the Classical scholar Marcel Detienne, is about what lies outside marriage: the hero, doomed to his premature death, is born of hot, dry, incestuous, and godlike myrrh, and ends his life in cold, wet, sub-human lettuce. (The Greeks called one lettuce variety *adoneis*.) The plants of marriage, completely different from either lettuce or myrrh, were the cereals which men raise by the sweat of their brow: cultivated plants, civilized, balanced and domestic. Adonis was a seducer, sometimes above marriage, sometimes below it, either godlike or sub-human, and doomed therefore to impermanence and no issue.

The Adonia in ancient Athens was a festival for courtesans. It took place during the Dog Days, the hottest time of the year. The courtesans would dance with their lovers on the flat rooftops of their houses, where they also grew miniature "gardens of Adonis": pots planted with lettuce, fennel, wheat, and barley. After shooting up quickly, the plants would shrivel in the heat and were then thrown into a river or the sea. Spices, on the other hand, came to maturity under the Dog Star, and these the courtesans carried down from the rooftops and piled onto incense-burners in honour of Aphrodite and Adonis. The "gardens of Adonis," Detienne explains, were like Adonis himself – not serious or built to last, not real agriculture, and not like marriage, which is what human beings are meant for.

SALAD

When the festival of Passover was instituted by the Lord God in Egypt, Moses and Aaron were told exactly how the Jews were to commemorate the escape from bondage which they were about to experience: a lamb without blemish must be ritually killed and then eaten "not . . . raw, nor sodden at all with water, but roast with fire." It must be accompanied with "unleavened bread, and with bitter herbs." The bitter herbs in question are commonly agreed to have been chicory, watercress, sorrel, dandelion leaves, and lettuce. All of these were common plants and could easily be found in the wild. All of them, especially when wild, are bitter. It was only much later (200 AD at the earliest) that the bitterness was first said to symbolize the embitterment of the Jews when they lived in Egypt. They had no reason to dislike eating bread with bitter herbs, as any gourmet who has tried it will testify. The meaning of the ritual expressed most importantly the speed with which they had to leave: "with your loins girded, your shoes on your feet, and your staff in your hand; and ye shall eat it in haste." There was no time to let the bread rise or the vegetables cook. Only the simplest and quickest preparations were possible, and therefore ritually appropriate, for the meal of the Lord's Passover.

Because lettuce is usually eaten raw, it constitutes, in the modern world as it did in the ancient, a "fast food." This important office it holds in addition to its status as a fresh, green, crunchy element in sandwiches and hamburgers, and as the background to every kind of cold plate. The modern "salad bar," offering variety as well as personal choice made on the spot, virtue for those who know it is estimable to "think thin," and cash-and-carry speed, is a perfect expression of several of our basic cultural values. "Something salted" is the meaning of the word "salad" (from *sal*, the Latin for *salt*). So important is lettuce both as one of the ingredients in salads and as alone constituting a salad, that words related to *salad* have become more commonly used for lettuce in many languages than are cognates of the term *lettuce* itself.

In case salad is being served together with the meat, says Emily Post, the doyenne of etiquette, each person should be provided with a separate plate for it, otherwise the gravy might mix with the dressing into "an unsavory soup," and the lettuce will wilt on the plate heated for meat. Wilted salad is utterly unacceptable: everyone wants freshness and either pliancy or crispness where raw leaves are concerned. (Lettuce can also be stewed and eaten as a soft vegetable, which converts it into something belonging to a quite different category.) The dressing we put on lettuce wilts it very quickly, which is the reason why salad must be tossed just before it is eaten.

The rigidity of lettuce depends on the hydrostatic pressure of the water in each of its plant cells. When the cells are full they become turgid and the lettuce is succulent, but when water intake is exceeded by water loss the cells collapse and the lettuce turns limp. (Iceberg lettuce, to which this rarely happens, has been especially bred for tough cell walls.) The osmotic pressure of vinegar or lemon juice and oil destroys the cell wall's ability to hold in its water, which pours out to dilute the dressing; heat gradually weakens the membranes by coagulating their protein; freezing punctures them by forming sharp ice crystals inside the cells (something similar happens to human ears and fingers when they become frozen). Water can pass by osmosis right through lettuce cell walls and replenish the liquid inside them, which is why lettuces soaked in cold water firm up so satisfactorily, provided the cell walls have not been damaged.

The bitter taste of lettuce is due to an aromatic compound called *lactupicrin*, found in the sap. Wild lettuce can be very bitter indeed, but the cultivated varieties of the plant, *Lactuca sativa*, have little bitterness left in them, although their taste becomes more acrid as they become overgrown. The stalks of bolted (overgrown) lettuce, which reach sixty centimetres (2 ft.) high and more if they are left long enough, were once sliced and boiled in a sugar syrup to produce a popular candy, sweet but faintly bitter, like the angelica which is still commonly preserved in the same fashion. A favourite method of making leaf vegetables more succulent and less bitter is that of blanching them – tying up the leaves as they approach maturity so that they whiten as they grow. This used to be a common practice in raising lettuce.

Lettuce is a plant of the daisy or *compositae* family (its blossoms contain many small yellow flowers crowded together), and it almost certainly originated in the Mediterranean area, probably in Asia Minor. Wild lettuce still grows all over temperate and southern Europe, and is described by one botanist as "a humble, obscure, roadside weed, inoffensive but unattractive." Cultivated lettuce quite often escapes from gardens and takes again to the wild. The three main kinds of wild lettuce, all of them capable of exchanging genes, are *serriola* or "prickly" lettuce (incorrectly but commonly called *scariola*, from which comes the word *escarole* for curly chicory or Batavian endive), the lettuce thought to have been one of the "bitter herbs" of the Hebrews; *virosa*, "smelly" lettuce, a larger version of *serriola* (it can grow over one and a half metres [5 ft.] tall) with a strong smell; and *saligna*, which means "like willow." From these evolved, with considerable help from mankind, the cultivated lettuce, *sativa*.

Much of the lettuce grown in the ancient world was raised for its seed, from which a delicious vegetable oil was extracted; indeed it is very likely that lettuce was cultivated in the first place for its seed, large quantities of which have been found in ancient Egyptian tombs. Lettuce oil was one of the favourite salad oils in the Classical world, and it is still used for this purpose in Egypt and in other parts of Africa. In 1954, a group of American scientists used seeds of the Grand Rapids leaf lettuce to show how light controls germination and dormancy in certain kinds of plants: red light promotes and far-red light inhibits the emergence of a shoot by means of their effects upon phytochrome, a protein plant pigment which is sensitive to light, at a photosensitive site in the seed. (In nature, most seeds are not covered by soil and germinate in the light.)

Lettuce is self-fertilizing by the sexual mode and hence has enormous gene plasticity. (It is not, like its relative the dandelion, locked into the evolutionary *cul de sac* of constantly similar asexual reproduction from an unfertilized diploid egg cell.) Lettuce is capable, therefore, of endless variety in size, shape, texture, and colour. Its versatility has made it the object of devoted attention by horticulturists through the ages. They have arrived at hundreds of varieties, which fall into four main classes. Asparagus lettuce or "celtuce" is grown for its thick succulent stem (the leaves are unpalatable); it is popular in China but grown in the west mostly as a novelty. Leaf lettuce is fragile and smooth-textured; it comes in many varieties including one with oak-leaf-shaped foliage and some tinged with red. The plant does not run to seed but produces a succession of leaves for cutting. *Radicchio* was apparently found, until recently, only in Italy. It is a speciality of Treviso in the Veneto region, although now it is being exported (with consequent deterioration in its quality) as a luxury product to many countries of the world. In its fresh and native state it is small and a beautiful variegated red – one Italian poet calls it "a flower you can eat" – with a texture like a delicate romaine.

The third class of *Lactuca sativa*, head or cabbage lettuce, falls into two types: butterhead (with soft, thick, and oily leaves) which includes Boston, Bibb, and many prestigious European types; and crisphead (hard-headed and crunchy), of which the most famous variety today is Iceberg, known as Webb's Wonder in Britain. Butterhead lettuces are what are called "truck crops" – nothing to do with trucks, but from the French *troquer*, "to barter or deal in small lots": they cannot be transported long distances without suffering, so they have tended so far to be grown close to their customers. Even in North America, small market-gardeners still deal in these vegetables locally. Iceberg lettuces can put up with comparatively rough treatment, and have therefore become a huge economic proposition; giant food businesses truck these (in the automobile sense) for thousands of miles to reach their points of sale.

The fourth class, cos or romaine lettuce, is tall and crisp. The name *romaine* is said by many to have originated when the lettuce was introduced into France from Italy by the poet Rabelais in 1537; alternatively it is said to date from its arrival in Avignon with the Popes when they took up residence there. (The latter explanation seems to have the backing of *Le ménagier de Paris*, about 1390.) The name *cos*, which is usually taken to refer to the Greek island, may attach to this lettuce because the Romans found it on Cos, and because the ancient Greek physician Hippocrates came from there. A more likely explanation is that *cos* means "big" (*gros* in French), and is the same, though phonetically altered by common usage, as the first syllables in *gooseberry* and *horseradish*.

King Cambyses of Persia (about 550 BC), who had not only married two of his sisters but had murdered many of his relatives as well, was accused by a wife of having stripped all the leaves from his house as if it was a lettuce, and of having left only the stalk. She showed Cambyses the bare stem of a lettuce and asked him whether he liked it better with or without the leaves. Cambyses angrily kicked her for producing this tactless parable, causing her to have a miscarriage from which she died. Herodotus thus gives us the information that Persians, as we would expect, knew the lettuce well. Greeks cultivated it assiduously too, none more so than the philosopher Aristoxenos of Cyrene, who practised the system of thought called Hedonism. A passionate food-lover – almost as devoted as Pithyllos, described as "The Picky," who kept his tongue in a bag between meals to preserve its sensitivity – Aristoxenos was so effete as to water his lettuces with salad-dressing the evening before he wanted to eat them, while they were still in the ground. The following morning he would pick them and exclaim that they were white pastries sent to him by Mother Earth.

The Greeks and Romans grew one kind of lettuce with flat stalks that were so tall, broad, and strong that they were used to make trellises and garden gates. The Romans had a great many named varieties of lettuce, and never failed to introduce their favourite kinds into the colonies of their empire. A result of this is that most European languages call lettuce by a name derived from the Latin *lactuca*. The medicinal uses of lettuce were highly regarded. The great physician Antonius Musa once cured the Emperor Augustus by prescribing lettuce, in opposition to a previous luckless doctor who had tried "hot" remedies. Musa was voted a statue in his honour, to stand next to that of the god of healing,

Aesculapius, and Augustus ordered that supplies of lettuce be kept pickled in vinegar and honey so that they might be available as medicine when out of season.

Exactly when lettuces were induced, by intensive selection of mutations, to form heads or tight balls of leaves folded upon each other, is as yet a mystery. The Romans did not know head lettuces, and neither, as far as we can tell, did people living in the age of Charlemagne (about 800 AD). In all likelihood, it was monastic gardeners, responsible for supplying a largely vegetarian diet and possessing a good deal of centralised horticultural expertise, in part inherited from the Romans, who produced both head cabbage (developed from kale and collards sometime during the Middle Ages) and head lettuce. The earliest known mention of *Lactuca capitata* (with an illustration) is in the *Kräuterbuch* of Leonard Fuchs in 1543. Head lettuce is dependent on man for its survival because the plant's tightly wrapped head restricts the development of inflorescence unless it is artificially aided.

It was the Dutch and Flemish who began market-gardening on a large commercial scale. From the early fifteenth century onwards, Amsterdam was famous for its vegetables as well as its dairy produce; the city went so far as to exchange its "night soil" (human waste) for garden produce in order to encourage agriculture, much as the Chinese have traditionally done for rice. Catherine Parr, Henry VIII's last wife, used regularly to send messengers to Holland when she required a salad; presumably the Dutch had plants to offer which were unobtainable in England. By the end of the sixteenth century the Dutch and Flemish were exporting all sorts of garden produce, including "salad herbes," to other countries in northern Europe. An influx to England of Dutch, Flemish, and Walloon refugees after Alva's reign of terror (1568-72), did a great deal to improve the agricultural practices of the English and to better their diet, which had never been strong on greens.

At the end of the seventeenth century, John Evelyn wrote a book on salads, called *Acetaria* (things in vinegared dressing): *A Discourse of Sallets*, in which he extols the reign of lettuce over the salad bowl. "And certainly 'tis not for nothing," he wrote, "that our Garden-Lovers, and *Brothers of the Sallet*, have been so exceedingly Industrious to cultivate this Noble Plant, and multiply its *Species*; for . . . by reason of its soporiferous quality, lettuce ever was, and still continues the principal foundation of the universal tribe of Sallets, which is to cool and refresh, besides its other properties," which include inducements to "morals, temperance, and chastity."

In the early nineteenth century, Sydney Smith wrote his famous versified recipe for salad dressing, which ends with a paean of praise for the result:

> Oh, green and glorious! Oh, herbaceous treat!
> 'Twould tempt the dying anchorite to eat;
> Back to the world he'd turn his fleeting soul,
> And plunge his fingers in the salad-bowl!
> Serenely full, the epicure would say,
> "Fate cannot harm me, I have dined today."

Lettuce seeds must have been taken to America almost immediately after Europeans arrived there, perhaps even by Columbus himself, since there is a record of lettuce being cultivated in the Bahamas in 1494. One American variety reported at least as early as the nineteenth century was a red-tinged leaf lettuce "of no commercial importance" which was called Iceberg. The name was adopted long after, in the 1940s, to designate the wonderful hybrid forms which from 1926 on were turned out by research laboratories in and near the Imperial Valley, California. The most popular type of lettuce with the public in the 1920s was named New York, so a lot of trouble was taken to ensure that the new variety looked as much like New York as possible. At first these lettuces, bred to combat brown blight, downy mildew, cabbage loopers, fleabeetles, thrips, armyworms, rotting in transit, wilting while waiting, and other hazards to which lettuce is prone, were all called Imperial (Imperial F, Imperial 1-13, Imperial 17, Imperial 152, and so on). But *Imperial* is not a word with desirable connotations in America. The name Iceberg – cold, clean and hard – was a winner.

LETTUCE AND LABOUR

Because American dollars are green, "a wad of lettuce" is slang for a roll of dollar bills. (The idea is quite old: the Italians used to call a gift of money "one of Sixtus v's salads," because the sixteenth-century pontiff, whose father was a gardener, is said to have helped an old friend by sending him a head lettuce, which when opened proved to be full of paper money.) Today the lettuce industry of the United States, 70 per cent of which is located in California and 15 per cent in Arizona, supplies North Americans and Canadians annually with three billion heads of commercial lettuce, principally Iceberg. (Home-grown and market-garden crops are not being taken into account.) That amounts to nearly thirty pounds of lettuce per person per year, or more lettuces than quarts of milk or loaves of bread. *Lettuce* can deservedly be thought of as synonymous with *money*.

It is said, however, that the great lettuce business conglomerates, which are called "grower-shippers" because they cover both aspects of the industry, are companies endowed with "the spirit of gambling." Their product is uniquely delicate, and economically risky. (Only strawberries, which are often mass-marketed by the same giant corporations as undertake lettuce, present comparable problems.) Cultivated lettuces are annuals, not perennials; they require constant reseeding, and the yearly clearing of the vast fields in which they are grown. Water-bills, tonnages of fertilizers, and quantities of insecticides and herbicides are enormous. Lettuces, even when sown together, grow at different rates, so that on any given day only a percentage of the heads (to be determined in the field) are ready for cutting. A field must be gone over recurrently. A good deal of research is being done into ways of transplanting the seedlings so as to increase uniformity of maturation.

A slight change in the weather can considerably speed or slow readiness for harvesting. The decision when to pick depends not only on the plants, but on the labour available and on the state of markets all over North America. Storage, even under refrigeration, can be for only a very short time, and distances travelled to points of sale are often in the thousands of miles; one small error in refrigeration levels can spell disaster. Lettuce from the south-west of the United States is supplied year-round to every region on the continent, and it must be shipped and received daily with positively no let-up. Demand for lettuce is what economists call "inelastic": people habitually buy a certain amount of it, but cannot normally be persuaded to purchase more than they usually do. This means that the price of lettuce, if weather conditions are bad, can skyrocket, sometimes within hours (the price which people are, if necessary, willing to pay for it being quite high), or it can plummet if there is too much highly perishable lettuce about.

Given the demand for year-round availability of cheap lettuce, the organizational difficulty which this entails, the capital investment in machinery required by modern agricultural methods, and the relative scarcity of the land and climate required constantly to produce lettuce, the concentration of the industry was almost inevitable. The same kind of food concentrations have occurred in Florida (citrus), Texas (onions and meat), and the American Pacific Northwest (potatoes). In 1976 twelve lettuce grower-shippers controlled 51 per cent of the California industry, and twenty-nine firms held 77 per cent of it. The four largest firms owned 40 per cent of California and Arizona lettuce. The numbers of companies are growing smaller not larger, a factor which presumably mitigates somewhat the anxieties of gambling.

The human labour for the lettuce industry is drawn from the "surplus" (unemployed) of the big cities, from the local rural towns, and from migrants to the Pacific coast, mainly from Mexico. Male Mexican and Philippino *braceros* (from the Spanish *brazos*, "arms") have worked the giant California lettuce fields since the 1920s; a continuing supply of labourers was assured by an agreement made between the American and Mexican governments in 1951. The rich soil required for the cultivation of lettuce harbours weeds in spite of herbicides; these have to be removed at least once during the crop's growing period, and empty or double lettuces have to be rooted out. Lettuce-field workers have to be constantly on the move, travelling with the harvest, holding themselves ready to go wherever hands are needed. At harvest time, the *braceros* walk along the miles of lettuce rows, judging which heads are plump enough, and cutting them. The heads used to be loaded into bins which would be hauled to the packing sheds to be iced for rail transport. The lettuces were packed in wooden crates with ice in between the layers of heads. The boxes were then moved on roller conveyors to railway cars, into which they were stacked by hand.

Soon the packing, as opposed to the gathering, of lettuce became the preserve almost entirely of North American "Anglo" labour; after considerable labour unrest in the late twenties and thirties, workers in the sheds were unionized, and by the end of the 1940s they were paid well. The Mexicans, both *braceros* (who were Mexican citizens) and native Mexican-Americans, stayed in the fields and were shamefully exploited. Their living conditions were appalling, they were poorly fed. Many of the *braceros* were *sindocumentos*, without papers and in the United States illegally, and they lived in terror of being caught and losing their jobs; there was no question of their complaining about cruel treatment.

In 1950 a revolution in lettuce technology occurred – and, as is usual with technological innovations, it benefited the grower-shippers rather than their employees, enabling them to overcome the inconvenience of having to pay their newly unionized packers well. Vacuum cooling had first evolved in Switzerland in the 1750s. An Italian physicist, G. B. Venturi, demonstrated how it worked in 1796 and the device was called the Venturi Tube thereafter. In 1948, Rex L. Brunsing of San Francisco had the brilliant idea of applying the Venturi Tube (which was being used mainly in carburetors) to the cooling of lettuce.

A steel tube fifteen metres (50 ft.) and two and a half metres (8 ft.) in diameter has pneumatically-operated doors at each end. It is filled with boxed lettuces and the doors closed, after which the air pressure inside is rapidly reduced. Free water is vaporized from the vegetables and carries the heat away with it; in a few minutes the temperature of the lettuces is reduced to the optimum −1°C. (30°F.). They are transported to pre-cooled trucks. No ice is needed, nor are heavy wooden crates. Vacuum cooling is much faster than refrigeration with ice. The portable steel tubes can be taken wherever convenient, which means that the ice sheds and the jobs that went with them were rendered obsolete. Packing could now be done right in the field by low-paid Mexicans, who were quickly taught how to trim the heads correctly, place them with the top layer's butts up and the bottom layer's butts down, and fill the boxes with the proper "squeeze," neither too tightly nor too loosely. New smaller fibreboard cartons, eventually palletized for mechanical lifters, took the place of the old crates on roller conveyors. The work ceased to be paid on an hourly basis: the more lettuce you picked and packed the more you made. Piece-rates are notoriously the remuneration of the underpaid.

Soon after the arrival of vacuum cooling, a plastic film was perfected which enabled the companies to have their lettuces wrapped before packing and delivery to the supermarkets. This meant that higher-paid workers in urban areas no longer had to be employed to trim and wrap lettuce before display on the produce shelves, since the California and Arizona Mexicans did it so much more cheaply. The costs of carting waste lettuce leaves as city garbage were also cut. Today more than 20 per cent of Iceberg lettuces are sold "source-wrapped." To the advantage of extra protection in transit is added what customers perceive to be the sheer prestige of buying something ready wrapped. (Unwrapped lettuce is referred to in the trade as "naked".) A further benefit is the possibility, which all vegetable and meat producers covet, of providing a natural object, like a lettuce or a chicken, with a brand name: subsequent careful advertising can convince customers that one "name" means better lettuce than another. The lettuce wrappers are mostly women, partly because the job requires a good deal less travelling than lettuce harvesting does, and partly because a lot of the work is seasonal.

Public criticism of the way the *braceros* were being exploited in California began to mount in the 1950s. In addition, local Mexican-American farm workers increasingly began to see in the poorly-paid foreigners a threat to their own job security. By 1960, the grower-shippers realized that they had two possible ways of keeping control over the labour supply: either the use of the *bracero* system must become further legalized, or they must mechanize the lettuce harvest and sharply reduce dependence on human beings. Money for mechanization research was provided by the California State Legislature, and the programme got as far as producing a mechanical lettuce gauger, a machine which could do away with the hitherto human task of judging the size and firmness of lettuce heads. A first project for a lettuce harvester was also developed.

These inventions were not put into use, however, because in 1964 an agreement was reached between the American and Mexican governments by which migrant workers could become "green-carders," with the right to reside legally, for the purposes of work, in the United States while remaining Mexican citizens, and even maintaining homes in Mexico where their families lived. The mechanization programme wound down as the cheap labour supply was further institutionalized.

But the farm workers of California were becoming restive: they found it harder and harder to obtain work, since, in spite of laws enjoining that American citizens should get preference in job vacancies, growers much preferred hiring the cheaper and more submissive, often still paperless, illegal, and therefore frightened *braceros*. The movement against the persistent exploitation of the *braceros* and the hard conditions of fruit and vegetable field workers generally began. Thousands of poor Chicanos, under the leadership of Cesar Chavez, "took on" the giant companies and formed their own union of workers from all the California farmlands, including the lettuce handlers. There followed the strikes, long marches, and non-violent resistance which captured the imagination of the world in the late sixties and early seventies. Middle-class students and intellectuals joined Chavez in the fight.

The great grape boycott against the intransigent grower-shippers began and spread all over the United States and into Canada. People gave up eating grapes, unless cartons could be produced which bore the black eagle designating their contents as having been picked by the California farm workers' union. Eventually the grower-shippers saw their largest markets for grapes completely shut down: Boston, New York, Philadelphia, Chicago, Detroit, Montreal, Toronto. The companies continued to refuse to accept the union, out of fear of having to raise wages. It had been the practice that workers were sent in to harvest only three days after vegetable crops had been sprayed with pesticides; rashes and stomach-aches were frequently reported among pickers. The union sought to increase the waiting period after pesticide application. They also wanted a health insurance plan and a fund created into which the companies would put two cents per man-hour, in order to cover workers' immediate expenses in case their jobs were made redundant through mechanization.

In 1970, just as the grape-growers capitulated in the face of the grape boycott (the struggle had taken five tumultuous and expensive years), the lettuce workers began to strike for a similar settlement. The response of the growers was to call in the Teamsters, an entirely different kind of union, and try to have them force the farm workers to join the huge and powerful transport workers' association instead of Chavez's United Farm Workers. There were fights, shootings, beatings, and threats. Chavez struggled to maintain unity and the non-violent principles of his followers.

Consumers throughout the United States and Canada, who were just beginning to enjoy grapes again, were asked now to abstain from lettuce. This boycott was much more difficult to put into practice, since table grapes are eaten as a luxury, whereas lettuce is an everyday salad staple and irreplaceable as such. Yet many people boycotted lettuce. An injunction was brought by the California courts against the organizers of the lettuce boycott. Chavez defied it and was jailed for contempt. Publicity surrounding this event enormously increased the effectiveness of the movement; even exports of Iceberg lettuce to Europe began to suffer. Finally the injunction was declared unconstitutional and the Supreme Court of California supported Chavez's union activities in the Salinas Valley lettuce dispute.

In May 1975, a California Bill of Rights for farm workers was passed. It remains to this day the most advantageous legislation which farm workers have achieved in the United States. Many of the objectives for which the union had fought for ten years seemed assured. In March 1977, the Teamsters signed a five-year agreement with the United Farm Workers to help rather than fight them.

A major source of contention between the union and the growers was the use in the field of the *cortito*, or short-handled hoe, used in thinning lettuces and in weeding. Growers argued that the short hoe was necessary to make workers bend closer to the lettuce; only then would they inspect it carefully enough. The other point of view was that bending over all day was inhumanly exhausting and painful: a long-handled hoe would save enormous amounts of labour. The union won the dispute, and the short-handled hoe was eliminated in 1975.

There was further unrest in the lettuce fields of California in 1979, when non-union labour was hired. The union struck and $5 million worth of Iceberg lettuce rotted away; prices rose to a dollar a head in California supermarkets. After two months the grower-shippers signed contracts. In spite of these attempts at accommodation the growers remain to this day almost solidly opposed to the farm workers' union. The other option – mechanization – still remained open to them. For several years, research had been going ahead which would allow the grower-shippers to bypass the union. After all, machines do not mind pesticides, and machines, as the growers say, "reduce uncertainty" and "increase productivity." Above all, machines don't strike.

By 1975, almost as soon as the workers had negotiated rights to the long-handled hoe, the growers had their first two mechanical harvesters ready. One of these machines emits gamma-rays and the other X-rays through the lettuce; any head which is sufficiently dense triggers a signal to the knife, which cuts it off at the base. Rubber fingers close on the head, lift it and drop it onto a conveyor which carries it to be mechanically packed and vacuum cooled. Four rows of lettuce can be harvested at a time, and at least seven hundred cartons packed in an hour. Drawbacks to the machines are that they are extremely expensive and their great weight causes them to compact the soil. If they come into general use, they will increase concentration of ownership since only ever-larger corporations would be able to find the capital necessary to buy and maintain them. Full mechanization is still only a threat but already it has meant that hundreds of thousands of farm workers throughout California, thousands of them lettuce handlers, have lost their jobs during the past decade.

Mechanization and the effect it has on employment is, of course, one of the great problems of our age. The big machines make the rich richer and rob the poor of their livelihood. Owners of factory farms argue that hand-picking a harvest is at best a gruelling task; doing away with it ought to be considered progress. To which one response is that picking carrots from a garden patch for oneself and one's own small vegetable stall is not hard: what is unbearable is sweating in a vast plantation doing the same thing all day long in order to make money for someone else. The task is dehumanized, in other words, long before the workers are displaced; farming has been artificially readied for the machine.

Perhaps the most important realization of all, although it is an uncomfortable one, is that the social ills attendant upon mechanized farming are the fault of the whole of society, and not only of the growers. The growers, after all, are trying to provide us with the two things we now demand: food which costs an unprecedentedly small proportion of our income, and the availability of the full range of all the varieties of food at all seasons of the year. For these reasons each kind of vegetable is raised in vast quantities where it will grow most efficiently; it is then shipped at the cost of enormous energy (to say nothing of detriment to the taste and nutrition of the food) to wherever the cities sit, voracious yet helplessly dependent upon the suppliers and their huge tonnages of food. The transport costs of a Californian lettuce bought in the eastern United States or Canada amount to 22 per cent of the whole. The entire growing process, including pesticides, herbicides, ploughing, and weeding, costs only 10 per cent; the rest is for harvesting, packing, cooling, loading, inspecting, storing, and retail profits.

There is no sign of this intense specialization and mechanization letting up. A new way of selling lettuce provides an example of recent trends: Iceberg lettuce is now being marketed ready shredded. It is cooled, then cored, chopped into "bite-sized" pieces, and packed into ten-pound (4.5 Kg) polyethylene bags, often together with cut carrots and cabbage. The air is then sucked out of the bags and replaced with gases ("modified atmosphere") which inhibit discolouration of the cut edges. Absolutely none of this is done by hand: shredded lettuce is a mechanizer's dream. The product is sold to fast-food chains, hospitals and prisons – and flown as far away as Hong Kong for use in fast-food franchises there.

In one limited but significant area new opportunities of work have opened up for farm workers in recent years. It should serve to remind us of the extent to which we, the public, control all the industrializing trends in the food business. For complex and far-reaching reasons (many of them not all that edifying), North Americans and Europeans have decided to become food-conscious. We have discovered Cuisine, at one and the same moment as we have found our Bodies. The trend-setting middle classes are already totally converted to wine with meals and cooking with olive oil (in countries where these have not traditionally been the custom), and to elegant food presentations, home bread-making, and exotic recipes of every conceivable kind and complexity. The new all-round Conspicuous Competence which is incumbent upon the middle classes also demands cooking skills of a high order for those who wish to rise and to shine.

Salads have become increasingly "creative," with the addition of "special" ingredients like arugula, radicchio, *mâche*, and herb mixtures almost unknown internationally less than five years ago. *Iceberg* became a dirty word overnight to large numbers of new gourmets. The crispy technological wonder was suddenly tasteless, nutritionless, and also much too easy to get (difficulty of access being one of the hallmarks of status). Nothing would henceforth do but Boston, Leaf, Bibb, and delicate European varieties – all the soft lettuces, which have in the past been considered incapable of travel and easily ruined in the handling.

But we reckoned without the ingenious agri-businessmen, not only in California but also in nineteen others of the United States, who do not even attempt to be lovable: they merely study our desires and set out to meet them. Middle-class neighbourhoods in the big cities now receive abundant quantities and varieties of the most delicate and refined lettuces, marketed by the giant food companies. They are picked by hand (no machine could manage these) and carefully packed in good strong boxes, by the million. They often travel as far as Iceberg lettuces have ever done: Boston lettuce from California is now quite common-place in the eastern United States and Canada.

"Gourmet" lettuce remains, nevertheless, a small proportion of overall output and consumption. There is no question that the culinary improvement, in its absolute sense of increased availability of lettuces with excellent flavour and textures, has been enormous; and the demand has been so competently met that status has already moved elsewhere.

Meanwhile, our own self-centred fastidiousness may be achieving at least some stay of execution for the farm workers whose previous suffering and fear were equally the result of our unheeding greed.

But, at the same time, another development has occurred in lettuce technology. The grower-shippers are beginning – particularly in the specialized new "gourmet" lettuce industry – to experiment with getting rid of soil, let alone workers, altogether. Lettuces are increasingly being grown in plastic foam cubes under bright lights. Nutrients are dissolved in water which is provided, in computer-calculated amounts, to every plant. Far less water is needed than for the irrigation of soil. It is possible to grow lettuces on almost vertical slabs of plastic foam, making them easy for a person to pick while standing up, or for a machine to take over the job. The practice saves plenty of space.

Air blows constantly through these lettuce-factories, cool in summer and warm in winter. It is therefore no longer necessary to confine lettuce growing to the silt-valleys of California with their mounting salt-pollution problems. The new factories can even be set up close to huge lettuce-consuming northern cities. The difficult standards of gourmet cuisine would appear to have been met head-on: production close to the point of sale in order to ensure freshness; the provision of delicate varieties which are impossible to harvest by machine; the ability to provide small crops of any type, to order, and almost immediately.

But the businessmen's triumph is to be short-lived, if the reactions of French gourmets to hydroponic lettuce are anything to go by. A recent French article on lettuce complains that all this technology results in a small, feeble, tasteless product; you can tell these sad creatures by their insistently green colouring, brought about by gases blown over them to activate chlorophyll production. They are so fragile that sellers are forced to wrap them individually (so much for the prestige, in France at least, of individually wrapped produce). The genuine gourmet, this article sternly concludes, will accept only lettuces grown in rich dark soil and in the open air; they must be eaten immediately after picking – if possible while they are still warm from the sun. And, apart from the romaines and some of the tougher leaf varieties, the very best lettuce is hardly worth bothering about at all, at any season other than springtime.

FRESH AND GREEN

Lettuce is an appetizer; lettuce clears the palate. At what point, then, should it appear on the menu – at the beginning or at the end? The ancient Romans puzzled a good deal over the issue. The great Greek gastronome, Archestratos, had recommended that lettuce be eaten "after the dinner, the toasts, and the smearing of perfumes" – in other words, after the meal and before the serious drinking or symposium began. Lettuce – cool, female, inert – would create a solid basis in the body before the "hot" vapours of alcohol began to take effect. (The same principle underlies the common belief that taking a glass of milk before setting out for a party will stave off drunkenness and a hangover: milk is calming, nourishing, female, and innocent in character, and always the opposite of hot, strong, masculine substances like blood, wine, or spirits.) The Romans began by following in general the Greek example, but in the time of Diocletian (first century AD) they decided to eat lettuce before the dinner, since a good deal of drinking took place during it, and since it was commonly agreed that lettuce makes you feel hungry.

The North American custom has traditionally been to eat salad greens before the meal, and the Roman decision is often invoked as a precedent. Emily Post thought the practice began with restaurants, which "wished to keep the customer happy while his entrée was being prepared, and people simply became accustomed to it." The waiting customer would whet his appetite while satisfying his impatience to begin eating. Lettuce is also served in America as a side dish, as a kind of vegetable to accompany the meal, but kept separate because of the heating of the main-course plates, and because of the dressing. Raw lettuce serves as a counterpoint to a hot cooked dish. The dressing would often be dispensed with entirely, since gravy can provide lubrication enough. As we shall see, an oily film over lettuce leaves has not been thought invariably appealing in northern European cultures.

In the 1930s, a crisis was provoked in the American lettuce industry because the promotion of canned and prepared foods bit largely into the domain of lettuce, the swiftly and simply prepared vegetable. Lettuce was in great danger, warned the industry, of becoming "merely a garnish" on the dinner tables of America. A campaign was launched, with contributions from all the grower-shippers, to avert this threat. Advertising emphasized the monumentality of lettuce bowls and the delights of tossing the leaves. The campaign may have done much to spread the use of salad dressings and the central lettuce bowl (as distinct from individual side-dishes of salad) in North America.

The French, on the other hand, serve fairly substantial though often cold hors-d'oeuvres first, and lettuce after the main course, to clear the palate before dessert. Lettuce tossed in dressing is a kind of interval, a pause to enable us to change the direction of our expectations. The rising of one's hostess solemnly to perform the tossing further heightens the caesura effect. Lettuce salad is half-way between the seriousness of the entrée and the frivolity of dessert. Its simplicity reminds us of the delights of the natural, particularly when a meal has involved considerable artistic skill, while its coolness begins to prepare us for the end of the drama of dinner: we collect ourselves in anticipation of the final confectionary flourish. A meal at which fruit is served for dessert is a much more everyday, informal affair, which repeats and re-emphasizes the "natural" theme enunciated by lettuce.

It was the custom in the past that the youngest daughter of the household had to turn the lettuce in the dressing with her fingers, maintaining the "fresh, green, female" mythology of lettuce. Dressing a lettuce made the anaphrodisiac plant "salad" (literally, "salted"); the sexual connotations of salt could add an extra erotic dimension to the girl's performance before the mixed company at the dinner table. The French used to say of a still young and beautiful woman, *elle retourne la salade avec les doigts* ("she turns the salad in her fingers").

Lettuce comes directly from the garden, simplicity and innocence itself, and its role is to "set off" the intricate or solid structures achieved through culinary skill. Lettuce, then, must be pure, that is unspotted, unbrowned, unwilted, natural, and uncontaminated by artifice. Its green colouring is one of our symbols of innocence, springtime, and paradisal gardens. Both tenderness and crispness, two typical qualities of lettuce leaves, mean to us life, spriteliness, health, and youth.

For modern food industrialists, the myth of lettuce is a headache – one among many arising from food mythologies in general. They work incessantly to provide us with what we say we want – only to come up against walls of incomprehensible prejudice and ingratitude. What do we expect? Food must be transported to the millions living in vast concrete cities, it must cost as little as possible, and it must be prevented from going bad while it waits for a sale. Why are people annoyed by the idea of pesticides, chemical additives, colouring agents, shape-holding powders, mouth-feel enhancers, artificial flavours, and shelf-prolongers generally? Insects, bacteria, rotting, sprouting, wilting, off-flavours, and oxidation are some of the main enemies encouraged by mass-production, lengthy transportation, and age. Food suppliers expend billions of dollars and all the intelligence and know-how which the scientific community can muster to fight back against these. In 1985, the food industry in the United States was said to have outspent all other commercial enterprises – and expenditures were growing faster than those of any other trade.

And now we have something new. Imagine being able to keep cooked meat, without refrigeration and without spoilage, for seven years. You could send it anywhere, and store it until someone was willing to buy it. This wonderful capability is already ours, if only the public could be made to see reason. The process is called *irradiation*. Scientists have been experimenting with it for thirty-five years, and food processors are absolutely convinced that this will give them opportunities hitherto undreamed of.

There are two ways food can be irradiated. The first uses gamma-rays or X-rays produced by a radioactive source such as Cobalt 60 or Cesium 137. The source would be housed in a cell with thick concrete walls, and/or kept at the bottom of a pool of demineralized water to protect workers from exposure to the rays. Conveyor belts would carry the food through the irradiation cell; the strength of the radiation dose would depend on the speed of the food's movement through the cell, and the distance between the food and the source. In the rival system, linear accelerators shoot electrons from commercially-produced radioactive substances. Until recently the electrons could be made to penetrate only the surface of products, but a new compact accelerator, which uses the electron beam to produce X-rays, is said to be faster and more powerful than the cell method. Also, its supporters point out, the accelerator can be turned off when not in use, and does not itself create radioactive waste, as the irradiation cell does. We are not told how the commercial producers of the radioactive substances required will get rid of their waste.

There are disadvantages to contend with when high doses of irradiation are used: colours change, smells arise, and flavours deteriorate, especially in bland foods with a high moisture content like milk products and vegetables. New chemical substances called "radiolytic products" are known to appear in irradiated food, and to increase proportionately to the dose of radiation delivered. Processors stress, however, that irradiation could do away with many chemical additives, and effectively kill trichina in pork. And the "positive" side of the degradation that occurs in protein and carbohydrates is that meat is thereby tenderized.

Irradiation kills bacteria and insects, prevents mould and off-flavours in aging food (when precisely the right amounts have been applied), delays ripening so that fruits and vegetables can conceivably be kept for months before eating, and prevents potatoes and onions from sprouting. Scientists have given the measurements of irradiation particularly unfortunate names: one hundred ergs per gram make one rad; one thousand rads make one krad (kilorad); one million (10^6) rads make one Mrad (megarad). Sprouting in potatoes is prevented by the application of five to fifteen krads. Russia has been irradiating its potatoes ever since 1958; Canada began in 1960. Even in these countries, however, irradiation is not common practice, for potatoes and onions do last quite a long time before they sprout. Up to one hundred krads would be required for bacteria destruction and long shelf-life assurance in lettuce and other vegetables. Meat and poultry, in order for the method to be "commercially viable," would have to be irradiated with between two and four Mrads. Irradiation equipment is enormously expensive; it would not be economically viable unless huge tonnages of vegetables were constantly fed into it. In other words, irradiation would greatly concentrate the already oligarchic food industry.

In 1981, the World Health Organization produced a report entitled "Wholesomeness of Irradiated Food." The food industry was elated — the moment, they thought, had come to irradiate. South Africa, the Netherlands, Belgium and Israel have actually gone ahead and routinely irradiate vegetables, fruit, prawns, frogs' legs, and spice. The South Africans label irradiated products with a logo advertised as "the symbol of quality and safety." In 1983, permission was given in the United States to irradiate spices: and already plans are afoot to triple the dose permitted in spice, making it three Mrads (three million rads) strong.

Nevertheless, in spite of what the food industry sees as a breakthrough, it sorrowfully reported in 1985 that "there is not a single canister of irradiated spice on the retail shelf in the United States." France had cleared some foods for irradiation, but no one there was using the method commercially. The United Kingdom continued to allow only low rad levels, except in hospitals for the special sterile diets prescribed for some patients.

The problem seems to be, according to the food processors, that irradiated food would have to be labelled as such. Market research has discovered that the American and most of the European public, unlike the Dutch or the South Africans, do not want to find out that their food has been irradiated, and modern food laws require that the public be told just that, wherever that is the case. No food distributors feel they dare try it. The difficulty created for them by these laws, and the intransigence of people's prejudice against irradiated food, dumbfounds the industry. They have argued (so far in vain) that irradiation is a treatment, not an ingredient or an additive, so they should not have to explain on a label what they have done to the food. So far irradiation label designs have been heavy on such symbolism as innocent green leaves and golden circles. The stickers are small enough to preclude statements like "this food has been irradiated." There are attempts being made to exchange the unfortunate term "irradiation" for "ionization," which most people understand less than they do irradiation, and would therefore (it is reasoned) worry about less.

The processors feel that irradiation is just around the corner, even though a Coalition to Stop Food Irradiation has been formed in the United States, and objectors are digging in their heels in other countries also. People appear to have learned not to embrace absolutely everything that is new. They are suspicious, and they doubt whether concrete walls and ponds of water, or safety gadgets in powerful accelerators, will always prevent gamma-rays and electron beams from attacking people as they attack bacteria. What are "radiolytic products" anyway, and why should we believe that the human frame was built to thrive on them? And what would happen to all the radioactive waste generated by routine food irradiation procedures?

Furthermore, the food processors have not succeeded entirely in appropriating for themselves the short but potent word "fresh." Freshness is one thing modern food supply systems deny us. Fresh corn is corn picked only when the water is already boiling in the pot, ready for the cobs as soon as they are snapped from the stalk. Freshness is a garden lettuce brought inside with soil clinging to its roots, dew on its leaves, and the risk of the odd caterpillar or bug. Fresh in supermarket parlance means "not rotten," or "this food was fresh when something was done to it to prevent it from deteriorating." But real freshness, for most people – and gourmets and food nutritionists concur in this – has a value in itself. Fresh food tastes better, and is almost always nutritionally better too. Of course we cannot expect supermarkets to give us anything really fresh; but it annoys us when they pretend they can.

Another dirty word for the American public, one advertising analyst warned recently, is "natural." People no longer trust anything with a label on it which says it is "natural," she tells us; we wonder, apparently, why we should have to be told such a fact. Advertisers should use "fresh" or "wholesome" instead. More than either low prices or nutrition, 95.9 per cent of the people who were surveyed for this particular report wanted freshness. People wanted dates on packages, so that they could know how long their food had waited on a shelf. Perhaps they will one day rejoice to find, along with the irradiation label, a date showing that their cold cuts are seven years old. The prospect does not look likely at present, but we can depend upon it that food processors will continue their efforts to make this dream a reality.

People demand that food should be the colour they like it to be. The anomalies that arise out of our insistence on the "correct" appearance of food are numberless. Excellent oranges which remain green when ripe cannot be sold unless they are first dyed or gassed an orange colour (it being always easier to dye a thing than to teach a person). People often refuse to eat dark chicken meat; bleach a leg, debone it, and they buy it as cheerfully as they do their favourite breast-meat. Lettuces must be a pure fresh green. Yet, more and more often, lettuce leaves are presented at salad bars already torn off the stalk and cut into pieces, and cut lettuce quickly turns brown.

The food processors looked about and found that if you spray sulphite (salt of sulphurous acid) onto lettuce, the browning effect disappears; a salad can wait all day and still look as if it has only just been prepared. This was a boon to every snack bar and restaurant. Supermarkets began to sell "serve-yourself" lettuce leaves by the pound, ready cut up for salads. Six sulphiting agents were declared GRAS (Generally Recognized As Safe) for spraying on salads, fruits, vegetables, and shellfish, and for dissolving in beer and wine. Soon faintness, shortness of breath and other allergic reactions to the new preservative were being reported in asthmatic people; more than a dozen people died as a result of sulphites. Even non-asthmatics developed rashes and stomach-aches. Demands were made that sulphite-treated products should be labelled and that if supermarkets or restaurants use the chemical, the fact should be posted. Sucrose fatty acid esters were also approved recently by the American government for sprinkling on fruit and vegetables. The coating, which contains only sugar and beef fat, slows ripening and wilting. But the very idea of it has enfuriated vegetarians, who have demanded posting for this product too.

It is true that laws enjoining food merchants to proclaim the presence of food additives are almost impossible to enforce. As one businessman put it, "When was the last time you saw a label for a waxed cucumber?" Having accepted the principle that food must inevitably be "fixed" in order to survive long enough to feed us, decisions about how far we should go in allowing food to be processed, and what we should disallow, become constantly necessary and endlessly complicated. The original decision, of course, was to divorce ourselves as completely as we have done from the source of our food, and thereby to make ourselves utterly dependent on agri-business, transport capabilities, and on the technological manipulation which serves both.

Once upon a time there was a greedy nun who came across a large and succulent lettuce in the monastery garden. She could not be bothered to say grace or to pause and bless the plant before seizing and eating it, with the result that she swallowed a small devil who happened to be sitting on one of the lettuce's leaves at the time. When she was finally cured of the fit which followed, the little devil came out of her mouth and addressed the exorcist in an aggrieved tone: "Why blame me? What have *I* done? I was sitting on this leaf, and *she* came along and swallowed me up." The story appears in the *Dialogues* of Gregory the Great (594 AD). For the parable-minded, it contains a lesson about greed, haste, and ingratitude, about cleanliness, and also about the possibility that all might not be well, even if our lettuces look fresh and green.

The story is also a clue to the fact that lettuces were well known at that date. Historians often claim that people ate almost no vegetables during the Middle Ages. This seems very unlikely, since vegetables grow easily and cheaply, and many people must have had access to a garden patch. Lettuces counted as "herbs"; and were probably also included among the food-plants which the English called "worts" – more correctly "cabbages," but the word may often have meant something like our "greens." Their status was not high, and they were, therefore, seldom thought worth mentioning – unlike meat and pastries, with their high price, complicated preparation, and conspicuous rank among the dishes presented at a meal. A person ashamed of his poverty and low status was made to feel "as potherbs among made dishes."

The English, it is true, have had an abiding contempt for green vegetables:

> Owre Englische native cannot lyve by Roots,
> By water, herbys or suche beggerye baggage . . .
> Give Englische men meate after their old usage,
> Beiff, Mutton, Veale, to cheare their courage,

wrote William Forrest, in *The Pleasaunt Poesye of Princelie Practise* in 1548. The claim, of course, is made on behalf of "princes," but another sixteenth-century document shows English maidservants despising French servants for eating so many vegetables and so little meat. In the seventeenth century, as we have seen, there was an upsurge of interest in green vegetables and salads. But right into the twentieth century smart English boarding schools for boys seldom provided their pupils with milk, fruit, or salads, largely because these were considered unnecessary luxuries, feeble and female foods which were unlikely to help in turning out real men.

Salads in our culture have always been considered women's food. This taste preference is, of course, invisibly bolstered by the ancient categorization of lettuce as "female." French lettuces seem most often to be given girls' names, such as Aurélie, Laura, Estelle, or Blonde de Paris. Light, green, and frilly lettuce goes with white wine, fish, chicken, soufflés, airy desserts, and refined dishes like strawberries and cream; red meat, potatoes, pies, red wine, and heavy puddings have been thought typically "male." Machines in modern life have robbed men of a good deal of the ancient necessity to prove themselves rough, tough, overbearing, and entitled to a rich and solid sustenance. As being lean becomes more difficult and more desirable, salads (and by "salads" we chiefly mean lettuce) become increasingly prestigious.

Both men and women, alike in this now as in so much else, agree that low-calorie, vitamin- and mineral-rich, cholesterol-free salad is what we ought to want. A recent survey has established that the top five "taste trends" in the United States are (in this order): salads, seafood, chicken, fresh vegetables, and fruit. The salad eaters, the report continues, were 45.1 per cent of them wine drinkers; they ate in restaurants often, were either single or came from households where the woman had a job, were heavy spenders, saw themselves as adventuresome, and undertook lots of jogging and weight-lifting. In other words, lettuce, once the standby of the rustic poor, has become an emblem of urban middle-class prestige and affluence.

CHAPTER SEVEN

Olive Oil: A Tree and its Fruits

F OR THOUSANDS OF YEARS the olive tree, its fruit, and its oil have been central to the ritual and the poetic vocabulary, as well as to the eating habits of the Mediterranean region, which is the heart of the civilization of the west. The same oil that is gracing our lettuce salad has been used to bestow irrevocable kingship, to consecrate priests, churches, temples, and holy objects, to light sanctuary lamps, and to signify sacramental grace and strength – even in countries very far away from olive groves and presses. The olive tree is not a spectacular plant, but it is one of the most deeply loved of trees. Contemplating one for the first time, it is not at all obvious why it should have exerted such power over the human imagination.

Furthermore, the olive itself in its pristine state, picked straight from the tree and eaten, tastes horrible. It contains an extremely bitter substance called *oleuropein* (after the plant's botanical Latin name, *Olea europaea*), which must be separated by patient and sophisticated procedures from the rest of the fruit. When the oil in the flesh of the olive is pressed out, the oleuropein is siphoned off with the vegetable water, which is difficult to dispose of and may become a dangerous pollutant. The ancient Romans used to call this residue *amurca*: they used it as a weed-killer and insecticide, and for eradicating woodworm.

In order to be rendered fit for eating, olives have to be soaked in lye and carefully washed; they are then cured in brine. The timing of the various stages of the process is important, and the addition of herbs and flavourings is an ancient art. Dry-curing, oil-curing, and salt-curing are possible without the aid of lye, but these methods can take months to complete. Even before the fruit comes to be treated or the precious oil pressed out of it, the moment for harvesting has had to be judged with accuracy; the olives have to be picked and transported, in spite of their delicacy, with as little damage done to them as possible. The trees themselves, until they are old enough to survive on their own, have to be grafted, pruned, encouraged, and protected.

In other words, man and the olive are cohabitors, living in alliance with each other. It is related in the Book of Judges of the Old Testament that the trees once decided they needed a king. Being eastern Mediterranean trees, they immediately thought of the olive as the obvious candidate for sovereignty. But the olive drew himself up and said, "Should I leave my fatness, wherewith by me they honour God and man and go to be promoted over the trees?" The olive tree knew that he had been accepted into civilized society and given high status within it; he had left the wild behind him. (The unfortunate trees eventually had to lower their sights and ask a bramble bush to be king.)

The extreme utility which the olive has traditionally offered in the societies which have cultivated it is offset by the labour needed to take advantage of the fruit and its oil. The tree has continually caused men to wonder at their own ingenuity as they transformed a small and nasty berry into a rich gastronomic triumph and squeezed out of its bitter flesh the most delicious oil on earth. The olive tree became synonymous for its cultivators with civilization itself and expressive of the highest human ideals. It shares with bread a whole mythology which speaks of wisdom, patience, mysterious goodness, and technological expertise. Like rice and wheat, the olive must suffer in order to render up its riches; the fruit must be crushed or man will not profit from it. "Oil can be drawn only with the press," says a Sicilian proverb: nothing is achieved without sweat. The olive is a tree dwelling outside paradise:

its fruit belongs to a different category altogether from that of Adam's facile apple.

THE CULTIVATED TREE

The olive is the Mediterranean tree *par excellence*. As one approaches the Mediterranean sea, coming over the top of a hill or round a bend in the road, one suddenly knows that one has arrived, even before the sea itself comes into view. All at once, this is it: the white light, the rocks, the special strident blue of the sky. The first olive trees provide final proof that we have entered a region unlike any other.

Olive trees hug the Mediterranean coast so resolutely that it was believed in the ancient world that the trees depended in some way on sea water, and that they could not survive more than seventy-five kilometres (40 miles) from the coast. The second assumption is as fallacious as the first: it is of course not the sea itself which the plant craves, but the mild temperature to which the sea gives rise. In the Mediterranean region the sea is a cooling influence on the African shore, and a warming one on the north coast. Olive trees need long hot summers, but also a winter chill for setting the fruit (nothing, however, below 12° C. [54° F.]), and no spring frosts which would kill the blossoms. In addition, they will not tolerate the climate at heights greater than two thousand feet above sea level. These precise conditions can be met in places on earth other than the Mediterranean: *Olea europaea* has spread to California, South Africa, Australia, and is at present the object of special attention in China. But as long as the myth of the Mediterranean survives, the olive will remain representative of its place of origin.

The *Olea* family of trees includes the privet, the jasmine, and the lilac. There are over thirty species of *Olea* in the world, most of which are valued for their hard wood, which is used in making tools and furniture. Only *Olea europaea* is cultivated for its fruit. One relative, also common in the Mediterranean region, is known as the wild olive or oleaster. This is a hardy, spiny shrub with small meagre-fleshed fruit; it is often used as a stock upon which the cultivated olive is grafted. It used to be assumed that this wild olive was the original material from which man gradually bred the fruitful tree. It is now thought that *Olea chrysophylla* ("golden leaf"), a species found growing wild in Asia, Africa, and the Canary Islands, is the real progenitor. The oleasters would then be descendants of plants which have escaped from cultivation, and which have degenerated over long periods of time into their present state. (It is said that although there is very little oil to be squeezed from the fruit of the oleaster, what there is attains the highest quality.) Some scientists believe that *Olea europaea* is itself the original tree, having needed only careful nurturing to make it as fruitful as it is. The problems involved in deciding where the olive tree came from arise in part from the longevity of the plant. Little can be done experimentally to check hypotheses. By the same token, if human beings developed the olive tree, just how they did so, given the plant's long life span, remains a mystery.

All fleshy fruits with a single woody stone enclosing a kernel are known among botanists as drupes, after the "original" drupe, the olive. (The word for a ripe olive in both Latin and Greek is *druppa*.) The olive nut is uncommonly hard and may take years to germinate. Farmers sometimes remove the kernels from their shells, soak them in fertilizer and plant them, but preferred methods of propagation include rooting cuttings, grafting, and planting out suckers. Where the olive's root structure joins the trunk, the circulation of sap slows down and concentrates into bulbous growths called ovules. These can be cut from the trunk and planted out, and they will root and grow into separate trees.

Olive trees can live for centuries, sending deep tap roots down into the soil in search of water. If a tree is cut down or burned, the root survives and can spontaneously send out fresh suckers from the ovules at its base underground. For this reason the mythology of the olive includes ideas of regeneration and immortality: green shoots miraculously being born out of an old charred stump. The shoots of a plant are called "scions" – a word which came also to mean human offspring, sons of the parental "stock." "Thy wife," promises Psalm 128, "shall be as a fruitful vine by the sides of thine house; thy children like olive plants round about thy table." (The image here is perhaps that of a cut stump "table" surrounded by green scions.) This ability to "begin again" is also the reason for extreme longevity in the tree: ages of two thousand years and more have been claimed in certain cases. The eight gnarled olive trees on the Mount of Olives at Jerusalem ("Gethsemane" means "olive press") are said to have been there since the time of Christ, and this might be literally true, or true in the sense that they could share the root-system of trees living then.

A tree which proliferates from suckers can develop an enormous girth, made, in fact, of many trunks fused together. The trees on the Mount of Olives are six metres (20 ft.) in circumference. One hollow tree belonging to a nineteenth-century Provençal farmer is said to have been used as summer sleeping quarters for himself, his family, and his horse. Such ancient trees have often enjoyed a role in human society partly analogous to that of a pet animal: people have given them personal names (one famous tree near Nice was known as "Pignole"), loved them, honoured them, or treated them as sacred. A family might insist upon the quality of oil, unmatched by any other, which a specific tree could give. A tree could be thought of as gracious, or obstinate, or angry and therefore loath to give any fruit.

Olive flowers are tiny and greenish-white. The leaves are narrow, pointed, and leathery, green on the upper surface and silvery underneath. They grow in pairs along the stalk: it is one of the characteristics which make olive branches, even when extremely stylized, immediately recognizable in art. Because the tree is evergreen, one of its greatest benefits to man has always been the year-round shelter it provides from sun and rain. Olive trees can grow where there is very little water, thanks to their deep tap-root and because they lose almost no moisture by evaporation: the olive leaf is water-tight.

The fruit when young is an intense green; as it grows it becomes a brilliant yellowish light green, then violet with coloured spots; as the flesh within darkens, the skin gradually changes from violet to brilliant dark purple covered with a whitish bloom, and finally to black. Fully ripe black olives produce the most oil; but the best-tasting oil is from fruit only beginning to ripen. Olives which fall, as they naturally do when ripe, are often bruised and deteriorate very quickly lying on the ground; one or both of these conditions will destroy the quality of the olive oil. For these reasons fruit to be pressed for oil should wherever possible be picked from the trees before it is ready to drop off.

However, olives are highly resistant to separation from the tree before they are ripe. It follows that picking this fruit is extremely onerous work. For the finest olive oil, the fruit ought to be picked one by one, and by hand. The olives should be deposited in sacks or baskets carried by the pickers up into the trees. Any fruit which does fall should be collected at once – daily if possible. The work is intensely seasonal, lasting a few weeks in the year at the most. These facts alone are almost enough to cause any self-respecting modern food industrialist to throw up his hands in frustration and transfer his capital to more easily profitable fruit.

None of these factors was a serious problem in the past, although the olive was always acknowledged to be a plant which demanded a great deal of effort from its owners. Olive harvesting took place in the winter when other farm chores were relatively few. The pressing of the oil (often by human strength alone) was traditionally carried out by sailors, who could not go to sea in winter. There would be perhaps scores rather than hundreds of trees to be harvested, and all the families of a village might pitch in to help, afterwards sharing out the results of their work. Most oil was produced for personal consumption.

The olive harvest (known as the *olivades* in Provence, and given equivalent names in other regions) was considered to be one of the high points of the year, comparable with the grape harvest. It was a social event complete with picnics, and a climactic tasting of the famous *frotte d'ail* or *bruschetta* (toasted bread rubbed with garlic and doused in the new oil), when the quality of the new stores was finally appreciated. We hear, too, of elaborate song cycles, with themes ranging from the epic to the jocular which had evolved over the centuries to be sung while picking the olive harvest. Some of these have been preserved, thanks to the efforts of folklore collectors. The work of harvesting and pressing the oil was hard, and the monetary reward nothing like what it would be today. It was accepted as part of the yearly round, and celebrated as a triumph. The rewards were immediate – and satisfying when times were good.

Even in idyllic circumstances, however, and even when people were more patient about manual work than we are, olive-picking was so tiring and difficult that short-cuts were sought. Olives should ideally be picked by hand, and often cannot be picked any other way; but near-ripe fruit can be beaten and shaken from the trees onto mats set out on the ground below. With some luck the bruising will not be too severe (one ingenious Italian idea is to use open umbrellas placed upside down on the ground to catch the olives: the fruit bounces, and bruises less), and provided that the fallen fruit is quickly removed for pressing, only slight damage can be expected. From the earliest times, people have been beating their olive trees in order to save time and trouble. In the Book of Deuteronomy, for instance, it is laid down that "When thou beatest thine olive tree, thou shalt not go over the boughs again: it shall be for the stranger, for the fatherless, and for the widow."

In the course of beating for fruit, branches were constantly being broken off the trees. People reasoned, however, that olive trees *liked* this kind of damage: farmers considered it important, interestingly enough, to feel that their labour-saving devices were helpful and not injurious to their trees. The beaters were in many cases actually encouraged by being given any wood they brought down for fuel, as part of their reward. Olive trees were pruned in order to augment their fruitfulness: surely, therefore, beating the branches would have a similar effect, whipping the trees into productivity?

Pruning has always represented a fascinating paradox: the cultivator reduces a plant in order to elicit increase from it. The German botanist Camerarius used as his emblem a drastically pruned tree, with the words *tanto uberius*, "so much the more fruitfully," written underneath. Camerarius himself doubtless understood the real science of pruning, but people have all too commonly assumed that cutting back is all there is to it. One Italian proverb pronounces that "An olive tree needs a sage at its feet and a fool at its head": it wants careful tending of the soil but mad pruning of its branches. Another folk riddle represents the olive as asking, "Make me poor, and I'll make you rich – who am I?" It has taken modern scientific hard-headedness finally to establish the fact that – in spite of aeons of folk wisdom – olive trees do best with only the minimum of pruning, and that indiscriminate beating can destroy a whole year's fruit.

One of the commonest problems of olive-growing has always been that the trees seem often to produce only every second year – and the better the crop of fruit in one year, the less likely the tree is to produce anything the following season. Great fruitfulness was thought to "exhaust" the tree's strength. This behaviour seemed annoying, but understandable. Today, biennial cropping has become economically intolerable: modern commercial practice cannot put up with abundance (low prices) one year, followed by a dearth and high prices the next. No longer does one olive tree serve the needs of one family: vast plantations are what we are after, to produce oil or fruit for thousands, and every tree must be regular, uniform, and constantly productive.

Modern agricultural scientists have discovered that the practice of beating the trees (*vareo* it is called, from the Spanish: the beating stick is called a *vara*) was largely responsible for biennial cropping. *Vareo* brought down, in addition to the slightly unripe fruit, a good deal of the new growth of twigs which would have borne the flowers and fruit of the following season; it was, in fact, systematic destruction of the tree's fruiting power. And the actual purposeful pruning, if carried out without expertise, was even more damaging to the tree: both men and olive groves paid for the ancient saw that the trees benefited from savage treatment. Careful and knowledgeable pruning, on the other hand, can (and presumably often did, in the past as well as the present) usually prevent biennial cropping altogether. The practice of *vareo* continues, although it is generally discouraged, but a machine has recently been invented for shaking olive trees. Nylon netting is spread beneath to catch the fruit, and the branches are vibrated until olives stop falling. The practice saves manpower, while comparatively little of the tree's new growth, which is vital for the next year's crop, is damaged.

Olive trees, traditional wisdom said, should not produce fruit at full strength until they have been growing for as much as fifteen or twenty years: a man tended saplings which might really benefit only his children and their descendants. He would cut back his young olive trees, training their trunks, preventing branching too low down, even forcing the branches to form ladders, useful for the pickers to climb later. Every country and region had its own traditional ideas about the size and shape of olive trees, the height of the trunk, the length of branches, and the space between trees. But about one thing everyone agreed: an olive tree could, and should, live for centuries. Early pruning to create a tall trunk and the prevention of early fruiting ensured long life for the tree. The ancient, gnarled, familiar, idiosyncratic, almost human olive tree survived in the place where the family had its roots. It gathered to itself all the connotations of peaceful constancy, historic continuity, and unshakeable dependability which were accepted as human ideals.

Nowadays, we cannot wait. Olive trees simply must not take more years than absolutely necessary to begin fruiting. We want them around only so long as they are intensely productive. Once they settle back into a less vibrant old age, then away with them: uproot them and start again. As a matter of fact, the olive, as twentieth-century man has discovered, is by nature more like a shrub than a tree. It is man, with his pruning and patience, who has created those twisted and massive grey shapes, those angular branches gesturing against the backdrop of the blue Mediterranean sea. If you leave an olive tree alone, its crown of branches will sprout very low down – it will scarcely produce a trunk at all – and it will begin setting fruit in five years, not ten or twenty. Ideally, very light pruning will then be required – though none at all is

likely to be the rule, since pruning is labour-intensive. True, the trees
will not last anything like as long as those grown in the past – but we
care very little now about anything lasting.

In the past, an olive tree was often a poor man's mainstay. It would
grow practically anywhere (which was where poor men tended to live):
on steep stony slopes, in dry hot places; if nothing else would grow,
the olive (provided the climate was Mediterranean) could be counted
on. The peoples of northern Europe ate butter and the peasants there
kept cows. In the south a family had its olives and olive oil; possessing
a tree was far less risky than owning animals. Even if it stood far away
from anyone's home and received hardly any tending it produced something; once it was established, it cost almost nothing to keep up.

We now know, however, that olives – like any other trees – do best
in correctly irrigated, rock-free, and fertile soil. In order to create a
profitable modern enterprise, we begin, therefore, by bulldozing the
land, removing the stones, and creating flat plantations for olives, to
ensure optimum drainage of the soil. The rooting of cuttings is speeded
up by a new mist-spray process. We plant the trees – shrubs really – in
serried ranks, so close together that their branches touch and they
become almost like hedges, with only enough space between rows for
the tractors to pass with herbicides and mechanical ploughs. Close-
planting facilitates the spraying of pesticides from the air, since no
chemicals are wasted on the gaps between trees (even though olives are
among the least amenable of fruits to many modern pesticides, because
their oil disconcertingly retains the flavour and smell of chemicals.)

Scientists urge the creation of large groves, bearing more than one
thousand trees per hectare, in order to justify the use of machinery and
the cost of remodelling the terrain. The terraces created on steep slopes
by the labour of generations of farmers should now be abandoned,
some say, unless piped irrigation is available and access can be created
for tractors. Not least among the momentous changes being advocated
is that of ownership: big companies alone have the capital, the access
to scientific research, and, above all, the unified leadership which mass
agriculture requires. In spite of these new ideas, it is still not uncommon
in the Mediterranean countryside for each olive tree in an ancient grove
to belong to a different family – even for many families to have inherited
shares in one tree.

The amount of work which olive cultivation still requires is a serious
count against it in the modern scheme of things; the ease with which

other oils are produced from tropical seeds, (as we saw when we read about margarine in chapter 3), causes fierce competition from these cheaper oils for profitable markets. Olive oil, unlike margarine, can come from olives and nothing else; and chemists, so far, do not seem to have made any claims to be able to reproduce its flavour. Meanwhile, people living in the rich countries of the world clamour more and more insistently for olive oil. This development is very recent, and, as we shall see, it is in several respects surprising. But the figures are unmistakable: demand for olive oil has gone up at least 2,000 per cent in North America alone during the past five years. The industry is suddenly being called upon to supply an increasing quantity of oil, just when olive cultivation was being comfortably thought anachronistic and, in many places, doomed to extinction.

Several things are being done to change the situation in the olive oil industry. "Rationalization," along the lines already described, is continuing apace. Old trees, abandoned by the farmers who used to tend them and who have now gone to live modern lives in cities, are increasingly threatened with destruction. This is especially true in countries like Italy and France, where people command high wages, and where it is often lamented that "nobody wants to tend the olives any more." The spread of the Common Market and of agri-business in Europe has already meant the ruin of many old olive groves, and the dismantling of many more is being predicted for Spain and Portugal. Prestigious centres of production like Liguria, Tuscany, Sardinia, and Provence are holding their own, while Spain and Greece continue to supply the world with large quantities of olives and olive oil. But olive production is increasingly being shifted to poorer Mediterranean countries, such as Turkey and Tunisia, where harvesters are content for the time being both to do the work and to accept lower wages.

PICKLED OLIVES

The word *oil* comes from *oliva*, the Latin for *olive*. The earliest Greeks had called the olive tree *elaiwa*; they later dropped the *w* sound, but Latin kept it, and handed on the term *oliva*, together with *oleum* for the oil, to the countries of the north which the Romans conquered, and to which the olive was exotic. The other main root for the name of the olive in the languages of the Mediterranean region is the Semitic *zayt*, which becomes *zayith* in Hebrew, *zait* in Arabic, and *aceituna* (*aceite* for the oil) in Spanish. (The holy oils used in church ritual in Spain are called *oleos santos*: the Latin name replaces the Semitic because of the association of the Church with Rome.)

The ancient Egyptians (who called the olive *tat*) grew and harvested olives mainly for eating, but preferred to leave the heavy labour of growing, harvesting, and pressing for oil to Palestine and her Levantine neighbours. The Egyptians imported enormous amounts of olive oil from this region, for lighting and for ritual requirements in their temples; olive crowns and branches are commonly found in mummy cases. It is thought by some that *Port Said* means "Port Olive," because it was the point of entry for Egypt's olive oil supplies.

It is easy to see how people learned to squeeze oil out of the olive; but the strange idea of seeking ways to make the bitter olive edible is, as far as we can judge, equally ancient. Pickling the olive preserves it in addition to adjusting its taste. The result turned out to be of great nutritional importance in the Mediterranean area, where olives have, from time immemorial, constituted an essential food resource, depended upon by the poor but also appreciated by the rich.

Olives were a favourite snack (another fast food) in the streets of ancient Rome, as they are in that city today. One would select olives from an array of different types, sizes, ripenesses, flavourings, and pickling brines, and carry them away from the vendor in cornets made of papyrus. For the Romans, olives were something quintessentially Italian and therefore civilized. They were also simplicity itself, and so satisfied a craving for rustic frugality: the Romans needed to see themselves as an austere people, content with little. Any foodstuff which can cover two poles of yearning at once (in this case both sophistication and simplicity), is bound to acquire great symbolic complexity for the society which so honours it.

Most people who have never encountered an olive before find the idea of eating one quite unpleasant, even repulsive. The blend of powerful and quite perversely difficult tastes – salty, sour, bitter – needs some getting used to. Ralph Waldo Emerson said that olives were like life at sea: exotic and distasteful. With perseverance, however, a liking for olives can be "acquired," and after that it is never lost. Taste is an extraordinarily complex phenomenon, not to be thought of as purely physical; human beings, indeed, are unique among omnivorous mammals in continuing to try eating foods they find repellent in the beginning.

Liking for certain foods creates a bond among people, and effectively excludes from the group those who have not acquired the taste. Learning to like something is in the nature of an initiation, of progress into a desirable position "beyond" the one formerly occupied. We prevent our children from drinking coffee because it is bad for them. A secondary but by no means negligible reason is that a coffee break becomes one occasion which beleaguered adults cannot share with their children; while we drink our unhealthy coffee, we can tell our children to "run along" with a clear conscience. As people grow up, they teach themselves to do what distinguishes adults from children: they will choke and cough until they have mastered the cigarette, or force themselves to down bitter beer until they are ready to join the group that actually likes it. Our television advertisements understand the lure of this "in" group, and with infinite cunning portray beer-drinkers as fit, extremely convivial, grown-up yet usually young; cigarette-smokers are made to seem sexy, sophisticated, and extremely healthy, even tough.

Eating olives, in our society (as opposed to that of the Mediterranean, where children are taught to like olives at an early age) is "sophisticated" behaviour. Liking them is proof of an adventurous readiness to try foreign foods, as well as of familiarity with an exotic yet universally acclaimed cuisine. Eating olives, one is grown up, broad-minded, and a person, as we say, "of taste." One really does like olives after a while: a new possibility for enjoyment has entered one's life, like an ambition achieved or an object possessed. Clearly, acquiring such a taste has many rewards, and once it has been acquired, we wonder how we could ever have forgone the treat. The taste of olives, once loathed because it was utterly unlike that of the pale, bland, sweet foods so obviously and effortlessly pleasant to us, now seems to be not only powerful and sophisticated, but also to possess a primary or fundamental character. Lawrence Durrell writes in *Prospero's Cell* that olives have "A taste older than meat, older than wine. A taste as old as cold water."

The ways in which olives are eaten in the Mediterranean region create a broad geographical division, separating the cuisines of the area into two parts. In the countries of the eastern half (Yugoslavia, Greece, Turkey, the Levant, Egypt, and Libya) olives are used as a garnish and for hors-d'oeuvres; they are eaten like a fruit, that is to say uncooked (except insofar as pickling them is "cooking" them) and often as small meals in themselves, accompanied perhaps by bread, cheese, and herbs.

In the west (Tunisia, Algeria, Morocco, Spain, Portugal, France, and Italy) they are very often cooked along with other foods. The reasons for these two attitudes towards the olive are to be sought in traditional mealtime structures, and perhaps in the likelihood, in the past, of there being little but olives to eat at certain meals. The countries where olives are often cooked are also those where green olives tend to be especially popular.

Olives may be eaten at the beginning of a meal or at the end; either way, they always make an excellent accompaniment for drinks. The modern martini pays homage to the olive's ancient role as enhancer of drinks by including one "swimming," as the ancient Greeks would have said, in the glass. In Spain, meals traditionally end with olives, so that a person who arrives on the scene when everything is over is said to "get there with the olives."

Spain produces more table olives than anywhere else on earth: two and a half million metric tons a year for export, about two-thirds of those being stuffed green olives. Factory-processed green olives get a short cure in lye, and are then fermented in salt brine. This means that the olives are treated with both of the methods used to discourage bacteria in food: lye gives the olives a pH level too high for most micro-organisms to live in, and the subsequent pickling brings the pH level down too low. Lactic acid, produced naturally by fermentation and sometimes added in the factory, together with salt, replaces most of the taste which was removed in the lye.

Firm-textured green olives are easily pitted (modern machinery removes seventeen hundred stones per minute) and keep their shape. The red "pimiento," or sweet pepper stuffing is a ground-and-reconstituted gelatinous pimiento paste which is extruded in ribbon form and squeezed into the olives with machine-tooled precision. It is even possible these days to replace the lid on a pitted olive so that no one would guess that the olive had ever been broached – as though it had grown seedless and ready-stuffed on the tree. Anchovy stuffing is funnelled like tooth-paste from tubes into the olives in the same fashion. Almond- and onion-stuffed olives have still to be processed by hand. Cracked green olives continue to be pickled at home or as a cottage industry. They are soaked for about two weeks in water with the stones left in them, and subsequently marinated in a salt brine with various combinations of flavourings, which include fennel, fenugreek, cumin, oregano, bay leaves, rosemary, chili peppers, and orange or lemon peel. Either vinegar or lemon juice may be added to the brine.

Black olives vary greatly in size, shape, texture, and taste. They grow especially large in the warm climates of southern Spain and Greece, reaching sizes over two centimetres (1 in.) long in some varieties. Greek olives are often not treated with lye, but cured only in plain salt or brine where, in time, they undergo lactic fermentation; the result in many cases has a strong and bitter taste. French olives from the cooler north shore of the Mediterranean are small, often with comparatively little flesh and a strong flavour; they are generally considered to be the best-tasting olives of all. Pickled Mediterranean olives are exported in large containers, in their brine, to America and to northern Europe. They continue to ferment in transit, so that valves have to be fitted to let gases out and prevent explosions. The alternative method, pasteurization to stop fermentation, is also practised, but it results in pickled olives lacking in *finesse*.

Ripe black olives cannot be factory pitted because their flesh is too soft; an olive pitter is, therefore, an inexpensive and useful kitchen gadget to own. In California, however, unripe olives are processed to make them turn black: the flesh then remains firm enough to allow destoning in the factory. They are picked green and then chemically blackened; the resulting dark colour is fixed with ferrous gluconate. A lye treatment is followed by washing, pitting, inspection, and immediate canning in a mild salt brine. There is no time taken for fermentation, which means that these olives develop no strong pickled flavour. They also need, as pickled olives do not, to be sterilized at high heat in the cans in order to become resistant to spoilage.

The oldest Californian olives are called Mission, because they were planted from Mexican stock at San Diego de Alcalá by Franciscan missionaries in about 1785. These are small olives, which may either be eaten black or pressed for oil. California produces hardly any olive oil these days, and small olives have not been greatly appreciated there for the last sixty years. The old Mission trees are often used for stock on which to graft large table varieties. Because many Americans like their olives large, salesmen of canned Californian black-ripe olives stress the size of their product with zeal; they have given the various dimensions of olives names which include Giant, Jumbo, Mammoth, Colossal, Super Colossal, and Special Super Colossal.

PRESSING FOR OIL

"Let the salad-maker be a spendthrift for oil," advises a Spanish proverb, "and a miser for vinegar, a statesman for salt, a madman for mixing." The best and freshest lettuce deserves the finest of oils, and plenty of it. The finest is unquestionably Cold Pressed Extra Virgin Olive Oil. (A less wide-spread tradition advocated walnut oil; but this has become these days, even in southwestern France, a luxury still rarer than top-quality olive oil.) Olive oil is called "Virgin" when it is the first oil to come out of the olive, that which is released from the fruit with the least pressure being applied. It is "Extra" to distinguish it from the merely "Superfine" Virgin oil: "Extra" has less than 1 per cent oleic acidity (0.5 per cent in the very best product), while "Superfine" has up to 1.5 per cent. "Fine" or "Regular" has between 1.5 per cent and 3 per cent acidity, plain "Virgin" or "Pure" has up to 4 per cent, and anything more acid than that is inedible lamp oil.

This classification, which is used on most olive oil labels, is a relic from the past. It can be completely misleading, because it has meaning only if the oil has not been refined by modern chemical and mechanical methods. An abominable olive oil can now be refined until its acidity easily ends up less than 1 per cent. The resulting oil will have no taste at all, let alone the matchless flavour of true "Extra Virgin." It can be made palatable by the addition of 5 per cent to 10 per cent of *frutada*, the strongest-tasting "Extra Virgin" oil; this produces what is called in the trade a "Riviera mixture," and it makes up most of what is sold world-wide as olive oil.

The real "Extra Virgin" oil is to be known by its taste, by the name of its supplier, or by the additional phrase "Cold Pressed," which indicates that it has not been refined. Top quality also commands a high price. In 1985, the finest Tuscan cold-pressed oils cost $20 Canadian per litre, which is between three and five times the price of olive oil as it is usually bought in the shops. Refining the oil and then replacing some of its taste is a compromise which most people must accept on account of the saving in money. A litre of cold-pressed oil is to be treasured, and used only for salads or as an added condiment, since heating it above 60°C. (140°F.) alters its flavour.

Olive oil "tastings," on an analogy with wine tastings, are one of the ways in which the olive oil companies are acquainting the public in non-Mediterranean countries with the range of their oils and persuading them to recognize the prestige of olive oil generally. About six small glasses containing oils ranging in colour from pale yellow to green-gold are savoured one by one, with unsalted bread and slices of apple between oils to cleanse the palate. One rubs oil on the back of the wrist – like perfume – to test the aroma. A fatty sensation in the mouth is a bad sign, acid in the throat another. Olive oil is intensely liable to pick up other odours and tastes, so the taster watches for the least degree of contamination, and also for any hint that the fruit was bruised in the harvesting, or was not precisely the right age for pressing. Then there are varieties of olives in the blend to be noted, the climate during growth being an important factor which improves or lowers quality.

Olive oil has good years and bad years, but it does not improve with age like wine. Five months' aging is needed for fruity oils like the Tuscan, which begins with a distinct peppery after-kick. (Some gourmets consider this pepperiness part of the oil's excellence, and do not wait for it to mellow.) Olive oil keeps well for up to two years, provided it is not exposed to sunlight; it can, on occasion and in the proper conditions, last for many years without deteriorating. The greenish colour of the best oils is a sign of their "extra virginity," but it is quite common now for manufacturers to add a few ground olive leaves in order to produce what they call a "green note," so that colour has lost most of its value as a distinguishing trait.

Cold pressing olive oil is a risky and labour-intensive process. The difficulties begin with the harvest, with fruit hand-picked at precisely the right moment (olives do not ripen simultaneously, even on the same tree), and with no bruises or damage in either transport or storage. Ideally, olives should not be held in storage at all before pressing because piles of fruit spontaneously heat up and begin to ferment, with increase in acidity and damage to the oil's aroma. But modern working conditions and the need for expensive modern machinery to be kept in operation makes storage, with its concomitant risk, almost inevitable. Stored olives are spread out as thinly as possible and must be kept cool.

The olive is the only fruit with a high fat content. Its precious burden of oil – 17 per cent of the olive's substance – is contained in pockets within the fruit's cells. The oil is removed by crushing the fruit until its vegetal structure is broken down. Metal crushers are economical, but they conduct heat; it is preferable to use millstones, each eight tons in weight. The softer the stone the better the oil – but, as usual, the best stone requires the most work, as it wears out quickly and needs to be recut and replaced. In the past, great care was taken to crush as few olive pits as possible; today we are less purist, but make up for this in part by providing more efficient filtering techniques.

The fruit is reduced to a paste so that the torn cells release most of their oil. In the cold-pressing method, the milled paste goes straight to the press, where it is spread, in loads of nine kilograms (20 lb.) of paste each, on round nylon mats. These are then mounted onto disks eighty to ninety centimetres (31 to 36 in.) in diameter, each with a hole in the middle. The disks are threaded one on top of the other onto a vertical spindle, and the whole column is then squeezed downward; oil and water pour down the perforated central shaft into the catchment basin. The method is essentially unchanged (except for the materials out of which the press is made) from that used three thousand years ago.

The first pressing, performed without the use of too much force and always in this method without heat, releases the finest olive oil of all. Second and third pressings, requiring increased power, produce successively inferior oils. Filtering, settling, and decanting to remove vegetable water follows. This process relies on the fact that oil is less dense than water, and therefore separates itself out and rises to the surface. Simple decanting pots, with a funnel at the bottom to drain off the unwanted liquid, have been found in Crete, dating back forty-five hundred years.

Next, the oil is stored for a few weeks in cool, dark, underground vaults, so that minute particles of remaining fruit can settle to the bottom. The oil is then filtered again. Many oil enthusiasts insist on very little settling and filtering: the taste is fruitier without it, but the oil deteriorates quickly and looks cloudy instead of a brilliant clear green-gold. The best oils are filtered through cotton; filtration through alkaline earth helps to lower the acidity of poorer oils. Sunlight spoils olive oil, so bottles should be opaque.

In modern mills which do not cold press, the crushed olive paste is heated slightly and then beaten with mechanical paddles. The purpose of this is to break down the membranes of lipoprotein which develop on the drops of oil freed in the crushing of the fruit, so that the oil drops run together as much as possible. Next, the mass is pressed with the help of heat and water. More and more commonly a centrifuge or spinning press is used; this saves time but damages the oil. Most of it, however, will be refined to remove acidity and used as the base for *frutado*-flavoured cheaper olive oil.

Modern producers of olive oil would dearly love to find an extraction method which would do away with the breakable disks and the labour-intensive cold press. Even where all the latest machinery is in use, they sadly compare their conditions of work with the cheerfully automated continuous screw-presses which the seed-oil industry can use to pour out vast quantities of cottonseed, rapeseed, peanut, soya, and other oils at a far smaller cost. Seed-oil can even be extracted by chemical solvents. But olive paste will not submit to the same treatment: the cold disk press, hot-pressing, or centrifuging the paste remain the only practical processes available for olive oil. Difficulties of harvesting and timing added to the non-continuous, multi-operational pressing methods account for most of the high cost and explain why olive oil, once a poor peasants' staple, is now a luxury.

People have always adulterated olive oil, or tried to, whenever other oils have been easier and cheaper to get. Today regulations are such that real, though refined, olive oil must be used as a base, with the addition of *frutado*, if the product is to be allowed the appellation "olive oil." Before a way of testing for saponification levels and other modern scientific methods of verification were available, tasteless vegetable oils were used to eke out the expensive "real thing." For example, an olive oil racket involving adulteration with tea-seed oil imported from the Orient was broken in the United States in 1936; the affair greatly encouraged the systematic inspection of oils in North America.

In May 1981, thousands of Spaniards became sick and hundreds died because rapeseed oil from France had been used illegally to adulterate olive oil which was then sold off at apparently "bargain" prices. The rapeseed oil, which was meant to be used only in steel mills, had been treated with aniline dye. It was bought up, bleached, recoloured, and reprocessed, and passed off as something like the refined olive oil base to which we are all accustomed. But in the process a deadly poison was created that killed or paralyzed human beings who ate it. Thousands of people demonstrated in Madrid, many of them on crutches and in wheelchairs; the tragedy was one of the most horrible food-poisoning disasters in modern western history. More than twenty people were jailed. The Spanish government introduced new laws making date-stamping obligatory, guaranteeing compensation for victims of food poisoning, and introducing fines for offences against public health. The twentieth century has unprecedentedly high standards of hygiene in one sense, but the dangers of chemical poisoning have escalated beyond anything imagined by our simpler and "dirtier" forefathers.

HEALTH, HEALING, AND ILLUMINATION

The ancient Greeks and Romans seem to have spent much of their lives pouring olive oil over themselves. They oiled after the bath, before and sometimes during meals, before and after doing physical exercise, before long journeys on foot and again upon arrival, and in general whenever they wished to relieve tension and fatigue. The prescription for health of the ancient Greek philosopher Democritus was "honey on the inside, olive on the outside." Later Greek and Roman versions of this adage prefer wine to be taken internally, but olive oil remains the external lubricant.

There were many professional anointers who offered massage for a fee to anyone feeling in need of relaxation, especially in the gymnasia and public baths. Every athlete who took his sport seriously (and every young man with pretensions to style was expected to frequent the gymnasium) had two trainers: a gymnastic master for physical training and an "anointer" who advised him about diet, gave him medical check-ups, and either prescribed massages and oil-rubs or performed them himself. The official in charge of the gymnasia of an ancient city considered one of his main tasks to be the provision of enough olive oil to make sport, as the ancients conceived it, possible.

Before wrestling naked, as was customary in the ancient world, one first did a few warm-up exercises to open the pores, then poured on oil and rubbed it in to make the muscles supple. Next one sprinkled oneself from head to foot with sand or dust, which stuck to the oil and provided a kind of protective second skin. This prevented the body from being too slippery for one's opponent to grasp; in addition, the oil and sand were thought to keep the body temperature constant and so to ward off colds and stiffness in the muscles.

After exercise, one was rinsed and scraped with an iron tool called a *strigil*, with more oil to soften the instrument's abrasiveness. After a bath in water and lye made from wood ash or lime, or a rubbing with Fuller's Earth to remove any remaining sweat, sand, and grease, one was ready for yet another generous application of olive oil to soothe the skin. An athlete's essential equipment (the equivalent of our soap and towel, sweat suit and sneakers) included a sponge, a *strigil*, and an oil flask with a flat disk round the opening with which to spread the oil as it poured out. The poet Martial, complaining about the young men of his day who refused to do any work, said they spent "most of their lives in oil," meaning that sport and luxurious massages were all they cared for.

The ancient Gauls, who may have learned the secret from the Phoenicians, made a kind of soap from goat fat and beech ash (potash). They used it mainly to redden their hair and make it fashionably stiff and waxy; but they also used it occasionally to clean themselves a good deal less painfully than the Greeks and Romans did with their scrapers and their lye and Fuller's Earth. Soap, which began to be imported into Italy in growing quantities in the early years AD, would eventually cut drastically the amount of olive oil which the people of the southern Mediterranean region used on their skins.

Olive oil became, however, the basis for making the highest quality soap, which came to be called "Castile" because this industry was centred in Spain. Other kinds of oil were used to make soap, but in Spain only olive oil was permitted. Castile soap is opaque, white, and glossy, with a faint natural fragrance. It became a world-famous luxury article from the eighth century AD onward. Marseilles, once the point of departure for exports of Gaulish soap to the Classical world, took over a good deal of the market in the thirteenth century. Marseilles often adulterated its soap by using other oils, until a law was passed in 1668 (it is still in force) refusing the name *Marseilles* to any soap containing oil not made from olives.

Olive oil is an excellent base for perfumes, and scented oils were used liberally on all social occasions in the ancient world. France, then as now, specialized in soaps, perfumes, and cosmetics generally; the industry depended upon French olive groves. Hair gleaming with perfumed ointment was greatly admired, as we saw to be the case among northern peoples who used butter rather than oil for this purpose. The ancient Egyptians used to set large cones of perfumed ointment, which must often have been made with olive oil, upon their heads at dinner parties; as the atmosphere warmed up the cones would gradually melt and deliciously drizzle scented oil down their hair and faces and over their bodies. (In butter cultures, as we saw earlier, butter was used in much the same way, for cosmetic basting of the human body.) Women in Greece and Rome perfumed themselves with scented oils, imitating Aphrodite (Venus) the goddess of sex, who was regularly anointed by the Graces on her sacred island, Cyprus; Hera herself, in the *Iliad*, enhanced her sexual attraction for Zeus by the application of perfumed oil to her person. Olive oil covered the bodies of dinner guests, and crowns of olive or bay leaves were worn at banquets as well. Excavators at Roman Pompeii found a shop which had specialized in perfumes and olive garlands: people invited to dinner could stop by on the way to the party and pick up the headgear and the oils which they needed for the evening.

Many people who live in the Mediterranean area today drink olive oil regularly in small amounts, one or two spoonfuls at a time, once a day, once a week, or once a month, for their health. The oil is a gentle laxative. There is some evidence that it has astringent properties as well, when applied externally. But it is health in general which many believe to result from taking small but constant doses internally of soothing, nourishing, softening oil. An Egyptian medical text of 1550 BC mentions olive oil seven hundred times as appropriate either to be taken orally or to be rubbed on the body. The use of oil as a shield against infection was a well-known precaution. The Good Samaritan, who is described as pouring wine and oil into the wounds of the man beaten up by robbers, first used antiseptic alcohol, then olive oil as protection from external contamination. Ground olive leaves can be used to cause fever abatement, and were an ingredient in ancient medicines given to combat malaria. It is now known that the olive tree contains salicylic acid, the active element in Aspirin. The hardened sap of the olive tree used to be chewed as relief for toothache, and "Lucca gum," as it was called, went into many medicaments, especially ointments for healing wounds and infections.

Light at night was most commonly provided in the ancient Mediterranean world by lamps filled with olive oil; an oil-soaked wick takes a good long time to burn. For sanctuary lamps, votive lamps, and any light which burned continually, olive oil was the preferred vehicle, since it smokes and smells so little. Until the early twentieth century it was customary in southern Europe to leave money in one's will for candles and lamp-oil for the funeral lights.

Olive oil has been used from time immemorial for dressing wool: it minimizes the breakage of fibres, prevents static electricity, and makes the fleece easier to handle as it is drawn and twisted in the spinning. It never causes discolouration, and is easy to wash out. Olive oil is now much too expensive to be used for this purpose, and is replaced with specially treated mineral oils. Olive oil is employed, or has been used in the past, for rust prevention, softening and lubricating leather, making ink, and diamond polishing. Fish has been canned in olive oil ever since Nicolas Appert perfected the canning process in 1804, although now soya oil is being increasingly used for cheaper products. In the ancient world, statues in danger of cracking because of the climate were kept constantly coated in olive oil. The huge image of olive-crowned Zeus at Olympia sat with a black marble pavement rimmed in white at his feet. Its purpose was to hold the oil which ran from the god's majestic gold and ivory form.

THE OLIVE BRANCH

The ancient Athenians were confident enough in their worth to believe that two gods fought for the privilege of being their patron. In front of the king of Athens and a panel of gods to judge the contest, Poseidon struck the rock on top of the Acropolis with his trident and produced a salt-water well or "sea"; then Athene miraculously presented her gift – an olive tree. The prize went to Athene, and Athens received her name. Poseidon, in a fit of pique, flooded one of Attica's plains, and sent his son to cut the winning tree down. The boy died by missing the tree and chopping himself down with his axe. From the day of the contest to the present time, pilgrims to the Acropolis have been shown the marks of Poseidon's trident in the rock (the salt "sea" was near by) and the "City Olive" growing on the hill among the temples which crown it.

The City Olive was believed somehow to embody the destiny of Attica. When the Persians besieged and then burned the Acropolis, the tree was left a charred stump. But almost immediately (the very next day, people said) it sent out a green branch: Athens was to rise again from the ruins. The tree stood at the psychological centre of Attica. From it, twelve suckers were taken and planted at the mythic "boundary" of Attica, in the Academy gardens (later to become the place where Plato founded his philosophy school), outside the city walls. These twelve trees were called the *Moriae*. They were constant and immoveable: expressive, with the City Olive, of the centre, the extent, and the boundary of the Attic state. They were also protected by a curse: anyone doing them damage would immediately find himself the object of supernatural rage. When the Spartans surrounded the city of Athens they laid waste the countryside, paying especial attention, as enemies did in the ancient Mediterranean world, to the destruction of olive groves. But they were sufficiently impressed by the curse to spare the Moriae. A single olive tree, planted to commemorate the Moriae and the site of Plato's Academy, now stands stranded in the middle of thundering traffic in the city of Athens.

There were many other sacred olive trees in the Attic countryside, all of them thought to be offshoots from the City Olive and its scions, the first twelve Moriae. They were fenced round, regularly inspected, and protected directly by the Council of State whose other main duty was deciding cases of murder. Anyone who damaged one of these trees, even if it appeared to be dead, was in the early days liable to be executed; in later times he was merely exiled for life and had all his property confiscated. From the fruit of the sacred olive trees was pressed the oil which was given to winners in the games held in honour of Athene, goddess of the olive tree and of Athens.

On the occasion of these games, once every four years, the citizens of Athens staged an especially elaborate procession up the Acropolis in honour of their goddess. Their goal was an ancient olive-wood statue of Athene which was dressed in a newly woven robe as a climax to the festival. A depiction of the procession, expressing as it did the totality of the people of Attica, was carved as a frieze round the great new temple which rose, a kind of man-made version of the green branch which grew from the charred olive stump, on the ruins left behind by the retreating Persians. The two great pediments of this temple, the Parthenon or Virgin's Temple, showed Athene's birth at the east end, and Athene winning the contest with her olive tree at the west.

Olive trees, as these myths and rituals exemplify, mean revitalization and continuity, as well as constancy. When Odysseus built his marriage bed, one post of it was the trunk of an olive tree, still rooted in the ground: it meant that his bed was immoveable, just as the Moriae were immoveable, and as is the marriage bond. His wife Penelope alone shared the secret of this bed, and in the *Odyssey* she cunningly tests the disguised Odysseus's identity by seeing whether he knows this crucial fact. When a male child was born in ancient Athens (a branch or scion issuing from his parents' wedlock and from the state), the family displayed an olive wreath at the front door of their house.

Olives are the most civilized of trees. The iconographical scheme of the Parthenon includes, in addition to the great procession frieze and the myths of Athene's birth and creation of the olive tree, a series of symbolic representations of Civilization conquering Barbarism. Tending olive trees requires experience and a technical mastery which makes them belong very clearly to the domain of Athene, the goddess of craftsmanship. Olive trees, like agriculture in general, suffer badly in wartime. In Attica, where olive oil was the country's chief export, burned olive groves spelled disaster. So olive branches, evergreen and civilized, came to mean "peace."

The olive tree represented wisdom not only in the sense of technical skill but also because peace is wise and can be preserved only through intelligence and civilized restraint. Olive branches were carried and worn as crowns by suppliants and heralds in the ancient world, much as a white flag signifies surrender and a non-belligerent attitude today. Suppliants, like sacred olive trees, should be safe from violence, no matter what the politics or what vengeful feelings may be rampant. They constitute a demand for self-control on the part of the powerful. Heralds used the olive to indicate their inviolability as they presented themselves in the camp of the enemy; in time the olive branch became a herald's badge of office. When artists of the Italian Renaissance depicted the angel Gabriel announcing the birth of the Saviour to Mary, he was usually shown holding a lily, symbol of purity and virginity. The lily was also the emblem of the city of Florence, however, and some of the Sienese painters decided that a flower representing a city which was their deadly rival was quite inappropriate for Gabriel to carry. They found a brilliant substitute: for Simone Martini and others, Gabriel holds an olive branch or wears an olive crown as a mark of Mary's purity, and also because he is a herald and peace-bringer.

Winners at the ancient Olympic Games received a crown of olive leaves for their prize. This honour implied that the victor possessed all of the civilized virtues associated with the olive branch. According to the Olympic ideal, any monetary reward would fall far short of the prize of recognition for true worth. The wreath was in some sense also the Fate of the wearer (as the City Olive embodied the destiny of Athens): Fate had ordained that this man should win, and Victory, represented as a winged goddess, bound his head with the triumph, in the form of an olive branch, in the sight of his countrymen. In medieval Europe, following a tradition going back directly to Jewish and Classical times, the anointing of a king or queen with olive oil would be completed by placing the crown of destiny upon the sovereign's head.

The olive wreath, and the bay wreath in honour of Apollo, were customarily worn by all the guests at banquets in the ancient world. Eating together is a sign of peace, trust, and civilized conviviality. For the Greeks, wearing olive and bay crowns at dinner also signified their acceptance of human limitation and abhorrence of *hybris*. *Hybris* meant insulting contempt for other people's honour arising from an arrogant misunderstanding of one's own worth and duties. Prometheus, the divine benefactor of mankind, had ordained the wearing of the wreath in memory of the day when he had been set free from bondage.

The olive tree, together with its oil, is a symbol of virginity, because its role is to preserve and to be constant, inviolable, and unchanging. Athene herself was a virgin. Olive-pickers, right into the Middle Ages in some places, had to keep chaste while the harvest was on. Olive oil, once pressed, is pure; it is golden and healing and gives light by preserving the flame of the lamp. In one of the parables of Jesus, the wise virgins were able to keep their lamps full of olive oil as they waited for the bridegroom, because they prudently took a supply of oil with them to top up their lamps if need be. They were humble (for in Christianity humility and wisdom are aspects of each other), and therefore not misled into forgetting what they were living for: they were able, as a result, to preserve and be constant. The foolish virgins got everything wrong, even their roles as virgins.

The modern phrase, "extra virgin olive oil," is a barbarism arising from the hectoring excess of advertising. "Virgin" here means merely "first"; the oil squeezed out in the first pressing of the fruit. But virginity, even when it is supposed to mean only the state of being first, is an absolute and superlative condition: it cannot become "extra" or more than itself. The misuse of the word comes about because the industry wishes to extend the use of it to oils inferior to the best: the best has therefore to be distinguished by means of an enthusiastic absurdity. Even though *virgin* is now used of olive oil in a technical rather than a mythic sense, the continued association of the word with the oil seems to be a remarkable – if unconscious – survival of an ancient linkage of ideas.

ANOINTING

When Noah decided that it was time to see whether the flood had subsided, he sent a dove out from the ark. She returned because there was nowhere for her to rest. He sent her away again a week later, and she came back bearing an olive branch; at the third try she flew away never to return. The olive branch in the dove's beak was a potent symbolic message: it meant that the most constant of trees, sure indicator of hope for the future and of the rebirth of civilization, had survived the flood. The dove was a herald from God, who was ready now to make peace with the world.

Christians from the earliest times understood the story of Noah, his ark, the flood, and the olive-bearing dove as a prefiguration of the Resurrection and of the sacrament of Baptism; they painted the scene with its new meaning over and over again in the catacombs. The dove and the olive branch are to be found especially often; they constituted a kind of shorthand for the whole story and its Christian meaning. The flood is the death of the old so that the new can begin afresh; it is a symbol of initiation. Noah and his ark "die" and are purified in the flood, as the Christian's old self is drowned in the waters of Baptism, so that he may be saved and rise again from them a new man. The dove, with its message of hope, wisdom, health, and peace as embodied by the olive, is the Holy Spirit, who appeared as a dove at the Baptism of Jesus. The olive twig stands for olive oil, which after the Baptismal washing anoints the Christian's head, completing his initiation and signifying the support of the Holy Spirit in his life. The oil also reminds the Christian that "Christ" means "Anointed" (*Christos* in Greek, *Messiah* in Hebrew.)

Anointing with olive oil was a sign of respect in the ancient world: one poured oil over the head of an honoured guest, and one anointed the dead. It was customary in ancient Greece to leave a jug of olive oil in a dead person's tomb as a friendly and respectful offering; if anything could be useful to the dead in the hereafter, oil was thought likely to be what they needed. The oil was apparently more costly than the beautiful container: the jug often held a tiny vessel inside the neck so that no more than a very little oil need be left in the tomb. Presumably the dead were thought to be weak, and were therefore to be cheated with impunity, even as the forms of ritual were being adhered to.

A host would offer oil for the feet of anyone who arrived at his house after having walked a long way. No one intending to travel a great distance on foot would dream of setting off without oil for tending his feet at the beginning and end of each day. When Jacob had his vision of angels, he rose the next morning, set up the stone he had used for a pillow, poured oil over it and called it Beth-el, "the House of the Lord." Jacob was travelling as lightly as possible at the time – but he had still thought it necessary to carry a flask of olive oil on his person. Later, Jacob returned to Beth-el, set up a second stone there, and poured wine and oil over it.

For thousands of years people have felt that it is right and necessary to pour oil over special or significant stones. Just why they have done this is mysterious. Perhaps these are some of the factors involved: The oil sinks into the stone, darkens it and makes it shiny; the oil seems somehow to have penetrated the stone, honoured it, perhaps even imparted some sort of life to it, adding dynamic power to the strength and duration of rock. "Fatness" always tended in the past to mean "life force." "Fat" land is fertile, whereas dry land and "dry bones" mean death. Oil made a man's skin "glow" (as we say) with life and happiness. The *omphalos* stone at Delphi, which claimed to be the centre or "navel" of the earth, was constantly anointed by the ancient Greeks; the sacred black rock of Islam, the Ka'bah at Mecca, is ceremonially drenched in oil. When Moses had the Tabernacle built at Sinai, God told him to anoint with olive oil, specially spiced according to a precise recipe, the Ark of the Covenant, the altars, and all the vessels and candlesticks. "You shall consecrate them, that they may be most holy; whatever touches them will become holy. And you shall anoint Aaron and his sons, and consecrate them, that they may serve me as priests." In memory of Jacob's action at Beth-el and of Moses at Mt. Sinai, all Catholic churches are consecrated as "Houses of God" and "Gates of Heaven" in a ceremony of anointing by a bishop: the twelve places of anointing are marked on the pillars and walls of the church by Greek (equal-armed) crosses. Altars are anointed with particular emphasis, and there are special traditional ceremonies for naming and anointing church bells.

Whatever is anointed – man, building, ritual utensil, or rock – is set apart; anointing initiates it into a new and singular state. Anointing the head of one's guest admitted him into one's house and into the number of one's friends. Dead people were anointed out of respect, and because they had entered a new state; when Jesus was anointed before the Passover by a woman as he reclined at dinner in the house of Simon the Leper, he interpreted the action as a preparation for his burial. A ceremonial application of olive oil could also be used as a way of distinguishing one group or society from another. The anointings at Mt. Sinai by Moses were designed in part to differentiate the Jewish Temple and Jewish ritual practice from those of the Egyptians and of the other peoples in Canaan.

Priests in the Catholic Church are ordained, as priests were in the Old Testament, by the pouring or rubbing on of oil. The image of oil as representing strength, constancy, and wisdom is present in all initiatory anointings, as it is in Christian Baptism, as well as Holy Orders, Confirmation, and the Anointing of the Sick. This last ceremony (which is not recognized as a sacrament by most of the Protestant churches) has recently been the subject of controversy in the Roman Catholic church. A decision was taken by the Vatican to emphasize the symbolism of strength over that of initiation: the oil is administered primarily as aid and comfort to the sick, and only secondarily as Extreme Unction, as it was formerly called, the "final anointing" or initiation into the "last journey" of death.

Consecrated olive oil, in both Jewish and Christian practice, represents the action of the Holy Spirit, whose other chief symbols are wind or breath ("life force"), the dove, and fire (we recall that olive oil was used for lighting). Oil flows, spreads, and penetrates, and then softens, nourishes, warms, strengthens, and provides illumination: it easily comes to signify what Christians call "grace," the "extra something" which God confers. When Samuel saw David, "the Lord said, 'Arise, anoint him, for this is he.' Then Samuel took the horn of oil and anointed him in the midst of his brethren; and the Spirit of the Lord came upon David from that day forward."

David instantly took on, with the Spirit, legitimacy, and also that personal inviolability which, in the ancient world, was the privilege of olive-bearing heralds and suppliants as well as oil-anointed kings. The change induced by anointing was permanent: even though Saul had been deposed as unworthy of the Lord, David rebuked the man who claimed to have killed him, for Saul had received the oil of consecration, no matter what his subsequent actions had been. "How wast thou not afraid," said David, "to stretch forth thine hand to destroy the Lord's anointed?" As Shakespeare put it many centuries later,

> Not all the water in the rough, rude sea
> Can wash the balm from an anointed king.

When a Jewish king was anointed by a priest or a prophet, he became a person permanently set apart, as the stone Beth-el was; he was granted the divine right of access to the throne because the oil expressed continuity and legitimacy. As king, he was permanently sacred and inviolable, and he had it in his power to radiate peace, civilization, and wisdom, and bring victory to Israel. In other words, the manifold meanings of the olive tree and its oil are all aspects of the Jewish idea of kingship.

Beginning with the Visigothic monarchs of Spain in the seventh century AD, and continuing with Charlemagne, who was anointed emperor by the Pope on Christmas Day, 800 AD, the medieval kings of Europe took over intact all of the symbolism of the Old Testament for their rites of coronation. King Solomon's anointing by Zadok has been especially singled out for commemoration: the anthem "Zadok the Priest and Nathan the Prophet" has been sung at every English coronation since 973 AD. Olive oil became, together with the crown, the embodiment of kingly authority. The consecrated oil also ensured that authority was not wrested from the original holders and guardians of it: once again, the olive tree and its fruits expressed continuity, in this case the preservation of the status quo.

For not just any olive oil would do. It was related in medieval France (the legend is believed to have been born in the ninth century) that when King Clovis, or Louis the First, was baptised in 496, the press of the crowd was such that the man with the oil had trouble reaching Bishop Remi, who was waiting to complete the King's baptism by anointing him. Suddenly the crowd saw a dove appear above the king; it descended with a small pear-shaped flask of olive oil in its beak. This was used to anoint Clovis and so initiate him into Christianity. When Remi died, a church was built in his honour at Rheims. In the church was preserved the original flask of oil, the *Sainte Ampoule*, as it was called. The kings of France were forever to be anointed from that store of oil (topped up at intervals: sacred oils do not dilute), and that alone.

The legend of the *Sainte Ampoule* was a political device, and a brilliant one. No upstart claimants to the throne could tear apart the fabric of the state: the royal line would be continuous and exclusive. Legitimacy depended upon the agreement of the powers (the Church and those who could persuade the Church) who controlled and guarded the sacred

symbol of sovereignty, the irreplaceable *Sainte Ampoule*. At the coronation of a French king, the procession of the Knights of the *Sainte
Ampoule* at dawn to get the flask was followed, in the great Cathedral
of Rheims, by the solemn showing of the flask to the people, and its
veneration. Then came the ritual anointing of the king on his head and
stomach, between his shoulders, on his right shoulder and his left, under
both his arms, at the elbow and the inner joint of each arm, and on
the palms of his hands. The king wore a special cloak with openings
at all these places. After the anointing the slits were closed up and gloves
drawn on over the king's oiled palms. (It was the anointing of the royal
hands with the sacred oil, a symbol of healing, which was believed to
give kings the power to heal scrofula by touch.)

The flask was smashed during the French Revolution at the sacking
of Rheims Cathedral, but a piece of it was salvaged. This was used at
the last French coronation, that of Charles X in 1825. The fragment of
the *Sainte Ampoule* was then retired from its long service, to the tomb
of St. Remi behind the high altar in the saint's Cathedral, where it
remains today.

Thomas à Becket had been driven into exile in France by King Henry
II of England when he received from the Virgin Mary a flask in the
shape of a golden eagle which contained sacred olive oil. This oil was
henceforth to anoint all the true kings and queens of Britain. Henry
II, anointed with oil which had no celestial origin, was by the same
token unacceptable to heaven. This "vision" was kept secret and the
golden eagle was hidden away for two hundred years. It came to light
only when the dream of a hermit led to its discovery – just in time to
anoint Henry IV as the rightful king of England. His predecessor,
Richard II, had been anointed, but with oil which had not come directly
from heaven.

Some sceptical people at the time thought that the legend and the
oil had been invented in order to support Henry's dubious claims to
the throne, and to compare Richard with Thomas à Becket's enemy,
Henry II. Some malicious chroniclers even reported that the miraculous
unction gave Henry IV head-lice. But the golden eagle, known as the
Ampulla, has been employed in England for every royal anointing since
1399. The Ampulla and the ancient ritual Oil Spoon were among the
few objects of the regalia to survive the Civil War in England in the
seventeenth century. They are both now to be seen in the Tower of
London.

A bitter conflict arose during the twelfth century over the increasing insistence of kings that they were in some sense priests as well as temporal rulers: that anointing and coronation constituted a sacrament. In the early thirteenth century Pope Innocent III decreed that there was a difference between bishops and kings, and he tried to insist that bishops could be anointed on the head with chrism (consecrated olive oil mixed with scented balsam), while kings received simple unscented olive oil on their arms and shoulders only. (The English and the French blatantly ignored the Pope and continued to anoint kings on their heads.) The coronation ceremony was further said, by Pope John XXII, to lack the permanent mark on the soul which priestly ordination conferred. This was potentially very damaging, because it suggested that kings could be unmade, whereas one of the chief meanings of anointing had always been that they could not. The details may appear to be merely picturesque, but they represent a deadly serious battle for the right of the Church to confer or withhold authority, over whether temporal authority should be thought absolute at all, and over the power of kings to interfere in what the Church saw as its own domain.

Anointing today is almost entirely restricted to religious symbolism, and even there its role is often largely traditional and either misunderstood or greatly reduced in meaning for many people. The modern secular state has no truck with absolutes such as inviolability and indelibility: our political ideals have rather to do with reducing the claim of anything or anybody to be unique or irreplaceable, while value is expressed as far as possible by means of money. We are committed to mobility and change, and these must always militate against both continuity and irrevocable status. The idea of things or persons being sacrosanct or "set apart" is not a feature of our mythology – not consciously or officially, that is. The imagery associated with the olive tree has, therefore, tended in modern times to limit itself to intimations of virtue (peace, strength, wisdom), and to be downplayed as a mark of permanent initiation and of exclusive and unquestionable status.

FROM GREASY TO MONO-UNSATURATED

The peoples of northern Europe belong to the butter cultures: sauces are traditionally made with cream, salads are dressed with salad-cream or even cold sugared water, and vegetables are often boiled because butter burns at a lower temperature than oil does, and is therefore unsuitable for long pan-frying. The olive-oil cultures to the south have traditionally distrusted and despised butter. As we saw in Chapter 3 the ancient Greeks thought the barbarians who ate butter were primitive and weird; the Japanese complained that butter-eaters stank. Plutarch tells us that when a Spartan lady paid a visit to Berenice, the wife of Deiotaros, one of them smelled so much of scented olive oil and the other of butter that neither of them could endure the other. For the opposite is equally true: the English have long shuddered at southern European food, calling it greasy, "reeking" with garlic, and "swimming in olive oil." Olive oil and garlic in combination was, of course, almost hilariously dreadful.

One typical story among many of how the image of olive oil has recently changed for people whose cuisine was traditionally based on butter, is associated with the history of the Greeks who came relatively late to North America, arriving in large numbers only after 1905. These people imported olives, olive oil, sharp cheeses and *feta*, spices, and dried figs for their own use: they had heard from the earlier Greek-Americans that these things would be hard to find in their new country. (The Creoles of New Orleans were an exception: they had always brought in plenty of olive oil, together with other French foods, for themselves.) According to R. J. Theodoratus, who has studied the evolution of Greek cookbooks in the United States, the new Greek-Americans' eating habits, together with their religious rites and language, kept them very isolated as a group for several decades.

Nevertheless, many Greek-Americans became café-owners, quickly learning what their clientèle would find acceptable. They carefully censored their menus, keeping such intensely national and strong-tasting dishes as *skordalia* (olive oil and garlic) a secret, to be shared only in their own houses, among themselves. Before 1960, cookbooks written for Greek-Americans regularly warned their readers not to eat *skordalia* before going out into the Anglo-Saxon world. The immigrants did, however, introduce a few dishes which pleased and educated American palates: the hand-held shish-kebab, or meat on a stick, for instance, was cheap, fast, and acceptably "interesting," with its flavourings of oregano, rosemary, lemon, marjoram, and bay leaves.

After the invasion of northern Greece in 1940, Greeks went to the United States in steadily increasing numbers. It was difficult to get olive oil during the war, so they used American cottonseed, peanut, and corn oils in their cooking. The result was that many more Americans began to eat and like Greek food. Greeks, on the other hand, began to adopt

American ways, shifting away from eating organ meats and the goat (taboo and rare in America), learning to like more "northern" dishes, and cutting down on oil for the purposes of slimming.

American acceptance of southern cuisine accelerated in the 1960s. Garlic arrived. "Ethnic" cooking was increasingly perceived by middle-class North Americans in general as alluring rather than revolting; adventurousness became good taste. Experimentation with "Mediterranean" foods (beyond the already acceptable shish-kebab), began in the Greek case with *stifado*, a stew with herbs and spices, from which all traces of oil could be meticulously removed before eating. *Moussaka* (almost unknown before the 1950s, when North America first took an interest in the eggplant and eventually began growing it) was suddenly on every open-minded, sensuous and hearty, intelligently money-saving table. Greek and other Mediterranean dishes required oil, not butter, and Americans quickly learned to like oil; a taste for olive oil in particular grew simultaneously, quietly, and naturally. *Skordalia* was brought out of hiding; it was soon being referred to in cookbooks as nothing more sinister than "a zesty sauce."

Disapproval of oil entirely on grounds of taste (finding oil "disgusting") still lingers among people of northern European descent, but in North America, the middle classes have on the whole become unprecedentedly eclectic about food: oil, like garlic, is now perfectly acceptable. Oil actually has an advantage over butter: it is largely "unsaturated" and therefore believed to be healthier.

It was first suggested by scientists in the 1950s that daily consumption of polyunsaturated fatty acids (known in the journals as PUFA) might actually lower blood cholesterol; and high blood cholesterol was known to be one important factor contributing to the risk of coronary heart disease. People began to turn from butter to margarine (the restrictions on the appearance of which had been lifted in 1950). Margarine was partly made of seed-oils whose fat is polyunsaturated, unlike saturated and cholesterol-carrying butter. Soya, corn, and sunflower-seed oils in particular could boast 55 per cent PUFA, and no cholesterol at all.

The most recent research (Mattson and Grundy, 1985) begins from a new realization that habitual large intakes of polyunsaturated fats may not, in fact, be healthy. Experiments in which animals were fed on it resulted in cancer. The composition of cell membranes has been shown to be altered by polyunsaturated fats, and the risk of gallstones may be increased. There are two types of lipoproteins: high density (HDL) and low density (LDL). While it may be beneficial to lower the incidence of LDL, it is not desirable to cut down on HDL. Polyunsaturated fats reduce both.

Saturated fat molecules are chains of carbon atoms which connect with hydrogen atoms until no more hydrogen or any other gas can be accommodated. (One reason for artificially saturating fat, as in margarine, is to prevent oxygen getting in and turning the fat rancid.) Polyunsaturated fat (with linoleic acid) has room for four or more additional hydrogen atoms per molecule. In between polyunsaturated and saturated fats is an intermediate type: that containing oleic acid. The fat is called mono-unsaturated, because it has only one double bond (polyunsaturated fat has several: saturated fat has none) and can absorb two additional hydrogen atoms per molecule. Olive oil is a mono-unsaturated fat.

Until now, mono-unsaturated fat has been largely ignored in the great cholesterol debate. It has been called neutral or intermediate in effect and lumped with saturated fats: people have been advised quite often to avoid it wherever it is possible to choose a polyunsaturated substitute. Experiments have now suggested, however, that mono-unsaturated oil may well be the "healthiest" choice of all.

Oleic acid, according to these experiments, reduces total LDL cholesterol (the "bad" kind) as the polyunsaturates do, but it reduces the "good" HDL appreciably less. It has long been known that mammals form mono-unsaturated fat in their bodies by directly removing two hydrogen atoms from saturated chains. It is also known that people from the Mediterranean region have a curiously low rate of cardiovascular disease. One reason for this may be their preference for mono-unsaturated olive oil.

This kind of research can produce great problems for the food industry: just when margarine was getting its powerful polyunsaturated message across, along comes olive oil to snatch away the prize. To make matters worse, olive oil has come a long way in public esteem lately: if health can be related to a product already considered to be a luxury, there is no telling how far the product could run. But the polyunsaturated oil men need not despair, for chemistry can still save them: if the public should become determined to buy mono-unsaturated oil, they can quite easily add some hydrogen to their oil, lose a double bond or two, and soya oil or corn oil too could end up mono-unsaturated – and still be much cheaper than olive oil. The only problem remaining would be the hopelessly complex flavour of olive oil, and the public's growing predilection for it.

CHAPTER EIGHT

Lemon Juice: A Sour Note

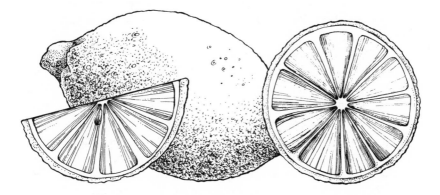

THE ACID JUICE of a lemon arouses our taste-buds, sensitizes them, and causes our mouths to salivate on the instant. Indeed, once we have known the taste of a lemon we never forget it and are liable to salivate at the very sight of anybody sucking one. It is said that a small boy with the aid of one lemon can reduce a brass band to helpless mouth-watering incompetence in a matter of minutes. When behavioural scientists (who claim to have shown that introverts salivate more in response to lemon juice than extroverts do) conduct salivation experiments, they have to hide the fruit away because subjects seeing a lemon in addition to tasting one are liable to react in a manner which ruins the saliva measurements.

The surprise of the sour on the human tongue inspired Plato (who had, of course, no knowledge of the nervous system) to speculate that it must arise from the action of extremely fine particles which lock into and mobilize cubical and octohedron-shaped granules in the tongue, churning them about and turning them into frothy bubbles. This disturbance must have been what communicated the powerful "acid" message to the heart, where Plato thought, reasonably enough, that we probably registered the sense of taste. Modern scientists tell us that sour things have a strong concentration of protons, which are active and mobile particles bearing a positive electrical charge. These, when on the loose, attach themselves quickly to nearby molecules and immediately change them. The tongue, nerves, and brain interpret proton concentration and activity in terms of what we call the sensation of sourness.

A few drops of sour lemon juice can tweak us into a heightened awareness and appreciation of a myriad different flavours. Almost everything we eat contains at least a tiny amount of acid, or we would find it insipid. Lemon juice or a twist of lemon peel can intensify the savour of vegetables, meat, staple grains, and sweet dishes; enlivening everything from cabbage to fish and ice cream, and all kinds of drinks from gin or pop to tea and coffee. Our simple lettuce salad, "raised," as the French put it, with salt, and accompanied by rich, complicated, smooth olive oil, and lemon juice, sharp and rousing, turns into one of the great irreplaceable culinary classics.

The yellow, oval, nippled shape of the lemon is both attractive and utterly unmistakeable: an image-creator's dream. Because its beauty conceals a sour interior, we describe a car as a "lemon" if it looked good when it was bought, but gave us an unpleasant surprise later. (The Citroën automobile people do not emphasize the fact that their product's name means "lemon.") But the comparison is unfair: we buy a lemon precisely for its endlessly useful acid juice; we would be very annoyed to find it sweet inside. Handy in size, available all year round, inexpensive, long-lasting, and perfectly packaged in a tough skin which is as valuable as the juice it contains, a lemon is the ideal household implement, an honorable standard against which all patented inventions might be measured. A modern kitchen without a lemon in it is gravely ill-equipped. "Life is a difficult thing in the country," exclaimed Sydney Smith in early nineteenth-century England, "and it requires a good deal of forethought to steer the ship, when you live twelve miles from a lemon."

THE GROWTH AND SPREAD OF THE LEMON AND ITS TRIBE

Oranges, lemons, mandarins, grapefruit, limes, pomelos, kumquats, and citrons are the main categories of citrus fruit. Many of us are familiar with hybrid forms, such as the tangelo (mandarin/grapefruit or mandarin/pomelo), the tangor, the chief variety of which is temple (mandarin/orange), the Meyer (presumed to be lemon/orange), or the greenhouse ponderosa (lemon/citron) and calamondin (sour mandarin/ kumquat). The grapefruit itself, which has only been cultivated since the 1750s, is thought to have been a mutation of the pomelo, or perhaps a hybrid of the pomelo with some other as yet unidentified citrus form.

Human beings have selected and bred all these fruits, and honoured them with names. There are in the world endless varieties of citrus fruit, bred from mixtures among species which number from 8 to 145, depending on the categorizations used by botanical authorities: these plants hybridize with exceptional readiness. In addition, citrus seeds are liable to what is called *nucellar embryony*: some of them (all of them in some types) contain more than one embryo, and grow several seedlings – all of which might be very different from one another. It is impossible to foretell the characteristics of fruit from a citrus tree grown from seed, until the first fruit ripens.

Outside the huge controlled citrus farms, in places where citrus is plentiful and people take life easy, most people simply learn what varieties and flavours are available on the trees growing near by, and make arrangements with the owners to have access to the kinds they like. It might be difficult to know quite what to call any particular fruit; modern commercial names like "limequat" and "citrangequat" give some idea of the complications. What all this means is that the history of various kinds of citrus fruit is very muddled indeed until recent times: when ancient writers refer to a citrus fruit by one name or another, we cannot know precisely which form they mean.

The ancient Greeks, for instance, called any strange fruit an apple, distinguishing it only by the name of the country they believed it came from, until it became familiar to them. It is still common for people to think of the ancient Greek myth of the Golden Apples of the Hesperides as concerning oranges or lemons. The Greeks themselves suggested this possibility, at about the time of Christ, when citrus fruit was first becoming well known in the Mediterranean region. The conjecture seems unlikely to be correct, however, because for one thing early Greek artists appear to have been quite happy to think of the wonderful Golden Apples as quinces, and for another the nymphs called Hesperides lived (as their name suggests) in the west, and it now seems certain that citrus fruit originated in the region of the Himalayas.

Did citrus fruit come from northern India or from south-central China? Both countries claim precedence, each with some justification. According to the explorations of the Japanese botanist T. Tanaka in the 1920s and 1930s, most cultivated citrus originates from a small area in Assam and northern Burma, and radiated from there to China, India, and Malaysia. The kumquat was, until relatively recent times, unique to China and Japan; and it is thought that the rest of the "orange" citrus strain evolved in China too: bitter oranges, mandarins, sweet oranges, and the Poncirus or trifoliate orange. Malaysia seems to be the producer of limes, pomelos, and their relatives. India is the most likely source of the citrons, some types of the bitter orange, and lemons. An earring in the shape of a lemon, or perhaps a citron (from about 2000 BC), was found at Mohenjo-Daro in the Indus Valley.

The first known reference to the lemon in Chinese literature, on the other hand, dates from as late as 1175 AD, when Fan Ch'en-ta described what he called the *li-mung* as "the size of a large plum . . . it resembles a small orange and is exceedingly sour to the taste." His words imply that oranges were common in China, as were plums, but lemons (if the *li-mung* was a lemon) were new. A Chinese emperor was solemnly presented with two bottles of what might have been lemon juice, also during the Sung period; and again this juice must have been rare in order to have been chosen as a royal gift.

A very early spreading of citrus to the three Asian centres must, according to this theory, have been followed by almost no exchange among them for many centuries, during which time the main citrus strains were developed in separation. No lemons of the common Mediterranean type have been found growing wild in any of those regions – or elsewhere; the lemon is, therefore, thought to be a relatively late hybrid, one of whose constituent strains is certainly the citron. Citrus fruit of the Indian (lemon-citron) type was growing in Iraq in the third millennium BC, if the dating of a find at Nippur of citron or lemon seeds is correct. A very early contact by sea between the Indus Valley and the Mesopotamian civilizations has been proven: citrus fruit could well have arrived in the Fertile Crescent from India via this route.

The citron, which is commonly believed to have provided some of the lemon's ancestry, is a knobbly, oval yellow fruit, usually between ten and twenty centimetres (4 to 8 ins.) long – though it has been known to grow until it weighs between three and a half and nine kilograms (8 and 20 lbs.) – with a protuberant nipple like a lemon. The tree, like the lemon tree, flowers all year round and is highly susceptible to frost. Its flesh is very scanty, most of the fruit's girth being taken up by white pith an inch or more thick. This skin is made into an aromatic candied peel, which constitutes the fruit's main value today. Most of the world's commercial citrons are now grown in Tunisia and in Puerto Rico. On the island of Corsica, a liqueur called Cédratine, made from citrons, is a traditional speciality.

The Jews called this fruit an *etrog*, and still use branches of the tree and its fruits symbolically, together with myrtles, palms, and willows, in their annual harvest Festival of Booths. They interpreted a passage in the Book of Leviticus which speaks of the "goodly tree" as referring to the *etrog*. Controversy has raged over when the Jews adopted the *etrog* as the "goodly tree." Did they come into contact with it for the first time in Babylon during their exile there (586 – 539 BC)? The Hebrew names for the fruit appear to have Assyrian and Persian origins, but Palestine could have received the citron from the east long before the sixth century BC. Some think it could have come from southern Arabia; there is even one theory that citrus fruit actually originated in the Arabian peninsula and spread from there. The idea that the Biblical "goodly tree" was some other plant entirely, and that the citron replaced it in ritual later, is discounted by many investigators on the grounds that the Jews were extremely conservative in matters concerning religious tradition.

But whenever and wherever the Jews found and adopted the citron, it became for them a fruit of enormous significance. Use of it distinguished Judaic harvest rituals from those of all the other religions of the Middle East. The *etrog* became for the Jews a kind of symbol of national and religious identity. After they rebelled against Rome in 66 AD, they were dispersed to various parts of the Roman Empire. Wherever they went they planted citrons, so that supplies would always be available for the harvest festival; it seems reasonable to suppose that oranges and lemons were cultivated in association with the *etrogim*. For ritual purposes citrons had to be from an ungrafted tree, of a certain size and shape, fresh and unblemished. A great many of them had to be grown in order for a few to be found perfect; the rest were presumably sold in local markets. The Jews were famous for their horticultural expertise in the first centuries AD: they planted orchards round the great cities in Spain, and worked the lands – partly for the benefit of their own community – round Alexandria. In this manner they were responsible for spreading citrus plantings around the Mediterranean.

Italy seems to have received its first citron trees, and probably other citrus varieties as well, in the first century BC, perhaps from Alexandria just before and after the annexation of Egypt by the Roman Empire in 30 BC. The Greeks had always referred to citrus fruit vaguely as "Persian" and "Median" apples. The Romans followed their lead, until about the middle of the first century AD, when they, and then the Greeks, began calling the citron *citreum*, *cedrium*, and other similar terms. The reason for this is a mystery: there seems to have been some confusion between the very different cedar (*cedrus*) and the citron. Among several theories accounting for it, perhaps the most likely is that the aromatic quality of the trees' wood was what these two species were perceived to have in common. The implication seems to be that the Romans had citrus trees but usually failed to get them to fruit; they grew them for their exotic scent and their wood, the smell of which was thought to discourage moths. In a fresco of the Villa of Livia at Prima Porta (38 BC) a tree carefully enough painted to be recognizable as citrus is provided with quinces, presumably to replace the fruit which had not matured. Oranges, lemons, limes, and citrons were all known to the Romans, for we see the fruit depicted on several mosaics, paintings and bas-reliefs. Citrus fruit remained rare, however, and perhaps mainly confined in Italy to the gardens of the rich.

What is certain is that all traces of citrus fruit other than the citron, which survived owing to its religious importance for the Jews, died out after the Barbarian invasions of Italy from the end of the fourth to the sixth centuries AD. The Arabs and Persians continued to cultivate citrus fruit, but it did not spread to the west again until after Islam was founded (sixth century AD) and began its conquests in the Mediterranean Basin. The oranges which the Arabs brought with them from Persia and Mesopotamia, and from their forays into India in the eighth century, were bitter. Sweet oranges were discovered in China and brought to Europe for the first time by the Portuguese in the sixteenth century: there is in addition one reference to a sweet orange in Sicily in 1480.

The Arabs cultivated citrus trees as ornamental plants, especially delighting in the scent of their leaves, flowers, and fruit. They shredded

the ends of twigs from orange, lemon, and other aromatic trees and
used them as disposable toothbrushes. They ate citrus fruits raw and
sweetened, candied the peel, and preserved bitter Seville oranges and
their skins in sugar (the ancestor of our marmalade), and lemons in
brine (a practice which remains one of the characteristic specialities of
Moroccan cuisine). Citrus oil was a favourite perfume, and went into
soaps and medicines. The Patio of the Oranges was planted at the Great
Mosque of Cordoba in southern Spain in 976; the courtyards of the
Alhambra in Granada were filled with oranges and lemons. After this,
citrus trees became favourite plantings in Spanish mosques, and then
in palaces, cloisters, and kitchen gardens throughout the Mediterranean
world. Huge citrus plantations were created in Spain. It is thought to
have been under the Normans in the twelfth century that Sicily, which
is still the world's largest producer of lemons, received its first lemon
trees.

THE LIFE OF LEMONS

The first clear literary reference to lemons is, as far as we know, an
Arab document of the early tenth century, where the *laimun* tree is said
to be very sensitive to cold. After citrons and limes, lemons are the
most vulnerable of the citrus fruits to frost. Ripe fruit on the tree is
destroyed by a temperature of $-1°C$ ($30°F$); even immature lemons
suffer internal drying at $-3°C$ ($26°F$), and the trees which bear them
can take only four more degrees (Celsius) of frost. The lemon is a sub-
tropical tree, and the fruit in its natural habitat is green in colour even
when ripe, and scarcely sour at all. The "orange" family of citrus fruits
show by their behaviour that they come from semi-tropical climes,
further north and cooler than the sub-tropical home of green, sweetish
lemons.

The warm, humid climate of northern India, where lemons most
probably came from, almost never gets colder than $10°C$ ($50°F$). But
the quality of acidity which we prize in the lemon, and also what we
think of as its characteristic colour, develop only when the fruit gets
cold (though not freezing) from time to time; less than $10°C$ ($50°F$) is
needed to begin decomposition of the chlorophyll in the peel. If we
want lemons sour and bright yellow we are compelled to grow them
quite close to their threshold of cold tolerance, which is why lemons

can be "tricky" trees. Modern lemon plantations are provided with wind machines and oil-burning orchard heaters in case of frost; personnel must constantly monitor temperatures and weather predictions, and maintain readiness to adjust the heat in the groves artificially at any moment. The cost of heating has become so heavy recently that low-energy methods are under study; running water in furrows and under-tree sprinklers can provide some protection from frost.

Lemon trees love plenty of water, but not a lot of rain: if the fruit gets wet its skin becomes puffy and prone to disease. The reason is thought to be that lemon trees evolved in forests where they lived in the shade of larger trees, so that little water actually fell on the lemons. The trees' trunks and branches are extremely sensitive to sunburn: in certain climates their limbs have to be protected by being wrapped against the sun, or painted white to coat them and reflect the light and heat off their bark. They have a very shallow root system for their size, and they need more fertilizer than most crops; again these characteristics are thought to have developed because of their origin in rich forest soil.

The lemon tree (*citrus limon*), like the closely-related citron (*citrus medica*), has purple buds and white flowers tinged with purple. It blooms and fruits all year round if the temperature is ideal: a tree often bears buds and flowers (white and purple), developing fruit (green to silvery) and mature fruit (yellow) all at the same time. The flowers, only 10 per cent of which actually set fruit, usually grow in clusters; each one may be accompanied by a single thorn. The lemon tree is naturally upright and spreading; its overall shape, like its fruit, is oval rather than round like the bushy orange tree and its spherical progeny. Lemon trees, unlike orange trees, have to be severely pruned every year, a labour-intensive and costly process which is necessary to encourage fruiting.

Citrus trees are evergreen, and the number of their leaves is directly related to the amount of fruit they produce, for the leaves manufacture the trees' food and help store any excess. Lemon leaves are paler than orange leaves, and, like them, dotted with tiny sacs containing volatile aromatic oil. The sacs can be seen by the naked eye if you hold a leaf up to the light; they burst and release their fragrance when the leaf is crushed. The leaves of all citrus trees contain d-limonene, which means that orange, grapefruit, or tangerine leaves all smell of lemon. Lemon leaves breathe on their under-sides, which is a highly useful trait when the environment is dusty.

A lemon is actually a large and rather unusual berry, of the type known, after the Golden Apples of the Hesperides, as a *hesperidium*. It has concentrated the solidity of the pulp of ordinary berries in its leathery rind, and given over its interior to membrane and juice. It is the outer rind, the *flavedo*, which turns yellow in cold conditions. The inner spongy white pith is the *albedo*, enclosing between ten and thirteen membrane-covered compartments containing vesicles full of greenish-yellow juice. There may be up to eight seeds, or none. The *flavedo* (from the Latin for "yellow") is dotted with oil sacs which are self-contained and without communication with surrounding cells or the fruit's exterior; this enclosure preserves the oil until its volatile fragrance is released when the peel is pressed or cut.

In North America and Europe the peel of citrus fruit is used quite differently from the flesh: we eat it only when it has been grated or cut in tiny pieces and mixed with herbs to be sprinkled over food, or we soak a twist of it in liquid as a flavouring. In other cultures, in Africa for instance, citrus fruit is quite commonly eaten whole, without peeling: it would be considered a waste to forgo the strong sensations afforded by the rind. Ripe tropical lemons are much less acid than ours, so that lemons as well as oranges can be eaten whole. In Athol Fugard's play, *The Island*, an African eats an orange whole; at the play's opening night in London, the audience sat coolly through the nude scenes on stage, but there were gasps of horror at the sight of a man enjoying a whole unpeeled orange.

Citrus fruits comprise the third-largest fruit crop on earth, after grapes and bananas. About 10 per cent of them are lemons and limes (which for some reason are not differentiated in world citrus statistics); most of the rest are oranges. There has been an enormous increase in worldwide lemon production, which more than doubled between the 1930s and the 1960s. Today about three million tons of lemons are grown annually, roughly two-thirds of them in Italy and the United States. The rest are grown in the Mediterranean region and in Mexico, Argentina, Chile, Brazil, Australia, and South Africa. Unknown quantities of lemons are raised for personal and non-commercial use, mainly in Africa, India, and the non-Mediterranean Middle East.

Nearly all the lemons in North America are grown in California. Florida tried hard to achieve commercially viable results in lemon-raising, but periodic frosts, in particular the disasters of 1835 and 1895, killed off the plantations. Some lemons are now grown in the southern part of the state, but the semi-tropical climate and the humidity of the Florida peninsula easily cause lemons to become puffy and relatively tasteless; their colour is never as brilliant as that of fruit grown on the cool, sub-tropical coastlands of southern California.

A wider daily temperature fluctuation gives all California's citrus brighter colouring, thicker rinds, and more of both sugar and acid than Florida fruit, which is rounder, juicier, and thinner-skinned. Oranges with an inherently high acid content may be too acid for many people's taste when grown in California, whereas Florida lemons may not be acid enough. It has been found practical and economical for California to grow most of the citrus eaten fresh and whole in North America. The thicker rinds of its fruit are an added advantage, providing extra protection for the transport of fruit across the continent. Florida provides the huge quantities (mainly of oranges) demanded for the juice and concentrate market, and for processing generally.

When the Spanish ceded Florida to the United States in 1821, they left behind them many wild citrus trees which had escaped from the plantations and could survive the sudden Florida frosts. Among these were various kinds of sour oranges and rough lemons: the latter tall trees covered with small thorns, bearing large, unpleasant-tasting lemons with thick skins and rough nipples. The rough lemon is believed to have been brought from India by Vasco da Gama or his Portuguese successors in the sixteenth century and planted where it is now found, in Africa and America.

Citrus trees, especially lemons, when raised from seed are ferociously thorny and take fifteen years to begin producing fruit; buds grafted onto already growing rootstock, however, begin to bear within five years and are far less prickly. Because of this, and because of the unpredictability of citrus fruit when the parent tree has been grown from seed, modern plantations invariably propagate their trees by budding or grafting fruit-bearers of known excellence onto rootstock, which should be tough and resistant to cold and disease. Oranges develop the finest, slightly acid taste when their rootstock is sour orange, but sour orange trees have been found to be subject to *tristeza* or "quick decline," a serious and so far almost untreatable citrus disease which is dreaded all over the world. Rough lemon rootstock gives an orange with less of the acidity required for the finest taste, but with resistance to *tristeza* as well as to drought. In addition rough lemon roots cause oranges to bear more fruit. For these reasons rough lemon is today the rootstock of millions of orange trees, especially in North and South America. Rootstock is toughest when it has grown from seed; Seminole Indians, who received citrus stock from the early Spanish missions, still pick rough lemon fruit, much of it growing wild in the Everglades, and sell it for rootstock seed to the giant orange corporations of Florida.

California lemons are budded onto orange rootstock because orange trees are far sturdier than lemon trees being grown for acid fruit, and less prone to crown- and root-rot diseases. Lemons grown from seed are also the most unpredictable of the already erratic citrus tribe. Sweet orange, grapefruit, mandarin, sour orange, and tangelo stock are all used to support lemon scions.

There are twenty-one officially named kinds of lemon. Verna makes up 90 per cent of the lemon production of Murcia in Spain; Femminello Ovale is 75 per cent of that from Italy. The two main varieties grown in California (and therefore the two commercially available throughout North America) are Lisbon, originally from Portugal but introduced into California from Australia in 1874, and Eureka, which was propagated from a single tree discovered in California in 1858.

The Eureka lemon is very similar to the Lisbon, but its tree is smaller and almost thornless, making the fruit especially easy to pick. An extremely important point is that it stores well. Both Eureka and Lisbon produce medium-sized fruit, very yellow, highly acid, and containing few seeds. A close relative which used to be grown a good deal in California, the Villafranca, has been almost abandoned now because it takes one year longer to bear than the two winners in the highly competitive commercial stakes. Eureka predominates two to one in the coastal regions; most of its fruit tends to mature in summer when demand is highest. Lisbon withstands frost, heat, and wind better, and is chosen for inland locations; its shorter, though heavier, main harvest is picked mostly in the fall and winter. The two types of lemon are hard to tell apart, except that a dimple or crease at one side of the nipple probably (but by no means certainly) means it's a Lisbon.

A lemon tastes best when it has been left to turn fully yellow on the tree and is picked as soon as possible after that. Anyone who can obtain such a lemon is fortunate indeed; it would be almost worth moving somewhere with a citrus-growing climate or buying a greenhouse just to be able to control one's fate in this respect. For most people outside the tropics, lemons have to be bought in grocery stores and in supermarkets. They have deliberately been picked green, when the acid content is highest; the acid is what makes ripe lemons last longer in storage than almost any other fruit, and immature lemons are more indestructable still.

Lemon-pickers go over the trees as many as six times a year, carrying five-centimetre (2 in.) ring gauges and taking from the tree only green lemons too large to pass through the ring. (Any yellow fruit is immediately processed or used locally.) They wear gloves to protect themselves from thorns, and take care not to scratch or bruise the peel in any way; fruit on the tree has a tender skin which can be damaged by the merest scrape of a fingernail. It must never be picked wet, because a wet lemon's rind is turgid and extremely easy to spoil by the release of its oil when pressure is applied. The eighty-eight kilogram (194 lb.) picking sacks for lemons are especially designed to allow gentle emptying from the bottom into boxes for transport to the storage sheds.

Green lemons have an FRF (Fruit Removal Force) of as much as nine kilograms (20 lb.) or more; this means that picking must be done by hand, with the aid of clippers. Research is being done into ways of chemically lowering the FRF of citrus trees in general, so that mechanical shakers or water hoses can be used to bring down the fruit. To date, the work remains manual, however: lemons in particular are especially hard to dislodge because they are not allowed to ripen on the tree, and would be at great risk of damage from their own thorns if shaken down. Moreover, the chemicals in question hasten the aging of the peel and reduce its resistance to decay. Pesticide use is also a problem for lemon growers, because the tree is never stripped of all its fruit: renewed applications of chemicals mean repeated doses for the lemons at their various stages of development.

Citrus, unlike most deciduous fruit, does not continue to ripen once severed from the tree. The next stage, "curing" the lemons, is carried out for aesthetic reasons alone and makes no difference to the juice inside. The lemons are washed and brushed and then made to turn yellow by being treated with ethylene oxide. The process was once known as "gassing," but "degreening" and "curing" have been judged to have less sinister connotations; "gassing" has therefore been dropped from the fruit-growers' terminology. Ethylene gas "degreens" by loosening the thin membrane that separates chlorophyll from its associated enzyme, chlorophyllase. This enzyme destroys chlorophyll on contact, leaving only the carotenoid pigment, lemon yellow. Ethylene gas is given off by many ripening fruits, so that this particular manipulation is considered to be almost natural; green lemons closeted with lots of ripening bananas, for instance, will turn yellow in a day or so.

Lemons are kept at the ideal temperature of 14°C (58°F) until needed for sale, often between three and six months after they have been picked. As they age, their skins become harder and more resistant to injury during transport. They are dipped in solutions containing copper, sodium carbonate, and other fungicides, and given a coat of wax to replace that lost in the scrubbing. This helps them withstand water loss, and keeps them looking shiny. Care has to be taken not to apply too much wax, for it would suffocate the lemons and ruin the taste of the juice. The tissue wrappers and cartons in which the fruit is packed are also impregnated with bactericides.

Before the invention and establishment of the processes of refrigeration and efficient rail transport, even the sturdy lemon was hard to obtain and expensive in cold northern countries. One ingenious answer to part of this problem was the creation of the lemon pavilions of Lake Garda in Italy, the northern-most citrus-growing plantations in the world. The lake is deep and itself a warming influence, and the lie of the surrounding land, which includes mountains screening off the cold of the Alps, creates a mild enclave. Even this is too cold for lemons, however, since temperatures drop below 0°C (32°F) for about twenty-one days in the year. The solution adopted for this problem was a cheaper version of the glassed-in galleries known as *orangeries* which were all the rage at French châteaux from the sixteenth century onwards.

The lemon gardens at Lake Garda were protected with high walls on three sides. Concrete and stone pillars about ten metres (33 ft.) tall were built at four-metre (13-ft.) intervals, with the trees growing between. In November when the cold weather arrived, gardeners would cover the sides and tops of the pavilions, fixing matting and wooden screens across the tops of the pillars and the open side, to enclose the trees completely. Glass panels let in some light; and stoves or fires were carefully lit inside on the coldest nights. The trees, in this manner, lived through the winter, and, the following April, the temporary parts of the lemon houses could be dismantled. Each tree produced about six hundred fruit a year, and would go on fruiting for over a century. The fruit was sold throughout northern Italy, and over the Alps in Germany and Austria.

This method of cultivating the lemon, one version of which is still practised in the region of Sorrento, dated back at Garda to at least 1500, and has been traced to the influence of the Franciscan monastery at Gargnano, founded in 1266. When D. H. Lawrence visited Lake Garda for the first time in 1912, he was told that St. Francis of Assisi himself had brought lemons to the region. He describes the lemon houses of Garda in his book *Twilight in Italy*, and relates his discussion with a worried proprietor who resented the threat to his trade of the lemons already arriving in increasing numbers from the south. And yet this very man, Lawrence thought bitterly, cared nothing for his beautiful lake or for the sun; he wanted railways, machines, and riches. "He did not know these mechanisms, their great, human-contrived, inhuman power, and he wanted to know them." Apprehension about the seemingly inevitable and probably ugly future results in a yearning for the past. "I sat on the roof of the lemon-house," Lawrence continues, "with the lake below and the snowy mountain opposite, and looked at the ruins on the old, olive-fuming shores, at all the peace of the ancient world still covered in sunshine, and the past seemed to me so lovely that one must look towards it, backwards, only backwards, where there is peace and beauty and no more dissonance."

Today lemon-pavilion colonnades still stand on the terraces above Lake Garda, their light, regularly-spaced pillars reflecting in the water and stitching serene patterns over the green mountainsides. They are a unique and magical part of this famous landscape. But only a handful of the pavilions still have lemons growing in them, and those only because their owners do it for pleasure and to keep up the tradition. Sicilian lemons have long ago put them all out of business. But there are movements afoot to preserve the lemon-pillars, even without the gardens, as a distinctive sight and a tourist attraction. Expensive resort hotels in the area like to incorporate the lemon-pavilion "look" into their architecture.

Lemons do play a role for people living in cold climates which corresponds to that of the faraway and longed-for Golden Apples of the Hesperides of Greek myth. Imported lemons arrive in our shops from the gardens of the fortunate south like golden missives from the sun itself. Northern Europeans, and especially Germans, have for centuries regarded the lemon juice, *limone spremuta*, of Lake Garda as their first taste of the south after the journey down from the Alps. The heart-stopping sight of the beautiful lake seemed to northerners like a glimpse of paradise, which would later ripen in their minds as a nostalgic and golden memory. For those who had only heard about it, the imagined splendour of this lake was symbolic of an equally ardent longing for the Future or for the Past, or for Elsewhere. Goethe evoked instantly the romantic desire of northerners for the south when he opened one of his poems with the words, *Kennst du das Land, wo die Zitronen blühn?* – "Do you know the land where the lemon-trees bloom?"

LEMONADE, POP, AND PROCESSED JUICE

The people of northern Europe had no knowledge of lemons until the Crusaders first tasted the fruit in the Holy Land at the end of the twelfth century. Not long after this, ships arriving in England from Spain and Portugal were including in their cargo a citrus sweet which they called *succade*; the lemon variety of this confection was specified as *sitrenade*. The fruit itself began to be regularly transported northwards for sale a hundred years later. The sour principle in cooking until then was supplied by tart fruits and leaves (crab apples, sorrel, green gooseberries, quinces) and vinegar; sour grapes gave acid verjuice. In France, the *marchands d'aigrun* sold everything sour, and monopolized the sale of citrus fruit as soon as it became available. Oranges, lemons, limes, and grapefruit are still called *agrumes* in French, from *aigre* ("sour"), even though sweet oranges now comprise most citrus in France as elsewhere.

One of the first uses for citrus fruit in northern European cooking was as an accompaniment for meat; bitter oranges and lemons would be stewed and served whole. Seville oranges were thought to be especially good with fish, while lemons were served with poultry. Lemons were for a long time unreliably acid; the earliest lemons mentioned in the north were mostly the "sweet," that is only slightly acid, *citrus limetta*, which the Sicilians called *lumie*. It is only in the eighteenth century that lemon juice (by now dependably sour) begins to be named regularly as an accompaniment for fish – a combination which today seems as obvious to us as that of butter with corn.

The Mongols were the first people recorded (in 1299) as enjoying lemonade (actually sweetened lemon-juice preserved with alcohol), although others must have discovered the drink before them. The English learned in India to like punch. The word comes from the Sanskrit for "five" because of its five ingredients: alcohol (originally arrack), tea, lemon juice (known in eighteenth-century England as "rob of lemons"), water, and sugar or honey. "Shrub," perhaps from the Arabic word *sharbia,* "drink," which also becomes "sherbet," was another popular English drink. It was made of brandy, white wine, lemon juice and peel, and sugar.

In the seventeenth century sugar became increasingly available in northern Europe, being shipped in from the new plantations in the West Indies. A fashion arose in France for lemon juice sugared and diluted in water. *Limonadiers,* who carried this drink in metal containers on their backs to sell it in the streets, became a familiar sight in Paris, much as fruit juice and water-sellers are today in Istanbul, Damascus, and other cities of the Middle East. Regular shipments of tropical fruit began to arrive in England from British colonies as well as from southern Europe; in 1703 oranges and lemons were being sold in the streets of London from "moveable shops that run upon wheels, attended by ill-looking Fellows." Oranges were a favourite snack, sold by female vendors at the theatres; Nell Gwynn, the mistress of King Charles II, was once an "orange girl."

A few drops of vinegar had always been added to water by the itinerant water-sellers, to help quench thirst; but sweetened lemonade was far more pleasing, though few people could afford it at first because both lemons and sugar were imported and costly. Parisian food connoisseurs at the same time added the claim, which has often been reiterated since, that lemon juice in salad dressing was less likely than vinegar to clash with the wine served at meals. (Lovers of vinegar in salad dressings respond that vinegar provides a "more complex" taste.) The *vinaigriers* of Paris began to see some of their trade being threatened; and the matter became serious for them in 1630, when a sudden drop in the price of sugar brought the price of lemonade down so that ordinary people could buy it, and demand for it started to grow.

In 1676 the French government granted a patent or monopoly to the lemonade men, creating a whole new guild, the *Compagnie des Limonadiers.* They set up permanent shops on the streets of Paris, and, together with the sellers of coffee and chocolate, gradually evolved the *café,* one of the great institutions of the modern city. Until the mid-nineteenth century, the owners of Parisian cafés were often known both officially and popularly as *limonadiers.*

Sometime in the eighteenth century, most probably in Switzerland, a method was found of "impregnating factitious waters with fixed air." At last it was possible to make ordinary water fizz, just as the delicious waters did from healthful mineral springs. Like so many culinary revolutions, the birth of carbonated beverages was thought at first to be a purely medicinal triumph; from the beginning carbonated quinine water was called "tonic," and drunk as one would follow doctors' orders or visit a spa. The next step was the sweetening of the "soda" water with another technologically perfected wonder, sugar; finally fruit syrups were created to be dissolved in the drink. Carbonated lemonade was one of the first of these concoctions, since lemonade itself was already so popular. At the Great Exhibition of 1851 in London, more than a million effervescent drinks were consumed, most of them soda water, ginger beer, and lemonade.

In the United States, where soda fountains became huge baroque architectural fantasies as well as centres for the social life of towns and cities, the new fizzy drinks achieved a reputation even loftier than that of a remedy for sickness: they were non-alcoholic, therefore safe and pure; they were an alternative to Evil. Coca-Cola—which started out as a medicine with a kick, combining extracts from the Bolivian Indian stimulant leaf, coca (from which cocaine is derived), and the African "Hell Seed," the kola nut—was advertised by its inventor in 1886 as "the Intellectual Beverage and Temperance Drink."

It was sold by its first great promoter, the devout Methodist Asa Griggs Candler, not only with the commercial instincts of a genius, but also with absolutely sincere missionary zeal. It was a *soft* drink: clean, wholesome, and entirely innocent. American medical journals began their attacks on the ready availability of cocaine in 1899; and very soon, in 1903, the Coca-Cola company without announcement removed all trace of the drug from its product, using from then on only spent (drug-free) coca leaves. The "healthy" image was quite sufficiently intoxicating to the buying public; any hidden "kick" had become not only redundant but a potential threat to the product's reputation.

"Pop" received its name in late nineteenth-century America. The word referred to the popping of corks which occurred when bottles were opened. In all probability *pop* has also come to connote in most people's minds the first syllable of the word *popular*. North Americans today annually consume 165 litres (36.3 Imperial gallons) of pop each—that is more than a bottle a day for every man, woman, and child. The amount has tripled since the 1950s; pop was said to have replaced water as America's favourite drink in 1983. Carbonated beverages contain water, sugar or aspartame, natural and artificial flavourings, natural and artificial colouring, acidifying agents, buffering agents, emulsifying and stabilizing agents, viscosity-producing or viscosity-lessening agents, foaming agents, and chemical preservatives. Several of the chemicals involved are derived from citrus fruits, or were once extracted from oranges and lemons but are now artificially synthesized.

Drinks containing predominantly lemon-lime flavours have long been overtaken in popularity by cola pop: they comprise 12.7 per cent of the American market, while the colas make up 63.2 per cent. The most famous of the lemon-lime drinks, Seven-Up, was produced by a family-owned-and-operated business until 1967. It began its career in 1929 with the unwieldy name, "Bib-Label Lithiated Lemon-Lime Soda," and was sold, in the moral and medicinal tradition, as a hangover cure "for home and hospital use." From the start, however, it was usually bought as a mixer for various kinds of liquor. In 1968, Seven-Up began an advertising campaign in which it proclaimed itself "the UnCola." Given the role of Coca-Cola and Pepsi-Cola in North American culture, this distinction implied a rejection of the establishment which amounted almost to profanity: it caught exactly the spirit of the rebellious young in the late 1960s. Lemon-lime drinks jumped from third to second place in North American sales, a spot they have held on to ever since.

Meanwhile, the idea of drinking fruit juices, an entirely different experience from that of eating fruit, was becoming increasingly attractive. Fruit juice in a glass is cleaner and easier to consume than the whole of the fruit; it is the refined and luxurious essence of the thing, produced by previously performed fastidious effort, like de-boned chicken or strained consommé. Perfectionist middle-class nineteenth-century households, with their high standards of both decency and comfort, demanded more and more lemonade for children's parties, drinks on the lawn, picnics, and family gatherings.

Until the end of the nineteenth century, the kitchen gadgets used to squeeze lemons were made in two parts, often fitted together with hinges, one bowl-shaped to receive the half-lemon, the other dome-shaped; the two pieces were squeezed together by means of long handles. They were made first of wood, then of cast-iron; the squeezing parts were often of porcelain, because of the fruit's acidity. After 1860, the bowl becomes cone-shaped to hold a lemon better, and then perforated to allow the juice to flow out without the pips and pulp.

The familiar object we all know as a lemon-squeezer was a stroke of genius, created by an unknown inventor before 1897, when it first appears in the Sears Roebuck Catalogue, complete with ribbed dome and

juice-catching rim; the teeth for catching the pips appear soon afterwards. The brilliance of this invention involves the realization that the
human hand, which can twist the fruit about and so get the maxi-
mum amount of juice from it, is far more efficient than a wooden or
iron plunger. The squeezer began its conquest of the world's kitchens
when an advertisement was placed in the *Saturday Evening Post* for
February 19, 1916, suggesting that we should "Drink an Orange" for
breakfast, and offering round glass orange-squeezers to readers for ten
cents each. This was an early sign of the coming revolution in American
breakfast-eating habits. It was just at this time that Will Kellogg was
beginning to promote corn flakes, the new cold breakfast cereal.

Lemon juice, which was once by far the most popular of fruit juices,
is now drunk much less than orange juice, especially since the discovery
in 1948 of a way to make frozen concentrated orange juice which retains
a good deal of its citrus flavour. Concentrated lemon juice is far less
successful, largely because of the poor integration of the added sugar
into the overall taste.

People still squeeze fresh lemon and orange juice for themselves, and
they know that the result is opaque in appearance. Within twenty-four
hours after squeezing (within four hours in the case of navel oranges)
the juice clarifies; at the same time, though for different reasons, the
fresh citric taste is lost. What has happened is that a pectic enzyme
called *pectinesterase* destroys the opaqueness, what the trade calls "cloud"
(which is associated in our minds with the distinctive, fresh citric taste)
in the juice. Extreme care is therefore taken with temperatures when
orange and lemon juice is processed. After pasteurization at 60 – 65°C.
(140 – 149°F.) for lemons (the fruit is extremely sensitive to heat – much
more so than oranges) the juice would turn as clear as diluted concentrate of apple juice: the taste would not have been destroyed, but
customers would never accept unclouded citrus juice. So lemon juice
is heated to 80°C. (176°F.) for exactly 3 seconds, or 85°C. (185°F.) for .8
seconds: this treatment is just sufficient to kill the pectic enzyme and
so prevent "cloud" loss. The slightest error in timing or temperature
impairs the flavour of the juice. There are also "clouding agents" available to the processed juice industry; these are made of coconut oil and
dearomatized cocoa butter, or methoxy pectin with starch and gum.

In spite of the lemon's excellent qualities of self-preservation and
handiness, people still find it worthwhile to add preservatives to lemon
juice and to package it in plastic lemon shapes. The size and form of

the lemon are so perfect and unmistakeable that they are kept; but square bottoms are sometimes added, because the lemon has failed to evolve a non-rolling feature. The same treated juice is also bottled for kitchen use.

One of the pioneers in this method of marketing lemon juice, ReaLemon, became engaged in 1978 in a long legal battle when its first real competitor found that it had to charge so little for its product in order to attract customers that it failed to break even. The case is a fascinating demonstration, not only of the attitudes governing competition in our society, but also of the behaviour of customers. Borden, the owners of ReaLemon, were told by the United States Court of Appeals in 1982 to cease and desist from pricing their product so low that the competition had no chance. They had, the Court judged, unlawfully monopolized the processed lemon juice market; the ReaLemon name had attracted too much power to itself.

Customers, it seems, are both "inert" about their shopping and tend to brand loyalty. Lemon juice is used in small amounts on all kinds of food. A poorly produced processed lemon juice could spoil the flavour of everything it is sprinkled on, so people who have found a brand of bottled lemon juice which they can put up with are cautious about trying another which might displease them and ruin a lot of food before it is discarded. They are actually prepared to forgo risking something new, especially since processed lemon juice is rarely high on the grocery list, and is not very expensive. ReaLemon had, in fact, priced itself so low in the first place because if it had asked a higher sum people might have remained satisfied with actual lemons.

Although profits to be made from the food-processing industry are huge, the headaches, as we have had occasion to remark before, are many: food can be machine-tooled, but people remain hopelessly irregular and difficult to predict. In this case they showed themselves to be lazy enough to buy a product which cannot match in taste the original; they were also too cautious to investigate the claims of something different. Perhaps we should marvel more at how much the industry persuades us to get out and buy – and then to accept when we have bought it.

THE ANSWER IS A LEMON

The lemon is perhaps the most versatile of fruits, not only in its range of culinary applications, but also in its general household and medicinal usefulness. The aromas and acids extracted from citrus fruit in general and lemons in particular are used in hundreds of different ways. Almost every kind of pop, for instance – not just those with obvious lemon flavourings – includes in its formula one or more extracts from various citrus fruits, including lemons. The anti-oxidant and flavouring agent d-limonene, extracted from the oil of lemon and orange peel, is one of the ingredients in the Coca-Cola formula which is kept such a celebrated secret.

Citral, a light yellow liquid with a citrus odour, is used as lemon flavouring in commercially-produced ice-cream and candy. It comes from lemon oil, but is now usually synthesized. Lemon oil and its products are also in packaged gelatin desserts, chewing gum, condiments, cereals, and many kinds of flavouring syrups. The fragrance of the concentrated oil (known in the trade as "folded" oil) is important in the soap, detergent, perfume, and cosmetics industries. Lemon oil is said from time to time to be cancer-causing, but complaints have not so far been sufficiently substantiated to elicit any action against it. Citrus peel causes allergies in some people; for this reason citrus products for infants never contain the constituents of peel. Frozen concentrated citrus juices, on the other hand, rely on peel-oil for a good deal of their taste.

Citric acid, an anti-oxidant and mild astringent, is the most widely used acidulant in the food industry; it is present in pop, candy, processed cheese, jellies, potato chips and other processed potatoes, and frozen foods generally. It is useful in curing meats and for firming-up such vegetables as peppers and tomatoes: it neutralizes odours and deactivates trace metals with their propensity to dull colours and cause off-flavours as foods age. When vegetables are mechanically peeled, the lye used to loosen skins is neutralized by citric acid.

More of this acid is found in the juice of lemons than in any other widely available fruit. Extraction of it, by boiling, settling, and screening the juice, or by freezing its water component and removing the ice so as to concentrate the acid, was once an important industry in Sicily, Cyprus, the Caribbean, and other sources of the world's lemon supply. Calcium citrate, marketed in powdered form, was also derived from lemons. But nowadays citric acid is usually prepared by mould fermentation of sugar solutions. The discovery of this process in the 1920s dealt a devastating blow to lemon and lime cultivation in the Caribbean. Citric acid is, in fact, found in most plants; this helps explain why the taste of lemon juice weds satisfactorily with the flavours of such a wide variety of foods: the lemon sharpens the acid already present in them.

Absolutely every part of a lemon is useful in some way, from its seeds to its outermost peel. Lemon-pip oil, unsaturated and aromatic, is important in the soap industry and in special diets. The pulp left over from squeezed lemons is evaporated and concentrated into "citrus molasses" which is sold as a base for making vinegar and as an ingredient in bland syrups and alcohol. The remains of the "rag" or pulp is also sold as cattle feed. Most of the pectin used to thicken and solidify jams, jellies, and marmalades comes from the white pith of citrus fruits. Among these, lemon and lime pectin has the highest "jelly grade" or capacity to thicken liquids. It is widely used in medicines taken to combat diarrhoea. The flavedo, or outer yellow layer of lemon peel, is invaluable for its intense taste and scent. (The word *zest*, which originally meant "skin or peel," then specifically "citrus peel," is now in common use as signifying "lively enjoyment.")

The chemical properties of lemons have been noticed and used for centuries, not only in the kitchen but as part of any knowledgeable housewife's medicine chest. Lemon juice is recommended in household manuals for hair and skin preparations; it is an ancient prescription for skin whitening and the removal of freckles, and is often claimed actually to promote slimming. It was a universally applicable bleach, a cold remedy, a relief for asthma and rheumatism, a laxative, and an aid for upset stomachs generally. The ancients had recommended citrus fruit as an antidote for poisons. Lemons have such high status as an all-round curative in modern Egypt that, according to a Coptic expression, a person convinced that everyone needs and adores him "thinks himself a lemon in a nauseated town." People used to chew lemon slices to relieve toothache (at least it could provide a distraction), and rubbed their teeth with lemon peel to whiten them. Determined women would bite into lemons or limes before parties, to sweeten their breath and redden their lips.

Lemon juice has been used to clean wooden furniture and silver, and the peel to get rid of mites, mosquitoes, and moths. Habitual sucking of lemons can corrode one's teeth to the gums, particularly if acid-softened teeth are brushed immediately afterwards with gritty dentifrice. The acid of lemons is strong enough to dissolve pearls. The resulting "salt of pearl" used to be thought an enormously powerful medicine: both magical enough and prodigally wasteful enough to cure even the diseases commonly attributed to possession by spirits. Benvenuto Cellini describes its use against epilepsy and hysteria; rich people could also demand that it be administered as a counteraction against suspected poison.

By far the greatest contribution of the lemon to human health has been its generous provision of vitamin C. A lack of vitamin C in the human body causes scurvy, which makes people depressed, weak, and anaemic. Scurvy victims are subject to internal haemorrhages and seepage of blood from the roots of their hair. Wounds refuse to heal, muscles ache, legs swell, gums bleed – the list of symptoms goes on and on. This horrible disease became a matter of focused concern in the sixteenth century, when long sea voyages of exploration were increasingly undertaken; the first account of an outbreak of scurvy at sea was written by Vasco da Gama, who discovered a passage to India via the toe of Africa in 1497. It was months of abstinence from eating fresh vegetables and fruits which, as we now know, resulted in scurvy.

Knowledge of how to cure the disease certainly existed long before vitamin C was discovered and understood. Jacques Cartier's sailors came down with scurvy on his voyage to colonize the coast of Newfoundland in 1535, and the Indians saved them by making them drink an extract of spruce needles, which are rich in vitamin C. An English herb was known as "scurvy grass" because of its remedial properties. Portuguese sailors during the sixteenth and seventeenth centuries were ordered to carry orange and lemon seed with them on all their journeys, and to plant citrus wherever they went. Victims among a Portuguese ship's sailors were once left behind on an island north of Venezuela. When the ship called back to pick them up on the return journey, the men were found to be in perfect health: they had eaten a good deal of citrus fruit during their stay on the island, which was named Curaçao, "cure," after this incident. A British ship on its maiden voyage for the East Indian Company in 1601 was able to stop off at Madagascar to take on orange and lemon juice as "the best remedy against scurvy" for the rest of its journey. The Dutch planted citrus at the Cape of Good Hope in

1654, for the use of passing ships. In the early eighteenth century a Hungarian doctor called Kramer treated scurvy by making his patients eat citrus pulp and green vegetables.

In 1747, James Lind, Physician to the British Royal Navy, performed what is thought to be one of the first clinically controlled experiments on record. Twelve scurvy victims were isolated and all given the same diet, in Lind's words: "Water-gruel sweetened with sugar in the morning; fresh mutton-broth often times for dinner; at other times puddings, boiled biscuit with sugar etc; and for supper, barley and raisins, rice and currants, sugar and wine, or the like." It was an eighteenth-century fantasy: their version of eating almost nothing but junk food. The men were then divided into six pairs, each pair's diet being supplemented by one of the following: cider; vinegar; a diluted sulphuric acid mixture; plain sea-water; a scurvy remedy in use at the time which consisted of garlic, mustard, gum myrrh, balsam of Peru, and other ingredients pounded into a paste; and two oranges and one lemon a day. Both of the men in the sixth pair were completely cured of scurvy symptoms six days after the experiment began. Even Lind, however, thought of citrus fruit as a *remedy* for scurvy; the idea was still to be conceived that nutrition might be so inadequate as to be the cause of illness, even when people have enough food comfortably to eat their fill.

The delay in making use of the accumulated knowledge of how to treat scurvy must be accounted one of the triumphs of bureaucratic isolationism and ineptitude. The British were nevertheless the first to take systematic steps to enforce anti-scurvy provisions for sailors. Forty-eight years after Lind's experiment and a year after his death, the British Navy, desperate for manpower which it still constantly lost to scurvy, decided at last to act. Ships' captains were ordered to carry enough lemons on board for every sailor to receive a daily dose of juice, beginning when the ship had been at sea about five or six weeks.

Until that date, sailors had been given rations of rum diluted with water. The water was the idea of Admiral Vernon, who saw that neat rum caused more trouble than consolation. The sailors called the watered rum "grog," describing the state of mind it induced, even after dilution, as "groggy." They named the drink after the Admiral's famous old cloak which was made of *grosgrain*, anglicized as "grogram"; the Admiral himself was known to his men as "Old Grog." Now, in 1795, grog became a mixture of rum, water, and lemon juice – which is still sold as a hot drink called *grog* in Paris cafés during the winter.

The British Navy ceased to be attacked by scurvy. Its fighting force had doubled by the beginning of the Napoleonic Wars, and lemon juice has been cited as one of the reasons for Britain's victory in that conflict. Lemons were chosen over oranges because they keep much better, especially when picked green. (We now know that lemons have roughly the same amount of vitamin C in them as oranges do, and four times as much as there is in limes.) Lemons and limes were often confused by name, lemons commonly being called "limes." British sailors soon acquired the nickname "Limeys," while the area where lemons were loaded and unloaded at the East London docks was called "Limehouse."

It has been known for centuries that a few drops of lemon juice sprinkled over cut vegetables, apples, or bananas will prevent them from browning, and citrus fruit itself does not discolour when sliced. It was an investigation into just this phenomenon which led to the discovery of vitamin C by a young Hungarian biochemist called Albert Szent-Györgyi, who published his findings in 1928. What non-browning plants had in common was an acid which turned out to be the substance which prevents scurvy – ascorbic (anti-scurvy) acid, or vitamin C. Lemon juice prevents browning by means of two acids, citric and ascorbic. These slow down the action of the enzyme set free by the rupture of plant tissues, and prevent it from combining with phenolic compounds and condensing them into brown polymers. Acid from other plants would perform this function just as well, but lemon juice is easy to apply and does not spoil the taste of the food it is protecting. Only man, other primates, and guinea pigs must consume ascorbic acid in their diets: all other animals make their own vitamin C. The acid plays a vital function in the connective tissue of our bodies, in the elimination of toxins, and in resistance to infection.

Just before he received the Nobel Prize for his work on vitamin C in 1937, Szent-Györgyi reported that he had found yet more gold in the peel of citrus fruit. He had isolated a substance which he called "citrin," which was a mixture of bioflavonoids, companions of vitamin C in the peel and pulp of oranges and lemons but not present in synthetic vitamin C. He thought they might provide additional help in the main-tenance of the body's smallest blood vessels, the capillaries. Szent-Györgyi himself withdrew his claims and suggestions as early as 1938, but the new substances, named vitamin P, became the subject of heated interest all over the world.

There are now known to be about eight hundred bioflavonoids, natural pigments which occur in most plants; about thirty of them are found in lemon peel, three of the best known being hesperidin, naringin, and rutin. Great hopes were raised that they could be used to help people suffering from diseases involving bleeding, skin disorders, frost-bite, diabetes, and abortion. In the west, disappointment with bioflavonoids was heavy. Experiments failed to prove any positive effects of these substances, but believers in their beneficial qualities could point out that anyone taking natural vitamin C always did so together with bioflavonoids, so that the power claimed for them was not easy to isolate.

In 1950 the term *vitamin P* was dropped from the medical vocabulary, though it was kept in France and Russia. In the late 1960s the U.S. Food and Drug Administration pronounced that bioflavonoids "were not a vitamin" and "lacked all nutritional value." The controversy has ended in a division between eastern and western medical practice: Russia and the Eastern Block countries prescribe bioflavonoids and market them in tablet form, but most western doctors have dropped them from the official medical repertoire, although they are still being offered, along with vitamin C, in cases where the combination just might be helpful. The dossier is not quite closed on the latest in the lengthy and ancient list of blessings which are claimed to be derived from oranges and lemons.

The manifold practical and scientific aspects of lemons can never claim all our attention, however: the poetic and evocative power of this fruit always has the last word. The German poet Rainer Maria Rilke was all his life captivated and inspired by the smell, taste, and beauty of lemons, as well as by their aura and promise of the warm south. "How I *live* it, this fragrance of lemons," he wrote once. "God knows how much I owe to it at times." In a letter to his wife dated 1901, he imagines a simple country repast which turns into a romantic seascape at sunset: "There would have to be bread, some rich, whole-grain bread and zwieback, and perhaps on a long, narrow dish some pale Westphalian ham laced with strips of white fat like an evening sky with bands of clouds. There would be some tea ready to be drunk, yellowish golden tea in glasses with silver saucers, giving off a faint fragrance. . . . Huge lemons, cut into slices, would sink like setting suns into the dusky sea, softly illuminating it with their radiating membranes, and its clear, smooth surface aquiver from the rising bitter essence."

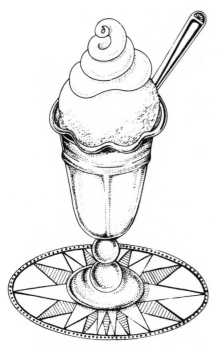

CHAPTER NINE

Ice Cream:
Cold Comfort

*M*ANKIND, thought Zeus, was a failed experiment. The creature had no fur, no claws; he was weak, fearful, inadequate, and generally hopeless: it would be better for his maker simply to cut his losses and start again, learning this time from his mistakes. But Zeus reckoned without his uncle Prometheus, the philanthropist or man-lover. The mischief-making Titan stole fire from Zeus. Then, not content with giving man what he had no business possessing, he proceeded to "place within him blind hopes" and to teach him technology: how to keep warm, to cook, to bake pottery, and to mould metals. People could then begin to live in houses instead of caves, to tame and exploit animals, to mine, to write, to compute, and all the rest.

Man in possession of fire was a thing existing in a state of permanent transgression. He encroached ceaselessly upon the rights of the rest of the universe; his weakness combined with his greed and his techno-logical know-how gave him what the Greeks called *daemonic* characteristics: he was neither one thing nor the other, a hybristic and troublesome mixture of beast and god. He was a perpetrator of nasty, dangerous, and pollution-causing acts, such as raping his Mother Earth by ploughing her up, and travelling over the seas where only fish belonged. It even occurred to him that he could find out how to fly.

The whole unfortunate yet fiendishly exhilarating saga began when Prometheus deceived the gods and let man get his hands on the secret of fire power – perhaps at the time when flint flakes emitted sparks as they were chipped into the first manufactured tools. The early stages of technological progress we call the Stone Age, the Bronze Age, and the Iron Age. Each of these was characterized by an increase in mastery over heat: human beings found out how to attain and use higher and higher temperatures. Later came insights into the uses of steel, steam, electricity, and nuclear power: all of them manipulations of heat.

Very recently we have begun a new journey of exploration, this time into the realms of cold. Heat is still the essential tool, however, for heat must be used in order to make cold. The science of low temperatures began seriously to affect people's everyday lives only about a century ago. Within one hundred years, cold (which had previously been almost always synonymous with death, evil, and the inhuman) has become essential to the lives we have chosen to live, in vast agglomerations of people cut off from what we need to nourish ourselves.

Cold preserves food until it is within our reach; cold enables us to get food from anywhere on earth at any season of the year. It therefore helps modern man to reduce the dominance that space and time hold over him. Robbed of cold, a modern city would be beaten to its knees within weeks. Blood banks, sperm banks, cryomedicine, plant libraries, rockets, and satellites are some more of the applications of cold to modernity. It would be wise perhaps to remember that these are all expressions of our need as well as of our resourcefulness.

We now know that it is impossible for anything to get colder than $-273°$C. ($-459°$F.). There is a great deal more about cold that we do not know, for cold science is still in its adolescence. The promising young technological giant had humble origins. Our realization that cold could be systematically used, even created, to prevent the putrefaction of meat and other foodstuffs came only after thousands of years of seeking out and saving ice merely to satisfy a desire for cool drinks in summer. Scientific enterprise also received modest but sustained support from the discovery that ice cream, a luxury dessert which had long been known, but only to the rich and by hearsay to everybody else, could in fact be made quite easily and cheaply by – and eventually for – everyone.

The democratization of ice cream depended on far more than cold science, however: it also required a great breakthrough in medical knowledge, as well as deployment of all the technological and social systems and structures which constituted the Industrial Revolution. Ice cream is, therefore, much more than merely its firm, sweet, frozen self. In its present form and widespread availability, it is a peculiarly modern phenomenon. For this reason, and also because of the ancient and still vigorous connotations of milk and of cold, it has become invested, in European and American cultures, with what amounts to mythic power. Ice cream is an appropriate and inevitable symbol of the yearnings, satisfactions, and contradictions inherent in modernity.

THE HISTORY OF ICE

A crowd never failed to collect, day after day, outside the window at 164A, The Strand, in London. It was the mid-1840s, and London was a densely populated, dirty, sprawling city, the largest the world had ever known. In the window sat a miracle, or rather the fruit of many miracles, the most perverse and delightful sight many of the crowd could imagine. It was a block of pure ice, and as it melted it was constantly replaced, from within the office building, from an unending supply of similar blocks. The ice had been brought by ship and rail all the way from America, and had successfully weathered a journey lasting over a month. Queen Victoria was pleased to express her admiration, and after that the royal household was always given ice by the American trading company, on request.

The sight of ice was surprising because it was in downtown London in the mid-nineteenth century. For thousands of years people have known how to collect ice from ponds, rivers, and mountain tops, and to save it, packed in heaps and insulated, for hot days when cool drinks are delicious. It has been suggested that mysterious pits found in Iron Age villages in Britain were intended for ice storage, and experiments have shown that they could have been used for this purpose. At the beginning of his great work, *The Mediterranean*, Fernand Braudel discusses the importance of the presence of mountains throughout the region, and shows how through the ages men have mined the summits of the Alps, the Pyrenees, Taygetus in Greece, and the mountains of North Africa for ice and snow, and carried these treasures down to the hot Mediterranean coasts and plains for sale.

In the fifth or early fourth century BC, Xenophon complained of people who "drank before they were thirsty," and therefore needed such effete titillations to thirst as costly wines and snow in summer. When Alexander the Great besieged the Indian city of Petra he had thirty "cold pits" dug, filled with snow, and covered with oak planks, so that his army could cool their wine and wait out the summer for their victims in relative comfort. Alexander had learned this technique (which was probably also known to the Indians) at his home in Macedonia. Roman emperors had ice brought to them by donkey-pack, sometimes from as far away as the Alps, over the excellent Roman roads. Seneca railed against the drunken habitués of the "shops and storehouses for snow" in the city of Rome.

The Arab word for "drink" is *sharbia*, which, as we saw earlier, gave us the word *sherbet*, so common was it to ice fruit drinks in the middle east. In 1494, the owner of a pilgrim boat received as a gift on his arrival in the Holy Land a sack full of snow, to the surprise and delight of his hot and thirsty passengers. The Turkish Empire was especially addicted to iced drinks, and was so well organized that ordinary citizens and not merely the military or the élite could enjoy them. Merchants sold snow water, pieces of ice, and fruit ices cheaply in the streets of Turkish towns. Boatloads of snow from Bursa arrived frequently in Istanbul (then known as Constantinople) during the sixteenth century, and the Pasha Muhammad received an income of 80,000 sequins for his ice mines in 1578.

Underground ice houses were known in China from at least 1100 BC, when a hymn addressed to the Goddess of Cold included these words:

In the days of the second month, they hew out the ice with
  harmonious blows;
And in the third month, they carry it to the ice houses
Which they open in the days of the fourth, early in the morning,
Having first offered a sacrifice: a lamb with scallions.

Relays of horsemen brought snow and ice down from the Hindu Kush to Delhi to ice sorbets for the Moghul emperors of India during the sixteenth century. Mrs. Fanny Parkes, a nineteenth-century Englishwoman, described an ancient Indian method of collecting ice on the Hooghly plain near Calcutta. Shallow lined pits were filled with unglazed pottery pans. When it looked as though the temperature would dip to freezing, a gong sounded and Indians streamed out from the Calcutta bazaars to fill the pans with water. At 3:00 A.M., if ice had formed, the gong was beaten again and the workers got out of bed and knocked the ice out of the pans into baskets, which they carried to the underground ice house. After having been supplied with blankets, shoes, and heavy wooden mallets, they went down into the pit and beat the ice into a solid mass before receiving their pay and returning home.

Insulation was understood very early. Everything from sawdust, leaf matting, and straw to sheepskins and rabbit fur was used to keep the ice from melting. Ice packed together in large stocks, especially in stone-lined vaults, keeps for more than a year without much trouble, provided the ice pit is drained, ventilated, and kept well covered. The Italians and Spanish piled snow in stone wells and cellars under their houses, tamped it down hard, covered it, and saved it for the summertime.

It was of course in hot countries that ice-collecting was not considered too much hard work; in the temperate north, summers were bearable without ice. But in the seventeenth century, when rich Englishmen started to travel extensively in Europe, it began to be thought amusing and profitable for mansion-owners to build themselves ice houses. Water coolers in the shape of ornamental urns with ice compartments became all the rage. Until this time there is little mention of the uses of cold for preserving food, except in China where ice houses had long been depots for keeping fish and fruit. Food in the west was either eaten immediately, or was salted and stored during the winter months.

Towards the end of the eighteenth century ice houses on English estates were fitted with shelving for fruit and later for meat. By the early nineteenth century there were commercial ice houses on all the principal salmon rivers in Britain, so that salmon preserved in ice could be taken to London for sale. Soon after this, ice began to be loaded into the fishing boats as they set out to sea; fish would be packed in ice for transport back to shore and then to its final destination. As iced fresh fish became increasingly available, the long decline in the popularity of dried, salted, and pickled fish began.

In early nineteenth-century Peru, blocks of ice were cut from glaciers by the Indians in the Andes. The blocks were lowered by ropes down the mountains to waiting women and children, who covered the ice with grass and packed it onto the backs of mules, which then began the hurried ninety-kilometre (56-mile) journey to Lima. By the time the ice arrived, at least a third of it had melted. What remained was sold in the streets of Lima by Indians carrying trays of ice on their heads and shouting, *Helado!* It was bought mainly for making iced drinks and ice cream, which were so popular that people would riot if their ice supply were to be cut off. Even when revolutions flared, no one dared commandeer the ice mules for any task other than their normal duty.

The United States of America was a country with wide extremes of climate. It had a huge hot south, which longed for ice in the summers. Southerners could be provided with ice from the northern regions of their own country, with its unpolluted stretches of water which froze in winter into huge supplies of excellent ice. The challenge of marketing northern ice to the south was to stimulate both trade in ice and solutions to the problems of transporting it. On the western coast of North America in the mid-nineteenth century, Russians in Alaska shipped cargoes of ice to California.

English interest in ice houses had no sooner been aroused in the seventeenth century than the American colonies began to take advantage of the ancient but (in England) newly fashionable expertise. On December 22, 1665, the Governor of Virginia, Sir William Berkeley, was granted "licence to gather, make and take snow and ice . . . and to preserve and keep the same in such pits, caves and cool places as he should think fit, saving the king's loving subjects liberty to make and preserve snow and ice necessary for their own proper use."

Enlightened wealthy landowners in America, as in Britain, continued to experiment with ice houses during the eighteenth century. George Washington and Thomas Jefferson both took a keen interest in the building and stocking of their own ice houses at Mount Vernon and at Monticello. By the 1800s, ice had begun in America to descend the social scale: merchants were making profits from supplying solid cold to more and more customers. In 1799, Charleston already had a street market in ice, and ships which had carried southern products to the north-eastern cities would fill up with ice at Boston for the return journey.

One of the earliest uses for ice, in the north as well as in the cities of the American south, was to cool fevered patients in hospitals. In 1805 an outbreak of yellow fever in Martinique inspired one of the pioneers of the ice trade, Frederick Tudor of Boston, to transport the first load of ice known to have been delivered to the tropics. He went on to build an experimental insulated ice house at Havana. He then established a trade in ice with Cuba and with Jamaica, Georgia, and Louisiana. Having enormously improved techniques of ice insulation on ships, he succeeded in landing Boston ice in Calcutta in 1833. Almost half the ice had melted before it arrived, but it could still be sold at half the cost of the native ice from the Hooghly plain.

For over a hundred years, from the early 1800s on, ice-harvesting in Canada and the United States provided employment for fishermen, farmers, and other country people during the winter months. Like hog-killing, corn-husking, and barn-raising, it was often a local, communal effort for the benefit of everybody. The process was soon speeded up, regularized, and simplified by mechanical and organizational means; it could then be operated as a specialized and lucrative industry. The use of ships to transport ice, and later foodstuffs as well, meant that ice had to be provided in uniform blocks so that the cargo would not shift in transit.

Ice surfaces had to be scraped and kept clear of snow as soon as horses could venture onto the pond, so that the ice could thicken without the insulation of snow. When the ice had formed to the desired depth, the surface was marked with a toothed plough in blocks fifty-six centimetres by eighty-one (22 in. by 32). Another plough was then dragged over the grooves, back and forth until the cuts sliced through two-thirds of the thickness of ice. A channel was cleared across the pond by cutting through the ice with picks and handsaws, then lifting the ice blocks out with iron claws. Large sheets of ice were then separated from the field and poled or pulled by horses fitted with spiked shoes, along the channel to the storage area, where they were broken into blocks. These were then hoisted to the ice houses and stacked inside. By this time American ice houses were no longer underground pits, but tall, carefully insulated structures relying largely on the sheer quantity of ice they held to retain the cold.

Everything had to be done as quickly as possible. No water could be allowed to flow into the painstakingly-prepared grooves and to fill them with new ice. The channel had to be kept clear of ice overnight, often by means of towing ice-rafts through the water, up and down all night long. If necessary, ice-cutting would go on till dawn by the light of flares. The working horses wore rope nooses round their necks so that if one slipped into the water channel the rope could be drawn tight: the horse was then incapable of struggling while planks were placed underneath him and a team of men and horses dragged him out.

The animal then had to be dried, blanketed, and given strenuous exercise. There were often dozens of horses at work at a time on the surface of an ice pond, necessitating the constant removal (more or less scrupulous) of dung from the ice.

The Norwegians cut ice and sold it to most of Europe during the nineteenth century. In 1822, when the first Norwegian ice cargo arrived in Britain, it caused consternation at the customs house, because it did not fit into classification lists for import duties. By the time it was decided that ice was "dry goods," the whole cargo had liquefied. After this, in spite of occasional cold winters in Europe, the Norwegian trade flourished. Its interest clashed with American ice after 1844, when the Wenham Lake Ice Company of Boston began shipping ice to Liverpool.

American advertising specialists had already begun to realize how much power could lie in brand names, even for products as natural and as simple as ice cut from a pond. The public was encouraged to think of Wenham Lake Ice as synonymous with an extraordinarily good taste, clarity, purity, and cleanliness. The company's power and technological mastery was symbolized by the block of ice constantly melting in its office window in the Strand. Norwegian ice continued to be cheaper, however. The American company eventually bought the rights to ice which formed on the surface of Lake Oppegaard in Norway and shipped it to England at the lower price, first renaming their Norwegian property Lake Wenham, so that ice of "extreme purity" could arrive in England under the title which the company had worked so hard to provide with the correct connotations.

By 1832, North American home-owners were accepting ice as a normal household comfort – a luxury in summer, but one which many people could expect to enjoy. In that year Frances Trollope reported from New York, "Ice is in profuse abundance. I do not imagine that there is a home in the city without the luxury of ice to cool the water and harden the butter." In 1855, a writer in *De Bow's Review* called ice "an American institution – the use of it an American luxury – the abuse of it an American failing." It was one of the first "luxuries within the reach of everyone"; among the most successful of the rewards by means of which the Industrial Revolution continues to justify itself.

The art of making ice mechanically was advancing rapidly by 1868, but still ice was expensive: a ten-pound (4.5-kilo.) piece of it from a plant cost $1, at a time when the best beefsteak was 2¢ a pound. In New Orleans, bouquets of tropical flowers and silk-clad French dolls were being frozen into blocks of ice as table centre-pieces for dinner parties. Mark Twain, who appears to have been entranced by this notion, described in 1883 how these blocks were set on end in a platter, "to cool the tropical air; and also to be ornamental, for the flowers and things imprisoned in them could be seen as through plate glass."

CREATING COLD

"Heat we have in readiness in respect to fire," wrote the Renaissance scientist and philosopher Francis Bacon, "but for cold we must stay till it cometh or seek it in deep caves and when all is done we cannot obtain it in a great degree." It had long been known to alchemists and early scientists that temperatures could be lowered and ice created by means of "frigorific mixtures," some of which Bacon himself described as employed in making ice for royal households. These included salt and ice, and snow or ice together with saltpetre, calcium chloride, ammonium chloride, and other chemicals. But these methods were costly (common salt, as we have seen, was itself valuable) and could not, therefore, be used "in a great degree."

Ice would continue to be found, rather than made, until a need for huge quantities of cold became so imperious that cutting, chopping, and lugging could no longer supply enough of it where it was wanted. It was also necessary that the basic laws governing cold should be understood – but even when they were, natural ice was abundant enough to cause people to concentrate their ingenuity on getting, preserving, and transporting ice rather than on creating it. When artificial ice was finally invented, people treated it with deep suspicion: surely "natural" ice was better than "plant" ice? They refused to buy artificial ice if it had air bubbles in it, because these "imperfections" reminded them that the produce was man-made and therefore quite possibly tampered with. (Natural ice itself usually contains bubbles.) Airless ice was clear and therefore looked pure. Ice-makers quickly adapted to consumer preference by simply removing air (which is utterly harmless) from the ice. The age of distrust for food processing had begun, and with it the enforced agility of food processors, who have to keep calming what they see as the unreasonable, even downright ignorant, prejudices of their customers.

Francis Bacon lived to glimpse – though only just – the chief benefit which human beings have so far found in cold. He was travelling in

March 1626 near Highgate, north of London, and meditating on reports he had heard that cold could delay the putrefaction of flesh. He saw snow from his carriage window, stopped the driver and sent him to buy and kill a chicken. Bacon stuffed the chicken full of snow, but in the process caught a cold, which led to his death some weeks later.

Fifty years after Bacon's ill-fated experiment, Pepys expresses in his diary his fascination with claims from Baltic merchants that slaughtered chickens kept in ice could last the winter without rotting. In 1799, the Russians astounded the world with their reports of finding whole mammoths frozen in Siberian ice, their flesh still edible by dogs. Very soon after this date, the essential first steps were taken which would eventually lead to the ability of man to make cold for himself and freeze his own food. The discoveries revealed new aspects of the nature of heat.

Heat had always seemed to be a kind of invisible liquid, which could be forced into substances by association with fire, or transferred from one material to the other on contact. What revolutionary scientific thinkers, such as Joseph Black (in a work published in 1803) and James Joule in the 1840s, made us realize is that heat is a form of energy and not itself a substance, and that temperature is not the same thing as heat. The first two Laws of Thermodynamics were formulated: that energy can never be destroyed or created, only transformed; and that some of the heat (energy) in a working machine is always lost as heat to its surroundings.

These ideas were to form the principal foundations of modern refrigeration technology. A refrigerator works essentially by the vaporization and condensation of a refrigerant liquid. Vaporize the liquid and it sucks heat out of its surroundings, or the things in the refrigerator (this is the Second Law of Thermodynamics in reverse); condense the liquid and heat is released – refrigerators being built so that the heat cannot be released into the machine but must escape into the air of the kitchen. It is heat – either a gas flame for absorption refrigerators or electricity to run compression-pump machines – which causes the expansion and condensation of the liquid.

The first ice-making machines, created in the 1850s, were named after the "refrigerator," more commonly called an ice box or ice cream cabinet, which was already a common article of household furniture. (Many Americans still call a refrigerator an "ice box.") This was a wooden chest like a large trunk which could be filled with food. It had a tin container at the top to hold ice, and a pan into which water drained as the ice melted. The first model, patented in 1803 by Thomas Moore, a Maryland farmer, had a casing over it made of rabbit skins. Ice boxes were handsome, practical objects (food kept in them, especially fresh produce, did not dry out as food can in modern refrigerators), and, cooled increasingly often by means of ice made artificially, they remained far more common than mechanical coolers until well after the First World War.

The first widely distributed refrigerating machines for domestic use were being manufactured by 1916. They were horizontal at first, like the ice box (the vertical shape prevents the entry of warm air less efficiently, but modern restrictions on space soon overrode this consideration), and until 1928 their exteriors were of dark wood.

A Florida doctor had made the first simple cold-creating machine for air-conditioning his hospital in 1844. The first commercial machine which actually made ice, enormous and weighing five tons, was built in Australia in 1855. The Australians were pioneers in the creation of refrigerating techniques because they soon realized that Europe was the logical market for the vast tonnages of Australian meat – provided the problems of transporting it could be overcome. Australians had no easy access to ice harvests, so they had no choice but to manufacture their own cold. Gradually, with many disastrous failures, refrigerated shipping evolved, and the Europeans at the other end of the long journeys from Australia, New Zealand, and America were persuaded to eat thawed-out meat months old – and to want more of it.

So it was that by the 1880s yet another complex and revolutionary modern structure was in place: world-wide food transport systems, using the preservative properties of cold. In industrialized countries, there would now be year-round availability of meat, poultry, dairy products, and eggs. Even beer could be made in summer and winter alike – provided it was not ale but lager, which is made in cold conditions and lasts (*lagern* in German means "to lay down" and "to store"). The factory could now begin to impose its unending productivity and invariability upon the ancient cycles and differentiations of rural work and farm produce. The price of food relative to other costs fell in the first two decades of the twentieth century, and agriculture has never again recovered its former societal role or its status.

THE ORIGINS OF ICE CREAM

It is often said that cooking, like the incest taboo, characterizes what almost anybody would recognize as distinctively human behaviour. For some reason, (and whether or not cooking is important just because it involves the use of Promethean fire), the actual taste of edible substances which have undergone fiery treatment pleases us. But it is rather rare in the history of mankind to find people eating food while it is very hot. More rarely still do we hear of people eating anything very cold. It was for cooling drinks as a special treat, not for freezing them, that ice was usually so painstakingly sought. Most people, in most places and times, have preferred eating their food tepid, "slightly hot" and "cool" being the acceptable extremes for temperature.

The reason for this is that health has usually been thought to consist of balance, in temperature as in everything else: the human body should therefore avoid anything much hotter or much colder than itself. The ancient Greek physician Hippocrates wrote in his *Regimen* that "it is dangerous to heat, cool, or make a commotion all of a sudden in the body, let it be done which way it may, because everything that is excessive is an enemy of nature. Why should anyone run the hazard in the heat of summer of drinking iced waters, which are excessively cold, and suddenly throwing the body into a different state from the one it was in before, producing thereby many ill effects?" But he adds, "people will not take a warning, and most men would rather run the hazard of their lives or health than be deprived of the pleasure of drinking iced liquid." When coffee first arrived in London in the seventeenth century, it was shudderingly described as a drink "of a soote colour, dryed in a Furnace, and that they drinke as *hote* as can be endured."

People are often described as having died as a result of drinking cold water. We may suspect that it was the unsanitary contents of the snow water itself which might have killed Don Carlos, imprisoned in the Palace at Madrid, in 1568, but at the time everyone said he should not have taken in so much cold liquid. Water ices and ice cream, of course, are frozen until they turn thick, which makes them colder still and on this view even more dangerous. They were nearly always available only to the few, and eating them was often thought of as an act of bravado: most people regarded them as perilous as well as strange and expensive. As late as 1869, Catharine Beecher warned American women that ice cream reduces the temperature of the stomach and "stops digestion"; it should on no account be served after a heavy meal.

Nowadays very few people take this aspect of ice cream eating seriously. We know that ingesting ice cream makes the body warmer rather than cooler, because of the work it must do to balance the temperatures.

But this heat is not a cause for discomfort, and not enough to spoil the delight of a cold treat on a hot day. Eating cold, and also eating very hot food compared with what our ancestors would have found acceptable, is now one of the ways we experience culinary variety. We have all learned at an early age that the cold of ice cream is not very dangerous, and it is strange now to almost nobody. The great change in taste and attitude in our culture is not the least of the revolutions which the understanding and control of cold have wrought in our lives.

The water ices of the Turks and Arabs were soft and semi-liquid, rather like slushy Italian *granita*. They were often eaten between courses, as soup is in China, to refresh and clear the palate. The sherbets which were sold in European cafés from the seventeenth century onwards, either by Middle Easterners or by Europeans dressed up as Armenians, Arabs, and Turks, were often heavily laced with liqueurs and served frankly as cold drinks. Still they were regarded as exotic and new when first tasted in Europe. They arrived in force at the same time as did the appetite for lemonade, which often contained alcohol as well as sugar, and which was also kept cold with floating lumps of ice.

Three more new and exotic drinks, hot ones this time, were alcohol-free: tea, coffee, and chocolate. The fashion in Europe for taking these coincided with and helped to further a dawning revolution in human *mores*. The consumption of non-alcoholic drinks, adopted by the upper classes as an essential component of social gatherings, meant that men and women could, without impropriety, consort as they had never done before. They could meet in public places and talk. The public places were chocolate-houses and cafés, and the first of these to achieve influential and lasting fame was the Café Procope in Paris. Francesco Procopio dei Coltelli, who founded the Procope in 1686, was of course Italian, probably from Sicily, via Florence.

The French had by this time been learning about food and drink from the Italians for a century and a half. The Italian Renaissance had had its effect upon cuisine as much as upon the other arts. In 1533, when fourteen-year-old Catherine de Médicis came to Paris to marry the Duc d'Orléans, later Henry II, son of that admirer of all things Italian, François I, she brought a retinue of cooks with her whose culinary expertise and ultra-modern attitudes astonished the French court. One of the cooking specialists later brought to France by Marie de Médicis when she married Henri IV in 1600 was Bernardo Buontalenti (some say Buontalenti came seventy-seven years earlier, with Catherine de

Médicis). He showed off an Italian speciality (although we have no reason to believe that the French had not heard of it before): iced confections made with cream, called *gelati*.

It was said that Marco Polo had learned about freezing sweet cream when he was in China, and there is independent evidence that the Chinese emperors ate sweetened ground rice mixed with milk and frozen in porcelain bowls. The Indians too have an ancient iced dessert (*kulfi*) made with milk boiled down until it thickens, and frozen in porous earthenware. Certainly, Italians knew all about storing ice for culinary use. "The meanest person in Italy who rents a house has his vault or cellar for ice," according to the eighteenth-century edition of the *Encyclopaedia Britannica*; and the custom was by no means new. It has not been ascertained (and perhaps it cannot be) whether the Italians were inspired by travellers to ice sweetened cream, or whether they thought of it for themselves.

The French nobility ate *glaces* on special occasions. At one dinner given by Louis XIV, the great Vatel (the *maître d'hôtel* who was further to immortalize himself by committing suicide when he feared that the fish would not arrive on time for dinner) "caused to be placed before each guest, in silver-gilt cups, what was apparently a freshly laid egg, coloured like those at Easter. But before the company had time to recover from their surprise at such a novel dessert, they discovered that the supposed eggs were a delicious sweetmeat, cold and compact as marble." This was probably ice cream, and certainly (like the death of Vatel) the stuff of which culinary myth is made: ice-cold sweets disguised as eggs were extravagantly perverse and definitely not food for ordinary people.

Procopio dei Coltelli, after having been a prosperous *limonadier* for many years in Paris, acted in 1686 on one of those insights which occasionally enable businessmen both to understand and to promote previously latent social trends – and to make themselves fortunes. "Procope," as the French called him, saw that cafés, one of which he already owned, were a little primitive, dull, and limited; the *cabarets populaires*, on the other hand, were fun, but rough and wild. Neither kind of establishment could be frequented by respectable women. So Procope opened a new house in the rue des Fossés-Saint-Germain, now rue de l'ancienne Comédie: Procope's was opposite a theatre, an important ingredient of his success.

He provided his café with high-class décor: expensive and impressive mirrors, chandeliers, and marble tables. All of these, together with the hundreds of coloured liquids in gleaming bottles, are still part of the traditional appearance of Parisian cafés. He set himself up as distiller, apothecary, *liquoriste*, and grocer, providing also, as all the cafés did, the news of the day displayed on the pipe of the stove which heated the establishment. People would come to his café to meet their friends, gossip, and talk politics. He sold liqueurs and sherbets, but also perfumes, jams, conserved fruits, coffee, chocolate, and, most luxurious of all, ice creams, which could be bought and decorously eaten as only the nobility had previously eaten them, from silver dishes in the most exquisite café in Paris. There were water ices, many of them perfumed with flowers (as they still are in Iran and other parts of the Middle East), "iced cheeses" incorporating sweet cream and egg-yolks, and *glaces*, with less egg than the *fromages glacés*. To this day French ice cream is often distinguished from others by its egg-yolk base.

There were soon many different ways of eating ice cream in France: the *bombe*, made in a spherical metal mould (now it comes in a simple bowl shape) containing a thick rind of water ice with a lighter-textured cream centre; the many *coupes glacées* composed of one or more ice creams with fruit and *crème Chantilly*, or whipped cream sweetened and flavoured with vanilla, each combination bearing an honorific title; *mousses* (where the cream is first whipped and then frozen); *parfaits* (originally flavoured only with coffee); and the elaborate ornamental iced confections of classic French cuisine. The *omelette à la Norvégienne* (Norway was the chief purveyor of ice in Europe) was hot meringue enclosing ice cream; in 1868 Americans rechristened this perverse frivolity baked Alaska.

From 1804, yet another two Italians, Velloni (one of the first of the full-time Parisian *glaciers* or ice-cream makers), and after him Tortoni, ran the Pavillon du Hanovre, with gardens, balls, concerts, and firework displays among the many entertainments. At this restaurant was born the famous *biscuit Tortoni*, a frozen cream *mousse* with macaroons, almonds, and rum. At Tortoni's, women were banished again, being allowed only to sit outside the establishment, in straw chairs, to take the ices.

The history of ice cream in England appears to begin with the eating of "creme ice" at the court of Charles I; a probably apocryphal story relates that Gérard Tissain, the French chef who made ice cream for the King, was given a pension of £20 a year to keep the formula secret. When the King was beheaded in 1649, a group of noblemen bought the coveted information from the chef. The English had, in fact, always been fond of creamy desserts: custards, syllabubs, trifles, fools, and "whitepots" made from milk products which the English called "white meats." There is even a record of "creme frez" (is that *fresh* or *frozen* or *with strawberries?*) being served at the coronation banquet of King Henry v. At the end of the seventeenth century the new interest in ice houses, in combination with the traditional English taste in puddings, must have made ice cream seem as much a natural development as an exciting Continental novelty. As we shall see, the creaminess of ice cream – the milk component – has always been considered more important in Britain and America than in continental Europe.

Coffee houses in England never became as elaborate as those in France which followed the tradition started by Procope. In 1662, a man was selling in London "sherbets made in Turkie, of lemons, roses and violets perfumed; and Tea or Chaa, according to its goodness." But I have found no record of English coffee houses offering ice cream. It was England, however, which produced the first cookery books for the middle-class housewife, as opposed to those intended for professional chefs employed by the nobility. One of the earliest of these, the *Compleat Confectioner* of Hannah Glasse (1760), explained how to make raspberry ice cream: a tiring and costly business, involving the shaking by hand of a pewter pot of the cream and fruit mixture over another pot containing salted ice, then letting it rest and periodically stirring it until the ice cream thickened. The first recorded use of the English phrase *ice cream* (previously *cream ice* and *iced cream*) occurred in 1769.

In Vienna, ice cream quickly became a common treat for the rich in the eighteenth century, eaten "winter and summer" as Lady Mary Wortley Montagu reported in 1716. Beethoven complained of the warm winter of 1793-94; "The Viennese are afraid it will soon be impossible to have any ice cream, for as the winter is mild ice is rare."

Italian coffee houses followed the French model, and sold *gelati*. A great many of them were opened, including two in the Piazza San Marco in Venice: the Caffè Florian, founded in 1720, and Quadri in 1775. Both of these, like Procope's, are still doing business today. Italian iced desserts included *granita* and *gremolata* (granular water ices), *coppe*, like the French *coupes*, Neapolitan *cassata* (an ice cream mould with diced fruit, nuts, and macaroons) and *spumone* (several layers of sherbets, ice creams and fruit in an oval mould), as well as the huge class of *semifreddi*, or "half-cold" iced confections.

Ice cream was known in North America at least as early as the 1740s, when a guest of Governor Bladen of Maryland wrote in a letter: "We had dessert no less Curious; among the Rarities of which it was Compos'd was some fine Ice Cream which, with the Strawberries and Milk, eat most deliciously." George Washington was an early American ice cream *aficionado*, having spent two hundred dollars on what must have been a great quantity of it at an ice cream dealer's in the summer of 1790. He also owned "a cream machine for making ice." Brillat-Savarin, the gastronome, tells how a French captain named Collet made and sold ices in New York in 1794 and 1795. He describes with satisfaction the surprise of American women at this technological and masculine feat: "nothing could be more amusing than the little grimaces they made when eating them. They were utterly at a loss to conceive how a substance could be kept so cold in a temperature of ninety degrees."

Dolley Madison used ice cream to make her famous White House dinner parties special; a guest enthusiastically described one such occasion when "an Air of Expectancy" which Mrs. Madison had propagated among those present was gratified by the sight, in the centre of a lavishly set table and high on a silver platter, of "a large, shining dome of pink Ice Cream." Mrs. Madison is said to have ordered custard pies for her husband's Second Inaugural Ball in 1813. They arrived frozen. One of the guests, horrified at biting into ice-cold custard, shrieked "Poison!" and the cook was seized by security guards. Mrs. Madison, with great aplomb, ate one herself and declared it delicious. This story (true or not) resembles one myth which often recurs in the history of gastronomy: that of the Accidental Discovery, preferably by a Famous Person, of a new combination of ingredients or a new way of cooking or eating them. Mrs. Madison was both breaking a taboo and creating taste. According to the first-century Greek writer Athenaeus, King Ptolemy of Egypt claimed to have demonstrated to his troops that an icy stream could be drunk without fear by coolly tasting it himself.

In 1846, an American named Nancy Johnson invented a machine for making ice cream which not only simplified the process but greatly increased control over the finished product. This was the portable hand-cranked ice-cream churn which beat the mixture of cream and flavourings with a paddle (known as a "dasher" on the analogy with butter churns) as it froze. The canister of cream sat in a wooden bucket full of the ancient "frigorific mixture," ice and salt. About twenty minutes of cranking is enough to thicken the ice cream. The stirring prevents the formation of large ice crystals and encourages the creation of tiny "seed" crystals in the mix; the cream, milk, eggs, and honey also coat the crystals and impede their growth by preventing water from adhering to their surfaces. The smaller the crystals, the smoother-tasting the ice cream. (Iced sherbets and creams made by stationary freezing generally require the addition of gelatin or egg-whites to inhibit crystal growth.) There is with the cranking method a single consistency throughout, and no lumps can form. At the same time the dasher incorporates just the amount of air required to loosen up the mix and help it melt quickly and deliciously on the tongue.

The invention of this machine marked a revolution in the history of ice cream: from this time on *anyone* could make the very best quality ice cream at home – especially since rock salt, which came to be commonly called "ice cream salt" until the early twentieth century, had become a cheap commodity. The visits of the ice man, with his horse and cart and his iron claw to heave blocks of ice, often meant the promise of a family treat: ice cream quickly became part of American folklore, as did the ice man himself. The new machine also made it possible to mass-produce ice cream and to sell it commercially. Until the 1880s even factory ice cream was turned out the same way as home-made: in hand-cranked freezers.

Just why is it that salt makes ice cream freeze – the very salt that is used to get rid of the ice on sidewalks? What takes place within the ice-cream machine, isolated from the surrounding air by its wooden bucket (plastic in modern versions of this system), is extremely complicated. Essentially what happens is that the addition of salt to the mixture of ice and water upsets the equilibrium of energy exchanges between ice and water (the movement and slowing of molecules) which naturally occur within half-frozen liquid.

The electric field of water molecules breaks up salt crystals into positive ions (sodium) and negative ions (chloride) and causes clusters of water molecules to form which cannot stick to ready-formed ice. Molecules still leave the ice as they have been doing, but new ice cannot form: the equilibrium is broken and the ice melts. The energy required for melting has to come from the kinetic energy of the water or liquid-phase molecules; they slow down and the temperature drops to below 0°C. (32°F.), even though ice is melting and not forming. Therefore, when energy (heat) moves out of the ice cream mixture and into the brine through the metal canister (for heat always moves from the warmer to the colder, and it moves easily through metal), the salty water stays cold even though energy is being added to it. When salt is sprinkled on sidewalk ice, on the other hand, it simultaneously melts the ice and drives down the temperature of the resulting water; but this temperature is quickly raised again to its previous level by the sidewalk itself and the circumambient air.

When the crank begins to stick, the ice cream is frozen, but still soft. Now the dasher is removed from the canister: the moment of magic when some lucky person is allowed to lick the dasher and know the quality of the ice cream. Next the repacked canister may be lowered back into the brine, the whole churn wrapped in a blanket for extra insulation, and the ice cream left to harden or "ripen" for an hour or so before being dished out (it should not become too hard: to solidify ice cream is to deaden a great deal of its flavour). The very best thing to do with ice cream when it is ready is to eat it at once – all of it. Keeping it always reduces the quality of its texture, consistency, and taste.

THE MODERN PERIOD: WE ALL SCREAM

Ice-cream vending in the streets is recorded as early as 1828 in America, when "a group of boisterous fellows with kettles in their hands" yelled "I scream, Ice Cream" to attract customers in the streets of New York. Italians had introduced the idea to Britain by 1850 at the latest, when Carlo Gatti was peddling ice cream to Londoners from a painted cart. He was so successful that he and others brought many more Italians over to join them. These immigrants were grossly exploited labour, often lodged in poor conditions and paid little; during the winter they often worked as hurdy-gurdy men. Every morning in summer they cranked and froze the ice cream mix they had made the previous night, and went their rounds in London, Glasgow, Manchester, and other growing industrial cities crying, "*Gelati, ecco un poco!*" It is thought to be because of their cry that ice-cream vendors were called "hokey pokey men" and the ice cream they sold "hokey pokey," a term which became common also in America.

Selling ice cream in the streets testified to the increasing ease with which ice could be obtained, and to the growing general popularity of ice cream. The dessert once the glory of banquets at court could now be carried about and shamelessly eaten by anybody in the street. Many are the claims to the invention of the first ice cream cone. The French and the Germans say they had metal and paper cones in the mid-nineteenth century. Carlo Gatti himself is said to have invented an edible horn or cornet (*corno* in Italian) for holding ice cream, by twisting pastry round his finger and baking it. A Syrian immigrant to the United States called Ernest A. Hamwi rolled up thin Persian waffles called *zalabia* and topped them with a ball of ice cream (a combination thought of on the spot and because of an accident – again that recurring theme) at the St. Louis World's Fair in 1904. He sold his confection as "the World's Fair Cornucopia." Other American inventors disputed his claim to be first.

The truth is almost certainly that containers and "holders," both edible and inedible and for many different kinds of food, already existed in most culinary traditions. This is not to discount the brainwave which discerned and immediately satisfied a wholly new requirement, that ice cream should become, at least on occasion, both portable and spoon-free. An automatic cone-rolling machine was invented in 1909; by 1924, 245 million cones were being produced per year in the United States alone, even though the cone had to share the field with other containers of individual ice cream portions.

No biological fact exerts for people a fascination which can compare with one that can underscore and therefore encourage an existing social trend. With the dawning, in the early twentieth century, of the age of self-sufficiency for the individual and the severing of social bonds, one decades-old campaign for better public hygiene at last began to make an impact: the old communal tin drinking-cups at public water-fountains began genuinely to seem both old-fashioned and insanitary. The Individual Drink Cup Company of New York was ready, as early as 1909, to cash in by supplying endless quantities of paper cups, one for each person whenever he felt like a drink. So successful was its clean white throw-away invention that the company could soon dispense with a title explaining its *raison d'être*: the name *Dixie Cup* was adopted instead because the sound of it was patriotic, musical, snappy, clean, and modern. The company doubled its profits in 1923 by developing a special version of its cup, each one to hold a single portion of ice cream. The cup had a round lid with a tongue to help pull it off; it was as deep as it was wide. Now you could either eat your ice cream, in a relaxed but still fastidious frame of mind, with a flat wooden spoon; or less delicately, more self-sufficiently, and in larger mouthfuls, by bending your lid into a scoop and digging the ice cream carefully, with an inimitably delicious hollow scraping sound, out of your own individual tub.

In 1919 a means was found of making a chocolate coating adhere to ice cream, and the result was marketed as the I-Scream Bar. Later the name was changed to Eskimo Pie, and the bar was provided with a holder and wrapper combined, made of disposable silver foil. The idea of the Good Humor Bar, an ice-cream block on a stick like a lollipop, was conceived in 1920; it was named and first sold by a man who adhered to the ancient belief that the humours of the mind could be controlled and improved by what one ate. Harry Burt Sr. made marketing history by having Good Humor Bars sold from vans equipped with bells to announce their presence, by an army of men in white uniforms with distinctly military-looking caps and belts. The Good Humor Man became a well-known and reliably invariable visitor to neighbourhoods all over North America. He had a strict code of rules and manners which his company had recorded in a manual; if he broke a rule he could lose his place in the ranks. The merchandising style of giant chain companies like McDonald's owes a great deal to various aspects of the Good Humor concept.

Pedal tricycles were one of the chief methods of ice cream vending in Britain. Thomas Wall, whose sausage and meat-pie business had been slow during the summer months, largely because refrigeration had not yet become efficient enough or universal enough, started mass-producing and street-vending ice cream in 1922. The Wall's ice cream man's slogan was "Stop Me and Buy One." The British launched into ice cream eating with unprecedented fervour. They began to forsake traditional English steamed puddings and tarts for the new, cold, and easy technological treat. By 1939, Wall's was the largest ice-cream manufacturer in the world, as it still is today, after the company's expansion into markets in western Europe and North America. Both Wall's and Eskimo Pie pioneered the use of solid carbon dioxide ("dry ice") to transport ice cream. This gas turns directly into a solid when frozen, and evaporates (with no messy melting stage) as it heats up. Its use greatly facilitated both street vending and the centralization of ice-cream manufacturing.

Ice-cream parlours opened in many cities of the United States during the nineteenth century; these echoed the tradition of Procope and his successors in France, Italy, Austria, and other European countries, where ice cream was decorous and to be eaten in appropriately elegant surroundings. Ice cream also came to be considered the *sine qua non* of American festive occasions. Brillat-Savarin was responsible for the re-pellent aphorism that "the *dessert* [the whole final section of a French meal] without cheese is a beautiful woman without an eye." An American magazine editor wrote in 1850, "A party without ice cream would be like a breakfast without bread or a dinner without a roast." The American comparison is less savage, but sufficiently earnest. Ralph Waldo Emerson was to complain of ice cream's role as a lazy social standby. "We dare not trust our wit for making our house pleasant to our friend," he wrote, "so we buy ice cream."

In 1851, Jacob Fussell, a Baltimore milk dealer who had noticed the rising fortunes of ice cream, decided to turn his cows' summer cream surplus into ice cream. This meant making as much ice cream at a time as he had extra cream; it was a much larger quantity than that of the confectioners and hotel managers who made only small quantities of it as required. But Fussell sold it at a much lower price – and found he could hardly keep up with the demand. He soon gave his company up to full-time ice-cream making (all hand-cranked), opened up plants in Washington, Boston, and New York, and then expanded to cities west and south. The first large-scale ice-cream manufacturing business had begun; Fussell has a plaque commemorating his achievement on the site of his factory in Baltimore. The young industrialist was greatly encouraged by a new craze which was to last until the 1950s: in 1874, cream sodas (an invention dating back to 1832) became ice-cream sodas; soda fountains and drugstores were from now on obliged to stock ice cream.

Meanwhile, ice-making machines were beginning to change the patterns of food preservation and transport, for artificial ice can be made where and when it is wanted. The Boston ice-harvesting business peaked in about 1870; thereafter "homegrown" or "natural" ice began to lose out. By 1914 the industry was broken, never to recover, although ice-harvesting operations continued into the 1920s. When it became common for many people to possess their own refrigerators, which happened first in North America, ice cream could be marketed in half-gallon bricks, to be taken home and kept cold until it was eaten for dessert. A new battle began: to transform the image of ice cream from something special, eaten as a treat, out of doors, or in fancy cafés and parlours, into something ordinary, a part of everyday home fare.

Ice cream, as its English name shows, is made with milk products, and ever since the seventeenth century in Europe (just when ice cream was becoming well known) milk had been suspected of being often disease-ridden, especially in the big cities. Milk, as we now know, is nutritious not only for human beings but for micro-organisms as well. The revelations of germ theory, and the elimination of infection in food by heat treatment, resulted from the investigations of Louis Pasteur into the fermentation of wine and beer in the 1860s. Milk was not systematically pasteurized in North America and England until the end of the nineteenth century. Before that, people preferred to add chemical preservatives and disinfectants to milk; it was simpler than keeping their animals and operations clean and free from contamination, and it avoided the nuisance of having to heat the milk. Ice-cream manufacturers relied also on the widespread belief that bacteria would die in cold, as they had been shown to be destroyed by heat.

As ice cream was eaten more and more frequently and widely, it was realized that it might well be a cause for outbreaks of disease. There was a terrifying "vanilla ice cream poisoning" in Norway as early as 1848; diphtheria, typhoid, scarlet fever, and intestinal diseases also pointed to ice cream as the culprit. In the early 1920s many careful scientific tests were carried out on ice cream, and it was discovered that pathogenic bacteria were not easily killed by freezing: some survived a temperature as low as $-250°C$ ($-418°F$) for ten hours with almost no effect; others grew and multiplied in deep cold. In fact, an ice-cream mix was shown to be even more conducive to bacterial growth than plain cream or milk.

After this, laws were passed that all commercially produced ice cream should be pasteurized before freezing. Pasteurizing destroys 20 per cent of the vitamin C in milk; some say that the treatment spoils the taste of milk by robbing it of irreplaceable volatile elements. Ice cream is now eaten on such a large scale, however, that the risk of disease outweighs other considerations. Today, a phosphatase test is routinely made on ice cream to ensure correct pasteurization, because the process destroys phosphatase in milk. Routine testing of cows for bovine tuberculosis is an important aspect of modern safety precautions for milk. Stringent regulations have to be enforced, in addition, to prevent recontamination of pasteurized ice cream, and to keep as germ-free as possible utensils, employees, vendors, scoops, and barrels, and even the air which comes in contact with ice cream.

Dangerous ice cream might have been sold without hygienic supervision from city carts in the nineteenth century, but it was always prized as innocent: ice cream, after all, was not liquor. As the Prohibition era got under way in the United States, triumphant lists were compiled in the dairy trade journals of American breweries which had converted to the production of ice cream. The Association of Ice Cream Manufacturers sang at their conventions in the 1920s the following verses, to the tune of "Old Black Joe":

> Gone are the days when Father was a souse,
> Gone are the days of the weekly family rows,
> Gone from this land since prohibition's here –
> He brings a brick of ice cream home instead of beer!

> *Chorus*:
> He's coming, he's coming; we can see him coming near –
> He brings a brick of ice cream home instead of beer!

Ice cream was a frivolity, however, and in the 1890s visits to soda fountains, and "sucking soda" in particular, were frowned upon in North America as unsuitable behaviour on Sundays. Ice cream merchants responded by selling a soda-less ice-cream concoction which they called a "Sunday." It is believed that the name was changed to "sundae" either to avoid any appearance of mocking the Lord's Day, or to persuade customers that the dish did not have to be eaten only once a week.

The ice-cream industry entered an entirely new phase in 1932, when Clarence W. Vogt invented the continuous ice-cream freezer. A pasteurized ice-cream mix is first homogenized so that the fat will not churn into butter. Then it is fed into this machine and quickly frozen, while being agitated, to a slushy consistency. A controlled quantity of air is pumped into the slurry, and the temperature lowered still further; the whole process can take a matter of seconds, although the mix is best left to settle between the two phases. Ice cream is extruded continuously from the machine onto a conveyer, then passed through a hardening tunnel, and mechanically cut and packaged. It is never touched or handled in any way, and the rapidity of the freezing helps ensure that the ice cream is smooth, because crystals have no time to grow. Speed and total control over the behaviour of the ingredients were at last within the ice-cream manufacturer's grasp. With the new technology in place, the giant ice-cream corporations became locked into fierce competition over prices: the public would buy whichever ice cream cost less.

Soda fountains, and the soda jerks who plopped balls of ice cream into fizzy glasses, with their colourful cries, personal style, and ice-cream-tossing skills, were quickly phased out. They had come to seem overdone, not predictable enough, not "cost-effective." Ice cream had been a Sunday afternoon treat, something one went "out" to eat. Now one bought ice cream in half-gallon (1.9-litre) blocks at the supermarket and took it home for supper, or routinely stopped by at one of the new chain stores where scores of ice cream flavours were laid out for the choosing. The sheer number of possibilities, ranging from chocolate to chili con carne flavour or marshmallow, made the act of selecting a cone a direct and awesome intimation of the power at the heart of techno-logical empire: it offered not only quantity, but a range and availability which outstripped both need and imagination. The parent company underwrote the quality of the ice cream which it supplied to all its franchises, as well as the expertise that went into its invention and production; every member store was like every other.

In the early 1950s, soda fountains dried up at the rate of twelve hundred per year. Universal domestic refrigeration and the use of cold for transport changed ice-cream making from a seasonal and local op-eration into a year-round proposition, with nation-wide marketing. Between 1957 and 1969, 1,656 North American ice-cream plants closed; big companies became huge corporations. Ice cream had become some-thing constantly in stock, taken for granted, and above all, cheap.

Ice cream in its natural state is a complex emulsion composed of solids (ice crystals), liquids, and air; also locked into the system are scattered fat globules, sugar, and egg and milk proteins. It had never been cheap to make; and as technology made the work easier, so the ingredients became more costly. The companies therefore, with the general goal of making ice cream more frequently consumed and easier to afford, moved beyond machine technology and sought the assistance of chemistry. The cream gave way to milk, and fresh milk was replaced by dried milk, concentrated skim milk, cheese whey, casein, and other milk fractions and derivatives. "Inert fillers" and "bulking agents" stood in for the substance of cream. Emulsifiers smoothed and "texturized" the result. Canadian scientists perfected the use of stabilizers. These are gelatins, and also chemicals derived from vegetables and from wood which have the property of thickening instead of relaxing as tempera-tures rise, so that the ice cream refrains from either dripping or melting.

One typical brand of ice cream at present on the market is composed of milk fat, nonfat milk, corn syrup, cheese whey, monoglycerides and diglycerides, carob bean gum, cellulose gum, guar gum, polysorbate 80, carrageenan, natural and artificial flavour, and artificial colour. By U.S. law at least 10 per cent of the mix must be milk fat by weight, and 2.7 per cent protein; a gallon (3.8 litres) of it must weigh at least four and a half pounds (2 kilograms), exclusive of micro-crystalline cellulose used as "fillers." Air bubbles (which are known in the trade as "overrun") can make up as much as half the volume of the ice cream. The standard is important, because all those gums could hold much more air than that. These rules were laid down in 1960, after a monumental battle: it took over fourteen years and thirty-eight thousand pages of hearings for an agreement finally to be reached between the American government and the ice-cream industry.

That there is a minimum milk component at all for ice cream seems outrageously backward to many food technologists. They complain because it "ties producers to particular ingredients" and "hampers flexibility." The dairy industry, in this as in the butter-versus-margarine controversy, has insisted on protection, and played on the automatic revulsion which any consumer feels when reading on his ice-cream package a list of polysyllabic chemicals instead of cream, sugar, eggs, and fruit.

Pleasure *can* be derived from the discovery that one has been deceived. Food is often served in disguise, or rigged to surprise the guests: an egg in its egg-cup might turn out really to be ice cream, or a pie to contain twenty-four live blackbirds. But the fun comes from a spirit of play: participation, sharing in the delight, is the essential factor. Admiration for skill was another component of such amusements, but admiration is a personal matter, and it is impossible to proffer it where there is a lack of trust. Today technology has tremendous prestige, but if its aim is perceived as being deception solely in order to turn a profit – in other words an impersonal "they" *might* enjoy it, but at our expense – our reaction turns quickly to contempt and anger, no matter how clever the trick. In addition, human beings have always been peculiarly sensitive about what they eat. To consume processed food is to hand over total control of one's diet to absolutely unknown other people. Trust, in these circumstances, is fragile. People today instinctively prefer that things should be what they look like.

This attitude could not be more irritating to those who have with great difficulty won the power to replace all the ingredients in food while maintaining a façade which looks surprisingly like the original. They are making food cheaper for us: why are we not grateful? Why should ice cream have cream in it just because it is called ice cream? And why is it that people would not buy it, in spite of the low price, if it were called iced milk derivatives with chemicals?

THE MYTHOLOGY OF ICE CREAM

In Anglo-Saxon countries, ice cream has always represented a kind of apotheosis of milk. The northern, butter-loving cultures reserved a special awe for milk; it is a food more than a drink, and it is innocent, pure, white, and wholesome. To freeze cream with fruit and sugar is to add an extra dimension of delight to the solid worth of milk. Ice cream has been heavy artillery to throw into the battle against liquor, a sound and tasteful alternative to the empty vulgarities of junk food, a country and childhood tradition to console our jaded and nostalgic city existences. In most of continental Europe, ice cream delivers an entirely different message. It has never lost its élite status: in Rome or Paris or Vienna ice cream is a very elegant dessert, served in an expensive café from tall *coupes* and tulip-shaped glasses, or moulded in layers into fancy shapes. Even when served in cones on the street, flavours are sharp and fruity, colours brilliant, and the milk component can be left out altogether without prejudice to the product's image.

In North America and in Britain, on the other hand, ice cream tends to come in pastel colours, pale because of the creamy white of milk. In 1942, the British decided to ban ice cream as part of the war effort, largely because it was perceived as a luxury item and austerity was the mood required. Yet even before the war, ice cream in Anglo-Saxon countries had come a long way towards achieving exactly the opposite image. It has concentrated deliberately on becoming democratic, universally eaten, and cheap. It is not merely a dessert, but an extraordinarily pleasant way of consuming semi-sacred milk. Its image is customary and comforting rather than exciting and sophisticated. In spite of their excellence and the admiration they inspire, French *glaces* and even Italian *gelati* are eaten in nowhere near the quantities reached by ice cream in "milk" cultures.

North Americans in particular have adopted ice cream as a food central to their mythology, a symbol almost of national identity. It was the Americans who had, in the nineteenth century, led the world in learning to enjoy the benefits of ice. They were the first, too, to insist on ice cream for everybody. From 1921, immigrants to the United States were served ice cream on their arrival at Ellis Island; it is related that many of them used knives to spread it on their bread. The story was repeated with delight by Americans because it seemed to show how distinctively American ice cream was in its luxurious modernity. It was classified as an "essential foodstuff" in 1917, and the U.S. Secretary of War considered it indispensable for the morale of the army.

During the Second World War the Japanese discouraged the eating of ice cream as behaviour which betrayed pro-western, and specifically pro-American, sympathies. The Japanese themselves, like the Chinese, will eat ice cream, but they do not like drinking large quantities of milk because the lactose is difficult for them to digest; in any case, in the view of their war commanders, the sweetness and the association of milk with babies made ice cream children's food, entirely inappropriate to men of military prowess. Americans, meanwhile, were forced to cut back on ice cream for economic reasons. They expressed their relief and joy at the end of the war by embarking on the largest ice-cream-eating splurge in history; over nineteen litres (20 quarts) of it were eaten in 1946 by every man, woman, and child in the country.

One American commander, General Lewis B. Puller, expressed the opinion that his marines would be tougher and more aggressive if they were given beer and whiskey instead of being molly-coddled with ice cream and candy. The Pentagon disagreed: during the Korean War American troops abroad were supplied with ice cream three times a week. Koreans did not eat it; Americans considered it a treat, an expression of their common identity and distinctiveness in a foreign land, and a sign that they were being remembered and cared for at home. When the American aircraft carrier *Lexington* was sinking, the crew brought all the cans of ice cream they could find out of the hold and gorged on the contents till it was time to go overboard.

To the connotations of purity which pertain to milk, ice cream adds the idea of cleanliness which we assume to be inherent in snow and in cold generally. Snow, like milk, is white, and everywhere thought of as a symbol of purity. Chinese texts of the T'ang period allude to the rare simplicity and cleanness of heart of the true Confucian gentleman, with whom they compare a fine jade vase full of snow. We have seen, however, that eating cold has been thought until recent times to be dangerous behaviour; when people die they turn cold, and evil is often pictured as exerting an icy grip. We probably still need to be reassured at some level about our new-found pleasure in eating frozen food.

We have also seen that milk has often been far from clean, even though cold does keep it from turning sour. Today, when the necessity of keeping milk contamination-free is better understood than ever before, we surround milk, milk products, and ice cream with symbolic affirmations of cleanliness. White-uniformed staff wielding scoops filled with antifreeze (the very word "scoop" sounds cold, clean, and delicious), gleaming stainless steel, polished marble, clear glass, and white enamel surfaces all assure us that the ice cream is technologically under control and safe, and simultaneously surround it with visual representations of the simplicity and purity which we desire. When one manufacturer recently tried using real vanilla beans in his ice cream, they showed up as flecks in the mix. The idea had to be discontinued because even that part of the market prepared to pay for the real thing rejected ice cream which did not look immaculate. (The incorporation of identifiable, or customer-chosen, additions such as broken cookies or fruit, may be perfectly acceptable.)

Ice cream is itself a technological feat, one of the triumphs of Promethean wit; if any society other than ours had invented it, they would have celebrated it in mythic legend, in painting, and in song. The ready availability of it presupposes all the organizational systems of a modern industrial civilization. Mechanical continuous freezing, pasteurization, and mechanical packing all contribute towards keeping the product "untouched by human hands" and therefore pure. Technology means safety. This is especially important in the case of ice cream, which, like any powerful mythic token, is potentially dangerous as well as beneficial.

No wonder then that people feel betrayed and more than reasonably irritated when they discover that technology has not contented itself with creating and preserving ice cream, but has reached a long arm into the image of innocence itself and subverted the very substance of what we trust it to protect. The gums, the cellulose, the casein, and the whey might look quite a lot like ice cream, taste fairly pleasant, and last indefinitely – but how can we be expected to approve of a symbol of purity which is shown to be an impostor, or an expression of simple verity which turns out to be an illusion?

Antonin Carême, the great French chef, is reputed to have remarked in the early nineteenth century that "the fine arts are five in number:

painting, sculpture, poetry, music, and architecture. And the main branch of architecture is confectionary." This statement certainly suited Carême's approach to his art: he meticulously designed on paper and then erected extraordinary edible edifices called *pièces montées*, entirely in order to delight dinner guests before they happily demolished them. Ice cream was an ideal medium for these miniature temples and monuments: it could be moulded to any required shape and then frozen, and its brilliant fruit colours were an asset to any design.

The fashion for elegant moulded ice-cream "pieces" lasted into the twentieth century. Albertine tells Proust's Narrator, in words which he considers "a little too well contrived" as well as enfuriatingly sexy, that she wants her ice cream "cast in one of those old-fashioned moulds which have every architectural shape imaginable; whenever I eat them, temples, churches, obelisks, rocks, a sort of picturesque geography is what I see at first before converting its raspberry or vanilla monuments into coolness in my gullet." And she continues describing ice-cream pillars, lemon-ice mountains, and strawberry Venetian churches for quite some time. Today we hear less of moulded ice extravaganzas, but the French and the Italians still enjoy producing complex ice cream follies.

In Anglo-Saxon countries ice cream is served in deliberately simple shapes, with emphasis upon its ability to stand free. The preferred form is rounded, by means of the scoop. A curled blob of ice cream (unless it is too mechanically smooth and over-doctored with emulsifiers) will crack deliciously and present a slightly rough and frosty surface which anyone with experience will immediately want to lick. Simple domed shapes are expressive of the generally mammary, motherly, babyhood connotations of milky ice cream.

The persona of ice cream will vary, depending on where and how it is served. Moulded, ice cream is prestigious and formal. Made at home and eaten as soon as it freezes, after the messy salt-and-ice business, the work, and the waiting, it is a family occasion and a treat. Served scooped onto simple dishes, and especially in dollops balanced on cones or in cardboard tubs, it is the food of relaxation, of crowds on holiday. In all these cases, ice cream is festive food. It may be flavoured outlandishly, covered in chocolate, sold on a stick like a lollipop; ice cream is "fun food" and easily lends itself to novelty. It can glory, too, in being perversely served with hot food – with steaming apple pie for instance, or enclosed in hot pastry or meringue. The idea of buying it in large bricks at a supermarket and keeping it in the refrigerator for constant servings at family meals must always represent an uneasy rejection of this aspect of the mythology of ice cream. It is a custom which could only have come about because of the milk myth: when ice cream is looked upon as above all nutritious, it begins to look a little solemn rather then festive or fun.

The sober and dutiful view of ice cream is also a consequence of everyone's owning a refrigerator: ice cream ceases to be evanescent. Transience, however, is the essence of festivity. The fun of being served an ice-cream obelisk lies largely in the fact that the structure will not last beyond this dinner-time: the shape chosen denotes permanence, and is given precisely to what cannot last. Crowds licking their cones in the hot summer sun enjoy themselves more intensely because they know they must go back to normal life soon. Ice cream melts; therefore it is perfect food for "time out."

This important aspect of what the trade magazines call "America's number-one fun food" is used to enormous effect by the American poet Wallace Stevens in his poem on the force which man exerts over the transient world – a force which is ultimately absurd because man is himself a part of the transitory world he rules. For Stevens there is cold, naked death at the centre of all life, and man can do nothing about this fact but see it and face it. He may divert himself while he lives, provided he is not taken in. Let him then enjoy the tasty, the transient, and the trivial in and for itself, for this is the only reality: "The only emperor is the emperor of ice-cream."

Thanks to the technology of cold, however, ice cream need no longer be truly evanescent, even though it is still best eaten soon after it has been made. A brick of supermarket ice cream can be kept on hand for weeks or even months, to be served at a moment's notice. It ministers to convenience: a need which modern man seems to find more to his taste than festivity. Ice-cream manufacturers have a puzzle on their hands nevertheless, deciding how to appeal both to fun and to daily habit, for ice cream continues to accommodate both terms of the contradiction.

It has also become an expression of nostalgia, in spite of the modernity and the technological prowess which it presupposes. There are today two main kinds of nostalgia, and ice cream appeals to both of them. The first looks back to past time. Ice cream is the delight of children and therefore evocative of childhood memories; eating it makes people feel young and at least temporarily secure and innocent. Ice-cream stalls are decked with striped awnings and gingham, merchants use clowns, stuffed toys, cartoon characters, and balloons, not only to please children but also to draw adults to indulge in childhood for a while.

Ice-cream sellers also like to pretend that they are very old-fashioned folks, and they give their premises not only a nursery air but a nineteenth-century look as well. Ice-cream parlours are making a comeback at present, almost all of them finding it profitable to provide "retro"-styled furnishings: black-and-white tiled floors (the tiles preferably hexagonal), bentwood chairs, "Tiffany" lamps, mirrors, cushioned booths, marble counters and so on. The very word *parlour* is evocative: one brand of ice cream advertises itself as offering "The Ice Cream Parlor Taste." Another finds it worth stressing that "We've been around since 1876."

The other nostalgia is for Elsewhere. For city dwellers, the ultimately Other place is the country. Ice cream accordingly insists on its rusticity – despite the continuous freezers and the polysyllabic chemicals. Rusticity in modern life is of course closely associated with the old-fashioned, so that the two kinds of nostalgia are interrelated. Both the past and the country are perceived as being somehow more trustworthy and certainly more natural than a modern ice-cream factory.

So ice-cream publicity gives us cows, emerald green grass, and churns, men in long white aprons, and drawings (rather than photographs) of mansions in the Old South. Gastronomic sections of magazines often carry articles describing authors' memories, typically of childhood on the farm. There is a sudden decision to crank out a barrel of ice cream, followed by the calling-in of uncles, cousins, and friends, the bustle of preparations, the sack of salt and the crushing of ice, packing the cream, turning the handle, and the ecstatic moment when the child is finally allowed to lick the dasher. These descriptions often convey basic information to their readers, who seldom know the details of all this folklore, let alone remember such a life. They also address a vague but nonetheless genuine nostalgia for a long-ago country past, with its family companionship and its simple pleasures.

Just when almost all the ice-cream parlours in America had closed, capitulating in part to the take-home ice-cream brick, Walt Disney opened one, in 1955, at Disneyland in Anaheim, California. This parlour was almost certainly the first of its kind: it was built specifically to be "old-fashioned" and advertised itself as such. True, the establishment was a museumizing recreation of an almost dead past, but Walt Disney, in this as in so much else, had his fingers on the mythic pulse of America. Five years later Reuben Mattus, whose story has been repeatedly described as "a capitalist folktale," began to market Häagen-Dazs Ice Cream.

He packed it in pint-sized round containers, not large bricks, and designed it carefully to satisfy nostalgia and fastidious taste ("an old world delight," the tub calls it, "especially for the most discerning"). There are no additives, emulsifiers, or stabilizers. It melts; it deteriorates if it is not kept frozen solid. Consumers are advised to let it soften a little ("tempering" it) before eating. It is also much heavier than it needs to be to satisfy the ice-cream standard, largely because it contains 16 per cent butterfat and only 20 per cent air.

On the lid appeared a map of Scandinavia; clean, sober, efficient, and technologically advanced Scandinavia, with a star marking Copenhagen and an arrow pointing impressively towards the star. The name Häagen-Dazs is a complete fiction, designed of course to attract the eye, to be seen rather than said: so much shopping is now self-service that buyers would rarely have to ask for it by name; when it became famous enough to be a household word, the pronunciation of it would look after itself. In any case, Mattus said, "the type of people we were looking for, if they mispronounced it, they'd think they were right and any other way was wrong." The name is meant to look vaguely but arrogantly Danish, with its double *a*, its hyphenation, and its impossible *zs*. The umlaut is especially effective, even though Danish has no umlaut. Mattus had absolutely nothing to do with Scandinavia; his factory was in the Bronx and later in New Jersey.

Mattus started small, and jealously guarded the "family business" image, even as his brilliant idea turned out to be exactly what the public had wanted without being able to formulate its desire. The firm prospered and spawned imitators. Frusen Glädjé, a concept created in direct competition with Mattus by his cousin Edward Lipitz, has a genuinely Swedish name which means "Frozen Delight." (The umlaut this time is correct, while the final French accent is a purely artistic touch.) Lipitz took the trouble to incorporate his company in Sweden (his tub has a map of part of Scandinavia with Stockholm marked in black), although his factory was in Utica, New York. The new company's innovation was an improvement in the container's design: not only small and round like the Häagen-Dazs tub, but in more emphatically smooth white plastic, with a raised rounded lid as well. Frusen Glädjé street-vending booths continue the smooth round white theme. The product aims at an extremely restricted market, describing itself as "A gourmet experience for those who prefer the best."

The Swiss and the Germans have also found their North American image pressed into the service of ice-cream sales. The allure of imported culinary *savoir-faire* does not operate everywhere in the United States, however. In the south, Rich 'n' Creamy was found to sell far better than a foreign name; as one Texas businessman put it, "We don't regard it as gourmet, but just a damn good product."

A totally different approach, "all-American" but laying much greater emphasis even than that of Häagen-Dazs on the nostalgic, the natural, and the rustic, was launched by "two Vermont hippies" in 1978. They called it Ben and Jerry's Homemade, "the only superpremium [ice cream] you can pronounce." Marketing strategy at the original store included an old ice-cream churn with salt and ice cranking before the customers, a honky-tonk piano, free movies, and apple-peeling, look-alike, and lip-sync contests. Customers were made to stand in line and wait for the ice cream to be ready. People would become frantic if a batch was sold before they got any: the impression that "everybody wants it so you might not get some" is one of the oldest merchandising devices on earth. When the machine ground to a stop, the first in line got to lick the dasher.

The company started mass-producing. The list of contents on the container was in hand printing, and there was a photograph on it of Ben and Jerry: the personal element enormously enhanced the natural, rural image. A great deal of publicity was generated through an advertising campaign by Ben and Jerry's Homemade which attacked the bullying methods of "the giant Pillsbury Corporation" when it bought the Häagen-Dazs company; Americans (indeed, people of all cultures) love to see the little guy take on the faceless great. Ben and Jerry's made millions, but continue to cherish their rustic image: a large new plant in Vermont keeps live dairy cows grazing on the front lawn.

Häagen-Dazs ice cream and its "gourmet" competition contain real cream, skim milk, egg yolks, sugar, and natural flavourings. It really does taste better than milk derivatives with chemicals. It costs more, however, than the difference in price between chemicals and natural whole ingredients should warrant. One business magazine estimated in 1984 that "the manufacturer pays 22 per cent extra, and charges up to 400 per cent more." Stores which stock it regularly add more or less outrageous mark-ups to the already high price, and people buy it anyway: the "gourmet" ice creams are created for those who *wish* to pay a little more. People want to buy reality. Into the bargain they also want a certain ambience and connotation, a *je-ne-sais-quoi*, which is one of the meanings of the word "myth."

The new ice cream is designed for people who want status; and one of the most effective methods of gaining status is to surround yourself with suggestions that you already have it. An ability to recognize the finest quality just might show that you have been brought up with it. Being prepared to pay for it is an expression of certainty that it is the best; and certainties in matters of taste, provided that other people can be persuaded to defer to them, are part of the insignia of status. Even now, "gourmet" ice cream is marketed as though it is a prestige product for the exclusive and demanding few.

The figures give a very different picture. Since 1980, each of the citizens of the United States has consumed more than fifteen litres (4 gallons) of ice cream per year; the business is worth $6 billion annually. The world's largest consumers of ice cream are, after the United States, Australia, New Zealand, Canada, and Britain. The market in all these countries is considered to be saturated, only to be influenced by the growth or diminution of the population. Within that market, "gourmet" ice cream sales are increasing by at least 38 per cent per year. The small heretical group of those who, unlike the great unwashed, "prefer the best," is fast becoming a very substantial minority. People in the First World feel prosperous and want to experience luxury. "They may not be able to afford a Rolls-Royce," says one market analyst, "but everyone can afford gourmet ice cream." Others have a different perspective: "Like beer and movies, ice cream booms when people are most troubled. It beats going to your psychiatrist."

People prepared to pay a high price for ice cream embark on quests for the ideal brand. Food columnists frequently describe long car journeys which they say they undertake in order to buy a particular flavour from the honest little dealer whom they have discovered to possess that ineffable flair. Approached from this angle, finding and eating the very best ice cream can take on some of the mystique of antique collecting or adventure touring, where victory is only to the competent, the passionate, and, above all, the first.

Manufacturers understand this corner of their market. Many are the stories they tell of long and arduous battles to achieve the indisputably "best" ice cream. The founder of a company refused for years to market a strawberry ice cream that does not meet his exacting standards; intense searches and negotiations finally succeeded in running to earth "the world's finest vanilla" for flavouring ice cream; another expert "spent six months just perfecting his mocha," or "laboured two years to achieve his real chocolate coating." Another demonstration of efficiency, commitment, and extravagance in pursuit of the best is the custom of actually mailing by air to one's friends a package of the "ultimate" ice cream, once it has been found: happy the few who have the means to harness technology in the service of their own taste.

One of the bemusing paradoxes of western society today is the ideal of remaining slim, raised as it has been to dizzying heights just as we increasingly reach for the most expensive ice cream, the heavy one with the most butterfat. "Diet" ice creams are a new area of expansion for the industry, to meet the demands of those who want ice cream, but not to "pay" for it by becoming fat. The new soy-based ice "creams" use vegetable rather than animal fat in order to encourage those worried about cholesterol. Tofutti, for example, is marketed as "the nondairy ice cream substitute." It was originally designed for Jews keeping kosher dietary laws so that they could eat ice cream at a meal which featured meat. The discovery that a large percentage of people are congenitally lactose intolerant is also encouraging to producers of tofu or bean-curd ice "creams." The product costs as much as the richest "gourmet" confections: it continues the marvellous marketing bonanza in "lite" foods which we have already looked at, where people happily pay more for less. As one food technologist put it recently, "All the big companies want to buy premium-priced ice cream. But there are far stronger fads for slender waists and longevity," and he went on to point out that over 57 per cent of North American households now have "calorie conscious" members.

With "diet" ices, food processing comes once again into its own, substituting, subtracting, doctoring, and reflavouring – and all, this time, in the irreproachable name of Health. One recently created brand of tofu ice contains the following ingredients: water, sugar, corn oil, corn syrup solids, tofu, salt, citric acid, sorbitol, glycerine, cellulose gel, soy protein, carrageenan, guar gum, locust bean gum, natural flavours, polysorbate 80, coconut oil, microcrystalline cellulose, monoglycerides, diglycerides, and cellulose gum. A call went out recently for food technologists to come up with "a low-calorie bulking agent with pleasant mouthfeel, not needing a caution label for single servings over 15 grams." All kinds of special intensive sweeteners and low-calorie fats are already on the production lines. "Lite" frozen desserts are expected now to parallel the enormous growth of sales in diet soft drinks. A $10-billion industry is projected for the end of the century.

"Gourmet" ice creams, on the other hand, proudly proclaim their heavy fat content and deliberately distend their prices. As competition among "premium" brands becomes fiercer, we are being offered not only pints of ice cream with silver and gold leaf mixed in at $6 a pint and up, but more and more butterfat, less and less air. Manufacturers have had to stoop to technology to achieve some of the new features, since without the help of some science, less air and more than 17 per cent fat have the effect of inhibiting the strength of flavour upon the tongue. But, as an influential article which appeared in *Time* magazine put it in 1981, "When people break faith with their diets, as they always do sooner or later, they want to do it with a strumpet certifiably and wickedly luxurious."

Here we have yet another contradiction contained within the mythology of ice cream. (Contradictory messages do not undermine but rather augment the power of entrenched symbols.) Innocent, childlike ice cream is now an incarnation of voluptuous hedonism. It is rich and costs a lot; the price is a consequence and almost a symbol of its "richness." It is heavy too – which is exactly what people should try not to be, especially if they are middle class and rich. (The small container should not confuse us here: most people bracketed as "rich" in our society live in households of one or two members; the pint-sized container is designed for them.)

Ice cream, despite its childhood image, is eaten far more now by adults than by children – three times as much more, according to one California study – and more by men than by women. The sexy, voluptuous, even "sinful" image of ice cream has therefore been greatly accentuated lately. Ice cream (cold, milky, breast-shaped) has always been mythologically "female" in northern cultures. For example, the ragged edge which often forms where a round scoop of ice cream rests on the cone is called a "skirt." A good scooper is trained always to provide "a neat, inviting skirt." Ice cream can be a sexual symbol of ambiguous gender: in the 1930s starlets licking cones were especially popular as pin-ups. Ice cream has in fact always had adult aspects to its appeal –

one thinks of the sophisticated aura of formal, moulded desserts, for example. Stendhal declared ice cream to be worthy of an adult's attention by remarking, on first tasting it, "What a pity this isn't a sin."

A new "confessional" note is struck by ice cream enthusiasts today, who regularly speak as though their favourite dessert is some kind of obsession, even a drug. Their eulogies remind us of Michel Foucault's theory about sex: modern man is imperiously required to *speak* about it. "I am an unregenerate ice cream fetishist"; "this decadent delight, my drug of choice"; "when it comes to ice cream, my taste-buds know no shame"; "it is outrageously heavy and rich, sinfully delightful"; "I stood in line for my multi-calorie fix." There is, in addition, a constantly reiterated insistence on the "satisfaction" which ice cream affords.

At least some of these words, and many more like them, which pour daily into TV copy and magazine columns, are designed of course to make people buy more ice cream: a drug addict, after all, never has enough; he keeps buying. The obsession with the enjoyment of ice cream's "voluptuousness" sounds as though modern *mores* have changed, relaxed, become free at last from constraints and from the "uptight" past. But there is a sense in which the substitution of food (and especially food so easily bought) for sex constitutes a false and knowing ingenuousness, and even a flight from the challenges and responsibilities which sex entails. It could be the "puritanical" attitude to sex reasserting itself in a twentieth-century, comfort-obsessed guise: a modern version of the Victorians' reputedly having found piano legs suggestive.

It is likely that there is as well another truth: that ice cream has become a great indulgence precisely because its "innocent" myth remains intact. It is a *safe* drug, an antidote to anxiety – to the stress, for example, of having to be thin. We feel that reality is now something for which we have to pay a high price; but we doggedly, even touchingly, wish that reality could be innocent.

References

ENCYCLOPEDIAS AND DICTIONARIES

CONSIDINE, D.M. and G.D., eds. *Foods and Food Production Encyclopedia.*
N.Y.: Van Nostrand Reinhold, 1982.

COYLE, L.P. JR. *The World Encyclopedia of Food.* N.Y.: Facts on File,
1982.

DE BRUHL, M. *et al.* eds. *Dictionary of the Middle Ages.* (5 vols., continuing.) American Council of Learned Societies.

DUMAS, A. *Le grand dictionnaire de cuisine* (1844). Paris: Grobel, 1958.

ENSMINGER, A.H. *et al.*, eds. *Foods and Nutrition Encyclopedia.* (2 vols.).
Clovis, California, 1983.

ERICHSEN-BROWN, C. *Use of Plants for the Past 500 Years.* Aurora,
Ontario: Breezy Creeks Press, 1979.

FITZGIBBON, T. *The Food of the Western World.* N.Y.: Quadrangle, 1976.

GOODENOUGH, E.R. *Jewish Symbols in the Greco-Roman Period.* (13 vols.).
N.Y.: Pantheon, 1965-68.

HALL, J. *Dictionary of Subjects and Symbols in Art.* London: John Murray,
1974.

HASTINGS, J., ed. *Encyclopaedia of Religion and Ethics.* (12 vols.). N.Y.:
Scribner's, 1924.

HEDRICK, U.P., ed. *Sturtevant's Edible Plants of the World.* N.Y.: Dover,
1972.

LAPEDES, D.N. *et al.*, eds. *McGraw-Hill Encyclopedia of Food, Agriculture
and Nutrition.* N.Y.: McGraw-Hill, 1977.

LEACH, M. and FRIED, J. eds. *Funk and Wagnalls Standard Dictionary
of Folklore, Mythology and Legend.* (2 vols.) N.Y.: Funk and Wagnalls, 1972.

MASEFIELD, G.B. *et al.*, eds. *The Oxford Book of Food Plants.* Oxford University Press, 1973.

MONTAGNÉ, P., ed. *Larousse gastronomique* (1938). London: Hamlyn, 1961.

The New Encyclopedia Britannica. (32 vols.)

PAULY-WISSOWA, *Realenencyclopädie der classischen Altertumswissenschaft.* (48 vols.). Munich: Druckenmüller.

REES, A. *The Cyclopaedia.* (45 vols.). London: Longman, 1819.

ROOT, W. *Food.* N.Y.: Simon and Schuster, 1980.

SCHAUENBERG, P. and PARIS, F. *Guide to Medicinal Plants.* London: Lutterworth, 1977.

WINTER, R. *A Consumer's Dictionary of Food Additives.* N.Y.: Crown, 1978.

GENERAL

ANDRÉ, J. *L'Alimentation et la cuisine à Rome.* Paris: Klincksieck, 1961.

ARNOTT, M., ed. *Gastronomy: The Anthropology of Foods and Food Habits.* The Hague: Mouton, 1976.

ARON, J-P. *Le Mangeur du 19ème siècle.* Paris: Denoel, 1973.

ATHENAEUS. *The Deipnosophists.* (15 books). 2nd-3rd century AD.

BARER-STEIN, T. *You Eat What You Are.* Toronto: McClelland and Stewart, 1979.

BARKER, T.C. *et al.*, eds. *Our Changing Fare: Two Hundred Years of British Food Habits.* London: MacGibon and Kee, 1966.

BARRAU, J. *Les Hommes et leurs aliments.* Paris: Temps Actuels, 1983.

BARTHES, R. *Mythologies.* Paris: Seuil, 1957.

BEECHER, C. and STOWE, H. BEECHER. *The American Woman's Home* (1869). Hartford, Conn.: Stowe-Day Foundation, 1975.

BELASCO, W.J. " 'Lite' Economics: Less Food, More Profit." *Radical History Review*, 1984, pp. 254-78.

BERRY, W. *The Unsettling of America: Culture and Agriculture.* San Francisco: Sierra Club, 1977.

The Bible.

BONANNI, L. and RICCI, G., eds. *Cucina Cultura Società.* Urbino: Shakespeare and Co., 1982.

BOURDIEU, P. *La Distinction.* Paris: Le Minuit, 1979.

BRAUDEL, F. *Civilisation matérielle, économie et capitalisme*. (Tome 1). Paris: Armand Colin, 1967.

BRERETON, G.E. and FERRIER, J.M., eds. *Le Ménagier de Paris* (1390). Oxford: Clarendon, 1981.

BRILLAT-SAVARIN, A. *Physiologie du goût* (1826). Belley, France: Gustave Adam, 1948.

BROTHWELL, D. and P. *Food in Antiquity*. London: Thames and Hudson, 1969.

BROUK, B. *Plants Consumed by Man*. London: Academic Press, 1975.

BROWN, L.K. and MUSSELL, K., eds. *Ethnic and Regional Foodways in the United States*. University of Tennessee Press, 1984.

BRYANT, C. *et al*. *The Cultural Feast*. N.Y.: West Publishing, 1985.

BURNETT, J. *Plenty and Want*. London: Nelson, 1966.

CAPPON, D. *Eating, Loving and Dying: A Psychology of Appetites*. University of Toronto Press, 1973.

CARSON, R. *Silent Spring*. Boston: Houghton Mifflin, 1962.

CARTWRIGHT, F.F. and BIDDISS, M.D. *Disease and History*. London: Hart-Davis, 1972.

CASTELOT, A. *L'Histoire à table*. Paris: Plon, 1972.

CHAN, H.T. JR., ed. *Handbook of Tropical Foods*. N.Y.: Dekker, 1983.

CHANG, K.C. ed. *Food in Chinese Culture*. Yale University Press, 1978.

CONNOR, J.M. *et al*., eds. *The Food Manufacturing Industries*. Lexington, Mass.: Lexington Books, 1985.

COSMAN, M.P. *Fabulous Feasts*. N.Y.: George Braziller, 1976.

CUMMINGS, R.O. *The American and His Food*. University of Chicago Press, 1940.

CUNQUEIRO, A. *La Cocina Cristiana de Occidente*. Barcelona: Tusquets Ed., 1981.

CUSSLER, M. and DE GIVE, M. *'Twixt the Cup and the Lip*. N.Y.: Twayne, 1952.

DARBY, W.J., GHALIOUNGIU, P., and GRIVETTI, L. *Food: the Gift of Osiris*. (2 vols.). N.Y.: Academic Press, 1977.

DE CANDOLLE, A. *Origin of Cultivated Plants* (1886). N.Y.: Hafner, 1964.

DETIENNE, M. and VERNANT, J-P., eds. *La Cuisine du sacrifice en pays grec*. Paris: Gallimard, 1979.

DOUGLAS, M. *Purity and Danger*. London: Routledge and Kegan Paul, 1966.

———. *Natural Symbols*. London: Barrie and Rockliffe, 1970.

———. *Implicit Meanings*. London: Routledge and Kegan Paul, 1975.

DRIVER, C. *The British at Table, 1940-1980.* London: Chatto and Windus, 1983.

DRUMMOND, J.C. and WILBRAHAM, A. *The Englishman's Food.* London: Jonathan Cape, 1939.

ELIAS, N. *The Civilising Process.* (2 vols.). Oxford: Basil Blackwell, 1978. Reprint 1982.

FARB, P. and ARMELAGOS, G. *Consuming Passions.* Boston: Houghton Mifflin, 1980.

FENTON, A. and OWEN, R.M., eds. *Food in Perspective.* Edinburgh: John Donald, 1981.

FIELDHOUSE, P. *Food and Nutrition: Customs and Culture.* London: Croom Helm, 1986.

FOLEY, A., ed. *A Guidebook to California Agriculture.* University of California Press, 1983.

FORSTER, E. and R., eds. *European Diet from Pre-industrial to Modern Times.* N.Y.: Harper and Row, 1975.

FORSTER, R. and RANUM, O., eds. *Food and Drink in History.* Johns Hopkins University Press, 1979.

FRAZER, J.G. *Pausanias's Description of Greece.* (6 vols.). London: Macmillan, 1898.

GEORGE, S. *How the Other Half Dies.* Montclair, N.J.: Allanheld, Osmun, 1977.

———. *Ill Fares the Land.* Washington: Institute for Policy Studies, 1984.

GIEDION, S. *Mechanization Takes Command.* Oxford University Press, 1948.

GIFFT, H.H., WASHBAN, M.B., and HARRISON, G.G. *Nutrition, Behavior and Change.* Englewood Cliffs, N.J.: Prentice-Hall, 1972.

GOODY, J. *The Domestication of the Savage Mind.* Cambridge University Press, 1977.

———. *Cooking, Cuisine and Class.* Cambridge University Press, 1982.

GOTTSCHALK, A. *Histoire de l'alimentation et de la gastronomie depuis la préhistoire jusqu'à nos jours.* (2 vols.). Paris: Hippocrate, 1948.

GRIFFIN, K. *The Political Economy of Agrarian Change: An Essay on the Green Revolution.* Harvard University Press, 1974.

GRIGSON, J. *Jane Grigson's Vegetable Book.* London: Michael Joseph, 1978.

HARLAN, J.R. *Crops and Man.* Madison, Wisconsin: American Society of Agronomy, Crop Science Society of America, 1975.

HARTLEY, D. *Food in England.* London: Macdonald, 1964.

HAZELTON, N. *Vegetable Cookery.* Penguin, 1979.

HEHN, V. *The Wanderings of Plants and Animals* (1885). Amsterdam: John Benjamins, 1976.

HEISER, C.B. *Seed to Civilisation.* San Francisco: W.H. Freeman, 1981.

HEMARDINQUER, J-J. *Pour une histoire de l'alimentation.* Paris: Armand Colin, 1970.

HENISCH, B.A. *Fast and Feast: Food in Medieval Society.* Pennsylvania State University Press, 1976.

HERODOTUS. *History.* 5th century BC.

HESS, J.L. and K. *The Taste of America.* N.Y.: Viking, 1977.

HUXLEY, E. *Brave New Victuals.* London: Chatto and Windus, 1965.

JASHEMSKI, W.F. *The Gardens of Pompeii.* N.Y.: Caratzas, 1979.

JOHNSTON, J.P. *A Hundred Years Eating.* McGill-Queen's University Press, 1977.

KAHN, E.J., JR. *The Staffs of Life.* Boston: Little, Brown, 1985.

LÉVI-STRAUSS, C. *Mythologiques*: I *Le cru et le cuit.* II *Du Miel aux cendres*, III *L'Origine des manières de table.* Paris: Plon, 1964-68.

LEYEL, C.F. *The Magic of Herbs. A Modern Book of Secrets.* London: Jonathan Cape, 1926.

LOWENBERG, M.E., *et al., Food and People.* N.Y.: J. Wiley, 1979.

MAC FADYEN, J.T. *Gaining Ground: The Renewal of America's Small Farms.* N.Y.: Holt, Rinehart and Winston, 1984.

MC GEE, H. *On Food and Cooking.* N.Y.: Scribner's, 1984.

MC LAUGHLIN, T. *A Diet of Tripe.* Newton Abbot: David and Charles, 1978.

MEAD, W.E. *The English Medieval Feast.* London: George Allen and Unwin, 1931.

MENNELL, S. *All Manners of Food.* Oxford: Basil Blackwell, 1985.

MOLDENKE, H.N. and A.L. *Plants of the Bible.* Waltham, Mass.: Chronica Botanica, 1952.

MONCRIEFF, R.W. *Odour Preferences.* London: Leonard Hill, 1966.

MURCOTT, A., ed. *The Sociology of Food and Eating.* Aldershott, Hants.: Gower, 1983.

MURR, J. *Die Pflanzenwelt in der griechischen Mythologie.* Gröningen: Bouma's Boekhuis, 1969.

ODDY, D.J. and MILLER, D.S., eds. *The Making of the Modern British Diet.* London: Croom Helm, 1976.

PALMER, A. *Moveable Feasts*. Oxford University Press, 1952. Reprint 1984.

PARIENTÉ, H. and DE TERNANT, G. *La fabuleuse histoire de la cuisine française*. Paris: O.D.I.L., 1981.

PLINY. *Natural History*. (37 books). 1st century AD.

POST, E.L., ed., *Emily Post's Etiquette*. (1817) N.Y.: Harper and Row, 1984.

POWLEDGE, F. *Fat of the Land*. N.Y.: Simon and Schuster, 1984.

PRAKASH, O. *Food and Drinks in Ancient India*. Delhi: Munshi Ram Manohar Lal, 1961.

PRESTAGE, E. *The Portuguese Pioneers*. London: A. and C. Black, 1933.

PULLAR, P. *Consuming Passions*. London: Hamish Hamilton, 1970.

PYKE, M. *Food and Society*. London: John Murray, 1968.

RENFREW, J. *Paleoethnobotany*. London: Methuen, 1973.

RENNER, H.D. *The Origin of Food Habits*. London: Faber and Faber, 1944.

REVEL, J-F. *Un festin en paroles*. Paris: Pauvert, 1979.

RICHARDSON, W.N. and STUBBS, T. *Plants, Agriculture and Human Society*. N.Y.: W.A. Benjamin, 1978.

ROOT, W. and DE ROCHEMONT, R. *Eating in America*. N.Y.: William Morrow, 1976.

SAUER, C.O. *Seeds, Spades, Hearths and Herds*. Cambridge, MA: M.I.T. Press, 1969.

SCHERY, R.W. *Plants for Man*. Englewood Cliffs, N.J.: Prentice-Hall, 1972.

SCHWARTZ, R. *More Work for Mother*. N.Y.: Basic Books, 1983.

SIMOONS, F.J. *Eat Not This Flesh: Food Avoidances in the Old World*. University of Wisconsin Press, 1961.

SZENT-GYÖRGYI, A.V. *On Oxidation, Fermentation, Vitamins, Health and Disease*. Johns Hopkins University Press, 1939.

TANNAHILL, R. *Food in History*. N.Y.: Stein and Day, 1973.

THEOPHRASTUS. *Enquiry into Plants*. (10 books.) 4th-3rd century BC.

TRAGER, J. *The Foodbook*. N.Y.: Grossman, 1970.

TURNER, J.S. *The Chemical Feast*. N.Y.: Grossman, 1970.

UCKO, P.J. and DIMBLEBY, G.W., eds. *The Domestication and Exploitation of Plants and Animals*. Chicago: Aldine, 1969.

VAN DER POST, L. *First Catch Your Eland*. N.Y.: William Morrow, 1978.

WASSEF, C.W. *Pratiques rituelles et alimentaires des Coptes*. Cairo: Institut français d'archéologie orientale, 1971.

WATSON, A.M. *Agricultural Innovation in the Early Islamic World.* Cambridge University Press, 1983.

WELCHER, D.N. *et al.*, eds. *Food, Man and Society.* N.Y.: Plenum Press, 1976.

WHEATON, B.K. *Savouring the Past.* London: Chatto and Windus, 1983.

WILSON, C.A. *Food and Drink in Britain from the Stone Age to Recent Times.* London: Constable, 1973.

WOLFERT, P. *Couscous and Other Good Food from Morocco.* N.Y.: Harper and Row, 1973.

YUDKIN, J. and MC KENZIE, J.C. eds. *Changing Food Habits.* London: MacGibon and Kee, 1964.

ZEUNER, F.E. *A History of Domesticated Animals.* London: Hutchinson, 1963.

WHAT SHALL WE HAVE FOR DINNER?

BLOCK, E. "The Chemistry of Garlic and Onions." *Scientific American*, March 1985, pp. 114-19.

DEETZ, J. and ANDERSON, J. "The Ethnogastronomy of Thanksgiving." *Saturday Review* 55 (25 November 1972): 29-39.

DOUGLAS, M. "Deciphering a Meal." *Daedalus* 101 (1972): 61-81.

———. "Taking the Biscuit: The Structure of British Meals." *New Society* 30 (1974): 744-47.

———. "Food as an Art Form." In *In the Active Voice.* London: Routledge and Kegan Paul, 1982.

LÉVI-STRAUSS, C. "The Culinary Triangle." *Partisan Review* 33 (1966): 586-95.

PALMER, A. *Moveable Feasts.* Oxford University Press 1952. Reprint 1984.

CORN: OUR MOTHER, OUR LIFE

CUTLER, H.C. and BLAKE, L.W. "Travels of Corn and Squash." In Riley, C.L. *et al.*, eds. *Man Across the Sea.* University of Texas Press, 1971.

BOGUE, A.G. *From Prairie to Corn Belt.* University of Chicago Press, 1963.

BRESSANI, R. and SCHRIMSHAW, N. "Effect of Lime Treatment on In

Vitro Availability of Essential Amino Acids and Solubility of Protein Fractions in Corn." *Journal of Agricultural and Food Chemistry* 6 (1958): 774-78.

GILES, D. *Singing Valleys*. N.Y.: Random House, 1940.

GOLDBERGER, J. and WHEELER, G.A. "Experimental pellagra in human subjects brought about by restricted diet." *Public Health Reports* 30 (1915).

HARDEMAN, N.P. *Shucks, Shocks, and Hominy Blocks*. Louisiana State University Press, 1981.

HATCH, J.K. *The Corn Farmers of Motupe*. Madison, Wisconsin: Land Tenure Center, 1976.

INGLETT, G.E., ed. *Corn: Culture, Processing, Products*. Westport, Conn: AVI Publishing, 1970.

JUGENHEIMER, R.W. *Corn: Improvement, Seed Production, and Uses*. N.Y.: John Wiley, 1976.

KAHN, E.J. JR., *The Staffs of Life*, ch. 1. Boston: Little, Brown, 1985.

KATZ, S.H. *et al.* "Traditional Maize Processing Techniques in the New World." *Science* 184 (1974): 765-73.

LIMBURG, P.R. *The Story of Corn*. N.Y.: Julian Messner, 1971.

MANGELSDORF, P.C. *Corn: Its Origin, Evolution and Improvement*. Harvard University Press, 1974.

MIRACLE, M.P. *Maize in Tropical Africa*. University of Wisconsin Press, 1966.

POWELL, H.B. *The Original Has This Signature: W.K. Kellogg*. Englewood Cliffs, N.J.: Prentice-Hall, 1956.

REINA, R.E. "Milpas and Milperos: implications for prehistoric times." *American Anthropologist* 69 (1967): 1-20.

ROE, D.A.A. *A Plague of Corn*. Cornell University Press, 1973.

WADE, N. "A Message from Corn Blight: The Dangers of Uniformity." *Science* 177 (1972): 678-79.

WALDEN, H.T. II, *Native Inheritance*. N.Y.: Harper and Row, 1966.

WALLACE, H.A. and BROWN, W.L. *Corn and its Early Fathers*. Michigan State University Press, 1956.

WEATHERWAX, P. "The Popping of Corn." *Proceedings of the Indiana Academy of Sciences for 1921* (1922): 149-53.

WEAVER, M.P. *The Aztecs, Maya, and their Predecessors*. N.Y.: Academic Press, 1981.

ZEVALLOS, M.C. *et al.* "The San Pablo Corn Kernel and its Friends." *Science* 196 (1977): 385-89.

SALT: THE EDIBLE ROCK

BATTERSON, M. and BODDIE, W.W., eds. *Salt, the Mysterious Necessity.* Dow Chemical Co., 1972.

BERGIER, J-F. *Une Histoire du sel.* Presses Universitaires de France, 1982.

EDITORIAL STAFF "Salt: A New Villain?" *Time,* March 15, 1982.

FISCHER, L. *The Life of Mahatma Gandhi,* N.Y.: Harper and Row, 1950.

GOLDEN, F. "Hideaways for Nuclear Waste." *Time,* March 16, 1981, p. 68.

JONES, E. "The Symbolic Significance of Salt in Folklore and Superstition." In *Essays in Applied Psycho-Analysis,* vol. II. N.Y.: International Universities Press, 1964.

KAUFMANN, D.W. *Sodium Chloride.* N.Y.: Reinhold, 1960.

LESSING, E. *Hallstatt.* Vienna: Jugend und Volk, 1980.

MOLLAT, M., ed. *Le Rôle du sel dans l'histoire.* Presses Universitaires de France, 1968.

MULTHAUF, R.P. *Neptune's Gift.* Johns Hopkins University Press, 1978.

NENQUIN, J. *Salt: a study in economic prehistory.* Bruges: De Tempel, 1961.

NEUMANN, T.W. "A Biocultural Approach to Salt Taboos: The Case of the Southeastern United States." *Current Anthropology* 18 (1977): 298-308.

RALOFF, J. "Salt of the Earth." *Science News* 126 (1984): 298-301.

——. "Surviving Salt." *Science News* 126 (1984): 314-17.

SIMON, C. "Eating a hole in the salt dome solution." *Science News* 124 (1983): 292.

BUTTER—AND SOMETHING "JUST AS GOOD"

ANDERSON, A.J.C. and WILLIAMS, P.W. *Margarine.* Oxford University Press, 1965.

BALL, R.A. and LILLY, J.R. "The Menace of Margarine: The Rise and Fall of a Social Problem." *Social Problems* 29 (1982): 488-98.

BROWN, M.S. and GOLDSTEIN, J.L. "How LDL Receptors Influence Cholesterol and Atherosclerosis." *Scientific American,* November 1984, pp. 58-66.

FORMAN, H. "The Butter Gods of Kum Bum." *Canadian Geographic*, January 1948, pp. 39-50.

FUSSELL, G.E. *The English Dairy Farmer 1500-1900*. London: F. Cass, 1966.

JIGMEI, N.N. *et al. Tibet*. London: F. Muller and Summerfield, 1981.

KITTREDGE, G.L. *Witchcraft in Old and New England* (1929). N.Y.: Russell and Russell, 1956.

KRETCHMER, N. "Lactose and Lactase." *Scientific American*, October 1972, pp. 71-8.

LUCAS, A. "Irish food before the potato." *Gwerin* III, 2 (1960): 12-24.

MC CRACKEN, R.D. "Lactase Deficiency: An Example of Dietary Evolution." *Current Anthropology* 12 (1971): 479-517.

RIEPMA, S.F. *The Story of Margarine*. Washington: Public Affairs Press, 1970.

ROCK, J.F. "Demon Dancers and Butter Gods of Choni." *National Geographic*, 1928, pp. 585-95.

SIMOONS, F.J. "The Purificatory Role of the Five Products of the Cow in Hinduism." *Ecology of Food and Nutrition* 3 (1974): 21-34.

SNODGRASS, K. *Margarine as a Butter Substitute*. Stanford University Press, 1930.

VAN STUYVENBERG, J.H., ed. *Margarine: An Economic, Social and Scientific History*. Liverpool University Press, 1969.

WIEST, E. *The Butter Industry in the United States: An Economic Study of Butter and Oleomargarine*. Columbia University Press, 1916.

CHICKEN: FROM JUNGLE FOWL TO PATTIES

CARTER, G.F. "Pre-Columbian Chickens in America." In Riley, C.L. *et al.*, eds. *Man Across the Sea*, ch. 9. University of Texas Press, 1971.

DETIENNE, M. and VERNANT, J-P. *La cuisine du sacrifice en pays grec*. Paris: Gallimard, 1979.

GEERTZ, C. "Deep Play: Notes on the Balinese Cockfight." *Daedalus* 101 (1972): 1-37.

GOLD, M. *Assault and Battery*. London: Pluto Press, 1983.

HAMM, D. *et al.* "Meat Yields from Hot Deboned Noneviscerated Broilers." *Poultry Science* 63 (1984): 497-501.

HOEFER, J.A. and TSUCHITANI, P.J., eds. *Animal Agriculture in China*. Washington: National Academy Press, 1980.

KOTTAK, C. "Ritual at McDonald's." *Natural History Magazine* 87 (1978): 75-82.

KUMMER, C. "Roast Chicken." *Atlantic Monthly*, November 1985, pp. 122-24.

MC ADAMS, C. "Frank Perdue Is *Chicken!*" *Esquire* 79 (April 1973): 113 f.

O'LAUGHLIN, B. "Mediation of Contradiction: Why Mbum Women Do Not Eat Chicken." in Rosaldo, M.Z., and Lamphère, L., eds. *Women, Culture, and Society*. Stanford University Press, 1974.

SIMOONS, F.J. *Eat Not This Flesh*. University of Wisconsin Press, 1961.

SMITH, P. and DANIEL, C. *The Chicken Book*. N.Y.: Little, Brown, 1975.

TALBOT, R.B. *The Chicken War*. Iowa State University Press, 1978.

TWIGG, J. "Vegetarianism and the Meanings of Meat." in Murcott, A., ed. *The Sociology of Food and Eating*. Aldershott, Hants: Gower, 1983.

URQUHART, J. *Animals on the Farm*. London: Macdonald, 1981.

ZEUNER, F.E. *A History of Domesticated Animals*. London: Hutchinson, 1963.

RICE: THE TYRANT WITH A SOUL

BEFU, H. "An Ethnography of Dinner Entertainment in Japan." *Arctic Anthropology* XI (suppl.) (1974): 196-203.

BRAUDEL, F. *Civilisation matérielle, économie et capitalisme*. (Tome 1). Paris: Armand Colin, 1967.

BUDDENHAGEN, I.W. and PERSLEY, G.J. *Rice in Africa*. London: Academic Press, 1978.

CHAN, H.T. JR., ed. *Handbook of Tropical Foods*, ch. 13. N.Y.: Dekker, 1983.

CHANG, K.C. "Food and Food Vessels in Ancient China." *Transactions of the New York Academy of Sciences* 35 (1973): 495-520.

———, ed. *Food in Chinese Culture*. Yale University Press, 1977.

CHANG, T.T. "Conservation of Rice Genetic Resources: Luxury or Necessity?" *Science* 224 (1984): 251-56.

CONDOMINAS, G. *Nous avons mangé la forêt*. Paris: Mercure de France, 1957. Reprint 1962.

FALASSI, A. "I percorsi del risotto." In Bonanni, L. and Ricci, G., eds. *Cucina Cultura Società*. Urbino: Shakespeare and Co., 1982.

GRIST, D.H. *Rice*. 5th ed. London: Longman, 1975.

HANKS, J.R. "Ontology of Rice." In Diamond, S., ed. *Primitive Views of the World*. Columbia University Press, 1964.

HANKS, L.M. *Rice and Man*. Chicago: Aldine, 1972.

HIGHAM, C.F.W. "Prehistoric Rice Cultivation in Southeast Asia." *Scientific American*, April 1984, pp. 138-46.

HILL, R.D. *Rice in Malaya*. Oxford University Press, 1977.

HOUSTON, D.F., ed., *Rice: Chemistry and Technology*. St. Paul: American Association of Cereal Chemists, 1972.

KAHN, E.J. JR., *The Staffs of Life*, ch. 4. Boston: Little, Brown, 1985.

KING, F.H. *Farmers of Forty Centuries*. Madison, Wisconsin, 1911.

LITTLEFIELD, D.C. *Rice and Slaves*. Louisiana State University Press, 1981.

LOEB, E.M. "Wine, Women and Song." In Diamond, S., ed. *Culture in History*. Columbia University Press, 1960.

MARTIN, M.A. "La riziculture et la maîtrise de l'eau dans le Kampuchea démocratique." *Etudes rurales* 83 (July-September 1981): 7-42.

RABBITT, J.A. "Rice in the Cultural Life of the Japanese People." *Transactions of the Asiatic Society of Japan* 19 (1940): 187-258.

RUTGER, J.N. and BRANDON, D.M. "California Rice Culture." *Scientific American*, January 1981, pp. 42-51.

SWAMINATHAN, M.S. "Rice." *Scientific American*, January 1984, pp. 82-93.

THORNTON, H.J. *History of the Quaker Oats Company*. University of Chicago Press, 1933.

UNESCO. "Rice-land Civilizations." *The Courier*, December 1984. (Special issue.)

LETTUCE: THE VICISSITUDES OF SALAD

Anonymous, "Food Irradiation." *Nutrition and Food Science*, September-October 1984, pp. 16-18.

BORTHWICK, H.A. *et al.* "Action of Light on Lettuce-Seed Germination." *The Botanical Gazette* 115 (1954): 205-25.

CURRIER, R.L. "The Hot-Cold Syndrome and Symbolic Balance in Mexican and Spanish-American Folk Medicine." *Ethnology* 5 (1966): 251-63.

DETIENNE, M. *Les Jardins d'Adonis*. Paris: Gallimard, 1972.

FRIEDLAND, W.H. *et al. Manufacturing Green Gold*. N.Y.: Cambridge University Press, 1981.

GAUTHIER, H. *Les Fêtes du dieu Min*. (2 vols.). Cairo: Institut français d'archéologie orientale, 1931.

Institute of Food Technologists. "Radiation Preservation of Foods." *Food Technology*, February 1983, pp. 55-60.

LEVY, J.E. *Cesar Chavez*. N.Y.: Norton, 1975.

LINDQVIST, L. "On the Origin of Cultivated Lettuce." *Hereditas* 46 (1960): 319-50.

MADSEN, W. "Hot and Cold in the Universe of San Francisco Tecospa, Valley of Mexico." *Journal of American Folklore* 68 (1955): 123-39.

PROULX, E.A. "Belle Lettuce." *Horticulture*, August 1983, pp. 34-44.

SUN, M. "Salad, House Dressing, but Hold the Sulfites." *Science* 226 (1984): 520-21.

WHITAKER, T.W. "Salads for Everyone – a Look at the Lettuce Plant." *Economic Botany* 23 (1969): 261-64.

——— and BOHN, G.W. "Contributions of Applied Science to the Lettuce Industry of the Southwest." *Economic Botany* 7 (1953): 243-56.

OLIVE OIL: A TREE AND ITS FRUITS

COUTANCE, A.G.A. *L'Olivier*. Paris: J. Rothschild, 1877.

DETIENNE, M. "L'Olivier: un mythe politico-religieuse." *Revue de l'histoire des religions* 78 (1970): 5-23.

Food and Agriculture Organization, Rome. *Modern Olive-Growing*. 1977.

GOOR, A. "The Place of the Olive in the Holy Land and Its History Through the Ages." *Economic Botany* 20 (1966): 223-43.

HARTMANN, H.T. and BOUGAS, P.G. "Olive Production in Greece." *Economic Botany* 24 (1970): 443-59.

HOFMEISTER, P. *Die heiligen Öle in der morgen-und abendländischen Kirche*. Würzburg: Augustinus-Verlag, 1948.

JASHEMSKI, W.F. *The Gardens of Pompeii*. N.Y.: Caratzas, 1979.

KANTOROWICZ, E.H. *The King's Two Bodies*. Princeton University Press, 1957.

KLEIN, M.B. *The Feast of the Olive*. Berkeley: Aris, 1983.

LYSIAS, "On the Olive-Stump." 4th century BC.

MATTSON, F.H. and GRUNDY, S.M. "Comparison of effects of dietary saturated, monounsaturated, and polyunsaturated fatty acids on plasma lipids and lipoproteins in man." *Journal of Lipid Research* 26 (1985): 194-201.

MITCHELL, R.W. *Castile Soap.* Boston, the author, 1927.

PARKER, B. *The Symbols of Sovereignty.* Newton Abbot: Westbridge, 1979.

ROBBINS, E. "Heracles, the Hyperboreans, and the Hind: Pindar, *Olympians* 3." *Phoenix* 36 (1982): 295-305.

SALOMONE-MARINO, S. "The Olive Harvest." In *Customs and Habits of the Sicilian Peasants* (1897). Associated University Presses, 1981.

THEODORATUS, R.J. "Greek Immigrant Cuisine in America: Continuity and Change." In Fenton, A. and Owen, T.M., eds. *Food in Perspective.* Edinburgh: John Donald, 1981.

WOLFERT, P. "Olives." In *Mediterranean Cooking.* Pp. 45-7. N.Y.: Times Books, 1977.

LEMON JUICE: A SOUR NOTE

ANDREWS, A.C. "Acclimatization of Citrus Fruits in the Mediterranean Region." *Agricultural History* 35 (1961): 35-46.

CHAN, H.T. JR., ed. *Handbook of Tropical Foods,* ch. 5. N.Y.: Dekker, 1983.

CORCORAN, D.W.J. and HOUSTON, T.G. "Is the lemon test an index of arousal level?" *British Journal of Psychology* 68 (1977): 361-64.

FOSCA, F. *L'Histoire des cafés de Paris.* Paris: Firmin-Didot, 1934.

GADE, D.W. "Décalage in the Italian Landscape: The Lemon Gardens of Lake Garda." *Landscape* 26 (1982): 12-19.

HESS, A.F. *Scurvy Past and Present.* Philadelphia: Lippincott, 1920.

ISAAC, E. "Influence of Religion on the Spread of Citrus." *Science* 129 (January 1959): 179-86.

KROUSE, C.G. "Brand Name as a Barrier to Entry: the ReaLemon Case." *Southern Economic Journal* 51 (1984): 495-502.

MC PHEE, J. *Oranges.* N.Y.: Farrar, Straus and Giroux, 1967.

RAY, R. and WALHEIM, L. *Citrus.* Tucson: Horticultural Publishing/ Fisher, 1980.

RILEY, J.J. *A History of the American Soft Drink Industry.* N.Y.: Arno, 1972.

TOLKOWSKY, S. *Hesperides, a History of the Culture and Use of Citrus Fruits.* London: J. Bale, Sons and Curnow, 1938.

ICE CREAM: COLD COMFORT

ANDERSON, O.E. JR. *Refrigeration in America*. Princeton University Press, 1953.

ARBUCKLE, W.S. *Ice Cream*. 2nd ed. Westport, Conn: AVI, 1972.

BRAUDEL, F. *La Méditerranée et le monde méditerranéen à l'époque de Philippe II*. (vol. I). Paris: Armand Colin, 1949.

CUMMINGS, R.O. *The American Ice Harvests 1800-1918*. University of California Press, 1949.

DICKSON, P. *The Great American Ice Cream Book*. N.Y.: Atheneum, 1972.

ELLMAN, R. "Wallace Stevens' Ice Cream." *Kenyon Review* 19 (1957): 89-105.

FABIAN, F.W. "Ice Cream as a Cause of Epidemics." *American Journal of Public Health* 16 (1926): 873-79.

FOSCA, F. *L'Histoire des cafés de Paris*. Paris: Firmin-Didot, 1934.

GIEDION, S. *Mechanization Takes Command*. Oxford University Press, 1948.

HIPPOCRATES. *Regimen*. 5th-4th century BC.

JONES, J.C. JR., *America's Icemen*. Humble, Texas: Jobeco Books, 1984.

MASTERS, T. *The Ice Book*. London: Simpkin, Marshall, 1844.

SKOW, J. "They All Scream for It." *Time*, 10 August 1981, pp. 52-8.

TRILLIN, C. "Competitors." *New Yorker*, 8 July 1985, pp. 31-45.

WALKER, J. "The Physics of Grandmother's peerless homemade ice cream." *Scientific American*, April 1984, pp. 150-53.

WILSON, D. *Supercold*. London: Faber, 1979.

WRIGHT, M. "Ice Cream by the Mile." *Scientific American*, January 1934, pp. 10-11.

Index